PRODUCER OF CONTROVERSY

CultureAmerica

ERIKA DOSS

PHILIP J. DELORIA

Series Editors

KARAL ANN MARLING

Editor Emerita

PRODUCER OF CONTROVERSY

Stanley Kramer, Hollywood Liberalism, and the Cold War

Jennifer Frost

 University Press of Kansas

Published by the

University Press of Kansas

(Lawrence, Kansas 66045),

which was organized by the

Kansas Board of Regents and

is operated and funded by

Emporia State University,

Fort Hays State University,

Kansas State University,

Pittsburg State University,

the University of Kansas, and

Wichita State University.

Library of Congress Cataloging-in-Publication Data
Names: Frost, Jennifer, 1961– author.
Title: Producer of controversy : Stanley Kramer,
    Hollywood liberalism, and the Cold War /
    Jennifer Frost.
Description: Lawrence : University Press of Kansas,
    2017. | Series: CultureAmerica | Includes
    bibliographical references and index.
Identifiers: LCCN 2017038275 | ISBN
    9780700624966 (cloth : alk. paper) |
    ISBN 9780700624973 (ebook)
Subjects: LCSH: Kramer, Stanley—Criticism and
    interpretation. | Politics in motion pictures.
Classification: LCC PN1998.3.K73 F76 2017 |
    DDC 791.4302/32092—dc23 LC record available
    at https://lccn.loc.gov/2017038275.

British Library Cataloguing-in-Publication Data is
available.

Printed in the United States of America

10 9 8 7 6 5 4 3 2 1

The paper used in this publication is recycled and
contains 30 percent postconsumer waste. It is acid
free and meets the minimum requirements of the
American National Standard for Permanence of
Paper for Printed Library Materials Z39.48–1992.

For Luc, Jonah, and Gus

CONTENTS

ACKNOWLEDGMENTS

This book continues my long-standing interest in US politics and culture, adding a study of American liberalism to my earlier ones on the New Left in the 1960s and mid-twentieth-century conservatism. Over the past few years, I have had much assistance and support for this book. The University of Auckland, particularly the School of Humanities Research Fund, provided both time and money for research and writing. I was able to conduct extensive archival research in the United States, and I benefited from the knowledge and expertise of archivists and librarians in the Department of Special Collections, Charles E. Young Research Library, University of California, Los Angeles, California; the Margaret Herrick Library, Academy of Motion Picture Arts and Sciences, Beverly Hills, California; and the National Archives, College Park, Maryland.

When I could not make the overseas trip myself, I had expert help from Elisabeth Wingerter at the New York University Archives, New York, New York, and from Sydney Soderberg at the Dwight D. Eisenhower Presidential Library, Abilene, Kansas. Dolores Janiewski and Simon Judkins provided significant materials related to Stanley Kramer from the Hoover Institution Archives, Stanford University, Stanford, California. In New Zealand, I was fortunate to have research assistance from Jonathan Burgess, Shane Smits, Michelle Thorp, and Rebecca Weeks, and translations of sources in Hebrew and Russian from Ayelet Zoran-Rosen and Natalia Galvin, respectively. This aid not only made the process of completing this book easier and more enjoyable but also enhanced its content and arguments greatly.

Professional colleagues offered helpful materials and advice. As he had with my previous books, Paul Boyer once again guided my research and thinking before he passed away. Bob Abzug, Sara Buttsworth, Larry Ceplair, Kathy Feeley, Glenn Frankel, Andrea Friedman, David Gerwin, Nancy Isenberg, Dolores Janiewski, Alison Kibler, Giacomo Lichtner, Elaine Tyler May, Lary May, John Pettegrew, and Steven Ross all provided important insights at various points in the process. Tom Doherty and Robert Brent Toplin reviewed my book proposal for the University Press of Kansas and shaped the final manuscript in key ways, particularly with regard to the first and last chapters. I am also glad that anonymous reviewers of the final manuscript pushed me to strengthen the book's overall argument.

This book would not have been possible without several key people. The staff at the University Press of Kansas—beginning with Michael Briggs's first email to me soliciting the manuscript and continuing with Kim Hogeland, Kelly Chrisman Jacques, Lori Rider, and Michael Kehoe seeing the book through publication and promotion—have been consistently enthusiastic, supportive, and patient. Karen Sharpe-Kramer's encouragement throughout the research and writing spurred me on in the process. She also helpfully provided suggestions and photographs. I greatly appreciate that she always accepted the parameters I set for this book; that is, it is not a traditional biography covering her husband's private life but instead a study of his public life of career, politics, and films.

Finally, to my family and friends: Eftihia Danellis continued to provide a wonderful "home away from home" for me while I conducted research in Los Angeles. Kathy Tatar's company and, on one occasion, research assistance made a big difference. My father-in-law, Denis Taillon, continually surprised me with valuable materials gathered on his research trips to his local library and bookstore. My family, especially Lynne Baca, Jim Frost, Millicent Frost, and Joyce Taillon, never forgot to ask me how the book was progressing. At home, Paul, Cealagh, and Luc Taillon remained unfailingly positive . . . unless I was procrastinating.

I'm dedicating this book to Luc and his cousins Jonah Goodman and Gus Frost. Like all of us, Stanley Kramer was far from perfect, but he maintained his political convictions in challenging times. I hope this dedication will serve as inspiration.

PRODUCER OF CONTROVERSY

Karen Sharpe-Kramer and Stanley Kramer arriving at the 40th Academy Awards ceremony, where Guess Who's Coming to Dinner *(1967) received an Oscar nomination for best picture. Copyright © Academy of Motion Picture Arts and Sciences.*

Introduction:
"The Thinking Man's Producer"

In 1962 the Academy of Motion Picture Arts and Sciences bestowed on the politically liberal producer-director Stanley Kramer its highest honor for a Hollywood film producer. The Irving G. Thalberg Award is given to "creative producers" for "consistent high quality of production" and "contributions to the motion picture industry." This award recognized Kramer's achievements as an innovative, independent producer who made socially critical, and even controversial, films. The accolade is not offered every year, and Kramer received only the sixteenth to be given out since the Academy established the award in 1937. He joined the ranks of legendary producers such as David O. Selznick, Darryl Zanuck, Samuel Goldwyn, and Cecil B. DeMille, who had won the award named after Thalberg—a legend himself, the "boy wonder" of 1920s and 1930s Hollywood. "I was taken completely by surprise," Kramer recalled. "The members were usually much slower to offer such recognition to the kind of pictures I made, and I considered the Thalberg Award a signal honor."[1]

Yet, at the very same time, Kramer's critical reputation suffered. While many reviewers praised his "good, perhaps noble, intent," his "courage," and his "forcefulness" in addressing "matters of import today" in his recent films, others disagreed. In reviews of his films *Inherit the Wind* and *Judgment at Nuremberg* in 1960 and 1961, *Time* magazine accused him of "sluggish, confused manipulation of ideas and players" and "crudely mismanag[ing] both actors and camera."[2] Other critics condemned his work as "emptily pretentious," "hollow, falsely sentimental, overproduced," and, somewhat more kindly, lacking in "subtlety."[3] Criticisms of Kramer's filmmaking and politics mounted over the decade of the 1960s and into the 1970s. "Will someone please turn off Stanley Kramer's movie-making machine? It's running amok," wrote Gene Siskel in the *Chicago Tribune* in 1971.[4]

The two most influential film critics of Kramer's later career, Pauline Kael and Andrew Sarris, shared an intensely negative opinion of his work. The *New Yorker*'s Kael argued that Kramer's "reputation as a great director is largely based on a series of errors" in which films he had produced were erroneously attributed to his direction. She went on over the next two decades to use him as a negative referent for other film-makers suffering from "the Kramer syndrome."[5] Sarris fully agreed with Kael's criticisms. In a 1960 review in the *Village Voice*, he held nothing back, calling Kramer "one of Hollywood's worst directors." Then, in his influential and agenda-setting *The American Cinema* (1968), Sarris placed Kramer in the "Miscellany" category. "If Stanley Kramer had never existed, he would have had to be invented as the most extreme example of thesis or message cinema. . . . Unfortunately," the critic added sardonically, "he has been such an easy and willing target for so long that his very ineptness has become encrusted with tradition." From Sarris's "ruthlessly hierarchical ranking system," critic Phillip Lopate noted, "we learned to curl our lips" at filmmakers such as Kramer.[6]

Such critical evaluations shaped Kramer's subsequent reputation as a liberal filmmaker and have overshadowed his historical significance. Yet attention to the producer-director's career, politics, and films within his historical moment reveals his cultural and political importance and impact. Kramer enjoyed a lengthy and prolific career from the 1940s to the 1980s. During his career, he produced thirty-five films, fifteen of which he also directed. Together, Kramer's films earned eighty-five Oscar nominations across multiple categories. Six of Kramer's films received nominations for the best picture Academy Award. *High Noon* (1952) and *The Caine Mutiny* (1954) he produced, and *The Defiant Ones* (1958), *Judgment at Nuremberg* (1961), *Ship of Fools* (1965), and *Guess Who's Coming to Dinner* (1967) he produced and directed. "He did better than average," historian Thomas Doherty has declared, "and deserves better than a glib entry in the miscellaneous file."[7]

As one of Hollywood's earliest and most successful independent post–World War II producers, Kramer fundamentally shaped the system of moviemaking that emerged in this era. He began his career when the old studio system controlled by a few large companies was breaking up, and new ways of organizing film production solidified. He valued the creative freedom and business opportunity provided in the transition from so-called Old to New Hollywood, and he flourished. In the 1950s he negotiated unprecedented production and distribution contracts with Columbia Pictures and United Artists. "Never before has an arrangement of this kind been concluded between a major film corporation and a completely self-operating independent organization," announced Columbia head Harry Cohn about their 1951 deal. According to film scholar Yannis Tzioumakis, his achievements with United Artists later in the decade were "a major concession to a creative producer like Kramer and unheard of in studio agreements with independent producers."[8] His public persona as an independent filmmaker showed younger artists that such a career was possible. With his freedom and autonomy—contractually constrained as it was—he made movies that consistently challenged Hollywood's conventional approach to subject matter.

Instead, Kramer produced films that took on contemporary social and political issues and—even more—offered a consistently liberal position on these issues. This was no small achievement, given that his emergence and development as a liberal filmmaker occurred within the context of the Cold War. In contrast to scholarly and popular assumptions about Hollywood as a bastion of American liberalism, during the 1950s—the crucial years of his career—an anticommunist Red Scare and blacklist dominated the motion picture industry. The liberal Kramer faced constant opposition from a vocal, vociferous Right. As one of his political supporters put it in the early 1960s, "Today, super-patriotic groups in America are vigorously and militantly using the anti-Communist, anti-Semitic cry to discredit if not silence those voices that would speak and act in what are generally considered 'liberal causes.'"[9] Kramer's career reminds us that liberalism's political course over the mid-twentieth century was far from uniform. He arrived in Hollywood during a liberal moment—the 1930s—but started as an independent producer during a conservative one.[10] Liberalism only came to the fore again in the filmmaking capital from the mid-1960s on, a development he helped bring about. He also was criticized from the political Left, most conspicuously later in his career. But to understand his actions and appreciate his accomplishments as a Hollywood liberal during the Cold War, a recognition of the hostile right-wing political context in which he operated is necessary.

One of Kramer's accomplishments was the public impact of his liberal filmmaking, which allowed Americans to move, make, and criticize movies in a more open political environment in the 1960s and after. His movies tested the waters of public discourse and opened the way for liberal perspectives on the most significant issues of his day. This development occurred from the start of his producing career in 1947 and continued into the 1970s. But the historical moment when Kramer and his movies dominated Hollywood's political landscape was the "turn of the sixties," from 1958 until 1962.[11] During this period, he was dubbed "Hollywood's producer of controversy" for creating films that emerged from and shaped the industry's influential discourses about national politics, society, and culture.[12] In these years, the veneer of consensus and conformity in Cold War America began to crack, and the cultural, social, and political challenges and changes that characterized the sixties began to appear. The producer-director released a film nearly every year in this period. *The Defiant Ones, On the Beach, Inherit the Wind,* and *Judgment at Nuremberg* dealt with American race relations, the threat of nuclear war, violations of free thought and expression, and the Holocaust. They advocated for civil rights and civil liberties, nuclear arms control, and Holocaust remembrance.

The social and political messages of these four films made them highly relevant to contemporary national and international issues, and provoked much public discussion and debate. Granted, at this point, Kramer was making movies during a period of declining and relatively low Hollywood output. Their impact and influence may have been greater than films made earlier or today. Even so, these movies attracted prolific and often profound comment from film reviewers and filmgoers alike. One industry trade paper called Kramer's 1959 film, *On the Beach,* "the powerful peace propaganda screen drama," and a filmgoer considered it "a valiant and inspired enterprise [o]n behalf of world peace."[13] "I left the theater with the feeling that nothing, <u>nothing, nothing</u> is so important as stopping the next war before it begins," exclaimed another filmgoer. "Those who decry disarmament proposals as unrealistic . . . should be required to attend." In 1960 a reviewer for the *Guardian* considered *Inherit the Wind* to be a "cry for the freedom for man to think" and attributed the film's political message to Kramer's liberal perspectives. "He sees men afraid to deviate from the norm, afraid to disagree with accepted attitudes, afraid to think and act radically. The battle for this freedom . . . is one that he himself has had to fight." A letter writer declared to Kramer the same year, "Any man who stands as you do for the ideals on which our Government was founded deserves the 'Oscar' of us Common people for helping protect our liberties."[14]

By the start of the sixties, then, Kramer's achievements as a liberal filmmaker had earned him remarkable recognition and respect internationally as well as in the United States. His popular and professional reputation at home gained him the first star to be dedicated on the Hollywood Walk of Fame in 1960 and the Thalberg Award in 1962. His commitment to liberal internationalism and cultural diplomacy in the midst of the Cold War secured his reputation abroad. His films screened and won prizes in film festivals around the world. The producer-director's overseas efforts were opposed early on by US government officials concerned about projecting a positive image of America and avoiding political controversy. Nowhere was this situation truer than in the Soviet Union. But Kramer rejected such limits on his freedom of expression and action, limits paradoxically put in place to fight a Cold War in defense of freedom. "In the free world, the artist must have freedom of expression. This is basic—it must be whole, not partial," he argued.[15] He believed his movies demonstrated that freedom and thus played an important ideological role in the Cold War. Seeking cooperation and exchange rather than conflict with America's superpower rival, he was invited to the 1963 Moscow International Film Festival as an honored member of the festival jury. There he acted on his liberal, universal ideals, and he won accolades as a cultural diplomat from the Soviets and Americans, including the US State Department.

Kramer's evident cultural and political importance in his time and place has since been obscured, due to a series of contradictions related to his career, politics, and films. His professional ambitions and political commitments did not always complement each other, creating internal inconsistencies and external conflicts. These contradictions, in turn, have polarized critical opinion about him. An aim of this book is to explore these matters to explain the rise and fall of Kramer's critical and political reputation over the middle decades of the twentieth century. Understanding these contradictions can tell us about not only the challenges Kramer faced as a Hollywood liberal but also the cultural and political tensions existing in Cold War America.

Contradictions and Challenges

As a filmmaker, Kramer occupied a paradoxical position: enjoying praise for his producing successes and enduring criticism for his directing failures. His early accomplishments as a producer on films such as

Champion (1949) and *Home of the Brave* (1949) earned him acclaim as "Hollywood's wonder boy who's shown how to make good pictures with precedent-shattering economy." Many, including Bosley Crowther, compared him favorably to his prominent producing predecessors: "Not since the late Irving Thalberg and Darryl F. Zanuck burst forth as Hollywood miracle workers has there been such a whiz as this young man." Kramer learned and made his mark on the business side of film-making at a challenging time in the industry, during the "boom and bust" decade of the 1940s.[16] He innovated and excelled in the areas of film funding, casting, distribution contracts, marketing, and promotion. He also worked with a veritable "who's who" of post–World War II filmmakers: he gave actors Kirk Douglas and Marlon Brando their first starring film roles and hired respected directors such as Edward Dmytryk and Fred Zinnemann. Sidney Poitier credited him with hiring African Americans when no one else in Hollywood would. Kramer collaborated closely with his screenwriters, most famously Carl Foreman, one of his first business partners from whom he later acrimoniously parted. Known as a "creative" rather than a "managing" producer, Kramer participated fully in his films' creative teams. In 1951 he characterized this difference as that between a logistical, "push-button manager"—an analogy he drew from his favorite sport of baseball—and "something like the artist" with "the temperament of handicraft workers."[17]

Once Kramer began directing in 1955, however, his skills—apart from his handling of actors—were much criticized. Pauline Kael's first review of a Kramer film, *Ship of Fools* (1965), analyzed his entire career up to that point and addressed the contrast between Kramer's roles as producer and as director. "There was talent in his productions" early on, she observed, but "there was no more reason to think it was his talent." As a producer, Kramer needed "only the talent to buy talent," and his initial motion pictures "were often cleverly and economically directed" by others. But the "pictures he has directed himself are not skillful," she decided. His first self-directed film, *Not as a Stranger* (1955), "lacked what used to be called sensibility, and formally it lacked rhythm and development." To Kael's mind, the quality of Kramer's direction never improved but actually worsened over time.[18] Although Kael and Sarris were among the most vociferous voices raised against Kramer's filmmaking, they were joined by more restrained observers as time went on. "As his critics often noted, Kramer was probably the least visual thinker among Hollywood's major filmmakers of the time," writer Mark Harris suggests; "shooting a movie, for him, was primarily a matter of assembling a group of actors and executing the words in a script."[19] As a result, by the 1960s, Kramer's conventional visual style made his films such as *Guess Who's Coming to Dinner* (1967) feel old-fashioned and plodding, just as Hollywood filmmakers were experimenting with the new techniques associated with European art cinema.

Similarly, the producer-director's reputation as a Hollywood liberal waxed and waned with that of post–World War II liberalism. As he staked out his positions on a range of issues, his words and actions were attacked variously by the political Right and Left and sometimes by both at the same time. His embattled experience as a liberal during the Cold War demonstrated what scholars now see: the "liberal consensus" of Cold War America was anything but.[20] Kramer became well known locally, nationally, and even internationally for wearing "his liberal politics on his sleeve." His politics built on the foundation of President Franklin Delano Roosevelt's New Deal of the 1930s. He often commented that he came into political consciousness in the era of the Great Depression. "We wanted to take part in the drive for the creation of a better world."[21] He advocated for social welfare and the rights of labor, civil rights, and civil liberties.

But he also circulated among leftists during the 1930s and 1940s, when a Popular Front liberal-left coalition flourished, particularly in Hollywood. In the 1950s and early 1960s, Kramer's political advocacy and affiliations led to confrontations with the anticommunist Red Scare and blacklist in which he variously clashed and conceded. His clashes honed his reputation as an embattled liberal facing down the Hollywood Right. His concessions—most famously, his 1951 break with his screenwriter and partner Carl Foreman, a former communist and future blacklistee—undermined it. Kramer was opposed to communism, yet he also cannot be called anticommunist. He did not fear or attack communists or support the blacklist.[22] He also opposed nuclear weapons, as in his film *On the Beach,* and he forged a relationship with the Soviets. In the wake of the Red Scare and the blacklist, scholar Andrew Paul finds Hollywood liberalism becoming more libertarian than social democratic, developing into a politics "that emphasized individual liberties over matters of social justice."[23] Kramer still sought to synthesize both.

Underlying Kramer's liberalism was a belief in intellectual universalism. In this view, all human beings were the same "under the skin," equally deserving of the same rights—similarly conceived—and capable of building "universal human connections beyond race" and other differences.[24] The theme and message in four of Kramer's films about American race relations—*Home of the Brave, The Defiant Ones, Pressure Point* (1962), and *Guess Who's Coming to Dinner*—exemplified his universalism. His universalistic convictions meant he saw no difference in the substitution of an African American character for an initially Jewish one in two of these films. "I chose to believe—and I think rightly—that all prejudices have at least a common denominator."[25] In the late 1940s and 1950s, Kramer shared this belief in universalism with most liberals, especially Jewish liberals, and in his films and public pronouncements at home and abroad. But intellectual universalism would be found wanting in the 1960s, criticized for overlooking specificities of ethnicity, race, religion, nationality, and, later, gender and sexuality in favor of one standard. This standard—rather than being truly universal—was actually white and male, a political and intellectual understanding Kramer and other liberals eventually gained. "I've made films about the black man's struggle for justice," he recalled, but by the 1970s he saw them as "inadequate" and "naïve."[26]

Kramer's career and politics came together in his films, and he became known for making liberal films in the social problem genre. Social problem films took as their subject a problem or conflict in society, such as racism or corruption, and illuminated contemporary issues and conditions in the process. The genre had a long history in Hollywood. Within the early motion picture industry, as film historian Kevin Brownlow notes, these films were known as "sociological" or "thought" films. They were both topical and political, originating in the era of Progressive reform in the first two decades of the twentieth century and flourishing during the populist period of the 1930s Great Depression. By the 1940s, the genre was associated with liberalism.[27] The plots told the stories of an individual or a group dramatically confronting and successfully overcoming a problem or conflict. As a consequence, these films generally provided simplistic analyses of complex issues and personal, individual answers when political, institutional solutions were needed. They also were didactic. As scholars Peter Roffman and Jim Purdy argue, films in the genre "teach a moral lesson of social significance . . . in a didactic fashion." In this way, the impulse and purpose behind these fictional films were related to those of documentary film, that is, to inform and educate citizens. Social problem filmmakers also drew on the visual conventions of documentary films, with a realistic style matching the realism in subject matter.[28]

The substance and style of social problem films fit Kramer's aims as a liberal and his approach as a filmmaker. The genre offered him flexibility, allowing him to make films about contemporary topics and historical subjects. Social problem films are also known for "an extensive crossing of genres," and various types of films can fall within the category.[29] Kramer dealt with social problems in war films and westerns, courtroom dramas and melodramas. His body of work did include films outside the genre. "I do believe, however, that motion pictures, within the framework of entertainment, must have something to say," he stated in the early 1960s. "I try to make pictures which have a relationship to reality, and which touch on the world as it is today." "He has remained," critic Arthur Knight observed in 1961, "sharply contemporaneous, eschewing an easy popularity in order to handle such demanding subject matter as paraplegic veterans, refugees in Israel, prison reform, integration, and the atom bomb."[30] This commitment meant Kramer's films expressed liberal themes of racial and ethnic tolerance, freedom of thought and expression, and peaceful coexistence between the United States and the Soviet Union. "Naturally, I make pictures which reflect my viewpoint," he declared in 1960. The visual style of the social problem film genre further suited the producer-director. The "comfortable, non-self-demonstrative black-and-white form of realism à la Stanley Kramer" worked well with the social and political content of his movies, as did his use of a simple and straightforward narrative form.[31]

Yet Kramer's close association with the social problem film—what film scholar Matthew Bernstein assesses as "one of Hollywood's most pretentious and least profitable genres"—created considerable contradictions.[32] Film reviewers and filmgoers accepted his films' genre category. But they questioned whether his films addressed social problems sincerely or sensationally, whether they reflected more his social conscience or his commercial interests, and whether they succeeded or failed in their political aims. At the start of Kramer's career, most opinion fell on the side of sincerity, social consciousness, and success, and many respondents continued to feel this way. He was hailed as "one of the few men in Hollywood with the courage to face, discuss, and risk his time and money on pictures that *have* something to say." He received praise for "bringing to the motion picture screen significant problems that beset our world and in pointing the way, through the film medium, to greater understanding among all men."[33] As his career proceeded, however, critics wondered, did "exploiting such situations aid or retard progress toward solving the things being pictured?" Criticisms grew about the "gulf between honest intentions and commercial realization" of his films.[34] In the *Christian Century*, Ronald Steel wrote, "Stanley Kramer has the mind of a moralist trapped in the soul of a Hollywood businessman. His reputation for serious themes is sabotaged by his inability to resist embellishing them with the gaudy baubles of Hollywood." Over time, Kramer was found guilty of "entrepreneurial liberalism," in film critic David Thomson's pithy phrase. "Commercialism, of the most crass and confusing kind, has devitalized all his projects."[35]

Given the market realities of the motion picture industry, there were commentators who recognized but did not fault Kramer's commercialism. "He is essentially a combination of the businessman-artist who is talented enough to look out for both ends at the same time." The difficulty of balancing financial with social and political concerns while making Hollywood films appeared in contemporary accounts of his career. "Mr. Kramer has chosen to specialize in the most difficult, chancy, yet vital area that exists for films," Arthur Knight further observed. "It is no coincidence that, so far as America's filmmakers are concerned, he operates in this field virtually without challenge or competition."[36] John Howard Lawson, a screenwriter, a communist, and one of the first targets of the Hollywood blacklist, also understood Kramer's commercial context. Lawson seriously engaged with the role of "film in the battle of ideas." As a communist, he believed that film "has potentialities as people's art—when it is controlled by the people and serves their interests. . . . But," he argued, "no such democratization of the art is possible under capitalism."[37] In his critique of Kramer, Lawson emphasized the restrictions imposed "by the commercial system within which he functions," and he joined Knight in appreciating how "Kramer's concern with ideas makes him unique among Hollywood producers." Kramer himself often noted the limits to his much-publicized independence. "I didn't buck the Hollywood system," he recalled. "I was part of the Hollywood system, had to be."[38]

Within the industry, Kramer's social problem films were further categorized as "message movies," a term he hated. He felt it marginalized his work and undermined its market value as entertainment. "I can't accept . . . the appellation of message which the exhibitor, distributor, or financial people have made for years a mark of nondistinction at the box office." "If you want to send a message, call Western Union," or so goes an old Hollywood adage. Of course, as Kramer knew, all movies carry messages, and yet he felt he needed to deny that fact. "I do not believe in so-called message pictures," he argued. His movies' "commentary on the passing scene, the expression of a point of view is not a message."[39] No one bought his denial. Film reviewers and filmgoers readily identified the social and political statements in his movies. They also responded intensely and variously, depending on political perspective. "No other producer in Hollywood has so conscientiously set himself to attacking important and difficult themes, allying himself with the cause of progressivism," as Knight, a liberal reviewer, admiringly put it. But conservatives accused Kramer of "loading his films with the most brazen pro-Communist propaganda." Left-leaning respondents argued the opposite: "with Kramer's movies," as was true of social problem films generally, "the subject is safely controversial."[40] These conflicting opinions about his social problem films meant they often provoked public debate about the relevant issues. "Film is a primary force in mass communication," Kramer observed, "and it spills over into the political arena, like it or not."[41]

For Kramer, such public debate was—alongside good box-office returns—the best possible outcome for his productions. "I have attempted, and I hope succeeded, in making pictures that command attention . . . that hit people hard, force people to see them, to think and to take a stand." His films became known as "thinking entertainment." He was "accorded the title of the thinking man's producer," because he liked "to provoke his audience with thoughtful pictures."[42] Film reviewers credited his social problem films "with raising the intelligence quotient of motion pictures," and filmgoers agreed. "I like the intellectual stamp on your productions," wrote one to Kramer, while a second stated, "You're just a troublemaker. Why do you want to make people think?"[43] By the late 1950s, Kramer did not assume "that a film can change anyone's mind about any issue. But if a screen drama . . . leads people to say 'I never thought about it in exactly that way,' then the job has been worthwhile." "It is not necessary to agree," he went on to tell an audience in the early 1960s. "It is necessary to discuss." And world leaders, political commentators, film reviewers, spectators, and Hollywood insiders did discuss, as did Kramer himself. He energetically participated in public debates over the meaning and messages of his films, revealing his enjoyment of what he called "the deliciousness of head-on conflict of ideas."[44]

In this way, the producer-director and his motion pictures intersected with the larger public sphere and illuminated the play of ideas and interests in the twentieth-century United States. Whether contradictory or controversial, Kramer's films performed a crucial "agenda-setting" function, especially in the late 1950s and early 1960s. His movies prompted film viewers and reviewers on "what to think *about*" if not precisely what to think.[45] Kramer's ability to shape the public agenda testifies to his prominence and prestige at the turn of the sixties, even as his critical reputation began its decline. Italian critic Tino Ranieri captured the contradictory nature of Kramer's career at the time. "Stanley Kramer stands behind the camera as on a podium," Ranieri argued in 1961. The producer-director was more "like a critic for a widely circulated press" than "an authentic artist of the cinema world." But he "struggles and becomes full of sincere enthusiasm, like the good democratic person that he is."[46]

The public discussions and debates surrounding *The Defiant Ones, On the Beach, Inherit the Wind,* and *Judgment at Nuremberg* reveal the cultural and political impact of Kramer's filmmaking at the height of his influence. These four films form the core of this study, but they are placed in the larger context of the producer-director's career, politics, body of work, and impact at home and abroad. The chapters on the individual films focus on different aspects of production and reception. Tracing the development of these films from page to screen illuminates Kramer and his team's work process with a variety of contexts and content. But all of the chapters highlight the controversies sparked by the individual films. *The Defiant Ones* provoked disputes about race, racism, and the civil rights movement in America. *On the Beach* led to global dialogue on the Cold War nuclear arms race. *Inherit the Wind* prompted debate about the Hollywood blacklist and civil liberties; *Judgment at Nuremberg,* about Nazi war crimes and the Holocaust; and both films, about how history should be represented and interpreted on film.

Sources of discourse about all of Kramer's movies came from inside and outside Hollywood. Kramer, his filmmaking colleagues, industry insiders, the trade and mainstream press, film critics, public figures, and filmgoers commented on his films. The prominence of many of the respondents to his films during this period is striking. Comments came from US and foreign government officials such as President Dwight D. Eisenhower's cabinet and Willy Brandt, the mayor of West Berlin; politicians and Supreme Court justices; scientists and Nobel Prize winners such as Linus Pauling and Edward Teller; cultural icons such as writer James Baldwin, poet Carl Sandburg, and baseball player Jackie Robinson; plus many American and international celebrities. The various audiences for Kramer's films—critical, political, and popular—brought different expertise, experiences, and expectations into the movie theaters, which in turn shaped their reception.

With regard to the popular audience, the challenges of uncovering "real cinema spectators" from the past are well known in historical film studies. But included in Kramer's papers are letters from filmgoers and comment cards from preview audiences, particularly for the four films focused on here. More audience response material exists for these than for any of his other films (apart from his 1971 film *Bless the Beasts and the Children*). This material provides evidence of popular responses to his movies. "We were most impressed," wrote one couple. "It really had a message which we thought was worthwhile." "I have long admired your work," noted one man. "You are an asset to the 20th century." These respondents were mostly self-selected and, therefore, ready to engage with social and political issues. As a result, extant responses to Kramer's films cannot be taken as representative of the general public's opinion, but they do indicate the range of reception possibilities at the time.[47]

Taken together, this rich collection of historical sources allows for a close examination of the production, circulation, and reception of the political meanings of Kramer's films during his career. This approach fits well with recent methodological developments in historical film and genre studies, which consider films and other media texts as "sites of discursive practice." It builds on but also differs from that of earlier popular biographies of Kramer, his memoirs, and scholarly, mainly textual, studies of his individual films.[48] Many of Kramer's films have been the subject of scholarly inquiry, especially *The Defiant Ones, On the Beach, Inherit the Wind,* and *Judgment at Nuremberg*, which have been called "the essence of the Kramer canon."[49] Textual analyses and assessments of his body of work have tended to mirror those of critics, often leading to negative evaluations of both the content and style. Although I find these persuasive and integrate them into my discussion, they often fail to fully contextualize his films within their historical moment. Contextual studies have proved most useful, and works on the key Kramer films *High Noon* and *Guess Who's Coming to Dinner* have helped frame my study.[50]

Understanding and appreciating Kramer's historical significance requires attention to the discursive, political, and historical environment within which he produced and presented his movies. This book aims to achieve just that, focusing less on the texts of his films than on the historical contexts. This book also presents more of the producer-director's public life than his private self. In press interviews and his memoirs, Kramer also privileged his career and politics over his personal life. "Too much self-analysis is dangerous," he confessed later in his career. Yet he did recognize how his biography mattered at his career's start.[51]

From New York to Hollywood

In telling the story of his early life, Kramer emphasized how his youthful experiences shaped his subsequent Hollywood career and liberal political commitments. Kramer was born Stanley J. Abramson in New York City in 1913, "just a few months before my father separated from my mother, leaving her with an infant son and next to no money." His mother, Mildred Kramer, raised him, because "my father was long gone." "I have no recollection of my father, and no one in my family ever spoke about him." He and his mother went by her family name, and his new middle name came from his uncle Earl Kramer. His mother "preserved our family through a perilous time," Kramer recalled, and he conveyed the rocky economic conditions of his youth. She "had enough education to get a job as a secretary," but she worked long hours, and the income she earned was "meager." As a result, for most of his childhood, they lived with his grandparents, who provided childcare while his mother worked. He believed his Jewish grandparents "instilled good traditional values in me." Like many Jews in New York—the city where more than 40 percent of American Jews lived—his grandfather had worked in the garment industry. "Their apartment," as Kramer described it, "was really a hole in the wall, dark and airless, it seemed always crowded, with four people living there. There were really only two bedrooms, one for my grandparents and one for my mother, so I lived in a little fenced-off area next to my mother's door, which was called my room."[52]

Their apartment was located in an infamous New York neighborhood. "Where we lived, Hell's Kitchen, was a notoriously rough slum on the west side of mid-Manhattan." Officially designated the Middle West Side, the area was called by the name "that disorders, rioting, and crime won for it in the early days of its settlement," observed a social worker in 1912, the year before Kramer's birth. By the turn of the twentieth century, small numbers of Jews, African Americans, and other groups had moved into a neighborhood dominated by German and Irish immigrants. Although very ethnically diverse, the residents shared job insecurity, poor housing, and dismal urban conditions. They were affected by "disheartening inertia" and "social neglect," noted the social worker, and they apathetically "accepted the conditions of their environment." "The center of a boy's life," determined a 1914 study, "was the gang to which he belonged, almost of necessity, from an early age."[53] Kramer confirmed this finding. "To protect yourself, you had to belong to a gang," and gangs were defined by ethnicity. "I was Jewish and since we were always outnumbered and often outweighed, we solved our problems by making strategic alliances, usually with the blacks" but also "some Irish and some Hispanics." "That was our way of achieving integration, I guess."[54]

What Kramer had going for him was a sharp intelligence and strong family support for his education. Mildred Kramer was "always determined that one day her son would enjoy the opportunities she never had. She was constantly urging me to study my lessons, earn good grades, and prepare myself for a college education." His aptitude for learning was recognized by his teachers, and he advanced through his schooling quickly. Later, he attributed his skipping grades less to "brilliance on my part" than to overcrowded schools. "I have one major regret about my early life: I was shoved through Manhattan's schools, and through New York University from the age of fifteen to nineteen, so fast that I forgot my youth."[55] He attended DeWitt Clinton High School, and among his teachers and fellow alumni were prominent, liberal, and left-leaning figures. His former history teacher, Irwin S. Guernsey, called "Doc," later corresponded with Kramer. So did his former English teacher, Abel Meeropol, lyricist and composer of the anti-lynching song "Strange Fruit," communist, and active in Popular Front circles.

They praised him for his stances on civil rights and civil liberties. "I wonder whether your De Witt training had anything to do with that," Guernsey wrote. At New York University in the depths of the Depression from 1929 to 1933, Kramer considered careers in business and law. The latter "fit perfectly with my mother's wishes. 'My son, the lawyer,' was then a popular thing among the Jewish population of New York." Kramer himself admired the famous labor and criminal defense lawyer Clarence Darrow. "I had dreams . . . of becoming another Clarence Darrow," with the ability to right social wrongs.[56]

Kramer's sense of social justice and his liberal commitments were shaped by coming of age during the economic crises and political transformations of the late 1920s and 1930s.

> As I reached early manhood during the Depression, I was also developing a social awareness that influenced my thinking about many things. Franklin Delano Roosevelt's election in 1932 brought with it a new liberal philosophy quite different from the big-business-oriented, conservative Republicanism of Herbert Hoover. The New Deal, with its social legislation, was really a better deal for most Americans. Roosevelt's whole aim was to give the average person a greater share in society and to take care of those who couldn't take care of themselves. This represented an innovation in our government. I agreed enthusiastically with almost every bit of it.[57]

Kramer appreciated how Roosevelt's New Deal improved economic security and working conditions. In contrast, when he was growing up, "there were no eight-hour days or even two-day weekends at the time." He also valued President Roosevelt's "concern for the welfare of all Americans, including blacks," although the first lady's endorsement of civil rights made an even greater impact.[58] In 1939, when Eleanor Roosevelt resigned from the Daughters of the American Revolution in protest over singer Marian Anderson being barred from singing at Constitution Hall, "that changed the course of my life." As with his fellow American Jews, Kramer found an ideology in New Deal liberalism and an identity in the New Deal electoral coalition that would last the rest of his life. "I'm a product of the FDR era," he would often say. "I grew up with social consciousness, burning with it."[59]

Kramer also grew up in the movie business. Mildred Kramer's secretarial job was in the New York office of Paramount Pictures, and his uncle Earl Kramer worked in film distribution. His mother used to get passes to Paramount theaters. "My first contact with the movies was on Saturday afternoons. As a very small boy, Tom Mix was my hero, that's for sure."[60] At New York University, Kramer wrote for the student magazine, the *Medley*, and edited the cinema section for several issues over 1930–1931. The film articles and reviews covered major movies in Hollywood history. The antiwar *All Quiet on the Western Front* (1930), based on the international best-selling novel by Erich Maria Remarque, "is one of the best of the year." The film's "most dramatic moment" occurs when the young German World War I soldier, played by Lew Ayres, offers "his criticism of the war in general." In *City Lights* (1931), Charlie Chaplin "has proved himself the greatest comedian ever produced by Hollywood." Even so, the success of this silent film in the new age of talking pictures would not bring back "the old 'silents.'"[61] From this experience, Kramer applied for a paid internship in Hollywood. "For some reason I've never quite fathomed," he was selected, along with four other screenwriters-in-the-making. "I graduated on a Friday and headed for Hollywood on Monday," Kramer remembered. "That was 1933 and I have been here ever since."[62]

What an auspicious moment to arrive in Hollywood, even for a lowly intern. The year 1933, when President Roosevelt took office, put Kramer in the movie capital just as the industry and its inhabitants were in the midst of myriad transformations. The advent of sound film at the turn of the decade demanded more screenwriters, and a stream of writers flowed west from New York, gathering speed with the Great Depression. These "Hollywood New Yorkers," as historian Saverio Giovacchini labels them, brought a new aesthetic and political sensibility to southern California.[63] Also by 1933, the full force of the Depression had hit the industry, with cost-cutting measures, employee layoffs, closed theaters, and studios in bankruptcy. Employees began organizing in response. The talent guilds formed, with the Screen Writers Guild and Screen Actors Guild established in April and June 1933, respectively. The passage of a cornerstone of the New Deal—the 1935 Wagner Act legalizing collective bargaining—gave a boost to unionizing in Hollywood. In a company town run by fiercely anti-union studio executives and "virtually unorganized in 1929," the industry became "fully unionized from top to bottom" by 1945. During this period, the movie capital vote for Roosevelt was well over 80 percent, "making Hollywood solid New Deal territory."[64] It also was territory for European filmmakers fleeing the rise of Nazism. These developments affected the industry's product, and scholars find a burgeoning "Hollywood democratic modernism" and "cinema of liberal idealism" in the 1930s.[65] Kramer would fit right in.

After the three-month internship at 20th Century-Fox, "nobody had taught us anything and they kicked us out on the street," but Kramer did not leave Hollywood. "I didn't have the train fare to return to New York."[66] He also was not ready to abandon the movie business. "I had developed vivid dreams about what kind of films I would write and I did not intend to abandon those dreams." With some fortuitous gambling at the racetrack to tide him over, he began to work a series of jobs that helped him learn filmmaking from start to finish. He worked as a laborer on a "swing gang" at night and on a "backlot gang" during the day, shifting scenes, building sets, and performing general carpentry. He wrote screenplays on his own time and sold one, *Stunt Girl*, to Republic Pictures, but it was never made. A "fortunate connection" brought him to Metro-Goldwyn-Mayer, then the dominant studio in the industry.[67] Employed in the research department and then as an assistant editor, Kramer gained valuable experience. "The pay was low, the glory was small, but it was a good place to learn how to put a movie together."[68] After achieving the rank of senior editor in 1938, he left MGM and focused on his writing. He penned screenplays for films at Columbia Pictures and Republic Pictures and radio scripts for the *Lux Radio Theater*, *The Rudy Vallee Show*, and the *Big Town* series. In 1940 Kramer joined the independent production company of David L. Loew and Albert Lewin. He worked on two movies, *So Ends Our Night* (1941) as a production assistant and *The Moon and Sixpence* (1942) as an associate producer.

"So I was slowly working my way up"—from laborer, researcher, editor, and writer to producer—"when a little something called World War II came along." In 1943 he entered the US Army Signal Corps, which meant he would be staying stateside and making movies for the military. "Lewin and Loew very decently gave me the title 'associate producer,' a big boost in getting me assigned to a unit stationed in Astoria, Long Island, New York. You had to have a background in the film industry to get assigned to such a unit." After attending basic training, Kramer returned to New York to the old Paramount Astoria studio the army had commandeered and renamed the Signal Corps Photographic Center. He was just one of many Hollywood and documentary writers, technicians, and producers the Army Signal Corps enlisted to turn out more than 2,500 films for different purposes during the war.[69] "I worked first on the *Army and Navy Screen Magazine,* which was like a *March of Time* newsreel for the troops. Later I got into other projects, including training films. It was a good experience that furthered my education in the various uses of film." One lesson he definitely learned: "film is a weapon." Kramer's army days saw the reelection of President Roosevelt for an unprecedented fourth term and, according to a colleague, involved him in "violating the law by engaging in pro-FDR activities while in uniform."[70] He also met fellow soldiers who would become partners in his future filmmaking ventures, including Carl Foreman. Foreman, a very talented screenwriter and for several years a member of the Communist Party, would be central to Stanley Kramer's greatest film achievements and the most difficult political conflicts in the early phase of his career.

Stanley Kramer at Columbia Studios, early 1950s. Courtesy of Department of Special Collections, Charles E. Young Research Library, University of California, Los Angeles, with permission from Karen Sharpe-Kramer.

1 A Hollywood Independent

Stanley Kramer began his career as a Hollywood independent in his mid-thirties at a volatile time in the US motion picture industry. By 1947, the year Kramer formed Screen Plays, Inc., the company that would produce his first film, Hollywood was reeling from a series of post–World War II shocks. Labor unions in the movie industry participated in the great postwar strike wave, and a series of violent strikes and conflicts occurred over 1945 and 1946. Box-office receipts began to decline from a wartime peak as Americans moved to the suburbs, bought televisions, and stayed home. The US government's antitrust case against the big Hollywood studios and their control of movie production, distribution, and exhibition was wending its way to the Supreme Court; the case would result in the 1948 *Paramount* decision divesting the studios of their theater chains. And in October 1947, the House Un-American Activities Committee (HUAC) would hold its first post–World War II hearings to investigate communist "subversion" in the motion picture industry. These hearings would feature the Hollywood Ten and lead to the establishment of the Hollywood blacklist. That the old Hollywood studio system was under increasing pressure created opportunities for Kramer and a new postwar generation of independent producers. But it also meant that Kramer and his fellow independents needed to make their way within a highly unstable and unpredictable industrial and political context.

For the decade starting in the late 1940s, Kramer met these conflicts and challenges through a series of negotiations and compromises in an effort to maintain both his producing career and his political commitments. As an independent producer, he still needed institutional support for financing, studio facilities, and distribution. Given this fact, he often qualified his status as "laughingly called an independent." "Independence was, in this equation, never more than comparative and highly circumscribed," argues scholar Denise Mann.[1] But Kramer's ability to successfully manage his early career in these new and difficult conditions earned him a reputation as a "boy wonder" and a "genius."[2] As to politics in the blacklist era, Kramer's liberalism meant he sought a middle path between the Hollywood Left and Right. In the process, he earned compliments and criticisms from liberals and leftists. But of most consequence he became a target of conservative anticommunists. Missed or understated in earlier assessments of Kramer's career, relentless attacks from the Right shaped the commercial and political environments in which he operated. The producer-director was never able to act without a hostile reaction from conservative forces in the movie capital, who accused him of "coddling Reds and pinkos."[3] Instead, Kramer constantly needed to defend his commitments to civil liberties, social welfare, and liberal internationalism throughout these years and later.

Kramer's liberal politics and independent position in the industry contributed to his selection of subjects for his early movies. He gravitated toward social problems, although not exclusively, and made the genre his own. He produced his first significant and successful social problem films—*Champion* (1949), *Home of the Brave* (1949), and *The Men* (1950)—and parlayed this achievement into an unprecedented $25 million deal with Columbia Pictures in 1951. Social problem films ideally reflected his social conscience and fulfilled his commercial strategy. The reality of the resulting movies, however, did not always achieve this ideal. Kramer soon determined that to preserve his vision of his productions, he needed more control over his pictures. By 1955 he had decided to start directing. Unique among the Hollywood independents, he moved from production into direction, "rather than the other way around," as Mann points out.[4] The first decade of Kramer's career and films matched the volatility of the motion picture industry, veering between successes and setbacks.

Crafting a Career's Start

At the end of World War II, Kramer left the Army Signal Corps as a first lieutenant, briefly married radio and theatrical actress Marilyn Erskine—their marriage was annulled—and returned to Hollywood. "I found the whole town waiting to ignore me," he recalled. "I scurried and scrounged for some kind of job until I finally decided if I wanted one, I'd have to invent it myself. That's when I decided to declare myself a producer."[5] His new career direction fit with the transformation of the production system then occurring in Hollywood. Eight big companies still dominated the industry: five "majors" that owned the-aters (Loew's/MGM, Warner Brothers, Paramount, 20th Century-Fox, and RKO) and three "minors" that did not own theaters (Universal, Co-lumbia, and United Artists). But the old studio system, a factorylike sys-tem of mass production that required ongoing investments in person-nel, facilities, and equipment, was no longer economically efficient or profitable in the new postwar environment. Instead, the "package-unit system" used by independent producers such as Kramer worked better. The producer made one film at a time, bringing together the necessary elements for that particular production and then disbanding. This new system of production allowed for greater flexibility, creativity, and cost saving.[6] Kramer became adept at this new mode of filmmaking and rose to the top rank of the Hollywood independents.

But Kramer first needed a production company. He already had co-founded Story Productions, Inc., with Armand S. Deutsch, an heir to the Sears, Roebuck, and Company fortune. "He came to Hollywood in 1947 with the dream of more than one rich man: to get into the movie business. He needed an ambitious young fellow to show him the ropes, and I was elected." Although they managed to secure the rights to "a very hot property," they never proceeded with the production. Kramer believed that "Deutsch had second thoughts about me. To him I was just a kid." Kramer sold his interest in the film rights to Deutsch and started Screen Plays, Inc., in 1947, with Carl Foreman and Herbert Baker, writers whom he had met in the military; George Glass, a publi-cist who had worked with Kramer just before the war at Loew-Lewin; and Sam Zagon, an attorney. "So there we were—army buddies with a new film company!"[7]

Screen Plays became the first company through which Kramer pro-duced a film but not the last. In 1949 he organized Stanley Kramer Pro-ductions, Inc., and over the years he would form different companies for legal and financial reasons. For example, the Stanley Kramer Com-pany, Stanley Kramer Pictures Corporation, and Lomitas Productions received credits for various films at different moments in time over his long career. "Business as such does not interest him," reported Bosley Crowther in a major profile feature article on Kramer in the *New York Times* in 1950, but as a producer it demanded his attention and drew on his evident "entrepreneurial ability."[8]

Financing did as well, and Kramer was creative with funding his productions. Banks were unwilling to put up money without collateral, "and I had no collateral." "In other words, to attain a loan, the producer need only give tangible proof he has no need of one." At Bank of America, he also was told he had no reputation to bank on: *"Who are you, Mr. Kramer?"*[9] Despite such blows, he made it work. Early on he found investors, such as Deutsch, and later Hollywood studios would provide funding. He enjoyed telling tales about securing money for his movies, and journalists enjoyed hearing them. One of his favorite stories concerned an acquaintance, Willie Schenker, whom he had met in his early days in Hollywood. Schenker was supposed to invest money in opening a Chinese restaurant, but instead "I promoted Willie out of his seventy-five hundred dollars." "I suppose you could say that was a triumph of art over egg foo yung." Schenker's investment in Kramer's first picture, *So This Is New York*, failed. "My sense of guilt about Willie was horrible. I mean, the Chinese restaurant had gone up in smoke." But, with a stake in Kramer's next few films, Schenker's investment paid off at an estimated $300,000, "a pretty good return," Kramer added.[10] He convinced additional investors, such as John Stillman, whose son Robert became an associate producer for a time, and Bruce Church, a produce grower in Salinas, California's richest agricultural area and the so-called Salad Bowl of the World. With Church and his partners as financial backers, Philip K. Scheuer of the *Los Angeles Times* could not resist pointing out, Kramer "is thus assured plenty of lettuce."[11]

Even as Kramer became more established in the movie industry, he still needed to manage the nerve-racking negotiations of getting a production "greenlighted." "I've always claimed it was the most creative part of filmmaking." He described one instance, after he and his partners had a story and screenplay they liked: "Then started the almost impossible progression of events which goes into an independent production. We blew our publicity horn. We promoted bank backing. The bank wanted to know who the distributor, director and stars were. But you can't have the others signed until you have the bank set—it's a vicious circle. So you work on all of them at the same time."[12] Kramer later called these maneuvers "an advanced game of footsy," while others considered his machinations "a kind of diplomatic gamemanship."[13] Either way, the young producer excelled at pinpointing and persuading potential backers for his films. Financing also came through partnership deals with other independents and with individuals. New business partners such as Sam Katz, cofounder of the Balaban and Katz theater chain, brought funds into Kramer's companies ($2 million in Katz's case). Later, United Artists and Columbia Pictures provided financial backing for Kramer's productions.

Even with financing, Kramer and his partners needed to keep expenses low to ensure they could be covered. They developed several innovative strategies "to use brains instead of money" in their filmmaking. In the process, Kramer received recognition inside and outside the motion picture industry as a "genius on a low budget."[14] The fundamental strategy was solid preparation, including rehearsals, before shooting the film. "Wouldn't you rather we made our mistakes in rehearsal, with no expensive crew standing around," Kramer asked, "than make them during shooting at the cost of $2,000 an hour?" This innovation cut the number of shooting days and costs to half the amount of the major studios. "Every nickel [spent] must show on the screen," he wrote.[15] Although commentators such as Bosley Crowther found this strategy "very sensible," it was perceived as "revolutionary" within the industry. Kramer disagreed with this perception. "Changing an obsolete pattern which is losing money is not revolutionary. It is only good solid business. . . . Hell, it's conservative," he exclaimed.[16]

Kramer's company shared several strategies with other Hollywood independents. They kept overhead low. A small salaried team of Kramer as producer, Foreman as screenwriter, and Glass as production assistant, general manager, publicist, and salesman started. Later, the team expanded to include others, such as a production designer, Rudolph Sternad, and composer Dimitri Tiomkin. They kept only a small office—"If you want to talk to somebody, you just stick your head out the window and yell," Glass reported—and rented soundstages and equipment as needed.[17] Their salaries were often deferred until a picture made money. "It's murder," Kramer felt. Since the producer needed "to wait till everyone else is paid off, he may never have it at all!" But it got his movies made and set the pattern for the rest of his career. "That's smart business," Hollywood gossip columnist Hedda Hopper reported.[18] Deferment evolved into "participation," whereby the filmmakers—from the screenwriters to the actors—took a percentage of the film's profits in lieu of salary. Despite later conflicts, Daniel Taradash credited Kramer for this innovation. "It was a fine thing to do in those days, and made writers respect him very much."[19]

Another of Kramer's cost-saving measures was to cast lesser-known actors rather than Hollywood stars. Avoiding stars brought greater realism to independent productions, as the actors could subsume themselves into their roles and audiences would be more likely to believe them. In turn, Kramer's casting of Kirk Douglas in *Champion*, James Edwards in *Home of the Brave*, and Marlon Brando in *The Men* launched their Hollywood careers.

Using actors instead of stars also privileged the film's story. For Kramer, the "subject matter is everything" and was often—although not always—a social problem. In post–World War II Hollywood, social problem subjects had many advantages for Kramer and company as it did for other Hollywood independents. They "similarly sought to break the classical Hollywood mode by choosing challenging story material," Mann argues.[20] Such material differentiated their product from that of the big studios. Independent producers, Kramer wrote, "cannot be a small scale echo of what the majors are doing." Given limited budgets, they could not compete with the big studios in expensive genres, like the "lush, musical, co-starring comedies, or psychological mysteries." Kramer and his colleagues "pinned our faith in stories that had something to say" and ideally "something that other movies hadn't said before."[21] If chosen correctly, such stories could generate popular interest. Kramer believed filmgoers wanted "stories off the beaten track." "We are in competition with TV. It is necessary to have a commodity which will draw an audience into theater. It must have more controversy, more drama, more everything."[22]

Statements and a "self-conscious approach to theme and topic" were characteristic of the social problem film genre and were succeeding in the postwar environment. In 1947, a year in which an estimated one-fifth of Hollywood's output was categorized as falling into the social problem genre, *Gentleman's Agreement* won the best picture Oscar. The film denounced anti-Semitism in the United States, a much-charged issue in the wake of the Holocaust. Starring Gregory Peck—who would later make *On the Beach* with Kramer—and produced by Darryl F. Zanuck, *Gentleman's Agreement* was a box-office hit, demonstrating the mainstream appeal of social problem films. Three of the first five films Kramer produced—*Champion* and *Home of the Brave* in 1949 and *The Men* in 1950—fell into this genre and enjoyed tremendous success. A capacious genre, social problem films are known as a "hybrid genre," and these first hits comprised one boxing film, two about war, and three psychological dramas.[23]

With *Champion*, Foreman adapted a 1916 short story by sports and fiction writer Ring Lardner. The rise-and-fall narrative was set in the brutal, corrupt world of New York boxing, and "New York was my turf," Kramer recalled.[24] "Here was a story in which I deeply believed." Since his days in Hell's Kitchen seeing acquaintances enter boxing, "I had developed a hatred of it. . . . I could see the punishment and exploitation it represented." The screenplay's interpretation of the boxer Midge Kelly and boxing also reflected Foreman's leftist politics. Although he had since left the Communist Party, he drew "a parallel between the prize fight business and western society or capitalism in 1948."[25] The film starred newcomer Kirk Douglas as Kelly. He "looked the part," Kramer believed. "He was raw-boned and lean, yet muscular," and had been a wrestler in college. Douglas also had the personality to project Kelly's "tremendous drive and colossal will" as he works his way up to the championship, abusing everyone around him in the process, only to die at the end.[26] *Champion*'s antihero was a departure from the boxer-as-victim of earlier fight films, and Douglas's performance earned him an Oscar nomination. The film won compliments for Screen Plays, Inc., "as a go-getter among rising young 'indies.'" Even as *Champion* was in postproduction, Kramer and company were working on the next.[27]

Home of the Brave, another crossover or hybrid social problem film released in 1949, dealt with race prejudice in the US military during World War II. The film starred James Edwards in his screen debut as an African American soldier, Peter Moss. Based on a critically acclaimed 1946 Broadway play by Arthur Laurents, who would later write the book for *West Side Story*, the movie explored the repercussions of a dangerous reconnaissance mission to a Japanese island by American soldiers. The character of Moss is psychologically traumatized by racism and war, leading to physical paralysis, and he is aided in his recovery by a white army psychiatrist, played by Jeff Corey. Foreman's screenplay fundamentally altered the original plot by switching the play's Jewish American main character to an African American in the movie. Kramer, as a Jew himself, had experienced anti-Semitism growing up and in the military. But he felt "*Home of the Brave* could be made more powerful by shifting its focus to antiblack prejudice." Profit motives also shaped this decision. Given Hollywood's recent attention to anti-Semitism in *Gentleman's Agreement*, as well as *Crossfire*, another 1947 film, this cycle of films appeared exhausted. The "film people," Laurents reported, "said Jews had been done," and another film about the subject would not appeal at the box office.[28]

As it turned out, *Home of the Brave* was the first of a cycle of social problem films in 1949 about racism, followed by *Pinky, Lost Boundaries*, and *Intruder in the Dust*. "Film's leading box office star for 1949," *Variety* reported, was "a subject matter. And a subject—racial prejudice—that until very recently was tabu." To ensure his film was first, Kramer sped up production even more than usual and kept it mostly a secret: "no one would know they were stealing a march on their competitors."[29] Notably, all four films incorporated "more adult and serious representations of African Americans," according to scholar Donald Bogle. Edwards believed his role exploded "the myth that Negroes couldn't play straight dramatic roles." These new representations signaled a significant change from Hollywood's old stock black stereotypes such as "Sambo" and "Mammy." Civil rights activists, the black press, and African American actors and filmgoers had long denounced such caricatured, degrading images as hindering the struggle for black equality. They demanded instead "black dignity in cinema."[30] *Home of the Brave* and the rest of the 1949 cycle reflected this postwar politics of representation.

Scholar Thomas Cripps points out that these movies were made by white filmmakers, like Kramer, who considered themselves to be racial liberals. As a result, they condemned race prejudice and segregation as wrong and against American ideals. They also sent the message that a "color-blind" and integrated society was best for all Americans, black and white. A shot of Edwards cradling his dying friend, Finch—a "black and white pietà," in scholar Michael Rogin's words—projected integration and "elicit[ed] African American forgiveness" for white racism.[31] These racially liberal films thus presented a distinctly white and limited vision of race relations. As the first film in the cycle, *Home of the Brave* became the paradigmatic example, for better and worse.

On the plus side, the character of Moss and the acting of James Edwards were heralded by black and white film reviewers. The *New York Amsterdam News* praised Edwards as a "crusader" and "the first Negro to play a completely non–Jim Crow role in a big time Hollywood movie." The film was considered "brave," "honest," and "daring" for taking on a subject usually unaddressed and in a realist style, which included the use of derogatory racial epithets in the dialogue. "Hollywood has come of age," Bill Chase of the *New York Age* contended, "with Stanley Kramer's ingenious and adult treatment of the anti–Negro question." Lillian Scott of the *Chicago Defender* praised *Home of the Brave* as "the most outstanding and honest motion picture on Negro-white relations in history." Her newspaper called the film "Hollywood's boldest stroke for democracy."[32]

At the same time, Moss is victimized and debilitated by white racism, and his passivity perpetuates another stereotype. It "unintentionally implied cowardice of the Negro" and "could have the effect of confirming prejudice" among whites, wrote one reviewer. The film also made the case for racial equality by presenting an African American in an all-white environment—in this case, a historically inaccurate integrated military—and as "altogether similar to a white man," according to Kramer.[33] For critical commentators at the time and since, this plot implied that equality required sameness and integration on white terms and relinquishing black culture and community. Like many films in the genre, *Home of the Brave* located the social problem in individuals rather than institutions, so the solution to racism was psychological healing rather than structural reform. Playwright Lorraine Hansberry made this argument at the time. "Your oppression is in your minds" was the message of Kramer's film. "The source and the root of Negro oppression lies in the persecution complex of the Negro," rather than in institutionalized white racism.[34]

For some critics, the "psychiatric double-talk" and "abracadabra of psychiatry" in the film's plot undercut the racial theme, but *Home of the Brave* and Kramer's next film, *The Men*, reflected the contemporary cultural prominence and uses of psychology.[35] Released in 1950, *The Men* took on the subject of the postwar rehabilitation and reintegration of paraplegic veterans. This group constituted a new category of wounded casualties able to survive World War II due to advances in medicine. Kramer explained the origins of the film in his visit to the Birmingham Veterans Administration hospital in Van Nuys, California, with Kirk Douglas to screen *Champion* for the patients there. "It was then and there that I got the idea for a film and the problems these men faced."[36] After extensive interviews with the patients, Carl Foreman wrote the original story and screenplay about Ken "Bud" Wilocek, a soldier shot by a German sniper and paralyzed from the waist down.

The film's opening narration connected the battles of war and recuperation from the wounds of war. "In all wars, since the beginning of history, there have been men who fought twice." Confined to a wheelchair, Wilocek is depressed and detached until, prodded by his relationship with his fiancée, he begins his emotional and physical path to recovery. He progresses until he suffers a major setback on his wedding night, when it becomes clear that he and his new wife will never be a normal couple or consummate their marriage. Although a resolution eventuates, it is ambivalent, with his wife asking if he needs help, and Wilocek replying with the last word in the film, "Please."

This lack of a happy ending reflected Kramer and Foreman's commitment to a more realistic plot; additional elements in *The Men* similarly aspired to cinematic realism. To achieve greater authenticity, Kramer and the director, Fred Zinnemann, decided to cast forty-five paraplegic men. Zinnemann felt "a realistic treatment" benefited from performances by "people who have gone through a unique and powerful emotional experience." Furthering this sense of realism was the young Broadway star chosen for the lead role: Marlon Brando. Brando's "smash performance" in Tennessee Williams's *A Streetcar Named Desire* led to a "flood of film offers." But he accepted only one, for Kramer's *The Men.*[37] In keeping with his "method acting," a realistic style based on personal memories, Brando immersed himself in the paraplegic world. He spent several weeks living in the hospital, experiencing life in a wheelchair, and getting to know the patients. Brando "brought a new kind of humanity to acting," Kramer recalled. "It was the first time we had ever seen an actor like that." Reviewers lauded Brando's performance of Bud Wilocek as convincing. Bosley Crowther deemed his acting "so vividly real, dynamic and sensitive that his illusion is complete."[38]

The performance of the leading actress, Theresa Wright, also received excellent reviews, although her character as Wilocek's fiancée, Ellen, raised questions about Hollywood's postwar portrayal of women. Wright already had appeared as a woman aiding a veteran in emotionally readjusting to civilian life in *The Best Years of Our Lives* (1946). This box-office hit and Academy Award best picture defined the conventions for the post–World War II coming-home film. Wright's appearance in *The Best Years of Our Lives* enhanced her role as Ellen in *The Men*, as cinema spectators viewed and interpreted an actor's performance within the "intertextual" context of other movies and publicity.[39] Both films presented women as responsible for aiding men's postwar reintegration and, toward this end, self-sacrificing and subordinate. The character of Ellen also injected melodrama into *The Men*'s realist aesthetic. The most emotional dialogue in the film is expressed in Ellen and Bud's rocky romantic relationship. "Oh please, please, try," she urges Bud in working toward recuperation. "Don't you see? I need you."

Although a measure of melodrama also appeared in *Champion* and *Home of the Brave*—"Oh, Doc, I can't!" says Moss, during his psychiatric treatment—these three early successes secured Kramer's reputation as a producer of social problem films in the realist tradition. As it turned out, his productions throughout his career mixed elements of realism and melodrama, as he sought both social relevance and emotional resonance. They also were masculinist, telling stories with men at the center and women on the periphery. With a few exceptions, men's motivations, conflicts, and resolutions dominated the plots of Kramer's films. In this way, his early films contributed to the process of redefining American masculinity following the disruptions and dislocations of World War II and into the 1950s. His leading actors—Douglas, Edwards, Brando, and later Humphrey Bogart and Robert Mitchum—played their part by displaying a range of masculinities from rough and rugged to smart and self-reflective.[40]

The cultural and financial impact of Screen Plays, Inc.'s early movies was tremendous, with box-office returns more than twice the cost of production for *Champion* and *Home of the Brave*. *The Men* did less well with audiences, Kramer believed, because of the onset of the Korean War a month before its release. "Few people had a strong desire to see a movie about paraplegic war veterans when many of their own sons, husbands, and brothers were getting ready for another war." Yet outbreak of war in Korea prompted Bosley Crowther to write a second review of *The Men* to emphasize the "haunting symbols of war's cost." Crowther even likened it to the "old anti-war classic" *All Quiet on the Western Front* (1930), which Kramer had written about as a student at New York University.[41]

Such critical attention, combined with the tireless promotional efforts of publicist George Glass, contributed to the growing prominence of Kramer's company and his role as producer. Kramer enjoyed producing. He described the role as "a self-styled originator and quadruple-threat man who can move in several directions at the same time and wind up the day's work by expertly sweeping the studio after everyone has gone home."[42] "I became a producer," he told Crowther in 1950, "because, in the Hollywood scheme of things, there is only one man who can make a picture as he sees it and wants it to be. That man is the producer. He has the power of final decision." His fellow independents agreed with him. Otto Preminger stressed the virtue of "being autonomous; it is the individual's authority and his responsibility." Julian Blaustein spoke of the necessity of the "producer's concept" and of guarding "it all the way through the process."[43]

Equally important was ensuring that all the participants "understand fully what the picture is about and what it is trying to say." Kramer's commitment to making movies that "said something" meant they were called "message movies." "Every picture says something," Kramer argued. "Even a cowboy Western says that Good triumphs over Evil." Even his next film—the costume drama *Cyrano de Bergerac* (1950), starring José Ferrer in his Oscar-winning role—"stood for honor and against compromise of one's principles." But *message picture* "is a dirty word," Kramer commented. Industry insiders assumed such a film took on an "unpleasant subject" and "cannot possibly interest the mass population. Both of these are false."[44] For each of his films, he assembled a production team and a cast who agreed with him on this point.

Kramer began with the partners and employees in his company but also brought in outside filmmakers and actors for specific projects. Carl Foreman provided a critical consistency as screenwriter for their first five films, but then he only wrote one more. Kramer varied his screenwriters after that, although he hired several multiple times, such Michael Blankfort, Abby Mann, John Paxton, William Rose, and Nedrick Young and Harold Jacob Smith. "I work very closely with the writer," Kramer stated, given his own writing experience and his belief that "every conscientious producer and director should." Kramer also involved himself in the editing process. He believed a "picture is really written three times," by the writer, the director, and then the editor, where "mistakes can often be rearranged, eliminated, corrected—in fact re-written—in the cutting room."[45] Until Kramer started directing himself, his company had little consistency with directors. Their first five films had four different directors: Richard Fleischer for *So This Is New York*, Mark Robson for *Champion* and *Home of the Brave*, Fred Zinnemann for *The Men*, and Michael Gordon for *Cyrano de Bergerac*. Kramer hired Zinnemann two more times, Laslo Benedek twice, and Edward Dmytryk the most, for four films. Interpersonal conflicts and opportunities elsewhere led to an ever-changing set of colleagues and cast members typical in the New Hollywood system.

Beyond production, Kramer needed to concern himself with the distribution and exhibition of his movies. He was familiar with the distribution end of the business, given his uncle Earl's career in New York. He also struggled to find a distributor for his company's first film, *So This Is New York*. When that film ended up with United Artists, Kramer's company signed a deal to provide United Artists with another five to distribute. At that point, United Artists—"the company built by the stars" Charlie Chaplin, Douglas Fairbanks, Mary Pickford, and D. W. Griffith—was "coming apart at the seams," according to film historian Tino Balio.[46] United Artists needed Kramer's company as much as the reverse.

Kramer also actively involved himself with exhibitors whether at home or abroad. If he found his films not being exhibited properly, he took action. "He gets out on the road to supervise booking and exhibition, and while it's strenuous and time consuming, he's found it pays off."[47] Along with the rest of the movie industry, Kramer recognized the importance of the international market, and new sites for the exhibition of Hollywood movies overseas emerged with the expanding circuit of film festivals. Building on the growing prestige of the Venice International Film Festival, established in 1932, a film festival boom occurred after World War II. Festivals were launched at Cannes, Karlovy Vary, and Edinburgh in 1946, Brussels in 1947, Berlin in 1951, and Moscow in 1959. These festivals were international showcases for national cinemas, but Kramer believed "too few times our films have made a sufficient dent in festivals."[48] Throughout his career, he made it a priority to personally participate in and present his films at festivals.

With a distributor and exhibitors, Kramer could get his movies into theaters, but what got filmgoers there was advertising and publicity, as George Glass knew well. Their company worked closely with the distributor on detailed campaign guides to convey the "EXCITEMENT, IMPORTANCE, and absolute MUST-SEE qualities" of their movies. Kramer's publicity colleagues admired his promotional sense. They wrote with requests for "some ideas with typical Kramer thinking" or "the Kramer hit-and-run strategy."[49] Kramer's company and distributor clearly were not above using exploitation techniques, suggestive sexual references included. One advertisement for *Champion* presented images of Kirk Douglas embracing three different women, with the headline, "Every woman goes for a *Champion*." An ad for *The Men* pictured a clutching Marlon Brando and Theresa Wright. "Did she dare marry the man who might never be the father of her children?"[50]

From his career's start, Kramer also recognized the need to cultivate film reviewers and filmgoers to foster positive reception for his movies. Although he later stated that he was "loath to support the contention that . . . critics really influence mass attendance," he made himself available to film reviewers and critics throughout his career. Before, during, and after a film's production, he appeared in the print media but also on radio and television when opportunities arose. More generally, Kramer offered interviews, speeches, and publications about the state of the motion picture industry, and his opinion was frequently solicited. And he certainly cultivated the audience. He emphasized that filmgoers were "discriminating," and they "talk about serious themes." But he also admitted that, overall, "you can't tell" what they wanted. He made films for which there was "no barometer of public reaction," and so every film was "a gamble."[51] To minimize the gamble, Kramer's company did what all the Hollywood studios did: preview screenings for each film as well as trailers to gauge audience reaction. The preview cards provided filmgoers an opportunity to express their opinions of Kramer's moviemaking and the productions that resulted, whether positive—"Excellent movie. Stanley Kramer sure knows to pick the good ones"—or negative: "A great theme, a great cast but dull, Mr. Kramer, dull!"[52]

In their responses, film reviewers and filmgoers expressed great familiarity with Kramer, indicating his public prominence and celebrity status. They felt they shared an intimate relationship with him, because, consistent with celebrity journalism, Glass's publicity and subsequent media coverage began to mention his personal characteristics and private life.[53] The young producer was described as "an intense young man" and later as "energetic," "direct and rambunctious." "Kramer did not look like a Hollywood enfant terrible," noted a 1949 *New York Times* article profiling his rising career. "He is a dark-haired, good-looking young man who wears plaid shirts and denim jackets to work, lives in a modest apartment in Beverly Hills and drives a 1946 Plymouth coupe. He speaks earnestly and literately on a variety of subjects." The article quoted his motto as a producer, as stated on a sign above his desk: "Please, God, Make the Pictures Big and the Heads Small." Others presented Kramer as preferring "the simple life" to "glamorous living" in Hollywood. They provided low-key coverage of his 1950 marriage to actress Ann Pearce and the birth of his first two children, Larry and

Casey.[54] He became well known as a baseball fan and gained attention as a gambler, both professionally and personally. "It takes double barreled courage to gamble as Stanley Kramer is gambling," reported one feature article. But "by nature he is one to take chances . . . on anything from the weather to how soon a fly will light on his sandwich."[55]

Even with this attention to his personality and private life, Kramer and his publicity team always emphasized his professional work in interactions with the media. Moreover, his fame came from his filmmaking accomplishments, not from his "well-knownness," to quote historian Daniel J. Boorstin's famous formulation of celebrity.[56] And by 1949 Kramer was "cutting a swath as a producer." Heralded for his "toughness," as one of the "stubbornly creative men who have learned to work with the new system," Kramer reorganized and expanded Stanley Kramer Productions in 1950. He also won a *Look* Achievement Award as "Producer of the Year." His "B-budget" films, *Time* magazine confirmed, "rated A with both critics and the ticket-buying public" and "made Hollywood sit up and take goggle-eyed notice."[57] By March 1951 he cut a deal that made the front page of the *Los Angeles Times*: "Kramer, Columbia Sign $25,000,000 Film Deal." "This is the most important deal we have ever made," Columbia president Harry Cohn announced. The deal specified that the newly formed Stanley Kramer Company would deliver thirty films over the next five years, produced on the Columbia lot. "Kramer was lucky in his moment," observed one journalist, with his career starting "at a time when the need for economy had become sadly apparent to Hollywood."[58] For a liberal in Hollywood, however, the political moment was less fortuitous.

Stanley Kramer and Red Scare Politics

Kramer's early career as an independent producer in Hollywood was fundamentally shaped by the nearly simultaneous start of the Cold War abroad and its consequences at home. In October 1947, the same year Kramer formed his first successful production company, HUAC launched its postwar Hollywood hearings. Based on the premise that communists had successfully inserted "Red" propaganda into American movies, HUAC subpoenaed a range of industry insiders. Some testified willingly—"friendly" witnesses—but "unfriendly" witnesses did not. Of these, the so-called Hollywood Ten, all current or former members of the Communist Party USA (CPUSA), refused to answer questions about their political affiliations. They disagreed in principle with the investigation as a violation of their First Amendment rights to freedom of speech, assembly, and conscience. Contempt of Congress citations soon followed; trials and imprisonment came later. In late November the movie industry ownership and management then conferred at New York's Waldorf Astoria hotel and decided to blacklist them. "We will not knowingly employ a Communist," read in part the Waldorf Statement they issued in early December.[59] The establishment of the Hollywood blacklist in 1947 contributed to the stifling of social criticism and political dissent in Cold War America. As a political liberal committed to making films that reflected his social conscience, Kramer needed to negotiate a political landscape increasingly dominated by conservative anticommunists and their Red Scare politics.

Kramer's growing reputation as a bold, young, independent producer was matched by his political reputation as a liberal Democrat in the tradition of Franklin D. Roosevelt and the New Deal. Lillian Scott of the *Chicago Defender* praised Kramer as an "intelligent, pioneering liberal." When screenwriter Daniel Taradash sought a producer to make a film about free speech in the early 1950s, "I thought of Stanley Kramer, who was a known liberal." Throughout his career, Kramer never missed a chance to explain the importance and influence of Roosevelt on his life. "I got very involved in the things he was dealing with," Kramer declared, including improving race relations, social welfare, and working conditions.[60] His early years in Hollywood in the 1930s overlapped with union organizing drives spurred by New Deal reforms.[61] As Kramer recalled, "we fought like hell just to get union minimum, social security, retroactive pay, and vacations. We finally got these rights into contracts." As a producer, he felt "the cost of labor murders you," but he was "loath to relinquish any of it or duck it, because it was a fight of blood to raise the standard and give the working man in the film industry a dignity and a position."[62]

"All of this had a tremendous influence on me, not only on which films I made, but on the way I made films and the reasons I made them," Kramer remembered. Throughout his career, he remained committed to the New Deal project and admitted that "Roosevelt was in the front of my mind."[63] In fact, the former president had a presence in several of his films into the 1960s—much later than was true of other Hollywood films. Photos appeared as part of the set decoration, and dialogue mentioned Roosevelt's name. "I'm a rock-ribbed

Republican who thought Franklin Roosevelt was a great man," asserts Spencer Tracy's character in *Judgment at Nuremberg*. Kramer hoped to make a "biopic" about Roosevelt, "something I've wanted to do for a long time." In 1951 Kramer achieved a major professional and political achievement: he secured the screen rights to the former president's life from Eleanor Roosevelt. "I am happy that Mr. Kramer will be the one to produce this picture," the former first lady stated. "I am familiar with his work and have great confidence in his honesty and integrity, as well as his ability." Although that film never got made, moviegoers recognized Kramer's interest in subjects related to political liberalism. One offered a suggestion. "Make into a picture *One World* by Wendell Willkie. P.S. Mr. Willkie was a *Republican*"—although a decidedly liberal and internationalist Republican.[64]

Even as Kramer occupied the liberal middle ground in Hollywood, his affinities and affiliations were often left-leaning. Many of his colleagues were of the Left. Carl Foreman was the best known of the former communists working with Kramer, but others also had been party members or circulated in leftist circles. The Hollywood branch of the CPUSA, like the party nationally, was "a mobilizing center" for a wider range of causes and activists.[65] As a result, a number of Kramer's associates took part in campaigns organized by communists. This participation occurred especially during the Popular Front years of the Great Depression and World War II, when the social democratic liberal-left coalition flourished in Hollywood. José Ferrer, the star of *Cyrano de Bergerac*, lent his support to what he considered "good causes," such as the Joint Anti-Fascist Refugee Committee. Later, this support led to accusations of communist sympathies.[66] Others attended Communist Party meetings or discussion groups. A good example is Kramer's longtime partner, publicist, and, at times, associate producer, George Glass. In the 1940s Glass was active in the Screen Publicists Guild and subscribed to the *People's World*, a successor to the Communist Party's *Daily Worker*. He also offered a lecture on movie publicity for the People's Education Center, an organization later named as communist-affiliated. Glass later received a subpoena and testified before HUAC. When Kramer, Foreman, and Glass needed help to finish the production of their first film, they partnered with Enterprise Studios. Enterprise "attracted to it a number of radical or liberal artists," according to film scholar Brian Neve, including former communists Abraham Polonsky and Robert Rossen as well as liberal activist John Garfield. All three men became targets of anticommunist forces, as were actors on *Home of the Brave* Lloyd Bridges and Jeff Corey.[67]

Over the late 1940s and 1950s, Kramer worked with many liberals and leftists caught up in the Red Scare in Hollywood, and his connections, combined with the content of his social problem films, made him a target for conservative anticommunist forces. His most difficult years in the blacklist era were 1951 and 1952, when HUAC returned to Hollywood. This second set of hearings occurred within a heightened Cold War context. They came after the explosion of the Soviet atomic bomb and the establishment of Communist China in 1949, after the prosecution of spy cases including that of Ethel and Julius Rosenberg in 1949 and 1950, and in the midst of the Korean War. Also in 1950, Joseph R. McCarthy, a Republican senator from Wisconsin, had gained fame by, and given his name to, smearing and silencing targeted Americans with unsubstantiated accusations of communist sympathies.

With the 1951–1952 hearings, HUAC issued more subpoenas and called more witnesses, and the blacklist grew. Those subpoenaed who refused to testify about themselves or about others cited their Fifth Amendment protection against self-incrimination, rather than invoking the First Amendment and risking contempt of Congress citations and jail time, as had the Hollywood Ten. But they did not escape the blacklist.[68] Those witnesses who cooperated with HUAC—whether willingly or under great pressure—hoped to avoid the blacklist. But once they decided to cooperate, they could not limit their testimony to their own lives and politics. They had to answer any and all questions put to them, including providing information about the political involvements of former friends and colleagues. Such informing came to be called "naming names." "The intimidation of Hollywood, a process begun in 1947, was successfully completed in the early 1950s," writes historian M. J. Heale.[69]

Kramer never received a HUAC subpoena or appeared on the blacklist as happened to so many around him, but his activities and relationships led to inflammatory items in the files of the Federal Bureau of Investigation (FBI). The FBI had been investigating the motion picture industry since 1942. Like HUAC and other anticommunist allies, the FBI believed communist filmmakers were shaping film content to their own, as well as Soviet, ends. Given the ideological power of motion pictures—at the time the dominant form of mass entertainment in the United States—the FBI considered this situation a danger to American politics, institutions, and way of life.[70] Concerns about both the content of Kramer's social problem films and the backgrounds of Kramer and his fellow filmmakers appeared in FBI files.

The FBI reported on Kramer's associations. Like Glass, Kramer was linked to the People's Education Center, for teaching about screenwriting in 1947. Two years later, the FBI reacted when the *People's World* recommended *Home of the Brave* as worth seeing. Conflating civil rights and communism, the Bureau deemed the film "100 percent propaganda of a Communist radical nature" designed to "arouse more racial agitation." In 1950 and 1951 Kramer was further reported "to be a communist sympathizer" and—more ambiguously—to have "had the reputation of being sympathetic to communism." Also in 1951, Carl Foreman was accused of being "a practicing communist member," even though he had already left the CPUSA. Most damning was the contention that "the Kramer outfit is Red from the top to the bottom." Confidential informants supplied this information to the FBI, and, as was common in the blacklist era, many of these items were the result of hearsay, rumor, and gossip. They also were shaped by anti-Semitism, as Jewish Americans were often "red-baited," or accused of communism, whether they were communist or not. The FBI eventually and fully cleared Kramer of being a member of the CPUSA, but these items would be recycled again and again in reports into the 1960s.[71] Moreover, they would find their way into the right-wing popular press.

During this "insanely difficult period," as Kramer described the "Communist-hunting era," his company began dealing with the personal and political fallout from the second set of HUAC hearings.[72] The hearings began in late March 1951, within days of the announcement of the game-changing deal between the Stanley Kramer Company and Columbia Pictures. Kramer and his partners in the new company could no longer act autonomously, and they now were partnered with a signatory of the Waldorf Statement. As was happening at the major studios, their employees or potential employees began to submit "clearance letters." These letters were signed affidavits designed to "clear" their names of any association with communism, avoid the blacklist, and allow them to be employed in Hollywood, although there were no guarantees of success. That this clearance process prioritized the interests of the industry over those of the accused individuals was explicit in the stated purpose of a set of letters addressed to Kramer's company: "to safeguard your company and its product, as well as the motion picture industry, from infiltration by Communists." Anticommunists inside and outside the film industry supervised this process and held copies of these letters, demonstrating the extent of the surveillance network enforcing the Hollywood blacklist.[73]

Several potential employees of the Stanley Kramer Company participated in the clearance process, organized not by Kramer himself but by his business partner, Sam Katz. One of the earliest clearance letters came from Irving Reis, at the time negotiating a contract to direct *The Four Poster* (1952) for Kramer. Reis sent a signed affidavit on June 1, 1951, denying membership in the Communist Party, declaring his loyalty to the United States, and expressing his anticommunism. "I feel that every decent American must oppose Communism and Communists in every possible manner and wherever their evil designs and purposes can be discerned." Reis explained his involvement in various liberal-left activities, now deemed "subversive," during the late 1930s and 1940s. "All of us make mistakes. Perhaps one of my mistakes was not to have exercised discretion in examining the true nature or purpose of some of these organizations or activities." Additional employees or potential employees engaged in this clearance process, including Kirk Douglas and actress Marsha Hunt. But not all did. Director Joseph Losey, who came with Kramer to Columbia, chose not to. In mid-1951, when he heard he had been named as a communist and had a HUAC subpoena waiting for him, he left the country.[74]

As part of the 1951 hearings, Kramer's partner and screenwriter Foreman received a HUAC subpoena, which began the end of their relationship. With his lawyer, Sidney Cohn, Foreman decided to take the "diminished" or "qualified" Fifth Amendment. That is, he would testify that he no longer belonged to the Communist Party, but he would refuse to discuss his past membership or to "name names." "I knew I could not live with myself as an informer," Foreman told writer Victor Navasky.[75] Kramer and Katz wanted Foreman to testify fully, even if it meant naming names, as their partner George Glass would do when he testified in executive session in 1951 and then publicly in 1952. "I could understand and even sympathize with his dilemma," Kramer remembered. "My only problem with his stand was that it endangered our company. I realized his testimony would pull all of us under a shadow, and I had a responsibility I couldn't ignore."[76]

What followed this impasse has long been open to interpretation, and Foreman, Kramer, and their respective supporters offer very different versions. "I got kicked out of my own company by Kramer," Foreman told Navasky. "If Stanley had had the guts to ride it out we might have won. . . . But Stanley was scared. In the crunch he said he was not prepared to have his career destroyed by my misguided liberalism."[77] In Kramer's own recollections with Navasky and with historian Larry Ceplair, he expressed his feelings of mistrust toward Foreman. "If he had leveled with me, if I had known all the facts," Kramer told Navasky, "that would have been one thing. But he really didn't." In his memoirs, Kramer did not take responsibility for ending their relationship. Instead, he stated, "Foreman and the company mutually severed association, but I did not dismiss him."[78]

News reports at the time, however, put the onus for their break on Kramer and his business associates. In September 1951, after Foreman appeared before HUAC and was deemed an "uncooperative witness," Kramer appeared in the news: "Partner Turns on Reluctant Film Quiz Witness"; "Kramer Splitting with Film Partner." Newspapers quoted from a "prepared" and "carefully worded statement" later attributed to Columbia Pictures. "There is total disagreement between Carl Foreman and myself." References to the role of Columbia Pictures and pressure from Harry Cohn, who had signed the Waldorf Statement, also appeared. "Interests and obligations involved are far greater than his or those of this company." Kramer scheduled a future meeting of company directors and shareholders, saying, "Necessary action will be taken at that time." A month later the *New York Times* announced "Kramer, Foreman Sever Relations," "because of their disagreement over Foreman's attitude as a witness" before HUAC. "Kramer said he was dissatisfied with his associate's stand and requested that he quit the Kramer organization."[79] Kramer never confirmed this—technically, Foreman's—interpretation of events following their disagreement over Foreman's HUAC testimony. But the way he explained his position in his memoirs actually, if unintentionally, fit this interpretation. "I was never confronted with the question of sticking with him, but in fact I don't think it would have been possible. I'd have been blackballed and maybe driven out of the industry for something in which I had taken no part."[80]

The Kramer-Foreman conflict was emblematic of the political and personal fallout from the Red Scare, as was their last collaboration: the western film *High Noon* (1952). Directed by *The Men*'s Fred Zinnemann, *High Noon* succeeded at the box office, with critics, and at the Academy

Awards presentations. It won four Oscars and earned nominations for best picture, director, and screenplay. Bosley Crowther lauded *High Noon* in all three categories. "It is a picture that does honor to the Western and elevates the medium of films. . . . Mr. Zinnemann's direction . . . gives this picture magnitude and class," and the "dandy Carl Foreman script, is as honest and pertinent a drama as we've had on screen this year."[81] Foreman was writing the screenplay when he received his HUAC subpoena in 1951. The story features Hadleyville, a town in peril due to both an external threat and an internal weakness. The film could be read, as Foreman intended, as a critique of both HUAC's investigations and Hollywood's capitulations. The main character is Marshal Will Kane, played by Gary Cooper. Frank Miller, an outlaw Kane had sent to prison five years earlier, has been released and is returning to kill Kane. At this moment of crisis, the marshal is abandoned by the townspeople and by his new Quaker, pacifist wife, played by Grace Kelly. "Kane had to stand alone, literally, against the lawless," Cooper recalled. Kane ends up killing the gang with the help of his wife, newly converted to violence. Foreman related the subject of *High Noon* in his pointed HUAC testimony as about "a town that died because it lacked the moral fiber to withstand aggression."[82]

Along with Foreman, *High Noon* became a target of the Hollywood Right. The fact that Gary Cooper was a prominent anticommunist complicated the political meanings of the film. But his political credentials and his Oscar-winning performance failed to sway his compatriots. "Can't understand how Cooper got sucked in," wrote Paramount Pictures' Luigi Luraschi to his contact at the Central Intelligence Agency, a relationship that hints at the extent of surveillance in Hollywood. "He's a savvy guy, but I guess the Western cloak fooled him." Luraschi also named Foreman as "very much identified with leftist causes."[83] Public and private attacks on Foreman contributed to his blacklisting and expatriation to England. "I took the diminished Fifth," Foreman stated, "and when it was over I was finished in Hollywood." "I'll never regret having helped run Foreman out of this country," anticommunist actor John Wayne proudly stated, a variation of a western idiom he had used many times on screen. As for *High Noon*, Wayne said, "It's the most un-American thing I've ever seen in my whole life." Luraschi considered the film "full of messages" for "the Communist and for his propaganda purposes abroad." Kramer disagreed. Foreman "put no Communist propaganda into the story. If he had tried to do so, I would have taken it out."[84] Of course, Foreman's intentions with *High Noon* were never procommunist but rather *anti*-anticommunist, a distinction Kramer well understood even if anticommunists in Hollywood did not.

What Kramer's comment indicated was the deterioration of his political and professional relationship with Foreman over that period. Their fraught relations during the making of *High Noon* have been well documented with written and oral primary sources by Larry Ceplair and, most recently, writer Glenn Frankel. At one point, Foreman was "relieved" of his film assignments and then was partially restored.[85] "We had to distance ourselves," Kramer later stated, "or our picture would be lost." In an interview just a few years after the conflict, an unnamed colleague reflected on the producer's actions during this period. "Kramer did what he had to do, I guess, or go out of business. I'll tell you this, though. I'll bet he's had more sleepless nights over the affair."[86]

In the end, Foreman received his screenwriting credit on *High Noon* but, controversially, did not receive credit as an associate producer. Producing credit remained up to the production company, and, as part of Foreman's settlement with the company, he waived his producing credit. This important finding by Ceplair (confirmed by Frankel) mitigates accusations that Foreman's "producing credit was taken from him."[87] Foreman's settlement agreement accorded him writing credit as well as an estimated $250,000, considered generous at the time and since. Importantly, it was not until the following year, 1953, that the Screen Writers Guild allowed producers to deny credit to blacklisted screenwriters.[88] Although it is impossible to imagine that Kramer and his colleagues would have denied Foreman's writing credit in any case, due to both principle and prior public recognition of his authorship, they did not have a choice in the matter.

Kramer's disassociation from Foreman in 1951 did not prevent him from being a focus of anticommunist forces in Hollywood, however. He, his colleagues, and their movies continued to be red-baited by private figures and organizations engaged in "exposing Reds in the name of patriotism," including the American Legion. The Legion had been at the forefront of US domestic anticommunism from its founding in 1919 by World War I veterans through the Cold War.[89] In December 1951, two months after Kramer and Foreman parted ways, J. B. Matthews, a journalist expert on "communist subversion," named Kramer in an article in the *American Legion Magazine*. "Did the Movies Really Clean House?"

assessed the anticommunist impact of blacklisting the Hollywood Ten. "To come speedily to the point," Matthews argued, the "answer is 'no.'" He called for a "complete house cleaning job in Hollywood" to rid it of additional Communist Party "conspirators" as well as their nonmember "collaborators." His evidence for Kramer's collaboration was, as in FBI reports, his teaching at what he called "the Los Angeles communist training school in 1947" and three movies currently in production: *Death of a Salesman* (1951), *Four Poster* (1952), and *High Noon*. These films involved Foreman and Virginia Farmer, "named communists," but also playwright Arthur Miller and directors Reis and Zinnemann, who had supported the Hollywood Ten or communist-front groups. Former and future colleagues of Kramer, such as José Ferrer, Michael Gordon, and Michael Blankfort, were also named, the latter two as communists.[90]

This 1951 article intimidatingly increased the pressure to expand and extend the Hollywood blacklist, and the American Legion and its magazine would keep Kramer in their sights throughout the decade. The magazine's editor did not let readers forget about Kramer's relationship to Foreman. "When he was starting out as producer, Kramer got himself a partner named Carl Foreman, who, it turned out, was a communist. But," the editor, Joseph C. Keeley, continued sarcastically, "Kramer, being the innocent kind of guy he is, obviously had no inkling of this." He went on to warn Kramer of the danger posed by "the commies who go on his payroll."[91] The *American Legion Magazine* also would continue to review Kramer's future films, reminding their readers, "They can stay away in droves from movies when they disapprove of them" and naming "Kramer's latest movie."[92]

The American Legion was not alone in campaigning against Kramer as part of the Red Scare in Hollywood. Local "Red hunter" Myron Fagan issued pamphlets, such as *Red Treason in Hollywood*, that listed "pals and helpers and agents" of Soviet communism. "Unquestionably one of the most brazen of all Hollywood producers" was how Fagan described Kramer. "I won't attempt to review his entire background of pro-Communism on this page—that would require an entire volume. But I will mention just a few of . . . the stars and writers he employed."[93] Hollywood gossip columnist and fervent anticommunist Hedda Hopper also took part. With an estimated readership of 32 million in the mid-1950s, Hopper was a powerful figure in Old Hollywood. At the start of Kramer's career she gave him favorable coverage, but she soon began attacking "that Red Stanley Kramer," as she called him. She objected to his leftist associates and tried to link him to screenwriter Lester Cole, one of the Hollywood Ten. When she asked Kramer in an interview, "Is it true or not?" he responded, "For God's sake, Hedda! . . . It's completely untrue." "I never worked with him. This is completely erroneous and ridiculous."[94] Adding to the anti-Kramer attack was Jaik Rosenstein, Hopper's former employee. In his newsletter, *Hollywood Close-Up*, he red-baited Kramer, asking, "The question with Stanley Kramer is, is he or is he ain't a Red? Were you not, as a matter of fact, at one time an instructor of Communist ideology?" "Kramer," Rosenstein taunted, "has not come up with any of the answers."[95]

Conservative anticommunists not only publicly accused Kramer of communist sympathies but also worked behind the scenes to expose him. Ward Bond, a character actor and leader of the anticommunist activist group Motion Picture Alliance of the Preservation of American Ideals, was one. In 1951 and 1952 correspondence to George Sokolsky, a right-wing Hearst press columnist, Bond conveyed information he hoped would indict Kramer. Sokolsky functioned as an arbiter of the blacklist, putting people on as well as getting them off the blacklist. To Sokolsky, Bond described Kramer as the producer of *Cyrano de Bergerac*, with the director, Michael Gordon, "named party member in '51 hearings." Bond also raised the issue of Kramer's 1947 lecturing at the People's Educational Center, where "all such Commy fronters and party members" taught, including two of the Hollywood Ten. "For my dough that's enough." Kramer, Bond argued, "hires all the known fronters and members he can," and he mistrusted Kramer's break with Foreman. "Mr. Kramer has risen up in righteous indignation at his partner Carl Foreman, who was caught with his red pants akimbo." Bond kept detailed track of all of Kramer's productions. In 1952 he sent Sokolsky a "fairly complete rundown on the pictures that Kramer has produced, and showing in detail the list of CP members and sympathizers he has hired in the 11 pictures." Bond believed that "this record is the most damaging thing against Kramer."[96]

Bond and other anticommunists also believed that Kramer's social problem films conveyed communist ideology. "Some of his films, we believe, are pro-Commie in content. *Home of the Brave*, for instance." At the start of the Cold War Red Scare, the FBI and HUAC sought to prove communist subversion in Hollywood through analyses of film content. The lack of explicit propaganda in a medium designed collaboratively and for popular entertainment made this task impossible. As a result, between the first and second set of HUAC hearings, both entities shifted focus to the easier task of uncovering the political beliefs and affiliations of individual filmmakers.[97] Private beliefs rather than public acts became the definition of "subversion."

But this shift in focus did not deter anticommunist attacks on film content. The FBI warned that between 1935 and 1945 communists and sympathizers—or "fellow travelers"—"extolled a number of 'message' films which criticized or satirized various aspects of American life." The bureau believed communists had found social problem films "particularly useful" as a way to "wield their influence in Hollywood." Hedda Hopper certainly hated social problem films. "Emphasizing the negative," she argued, "can be just as effective as waving the Red flag." She especially worried when such films were exported, as she believed they presented an unflattering picture of the United States.[98] Myron Fagan indicted several of Kramer's films as procommunist but singled out *Home of the Brave,* as had Bond and the FBI.

The film of Kramer's early career that drew the most anticommunist fire—even more than *Home of the Brave* or *High Noon*—was *Death of a Salesman* in 1951. Arthur Miller's 1949 Pulitzer Prize–winning play told the story of the hopeless life and suicide of a failed businessman, father, and husband, Willy Loman. "Kramer had bought the play because he liked what it had to say," the director Laslo Benedek wrote at the time. Kramer cast Fredric March in the lead, and Miller "fully approved the choice."[99] Cast members from the original stage play as produced in New York and London also appeared. The film received positive, even glowing reviews, despite its depressing theme about "the treadmill pursuit of fickle fame and fortune." "To produce *Death of a Salesman* took substantial courage," stated reviewer Edwin Schallert, "and for this Kramer merits the accolade."[100] The film received five Oscar nominations, including three in acting categories for March as Loman, Mildred Dunnock as his wife, and Kevin McCarthy as his oldest son. Critical and industry respect contributed to *Death of a Salesman* screening at the prestigious Venice festival in 1952. In contrast to anticommunists such as Hopper, Kramer celebrated the foreign release of socially critical films like his, "on the ground that they best exemplify our strongest commodity: liberty." Kramer took seriously the central role American freedom played in the US rationale and rhetoric for the Cold War and sought to make it real.[101]

Anticommunists considered such freedom of the screen to be dangerous and criticized both the content of *Death of a Salesman* and the politics of the filmmakers. Bond indicted the film and Fagan cited it for "containing anti–Free Enterprise propaganda and debasing the American way of life."[102] The FBI had similarly commented on the original play "as 'a negative delineation of American life' which struck 'a shrewd blow' against American values," as scholar Nathan Abrams discusses. It did not help that the *Daily Worker* agreed and praised the play for showing "a social picture of a man who has struggled all of his materialist life, thoroughly indoctrinated with the American (capitalist) dream." The Soviet newspaper *Pravda* endorsed the play as well, according to Abrams. "The salesman's tragic destiny is depicted in the play as a logical consequence of the inhuman laws of the capitalist world."[103]

Even if Kramer's film softened this critique, anticommunist critics were not quelled. They red-baited seven participants in the film. Kramer, Miller, and March were named most prominently. Miller had long been a Marxist, attended Communist Party meetings in his youth, and participated in organizations later deemed to be communist fronts. Industry insiders testified that Miller was a "concealed communist." In 1956 he would be subpoenaed by HUAC.[104] The politically liberal star of the film, Fredric March, had been called before HUAC back in 1940 and criticized the committee and its actions. He continued to be monitored by the FBI. Additional targets were screenwriter Stanley Roberts, director Benedek, actress Dunnock, and actor Howard Smith for supporting the Hollywood Ten or other activities.

In the case of *Death of a Salesman*, anticommunists went beyond words and took action to confront the film and the filmmakers. The American Legion picketed the film in Washington, DC, stating "that we in the grassroots object to Hollywood subsidizing folks like Arthur Miller." The Legion's threats of picketing in Ohio led to some exhibitors breaking their contractual commitments with Columbia Pictures and refusing to screen the film. The most confrontational group was the Wage Earners Committee, a recently formed antilabor union and problacklist organization.[105] It promised to expose "the identities and operations" of "subversive propagandists" in Hollywood until the industry took action with "effective policing of the medium." Its publication, the *National Wage Earner*, listed ninety-two films "which employ commies and fellow travelers and contain subversive subject matter designed to defame Americans throughout the world." One film was *Death of a Salesman*, and the Wage Earners Committee deployed pickets and circulated leaflets outside movie theaters showing the film. The leaflets named Kramer, Miller, and March. In reciting the "true facts" about Kramer, the leaflet labeled him as "notorious for his red-slanted, red-starred films." It stated again his teaching at "the Los Angeles Communist training school" and his hiring of "Communist-front" employees.[106]

Kramer did not take this attack lightly. In a bold move within the context of the second set of HUAC hearings and a frightened, intimidated film industry, he filed a $1 million libel suit against the Wage Earners Committee in January 1952. His suit accused the committee of "wrongly and maliciously" identifying him as having communist sympathies. He asserted that he had "always conducted . . . himself with loyalty toward the government of the United States and to democratic principles and tenets." He held nothing back in charging the defendants with "evil motive and malice and ill will" and with intent to "injure, disgrace, and defame" him. In a public statement accompanying the lawsuit, Kramer called the accusations against him

> unmitigated lies [that] were known by the Wage Earners to be lies before they were made. . . . I will fight back at anyone who attacks my good name, my patriotism or motives behind my work. In hopes that justice would prevail of its own accord, I have remained silent for weeks, but the committee's baseless and ridiculous libel have given rise to whispers which have created genuine harm to me. I intend to get the record clear and obtain full indemnification.[107]

The response from his film industry colleagues was remarkable. "'It's about time' was the phrase heard all over Hollywood." Kramer had taken "the first courageous stand in our industry's history against the slanderous attacks of pressure groups." The major associations supported him, including the Motion Picture Association of America (MPAA). Ward Bond counted twelve "hoodwinked" organizations "backing up Kramer." Journalists credited Kramer with stirring "the industry out of its customary lethargy" and sparking an "unequaled display of courage and unanimity of purpose."[108] When MGM's head, Dore Schary, filed his own suit the following month, a court order soon stopped the picketing.

Kramer's successful legal action repelling anticommunist assaults reinforced his political image and credibility as a staunch liberal in Hollywood. His lawsuit made it clear that he was not a communist but a liberal. "By suing, Kramer is inviting a complete investigation of his own record," Hollywood columnist Jimmie Fidler contended, and "he'd hardly be doing that if he had anything to hide." Yet leftists expressed anger and a sense of betrayal. As Kramer recalled, "in living-room dialogues I was called a Red baiter."[109] This accusation gained traction during his conflict with Foreman and accelerated with his hiring of director Edward Dmytryk. A former member of the Hollywood Ten, Dmytryk "recanted" after serving his prison sentence for contempt of Congress. He admitted his past membership in the Communist Party, "named names" before HUAC, and came off the blacklist in 1951. Kramer was the first to hire him. "I was lucky. I was working for the most progressive filmmaker in Hollywood," Dmytryk recalled. Kramer "broke down the resistance to blacklisted filmmakers." But their association led to attacks from the political Left. "Dmytryk, gone over to warmongering and restored to the favor of Big Money, is now directing for Stanley Kramer Productions," accused the *Daily Worker*.[110]

Even as it left him open to political criticism on all sides, Kramer still held true to his New Deal liberalism as he moved into the middle years of his career. For example, the films Kramer made with Dmytryk often received political as well as film criticism: *The Sniper* (1952), a film noir thriller about a serial killer starring the anticommunist activist Adolphe Menjou; *Eight Iron Men* (1952), a World War II combat film; *The Juggler* (1953), the first Hollywood film to be shot in the new Israel about a Holocaust survivor; and *The Caine Mutiny* (1954), based on the Pulitzer Prize–winning 1951 novel by Herman Wouk about a US naval ship in the Pacific. Michael Blankfort, who wrote the original screenplay for *The Juggler*, commiserated about being attacked from the Right and the Left, not just by "the frenzied, marginal fascists but the others who thought they were the best voices of the future of man."[111] When Kramer assigned screenwriter John Paxton to a social problem film about a motorcycle gang terrorizing a town, *The Wild One* (1953), Ward Bond again took notice. Paxton "has long pro Commy record. Paxton's agent says Kramer doesn't want this known," he wrote George Sokolsky.[112] Despite Red Scare politics, Kramer had the opportunity to employ many talented filmmakers in the first half of the 1950s. He worked again with Marlon Brando, Kirk Douglas, James Edwards, and José Ferrer and for the first time with Humphrey Bogart, Julie Harris, Rex Harrison, and Ethel Waters. He made more social problem films, translated more stories from stage to screen, like *The Member of the Wedding* (1952), and explored themes he would elaborate on in later films, including the Holocaust.

The Caine Mutiny was the last film Kramer produced for Columbia Pictures—Harry Cohn "terminated" their contract in late 1953—and the last he made before becoming a director. Fortunately, this film made money at the box office, so much money that it offset the losses incurred by Kramer's other ten films for the studio.[113] "It bailed us out and kept me alive while I took time to decide what to do next." In hindsight, Kramer believed his arrangement with Cohn and Columbia "was a fiasco." "I was in a place I didn't belong, doing what I shouldn't be doing, and not doing it well."[114] Kramer was ready to step back from the production schedule demanded by Columbia and set his own pace; he was also ready to direct his movies himself "to protect his dream." "I always wanted to be a director."[115] Kramer returned to United Artists, which *High Noon* had helped make profitable. In the mid-1950s United Artists was succeeding, partly because it offered a winning "combination of creative control and profit participation, with little or no financial risk for the independent producer." Using a new company, Lomitas Productions, Kramer negotiated several deals for financing and distribution.[116]

His 1957 contract with United Artists stood out as unique and constituted a mark of respect for Kramer in his new status as a producer-director. United Artists provided financing from preproduction to completion. It retained the right to approve the production budget, schedule, and locations, as well as the stars, the producer, and director. But the contract did not require Kramer to seek approval of the screenplay from United Artists or to show daily rushes. This unprecedented arrangement spurred Kramer to offer his opinion that United Artists was "the greatest single operation for the independent producers" in Hollywood. Within this context, he aimed "to be independent in order to be able to do pictures the way I see them and then be able to survive."[117] But he was not off to an auspicious start with his first two directed films, both based on best-selling novels. *Not as a Stranger* (1955) was an exposé of medical practices starring Robert Mitchum, Frank Sinatra, and Olivia de Havilland. In the end, the film was a big hit with audiences but not with the critics. *The Pride and the Passion* (1957) was a historical epic set in Spain during the Napoleonic Wars and filmed there with Cary Grant, Sophia Loren, and Frank Sinatra. The movie was a "big picture," cost more than $4 million, and was, in Kramer's words, "a complete and utter bomb!"[118]

Although extremely mixed, the news coverage of these first two directing experiences confirmed Kramer's prominence as a filmmaker and political figure in the movie industry. By 1957 and 1958, newspaper reports labeled him a "Hollywood giant." He had "matured impressively as a film creator" and continued his "involvement in the ideological, social and business conflict that divided Hollywood into two warring camps for almost a decade."[119] As the Cold War continued at home and abroad, he purchased the rights to a 1948 novel, *My Glorious Brothers,* by Howard Fast, who had left the Communist Party only the year before. Although that movie would never be made, he also bought an original screenplay that would become *The Defiant Ones* (1958). The script was coauthored by Harold Jacob Smith and a blacklisted actor and writer, Nedrick Young. In 1953 Young resolutely refused to testify at his appearance before HUAC. "I invoke, I exercise and defend the Constitution of the United States against this body and all similar bodies." He considered "the existence of this committee a flagrant corruption of the Constitution," "designed to invade the right to think, to speak, to act, to assemble with people freely."[120] In his HUAC statement, Young invoked the American civil liberties his future producer-director, Stanley Kramer, also would seek to defend.

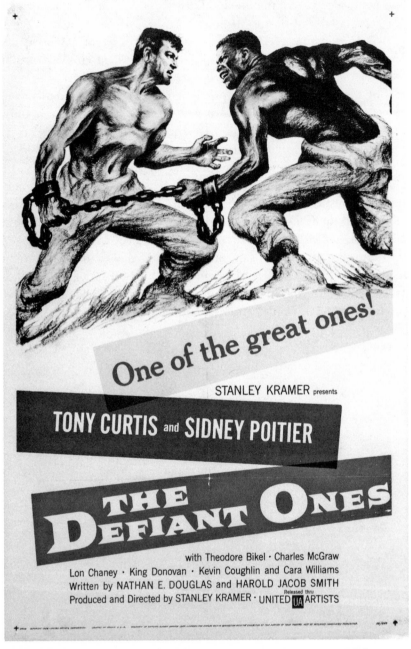

Poster for The Defiant Ones *(1958). Courtesy of Margaret Herrick Library and MGM/UA.*

2 Civil Rights Meets
The Defiant Ones

For his third venture as a director, Stanley Kramer returned to the film formula that had brought him success in his early career as a producer. The film was *The Defiant Ones.* Kramer's 1958 film starred Sidney Poitier and Tony Curtis as two prison convicts, chained together, as they try to make their escape. The plot functioned as an allegory for American race relations—due to the chain linking the black and white characters—at a key point in the modern civil rights movement. As a social problem film about racism, the movie sent a clear message. "My primary consideration," Kramer told Philip K. Scheuer of the *Los Angeles Times,* was that the characters "learn the hard way that they must depend on one another—regardless of color or any other difference." Another consideration, however, was financial. After he "splurged on two epics," Scheuer noted, Kramer needed to "return to the lower-budget milieu of his *Champion* and *Home of the Brave.*" He sought "to steer a safe course between multimillion-dollar epics and 'cheap' exploitation pictures," and he believed he had "hit on just the right compromise—with cash, not his conscience."[1] With *The Defiant Ones,* Kramer's reputation for courageously challenging the Hollywood system as an independent producer-director making films about important social and political issues was secured. Over time, it became one of his favorite films and so identified with him that he often was referred to as "the defiant one" himself.[2]

At the time, the film garnered Kramer artistic recognition, financial rewards, and political respect, particularly with regard to civil rights. Four years had passed since the historic 1954 Supreme Court decision *Brown v. Board of Education* that declared racial segregation in America's schools unconstitutional, and one year since the crisis over implementing the *Brown* decision began in Little Rock, Arkansas. In response to *Brown,* many white southerners mobilized to maintain legal segregation. They engaged in what they called "massive resistance" to integration and violently suppressed African American activism. As part of white resistance to black civil rights, in 1957 Arkansas governor Orval Faubus refused to allow nine black students to integrate Central High School in Little Rock. This action precipitated a major racial crisis that forced President Dwight D. Eisenhower to dispatch federal troops to the city, undertaking the first such military intervention in southern race relations since the Civil War and Reconstruction nearly a century before.

The Little Rock school integration crisis remained a point of reference during the production and exhibition of *The Defiant Ones*. Kramer reported being questioned overseas about the crisis, as the "incidents which took place in Arkansas comprised the biggest single news story to come from the United States in the past year."[3] In keeping with his New Deal liberalism, he believed in a "long" civil rights movement, beginning not in the 1950s but in the 1930s, arguing that the "current situation is the result of 30 years of progress toward a clear, just and constitutional status for the Negro." Kramer hoped his film—a story of shared humanity and universal values—would "provide some answers to some of the sorrowful situations created by racial bigotry." In "combating race prejudice," he contended, "motion picture technique, art, approach has a great deal to contribute."[4]

Kramer also deployed his latest movie to combat the Hollywood blacklist. *The Defiant Ones* began as an original screenplay called "The Long Road" written by the blacklisted Nedrick Young and Harold Jacob Smith. Young wrote under the pseudonym Nathan E. Douglas (the initials N. E. D. spelled his nickname), because he had been blacklisted after he was, as he put it, a "*very* unfriendly witness" before HUAC in 1953. "I will not answer your question because to answer your question would be to concede your right to ask it and this I do not do," Young told the committee.[5] Purchasing a screenplay Kramer considered the "most exciting original story I have ever owned" meant breaking the blacklist, at least covertly. He claimed to have "read and purchased within two hours," paying $75,000 for the rights, "a sum said to be the highest price paid for an original screenplay in 17 years."[6] In addition to paying Young and Smith well, Kramer gave them a share of the film's profits and cast them as drivers of the prison truck carrying the characters played by Curtis and Poitier. They appear at the start of the movie as the opening titles and credits roll, so their names as screenwriters are superimposed over their images on the screen. With this "sly cinematic joke," Kramer's film allowed Hollywood insiders to identify Young and his pen name and offered "a nice ironical thrust at the blacklisters." The blacklisters thrust back, however. Myron Fagan considered *The Defiant Ones* as proof of Kramer's "pro-Communism." It would "incite strife between Whites and Negroes by exploiting supposed grievances and prejudices," he argued.[7] Anticommunists such as Fagan brought together Red Scare politics and an anti–civil rights agenda, but in 1958 their attack on Kramer and his latest film would not succeed.

Writing Race from the Left

Kramer's production of *The Defiant Ones* started with Young and Smith's strong screenplay, which won multiple awards, including an Oscar for best original screenplay. Since then, their script has been seen as displaying "the promises and pitfalls" of post–World War II racial liberalism: against prejudice and segregation but offering only simplistic and superficial solutions.[8] Yet Young and Smith's leftist politics profoundly shaped the story and the style of *The Defiant Ones*. The movie tells the tale of two prisoners in the American South, Noah Cullen, played by Poitier, and John "Joker" Jackson, played by Curtis, as they make their break from the chain gang, through their time on the run, to their eventual recapture. For most of the film, they are hampered by being chained together at the wrist. The chain forces them to work with one another in overcoming natural obstacles, such as a rushing river, a slick clay pit, and an impenetrable swamp. They face human foes, including a posse composed of police, civilians, and dogs; a lynch mob; and an armed young boy and his lonely mother. Cullen and Jackson also need to overcome their mutual antagonism. Their anger stems from their lifelong experiences with racism and leads to harsh verbal exchanges and physical fights. Through a process of conflict and cooperation, they realize their commonality and choose to stand by one another, even after the chain is broken. Jackson does not let Cullen proceed through the swamp's quicksand to his sure death, and Cullen does not abandon the wounded Jackson when he cannot clamber onto their train to freedom. The film ends with Cullen cradling Jackson and singing an old blues song.

In crafting their screenplay, Young and Smith both reused and revised the Hollywood tradition of social problem films about race relations in the United States. As with Kramer's earlier film *Home of the Brave* (1949), *The Defiant Ones* puts a conflict between a white and black American at the center of the drama and achieves a resolution by the movie's end. The subject matter emerged out of the compassion and concern of the screenwriters, who aimed to teach a lesson and to spur social change. "Our simple thesis," wrote Young and Smith, "is that from common struggle toward a common goal, man realizes his interdependence with other men. The realization of 'brotherhood' is in itself a goal of the first importance." They explicitly connected their screenplay to the civil rights movement and referenced ongoing campaigns for school desegregation and the hope of success "today . . . in Virginia, perhaps tomorrow in Little Rock."[9] But in contrast to how the film is often remembered and analyzed, Young and Smith did not offer an easy or simple solution to the problems of race and racism in America.[10] Their original title, "The Long Road," indicated as much. There is not one cause or one villain. Instead of solely blaming Jackson for his racism, Cullen attributes it to the larger society and culture: "you breathe it in when you're born and you spit it out from then on." The film highlights a complex set of social relations perpetuating white supremacy, from the prisoner Jackson and the state police chief to the lynch mob and the boy's mother. The movie also hints at fissures in the social order, with divisions among the white characters over race.

The Defiant Ones thus avoided the "glib social analysis" of earlier social problem films, and this genre innovation owed much to Young and Smith's leftist politics. "The real triumph," they argued in defense of their screenplay, "lies in the two men overcoming a set of moribund mores learned from an abnormal social superstructure, which had originally made them think they were enemies."[11] Their use of the Marxist term "superstructure" is telling, even if they qualified it with "abnormal." Racism in the film is not only a moral or interpersonal problem as it was in most social problem films, including *Home of the Brave*. White supremacy is also institutional and structural, represented in the film by the police and the prison system. The relationship between base and superstructure, between a society's economy and relations of production and its ideologies and institutions, had recently been the subject of fierce debate within the Hollywood Communist Party. Although the debate had a different focus—could communists have a political impact through their work in film?—it heightened attention to the concepts of base and superstructure. American leftists understood racism as an ideology and, thus, part of the superstructure. Capitalists wielded "white chauvinism" as a weapon to divide the working class along racial lines. In this formulation, racism is embedded not just in individual psychology but in the American political economy.[12]

In fact, the pivotal moment in the film's plot occurs when Cullen and Jackson realize that, despite their racial differences, they share a similar position in terms of class and status. Jackson reveals his history of low-wage work, including a job as an auto mechanic: "there I was, back in that pit with grease in my eyeballs." Cullen conveys how hard it was to make a living farming, when he had to "scratch it out with hand tools and a mule." Economic oppression and class inequality also lead to their imprisonment. Cullen's confrontation with a debt collector—"Man come on my land cos I didn't pay the note"—led to a conviction for assault, and Jackson explains his jailing: "Because I didn't know how to be a big enough taker. I was just a stealer." Another scene that emphasizes their commonality occurs when the two men are nearly lynched by a small-town mob. Jackson exclaims in surprise, "You can't go lynchin' me. I'm a white man!" He discovers that his whiteness does not compensate for his degraded status as a criminal and convict, a status he shares with Cullen. This "appeal to sameness," this social message that "suffering is shared regardless of racial background," has been seen as *The Defiant One*'s simplistic answer to racial discrimination in the United States. This answer also can be seen as conveying the Marxist assumption that class exploitation trumped racial exploitation and overlooking the distinctive racial oppression experienced by African Americans.[13]

Yet Young and Smith's plot line tracing the characters' realization of shared experiences did not overlook racial differences, nor did it come to an easy resolution. When Cullen and Jackson argue over the use of racial epithets, Jackson contends that his being called "hunky" or "bohunk"—slurs that conflated central European ethnicity and working-class status—equates to his calling Cullen "nigger." Cullen puts a stop to this equation. "You ever hear tell of a bohunk in a woodpile, Joker? You ever hear tell of 'catch a bohunk by the toe'?" Moreover, at the film's end, they may be personally "liberated from hate," as the screenwriters explained, but they also are headed back to prison. Their film does not have a happy ending. The *New Republic*'s Stanley Kauffmann believed the "bitter ending" induced "a fatal sense of futility."[14] In the *New York Times*, Bosley Crowther considered it "uncertain and ambiguous" and sent "audiences away with questions in their minds." "Indeed," he asked, "are we to gather that the new-found brotherhood of the two is without hope of liberation?" For the screenwriters, this response was precisely what they sought with their film. "If," they responded to Crowther, "we find a larger question arising from it, then we have succeeded most fully in expressing our intention. The question of freedom in its broadest sense can only be resolved by the people everywhere in the land, not by the authors."[15] By conveying that transformative change in America's race relations would come only through grassroots struggle and that their role as creative artists was limited, Young and Smith encapsulated the debate among Hollywood leftists about the political potential of film. Like Kramer, they aimed to make "a comment on American social problems, such as race bias," rather than offer a solution.[16]

Young and Smith brought an artistic and political perspective shaped by debates and discussions on the Left to their collaboration with Kramer and the film's production team. Even though Young was on the blacklist and "there was such fear in the air," he still sought to write what he felt was "real and true" rather than what was "safe."[17] Like his leftist screenwriters, the liberal Kramer sought to make motion pictures that contributed to social change and reform. He hoped his purchase of Young and Smith's screenplay would "encourage young writers to develop new themes dealing with the world we live in." The high price Kramer paid for the screenplay made the new, so-called tyro writers into "a real Hollywood success story." This positive development came after they had failed to sell the screenplay for only $15,000 to blacklisted Hollywood filmmakers who had expatriated to England, one of whom was Cy Endfield. Endfield knew Young and was very sympathetic about his financial difficulties. In 1956 he had received word about the blacklist's impact on colleagues back in the United States. "Some guys are making it—others are doing badly, as Ned," wrote one of their mutual friends. Endfield "would have taken an option on" the screenplay "himself had he had the money." Young and Smith later used Ingo Preminger, brother of producer-director Otto Preminger and a "primary agent for blacklisted writers," to sell their screenplay to Kramer.[18]

Although the screenplay was credited to Young's pseudonym, Nathan E. Douglas, Hollywood insiders knew its backstory. Sidney Poitier recalled the writers as "very intense and committed progressives."[19] At the time Dalton Trumbo, blacklisted screenwriter and one of the Holly-wood Ten, wrote in a personal letter about the screenplay that "no secret at all was made of its origin. . . . Stanley Kramer bought it, and the sale is probably one of the most open that thus far has occurred." Trumbo expressed admiration for Kramer's attitude—"He appears not to give a damn"—and his view that this event signaled "the blacklist is breaking so very fast."[20] Trumbo's most recent biographers, Larry Ceplair and Christopher Trumbo, extend the discussion of Kramer's dealings with Young and his coauthor Smith. Josh Smith, Harold's son, later recalled that "Kramer did not insist on any credit fictions, fronts, or coffee shop exchange of rewrites." Instead, he treated and paid them well. Tony Curtis remembered Kramer's actions as wanting "to send a message to supporters of the late senator Joe McCarthy that he wouldn't be intimidated by the senator's anti-Communist rampage."[21] Kramer sent another important and very public message in 1958. As a guest on the NBC television show *Youth Wants to Know,* he implicitly challenged the Hollywood blacklist by admitting he had employed "many people who had been subpoenaed" by HUAC. "I personally have felt in terms of employment that those things are not things that are questions asked or lists made."[22] The production of *The Defiant Ones* went ahead under Young's pseudonym, but Kramer's hiring, treatment, and endorsement of the screenwriters signaled a change in Hollywood.

Picturing Black and White

In addition to a strong screenplay, Kramer produced *The Defiant Ones* with many of the same elements that had appeared in his earlier success-ful films, with a cinematic style in clear service to the compelling story. After purchase, the screenplay still had to go through the Production Code Administration's rigorous censorship process. The PCA's analysis of film content categorized the film as a social problem film and de-cided the ending was "Fatalistic," after rejecting "Happy," "Unhappy," and "Moral." Like Crowther, PCA administrators decided *The Defiant Ones* portrayed the two prisoners as relatively powerless before social and institutional forces. For the "Portrayals of 'Races' and Nationals," PCA documents only mentioned Sidney Poitier in a "prominent role" as a "Negro," played both "sympathetically and unsympathetically." They answered "both Yes + No" to the question "Does the story tend to enlist the sympathy of the audience for the criminal(s)?" Concerns about the depiction of violence—"Punch," "Hitting with chain"—were raised.[23] In the correspondence between the PCA and Kramer, Geoffrey M. Shurlock demanded that "excessive forms of brutality" be curbed or moved off screen and took issue with the idea of a sexual affair between Jackson and the single mother. "Any such suggestion would be unacceptable in the finished picture." With regard to language, Shurlock objected to the frequent use of "hell" and "damn" but agreed that "the use of the word, 'nigger,' is valid in these circumstances."[24]

For Kramer, the screenplay's language, violence, characterization, and plot made *The Defiant Ones* into powerful drama. It was "a story about the defiance of youth, of the defiance of the individual in our society and in all of the world," he contended. "Make no mistake about it, this is a controversial story." Kramer played up the film's racial conflict in heightened language. "The principals are a white boy who hates Negroes and then finds himself chained to one as both attempt to escape from a chain gang." He emphasized that the film dealt "uncompromisingly" with American race relations.[25] Kramer's pitch for *The Defiant Ones* built on his history of making movies that "forthrightly . . . treat[ed] themes far off Hollywood's beaten track" and of risk-taking. "Not long ago, audiences welcomed almost any film we called controversial, adult or offbeat," he declared. But "I don't think that controversy for the sake of controversy is enough. Not anymore." In his typical fashion, he praised—and pandered to—filmgoers who "are more selective than ever before" and acknowledged the need to make "a picture that says something," says it well, and is exciting. "It's a gamble," he once again admitted. "But with every film today we've got to gamble."[26]

With the story set, Kramer needed to cast his film. He recognized that the casting was going to be crucial to the success of this film. "If I am going to make a picture about a Negro and a white man," he noted, "I have to be smart about casting in order to sell it." And his smartest decision was hiring Sidney Poitier. Poitier made his name in Kramer's genre; these "so-called 'problem' pictures," he believed, "helped my career." By the late 1950s, Poitier was a much-respected actor and widely viewed by producers as a box-office draw. He also had emerged, in the words of his most recent biographer Aram Goudsouzian, as "popular culture's foremost symbol of racial democracy." His costar Tony Curtis believed Poitier "was to the movies what Jackie Robinson had been to baseball."[27] His success in Hollywood indicated to many Americans that racial progress was occurring in the 1950s and 1960s. Early in his career, Poitier had criticized stereotypical roles for blacks, turned down roles because the characters were "too passive" or "bereft of dignity," and instead cultivated an "educated, sophisticated, articulate" image.[28]

Kramer recalled concerns that the role of Noah Cullen, "an ignorant criminal," in *The Defiant Ones* threatened Poitier's star image, but neither he nor Poitier was worried. It was "an amazing film," Poitier later wrote. "It disturbed a lot of people—and it *informed* them." Participating in Kramer's movie "would represent for me and other black actors a step up in the quality of parts available to us, and at the same time afford the black community in general a rare look at a movie character exemplifying the dignity of our people—something that Hollywood had systematically ignored in its shameless capitulation to racism."[29]

At the time, the character of Noah Cullen and Poitier's portrayal of him were recognized as complex, but over the years Poitier's role has been remembered differently. For most scholars, Cullen joined the list of Poitier's roles as "restrained Black men who endure the indignities and injustices of racism with cool patience and dignified strength." His characters were "non-confrontational black men with whom white viewers could sympathize."[30] No one involved in the production of *The Defiant Ones* saw the character of Cullen as "restrained" or "non-confrontational," however. Kramer commented on the range of Poitier's performance in the film, from "a pathetic and even pitiful character" to "moments of overwhelming and savage emotional power," indicating an intensely expressive portrayal. Similarly, Poitier reportedly told Kramer at the time that the film "really has it. I can feel the pain, the animosity, the challenge two characters like ours would be feeling." Such understandings of Poitier's character recently received scholarly support from Roland Leander Williams, Jr., who argues that Cullen "looks angry and mean" at the start of the film, more "a fugitive from black bondage" than an "Uncle Tom."[31] But Williams is an exception.

Scholars also present the relationship between Cullen and Jackson as "an interracial friendship" and *The Defiant Ones* as an "interracial buddy film." The filmmakers avoided such statements about the two characters. Poitier told *Look* magazine about the movie, "It doesn't pretend to give a cure-all for hate-thy-neighbor." Instead, he summed up Cullen's feelings as "I'm going through a hell of a lot with you, and still don't dig everything about you, but in some ways you're not so bad after all."[32]

Tony Curtis, Sidney Poitier, and Stanley Kramer in a production still for The Defiant Ones *(1958). Courtesy of Margaret Herrick Library and MGM/UA.*

Poitier's costar, Tony Curtis, also readily signed on to the production and similarly steered clear of any mention of "friendship" between the two characters. "I liked the fact that the two lead actors were chained together until almost the end of the movie," Curtis recalled, noting that "these two convicts from different races had to accept each other as equals." He knew "the topic of race guaranteed that this film would be controversial." His strong commitment to the film included contributing crucial financing through his own production company. Just as the part of Noah Cullen was a departure for Poitier, the role of Joker Jackson meant Curtis—with heavy makeup altering his nose—would "escape the pretty-boy rut I'm in." "At first they said I was too good-looking for the part," he later recalled. "I didn't look enough like the asshole 'nigger-hater' I was supposed to play."[33] The filmmakers assumed that external appearance reflected internal character, and therefore a racist, especially a white, working-class, southern racist, needed to be ugly. This assumption revealed, as scholar Allison Graham pointedly observes, "the degree to which stereotypical imagery could inform socially conscious filmmaking," including that of Kramer and his colleagues. The character of Jackson epitomizes the "celluloid cracker" found in earlier Hollywood movies, a stereotype central to the popular and political depiction of the South as a backward region, filled with poverty and racism.[34]

Despite enacting a negative southern stereotype on screen, particularly at the start, Curtis believed in the film. He stated that *The Defiant Ones* "was important to me, because I was still building a case to be seen as a serious actor." The previous year, for example, he had taken on a dramatic role as a scheming press agent in *The Sweet Smell of Success* (1957). Curtis considered *The Defiant Ones* politically important as well, "a groundbreaking movie for its time. It also made me much more aware of racism in America." Curtis remembered joining Poitier to "sit and talk about the inequities that he had suffered from his whole life. As a Jew who'd dealt with plenty of anti-Semitism, I had some understanding of his situation." He insisted that he and Poitier share star billing, as to do otherwise "would contradict the entire premise of the movie." The names of both actors would appear above the title in alphabetical order; "Kramer Film Stars Equal," headlined the *Los Angeles Times*.[35] And, as it turned out, both men received nominations for best actor at the Academy Awards. Curtis's emphasis on equality rather than friendship between the characters of Cullen and Joker indicated an understanding that political, not just personal, relations mattered in the film's plot.

The portrayal of the supporting characters in *The Defiant Ones* similarly emphasized the significance of institutions as well as individuals in perpetuating racism in society. Two key characters are the law enforcement officials leading the search for the escaped convicts: Sheriff Max Muller and state police captain Frank Gibbons. The sheriff is "doing his job without hatred or rancor," "without redneck histrionics," recalled Theodore Bikel, the actor who played the part.[36] Bikel's Oscar-nominated portrayal countered the image of the racist, reactionary southern law official that existed at the time. This negative image was later reinforced in reality by men such as Eugene "Bull" Conner of Birmingham, Alabama, who shockingly turned police dogs and fire hoses on civil rights protestors in 1963. Instead, Muller is a humane man and wants to capture Cullen and Jackson without brutality or bloodshed. His posse is well armed, however, and includes a dog handler with bloodhounds for tracking as well as two vicious Dobermans. Muller's rival, Captain Gibbons, "wants to take the prisoners dead or alive, but Muller orders the dogs kept leashed, and warns the men about using their guns." "These are men," he says when a member of party likens their search to "runnin' rabbits."

The conflict between Muller and Gibbons has been analyzed as representing different approaches—cautious response or violent repression—among white Americans to the civil rights movement, including the Little Rock crisis.[37] Their conflict goes beyond the individual level, however. "To the two men, the sheriff represents law and oppression," noted the screenwriters Young and Smith. *The Defiant Ones* makes clear how institutions such as law enforcement functioned to disadvantage Americans such as Cullen and Jackson.

But as the search drags on, Sheriff Muller must make a choice reminiscent of Young's confrontation with the blacklist. When Muller is reminded he is up for reelection that year, the pressure on him to escalate the search party's tactics mounts. He faces the dilemma between using the dogs or losing his job. Young and Smith clarified their screenplay's depiction of Sheriff Muller's dilemma: "The sheriff represents an exploration of a character familiar to us all, the man whose humanist principles" conflict with "his own self-interest." In the end, Muller refuses to cater to what we assume is his mostly white, law-and-order constituency, and he recaptures the men without violence. His decision symbolized "the triumph of principle," according to the screenwriters.[38]

This decision and the larger principle recalled Young's own before HUAC in 1953. Over the decade, he remained firm despite his continued blacklisting. "I have been asked many times why I don't make things easy for myself and 'recant,'" he later explained. If Young admitted he had been a communist, recanted his earlier beliefs and activism, and "named names," he could get off the blacklist. But by doing so, he would be sacrificing his civil liberties, including rights to freedom of thought and expression, as well as his loyalty to former friends and colleagues. Young refused this arrangement. "I simply won't do it just to secure an economic advantage for myself."[39]

The actors in *The Defiant Ones* thus encountered complex representations of race, class, and politics in the film, but the same cannot be said of how gender relations were portrayed. Of the two main women characters—the single mother Cullen and Jackson encounter and Cullen's wife—only the former appears on screen. Cara Williams effectively played the part of the lonely, love-starved mother, and she received a best supporting actress Oscar nomination for her performance. The film's dialogue conveyed her character's motivations and backstory, yet the screenplay called her only "the woman." Leaving her unnamed reduced and essentialized the only female character prominently present in the movie. Williams's character also is needy, repeatedly asking Jackson to "take me with you," and she is treacherous, directing Cullen to go through a deadly swamp. She undermines the action and affiliation of the male protagonists, as does Cullen's absent wife.[40]

Early in the film, Cullen protests his wife's passive response to racial and class oppression. The message from "my wife: 'Be nice,'" he tells Jackson. "They throwed me in solitary confinement, and she said 'Be nice.' A man'd shortweight me. She'd say, 'Be nice, or you get in trouble.'" In this way, Cullen blames his wife for his exploitation and emasculation within America's social relations of power. As black feminists have pointed out, this charge unfairly makes black women complicit with the disempowerment of black men within a white racist society. "I never could get that woman to understand how I was feelin' inside," Cullen continues. The implication is that Jackson, although white, is male and does understand. Both plot elements involving women worked to forge a bond between the two men by excluding and criticizing the female characters.[41]

Even as *The Defiant Ones* continued the problematic portrayals of women in Kramer's films, it revived his practice of inexpensive filmmaking. Unlike his most recent film, *The Pride and the Passion* (1957), the movie had a modest budget of $778,000. Kramer also returned to shooting in black and white, and cinematographer Sam Leavitt was rewarded with an Academy Award. Not only less expensive than color film, black-and-white film stock reinforced the movie's theme. As Theodore Bikel noted, "It was a constant but subtle reminder we were dealing with a story that revolved around the friction and agony of black-white relationships."[42] They shot the film quickly, both on set and on location. Universal Studios provided the set, which Kramer closed to journalists and then advertised in the Hollywood trade press. The closing was presented as a "shocker" and nearly unprecedented in "an industry whose publicity-consciousness is second to none." "Closing the set was a difficult decision," Kramer acknowledged at the time. But he wanted "to hold back some of the shock values in the picture" and spark curiosity, as he had with *Home of the Brave*.[43]

In addition to the set, various locations in southern California, including a state park in Calabasas and a portion of the Southern Pacific railroad, provided a rugged landscape and experience for filmmaking. Because the film's locale was supposed to be in the South, not California, the setting remained unidentified and nondescript. As a result, Curtis felt the film "needed a stronger sense of location." "Nothing is really of the American South," noted one observer, so "overhanging the entire film is a non-authentic atmosphere." Still, the location filming was challenging. "Sidney and Tony were forced to fight, wade, swim, and climb through swamps, marshes, and other rugged terrain while chained together," commiserated the *Chicago Defender*. This "ordeal" was partly due to the fact "that Kramer [is] a perfectionist."[44] Winter weather complicated the filming; at one point a rare snowstorm delayed filming on the Kern River, near Kernsville, California. When filming restarted, Poitier and Curtis needed to wear rubber diving suits under their denim prison garb to withstand the river's thirty-eight-degree temperature. Shackled together, they were swept away by the swiftly running river and rescued by four stunt men on safety ropes, an example of what the *New York Times* called "the Curtis-Poitier heroics." "The location shots in the swamp and underbrush were not easy," Bikel recalled. "It got quite cold and there was a little rebellion going on until everyone was issued long johns." Even so, he added, "We all knew . . . that we were part of something out of the ordinary."[45]

As the film moved from principal photography into postproduction, decisions about editing and music reinforced the film's story and style. The editing involved simple cuts rather than dissolves or fade-outs, which kept the pace of the film consistent with the action of escaping prisoners, and editor Frederic Knudtson earned an Oscar nomination. The decision to omit a musical score and instead to use diegetic music (music coming from within the film world) throughout was effective. Ernest Gold's choice of music—a radio occasionally blaring rock 'n' roll music and a repeated blues song sung a cappella by Poitier—contributed a sparse but meaningful soundscape to plot developments. The song was adapted from "Long Gone (from Bowlin' Green)," which tells the story of a prisoner who makes his escape. Although different versions of the song and lyrics existed, Kramer's production company gave screen credit to a 1920 song, with music by W. C. Handy and words by Chris Smith. That version presents the main character, Long John, as "an escape artist of tall-tale proportions."[46] Like Cullen and Jackson, he flees bloodhounds but also a submarine and a "flying machine." What Poitier sings—or rather chants—in the film refers to a chain gang—"A twenty long years on a chain gang / Sweatin' and bustin' rock"—and escape—"Long gone / Ain't he lucky." The revised lyrics included a nonsensical riff on "a sewin' machine." Yet the song, "far from being a senseless one," Young and Smith argued, "is an individual expression of defiance." "I can assure you," music critic and historian Edward "Abbe" Niles agreed at the time, "this is *the* American escape song."[47] With decisions about music and the production work wrapping up, Kramer and his colleagues now shifted to the film's promotion.

Film Promotion, "Exploitation," and Race

As an independent producer, Kramer knew that the production of a film was only half of his job; the promotion of the film was equally important. In designing the promotion or "exploitation" campaign for *The Defiant Ones*, Kramer and his team consulted the leading exhibitor in the United States at the time, David B. Wallerstein, president of the Chicago-based Balaban and Katz theater chain. Wallerstein agreed the film was "powerful" and would "do business—provided the public is made aware that this is a strong, gutsy story with sex and suspense and all the commercial elements."[48] To build public awareness, the filmmakers utilized advertising, publicity, and promotional events, including newspaper display ads, posters, the trailer, press releases, the premiere, special screenings, and a series of stunts. These elements of a promotional campaign—what media scholars call "paratexts"—aimed to build anticipation and get audiences into theaters. They also established expectations and framed the story for filmgoers. In this way, film promotion both "sells and tells" the movie's narrative.[49]

Wallerstein further recommended "an exploitation ballyhoo campaign as well as a 'prestige' campaign." By the 1950s the term "exploitation" in Hollywood meant not only film promotion, as Kramer and his colleagues used it, but also applied to a category of films. Although their film fit few of the characteristics of the so-called exploitation film—cheap, sensational, aimed at teenagers—*The Defiant Ones* did "exploit" a contemporary and controversial topic: race.[50] Kramer took Wallerstein's advice and pursued a marketing strategy that combined both crass ploys and classy events to attract an audience to his movie.

The first decision to be made concerned the location for the premiere, and Kramer sought to capitalize on current events in the civil rights movement by opening *The Defiant Ones* in Little Rock, Arkansas. To explore this option, he approached Harry S. Ashmore, the executive editor of the *Arkansas Gazette*, a well-known liberal Democrat, and a racial moderate. During the Little Rock crisis in the fall of 1957, Ashmore wrote a series of editorials in support of school integration. These editorials won him a Pulitzer Prize for their "forcefulness, dispassionate analysis, and clarity."[51] Kramer also knew Ashmore's book charting the significant social and political changes occurring in the South. Boldly titled *An Epitaph for Dixie*, the book had just been published in early 1958 when Kramer wrote to him. "This is perhaps an unusual Letter-to-the-Editor," Kramer began, "but I wish to ask your advice." He described the plot of *The Defiant Ones*, although he downplayed the controversial content he had been playing up. "This is not a segregation (or integration) story per se," but a story about how "every man is a human being, whatever his color." Kramer explained his determination to screen his movie "against the widest possible shades of opinion," and he thought a "showing in Little Rock, the best-known site of U.S. social change today, might offer such a range of public reaction." He expressed his hope "to have an audience ranging . . . from Governor Faubus to the first nine Negro pupils of Central High School."[52] Ashmore responded favorably to Kramer's letter, and publicist George Thomas, Jr., traveled to Arkansas for further discussions.

But the many challenges involved in a Little Rock premiere for *The Defiant Ones* soon arose. In his report back to Kramer and his team, Thomas emphasized that their promotion campaign did not need to "exploit the explosive nature of the film" or "to tie it specifically to segregation or other issues." "Nevertheless," he argued, "Little Rock is a natural arena for a preview." He had received "a pledge of full and continued cooperation by Harry S. Ashmore. . . . He thinks very highly of our screenplay, both as a Southerner and an author." But Ashmore sensibly advised "against a 'premiere' with the usual hoopla, because it would appear to exploit local troubles." The school integration crisis that began in the fall of 1957 continued through 1958. The famous and courageous Little Rock Nine had integrated Central High School, but they faced constant harassment and violence, and federal troops remained in Little Rock. Although *The Defiant Ones* "might be helpful to the community in its segregation problems," Thomas wrote, "because of our picture's theme, the White Citizens Council would be against it, possibly boycotting or even demonstrating against it." Further complicating matters was the fact that "all Little Rock theatres are segregated." The choice open to the filmmakers was fraught: "an integrated showing at the civic auditorium," which would likely spark racial conflict, or "simultaneous showings in white and Negro theatres," which would severely undermine the film's message and compromise the filmmakers' integrity.[53]

With the Little Rock option foreclosed, Kramer and his colleagues chose Chicago for the film's premiere, but they continued to make contemporary American race relations central to their promotion campaign for *The Defiant Ones*. This strategy appeared in publicity aimed at one of the film's essential audiences: exhibitors. Reviews in the industry trade press often indicated how the filmmakers sought to convince exhibitors to book their movies, as they were more likely to be based on studio press releases than on independent journalistic assessment. For example, the *Motion Picture Herald* contended that the title and the story of *The Defiant Ones* combined with Kramer and his reputation made "a sort of guarantee this is a 'talk-about.'" This reference reinforced the idea that Kramer's social problem films made important contributions to public discussion and debate. The film "compellingly conveys the issues as well as the emotions of our times" and a "message of human dignity and principle." The review even claimed "some exhibitors [were] enlisting voluntarily to sell this picture on its general basis of good-will" and that "the avenues of public weal in the more populated centers lend themselves to the enterprising showman." In this way, exhibitors were called to embrace *The Defiant Ones* as a way to extend feelings of cooperation and friendship and enhance the general welfare in American society. This appeal departed sharply—and surprisingly—from the usual emphasis on commercial activity and profit making in the trade papers.[54]

The film's racial message also featured in several press releases from Kramer's publicists proclaiming the profound symbolism of the chain linking the two protagonists. The chain, "a 4 lb., 29-inch iron chain, costing $1280, virtually co-stars with Tony Curtis and Sidney Poitier in Stanley Kramer's *The Defiant Ones*," blared one press release. "One of the principal story points," Kramer stated in another, "is that the two antagonists learn the hard way that they must depend on one another to survive. Therefore the chain becomes a simple yet powerful symbol of our theme." "Perhaps," a third press release noted, the film "might inspire a campaign to rid the country of chain gangs where they still exist."[55] So much publicity for a movie prop risked overexposure and, as it turned out, sparked a spoof from industry insiders. In an Oscar campaign for *I Want to Live!* (1958), actress Susan Hayward and her director, Robert Wise, parodied their competition with a picture of themselves handcuffed together. But many media outlets picked up the press releases, almost intact. The chain was a "powerful symbol of racial conflict," noted the *Chicago Defender*. "The web of complicated human and cultural chains that link black and white America becomes . . . a single chain 29 inches long," summarized *Life* magazine.[56] The film's publicity made it clear: the meaning of the chain was the message of the movie.

Yet even as the filmmakers promoted their film's uplifting social and political message, they also publicized the sensational aspects of their movie. The newspaper display ads, the posters, and the trailer emphasized the movie's sex and violence. In the line drawing used for the ads and posters, Curtis's and Poitier's characters are bare-chested, exaggeratedly muscled, and snarling at each other like wild animals. The text for one ad exclaimed: "LOOK AT THEM! Toe to toe . . . clawing at each other's flesh . . . smashing steel in each other's face! And always behind them—the sheriff, the mob, and the killer dogs to finish the job!" Other ads focused on the sexual relationship between the characters played by Curtis and Williams. One ad included a drawing of the couple lying in bed kissing, with Poitier's character looking on, with the text: "There in the cabin the white man made love to the woman . . . and the black man waited—listening for the dogs closing in for the kill!"[57] The advertisement actually contradicted the plot, because Cullen sleeps during the night of the sexual affair between Jackson and "the woman," but this ad sought to evoke what film scholars call "the voyeuristic gaze."[58]

The anger, aggression, and action of the two men also dominated the trailer for *The Defiant Ones*, with shots of them running chained together, fighting, the threatened lynching, the pursuing dogs, and one quiet moment of intimacy between the couple. The trailer's dialogue and the titles reinforced the theme of violence: "Chained Fury! Chained to each other like animals! At each other's throats like animals!" The ads, posters, and trailer for the film reflected marketing maneuvers more consistent with an exploitation movie than a high-minded social problem film.

As with any movie in Hollywood—where the stars sell the movie, so the studios sell the stars—the promotional campaign for *The Defiant Ones* featured the two starring actors, although Poitier figured more prominently than Curtis. The movie ads and posters were one exception, as the name and image of Curtis appeared first, on the left, and slightly higher than Poitier's to the right. This positioning could be viewed as an effort to highlight the role and contribution of a white actor and downplay those of a black actor, despite the filmmakers' commitment to equal billing for the two stars. Yet Curtis was the bigger star at the time, his name came first alphabetically, and Poitier stood out in the rest of promotional material for the film. The trailer, for example, opens with a shot of Cullen speaking angrily and at length to Jackson, who is off-screen. The publicity designed for Poitier claimed that his "outstanding" performance in *The Defiant Ones* showed he was an actor "of unlimited power" and secured his stardom. "That's just the way it was," Curtis recalled. "Sidney was a helluva talent, no matter what color he was, and this was a time when Hollywood was just starting to realize maybe it could do something positive for civil rights."[59]

Poitier participated in many activities promoting *The Defiant Ones*, apart from one: he refused to record the song "Long Gone" for commercial release. Employees in Kramer's company, Lomitas Productions, approached Poitier about releasing an original soundtrack recording as a "substantial profit might be realized from the sale." But Poitier strongly objected. He did "not consider himself a vocalist of any kind and feels that this would not perform any service for the picture or for himself," reported one of Kramer's colleagues. When asked by the news media about his singing in *The Defiant Ones*, Poitier "said it was because his voice had just the right irritating quality for the story. . . . But he insists he's an actor, not a singer."[60] The actor's insistence on this point signaled more than a lack of confidence in his singing voice. It also posed a challenge to "white culture's perception of African Americans as fun-loving, 'rhythmic' people." This white perception fit with the minstrel tradition in American culture and contributed to Hollywood's long-standing black stereotypes.[61] By undermining the association of blackness with music, Poitier refused to be bound by racial stereotypes and furthered efforts to expand the types of film roles open to African

Americans. Against his wishes, he soon would be singing in *Porgy and Bess* (1959), but "his emphatic rejection" of recording "Long Gone" was heeded. "Mr. Kramer feels quite strongly that Lomitas should not exploit a sound track containing the voice of Sidney Poitier."[62]

Poitier's commitment to promoting *The Defiant Ones* more generally meant he played an important role in the events and publicity surrounding the film's premiere at Chicago's Roosevelt Theater on August 13, 1958. Known as a city where Kramer's "pictures always have been well received," Chicago became the focus of an energetic campaign to bring attention and audiences to the film.[63] To prepare for the premiere, Kramer's team organized advance screenings for specific interest groups and planted media stories to secure publicity and positive word of mouth. One influential marketing target, especially among African Americans, was the Johnson Publishing Company, the publisher of *Ebony* and *Jet* magazines, which was based in Chicago. "Tremendous reaction from Johnson group at capacity screening," publicist George Thomas wrote Kramer. "Believe will bring maximum results." Indeed, *Jet* gave extensive coverage to *The Defiant Ones* in its "Movie of the Week" feature and in subsequent stories. "Is Poitier Hollywood's Best Actor?" the magazine later asked, citing his performance in the movie as "alternately an embittered and warm human being, struggling to prove a man is to be measured by what he is, rather than what color he is."[64] Successful screenings occurred for other groups in Chicago, and—unlike what Kramer's colleagues feared in Little Rock—"audiences in Chicago were mixed, white and Negro. . . . The picture, obviously, calls for this," they stated.[65]

The advance screenings and media stories were augmented with extensive advertising, collaboration with exhibitors, and a Chicago visit from Poitier. With an ad campaign costing approximately $18,000, Thomas declared, "We expect to dominate next weekend's papers and will also do well the weekend after opening." Promotion of *The Defiant Ones* then received a big boost from Wallerstein and some thirty-five Balaban and Katz theaters. They launched "the circuit's largest cross plug trailer and lobby display in campaign for the world premiere" of what Wallerstein predicted "will be Kramer's biggest grossing film."[66] Kramer's colleagues also secured marquee advance for the first time ever in Chicago. Instead of the Roosevelt Theater's marquee displaying the film's title only once *The Defiant Ones* opened, the marquee began counting down the ten days until the premiere. These various promotional activities set the stage for Poitier's "smashing" visit. Over a period of several days, Poitier interviewed with newspapers, radio, and television, had lunch invitations at Johnson Publishing Company and with Mayor Richard J. Daley, and attended several church services. Finally, the actor headed up black Chicago's annual Bud Billiken Day parade to honor and celebrate children's education. The parade had thousands of participants and an estimated half million spectators, and Poitier received a "tremendous ovation." Poitier's visit was credited with "achieving what is regarded here as heaviest all time Chicago penetration" for *The Defiant Ones*.[67]

In addition to these "prestige" events, the promotional campaign in Chicago also included "ballyhoo" stunts and gimmicks. The most tactless stunt involved a reenactment of Cullen and Jackson's escape. Forthrightly labeled "exploitation" in the campaign outline, "a white youth and a Negro youth, with about four feet of chain between them," appeared in the Billiken Day parade. "They were dressed in torn shirts and jeans, and wore on their backs signs announcing the title of the picture and the date of the opening." Apparently "they got as much attention as did Poitier," Kramer's publicity team happily reported.[68] Another stunt listed under "exploitation"—but in better taste—was a beauty contest to name a "Miss World Premiere." The pretty and poised winner, Juaria Moore, greatly raised the status of this gimmick. Named "Miss Bronze America" of Chicago in 1955 and appearing on the cover of *Jet* as a debutante in early 1958, Moore did win admirable publicity for *The Defiant Ones*. Moore "will reign supreme at the opening" and help "ballyhoo the Stanley Kramer masterpiece," reported the *Chicago Defender*.[69] Another idea considered newsworthy by Kramer's team included finding "a Negro milliner" and having "a *Defiant Ones* hat created, which can be photographed." Thomas did act on one final brainstorm: sending a glowing review of the film to local ministers as "a ready-made sermon for them."[70]

After the premiere and as they readied for the film's general release, Kramer and his colleagues reported "record-breaking" box office at the Roosevelt Theater. In his final few press releases based on the Chicago campaign, Thomas claimed *The Defiant Ones* "has smashed all opening-day, weekend and first week's records in the 37-year history of the Balaban & Katz theatre, with a $53,500 first week gross that tops the previous record-holder by 25%." Not only were customers lined up "around the block" but we "are playing to all kinds of people—men and women—young and old." "The 'electricity' is in the air," he exclaimed. "This picture not only opened big—it has legs."[71] Following on from the Chicago campaign, Kramer's team widened their focus to the film's national opening and began to zoom in on New York as a location for promotional activities. In the process, they turned away from exploitation stunts and organized a high-toned event to reemphasize the social and political meaning of the film.

At a major luncheon in Harlem attended by media, religious, and political leaders, famed baseball player Jackie Robinson presented "The Defiant Ones Award" to pioneering African American journalists Jimmy Hicks and Ted Poston. The award recognized Hicks, then executive editor of the *Amsterdam News*, and Poston, a reporter for the *New York Post*, for "devoted service and deep interest in the principles of America and the promise of true democracy." Both men had covered the Little Rock school integration crisis for their newspapers, as well as other major events in the civil rights movement. The award citation credited both men with "devotion to duty in the face of overwhelming odds, mob violence, and man's inhumanity to man," making each man—as expected—"a defiant one." This successful event yielded a meaningful endorsement from Robinson, known for challenging racial segregation in major league baseball. "For years I have been saying that what is needed in our progress toward equal opportunity is the chance to know one another," he stated. "*Defiant Ones* illustrates this point very well."[72]

Audiences, Reception, and Race Relations

Kramer and his colleagues used Robinson's statement in advertising to attract audiences and affect their response. Due to United Artists' distribution network, *The Defiant Ones* reached a wide audience inside and outside the United States. The domestic respondents for *The Defiant Ones* included white and African Americans, northerners and southerners, and Hollywood insiders. The film's overseas respondents came most prominently through the film's appearance on the international film festival circuit. Audience response illuminated the consumption end, rather than the production end, of Kramer's film. Extant audience response commented more on its social message about American race relations than on its cinematic technique, and most evaluations were positive, often enthusiastically so. But some evaluations of the film, generally from the political Right and Left, were sharply negative.

In 1958 and 1959 the vast majority of the audience response strongly endorsed the movie and its liberal racial message. Film reviews appeared in all of the major newspapers and magazines in the United States: the *New York Times*, the *Chicago Tribune*, the *Los Angeles Times*, *Life*, *Time*, and *Newsweek*. The black press, including the *Chicago Defender* and the *Baltimore Afro-American*, and more specialized periodicals such as the *New Republic* and *Saturday Review*, also reviewed *The Defiant Ones*. Their headlines captured the main point of the reviews: "Film Hits Hard at Race Hate," "New Hollywood Movie Has Sensitive Racial Plot," "Links in the Human Chain," "A Forceful Social Drama," "Hollywood at Its Best," and "*Defiant* Is Great Kramer!" These positive evaluations shared an appreciation for the film's contemporary relevance. "This blunt, unpretentious film," noted Mae Tinee of the *Chicago Tribune*, "lays bare, with almost painful candor, a major problem in these United States." "What mostly impressed the assembled Negroes about this movie," reported her colleague Roi Ottley after a special screening, "was the forthright handling of one of the touchiest problems of our day."[73]

Black and white members of two preview audiences in Dallas agreed. "Most unusual—but tuned to the present thinking." "Very timely." "Has guts to treat a touchy subject." "We need to have more pictures on race relations such as this one." "Should be seen by every American." Just as audience members recognized *The Defiant Ones*' timeliness, they conveyed an understanding of the movie's message as realistic rather than optimistic. "Stark drama." "Treatment of racial themes brutal and effective." "Excellent portrayal of human emotions under stress fully shows the false front of racial prejudice."[74]

Confirming what the filmmakers intended, most reviewers and spectators also portrayed Cullen and Jackson's relationship as more restrained than close. For Philip Scheuer, "if love is perhaps too strong a word to describe the degree of their not hating, interdependence certainly isn't." "Interdependence" conveyed a common purpose and mutual support but less emotion, as did "comradeship," the term used in the *New Republic*. However, Bosley Crowther claimed "they are brothers under the skin," lending much more intimacy to their relationship.[75] A few responses romanticized and even eroticized the relationship between the film's protagonists. *Life* magazine saw Cullen and Jackson as sharing "an odd, reluctant love." For some observers, the film's final image, with Cullen holding Jackson, repeated the "black and white pietà" of *Home of the Brave* (1949) and captured this emotion.[76] An important contemporary literary critic, Leslie A. Fiedler, took this interpretation further in his 1960 book *Love and Death in the American Novel*, finding homoerotic undertones in the film. He was not alone. A letter writer to the *New York Times* offered an "off-beat" suggestion by "a Freudian psychiatrist" that the film presented "the triumph of homosexuality over the forces of conventional morality and law and order." This homoerotic reading has since been reinforced by scholars, but most contemporaries did not identify Cullen and Jackson's relationship as either sexual or sentimental.[77]

Similarly, few reviewers—whether white or black—read the character of Cullen as nonconfrontational or passive in relation to Jackson, as would later scholars. The *Chicago Defender* considered Cullen to be "the most powerful screen role ever written for a Negro," and the *Baltimore Afro-American* agreed. To support this assertion, the *Afro-American* pointed out the difference between how the two escaped convicts react to the lynching threat in the movie. "It may never happen in real life—a colored man and a white . . . facing a lynch-mob together," but "Jackson's nerve breaks and he pleads for mercy, while Cullen faces the mob courageously." Stanley Kauffmann in the *New Republic* focused on another moment in the film when Cullen prevails. "They quarrel about which direction to take; the Negro wins." Jackson wants to head south, but Cullen "ain't goin' south. . . . We goin' north," he declares. Kauffmann described Poitier's portrayal as "sprung with inner tensions, radiant with force." As "he speaks it carries several centuries' accumulated protest."[78] Of course, contributing to this interpretation of the character of Cullen as "cynical" and "proud" was the high quality of Poitier's performance. Film reviewers contended that the film solidified his stardom. "Sidney Poitier," the *Chicago Defender* reported, is expected "to become a firmly established motion picture star before 1958 is out." The *New York Times* agreed and headlined: "A 'Defiant One' Becomes a Star."[79]

Although most film reviewers and spectators responded positively to the story and message of *The Defiant Ones*, key critical voices—generally on the Left and both white and black—indicted the film's content and, especially, the characterization of Cullen. "The whites and the blacks of the South have been chained together for a good many years," wrote Robert Hatch in the *Nation*, "and they have not grown notably sweet toward each other because of the confinement." He went on to criticize Kramer for "oversimplification." The film "may give people the notion that prejudice is just a big, unhappy misunderstanding and that it can be solved by a little effort at a common goal."[80] Comedian Lenny Bruce made *The Defiant Ones* part of his routine and offered biting comments on what Allison Graham calls the "easy liberalism and veiled racism" of many social problem films of the era, including Kramer's. "To play the Star-Spangled Banner it takes both the white keys and the dark-eys," Bruce mocked. "Yessir," he continued, "it's gonna be a Message World." Bruce's style of humor reflected an increasingly ironic sensibility in American culture that contrasted with, and ridiculed, Kramer's sincerity.[81] Even as Kramer's efforts to address racial problems in his films can be seen as problematic, they were well-meaning. But Bruce's comedy routine revealed how old-fashioned and inauthentic Kramer's earnest approach to social criticism appeared to a younger audience by the late 1950s and early 1960s.

A few years later, a powerful critical analysis of *The Defiant Ones* came from James Baldwin, a prominent writer, public intellectual, and, like Kramer, a graduate of DeWitt Clinton High School. Baldwin demolished the entire premise of the movie's plot: the assumption of equality in emotion and experience between the two protagonists that provided the basis for their later mutual understanding. Their initial mutual hatred, Baldwin explained, "is not equal on both sides, for it does not have the same roots." The root of white hatred for African Americans "is terror," but "the root of the black man's hatred is rage." Poitier's performance conveyed this rage so vividly that "there is no way to believe both Noah Cullen *and* the story." Baldwin further pointed out the different racial readings of the film's interracial message. "Liberal white audiences applauded when Sidney, at the end of the film, jumped off the train in order not to abandon his white buddy. The Harlem audience was outraged, and yelled, *Get back on the train, you fool!*"[82] Comedian Dick Gregory used humor to express this same reaction in his routine. "So as the train moves down the track, I reach out my arm to him. Yes, I reach out and I wave my hand, and I yell, 'Bye, baby!'" These instances showed African Americans rejecting the "white-oriented 'black-as-martyr'" hero—as scholar Mark A. Reid puts it—prominent in social problem films, such as Kramer's earlier *Home of the Brave.* Baldwin's argument that the ending of *The Defiant Ones* aimed "to reassure white people, to make them know that they are not hated" would be endorsed by future scholars.[83]

But this reassurance failed to reach all white audiences in the American South, due to local censorship. Northern critics—black and white—called the film "this year's top interracial film," "aggressively anti-racist," and "a controversial interracialer." They recognized the movie, "because of its message, will undoubtedly have tough sledding in some sections of the country," meaning the South.[84] Official censorship bodies in the South had long been concerned with "policing cinematic images" that "questioned racial hierarchies."[85] Such bigoted censorship led some southern localities and theater owners to reject *The Defiant Ones* as part of the segregationist resistance to the civil rights movement. For example, a movie theater in Montgomery, Alabama—the site of the famous 1955–1956 bus boycott and home to Martin Luther King, Jr.—canceled its run, citing protests from the local White Citizens' Council. The local Montgomery council claimed the movie was "anti-Southern and pro-integration."[86] Theater owners in Jackson, Mississippi, were threatened with a boycott if they became "traitors to the South" and played any "motion picture with a racial flavor showing colored actors or opposing the South's 'way of life.'" As a result, *The Defiant Ones,* the *Baltimore Afro-American* noted, "is definitely taboo in Mississippi."[87]

Negative responses also came from white filmgoers at the Dallas preview: "I regard the story as propaganda." "Looks like a NAACP picture." And southerners wrote directly to Kramer vehemently protesting the movie. "I have just seen the *rotten* shot of a nigger and a white man fighting," one Arkansas woman wrote. "If there is *any* way we women can *stop* this filthy film from ever being shown in Ark. or the whole south—we will surely *do* it."[88]

Southern white reception for *The Defiant Ones* was not monolithic, however, a fact recognized by respondents in the North and South. There were special screenings for integrated audiences in the South. Church groups hoped to "use the film to prove that deep understanding and affection can exist between members of different races."[89] Similarly, white members of the Dallas preview audience mostly responded positively to the film: "Comes to grips with the South today." "Brings out some real aspects of the South that very often are ignored." But some liberal southerners took issue with the film for exploiting the race issue for commercial gain and for stereotyping the region. "This is disgraceful and an insult to all us down *South!*"[90] Acknowledging that racism was not only a "southern problem," the American Anti-Prejudice Society sponsored a premiere of *The Defiant Ones* in Joliet, Illinois. Hazel A. Washington of the *Chicago Defender* hoped that, wherever they are, "the right people 'get the message' sent their way via *The Defiant Ones.*" Stanley Kauffmann understood the film as challenging any "facile sentimentality" about "the road ahead" in American race relations or "the moral superiority of any of us, Northern, Southern, white, black."[91]

The film's racial content raised concerns with anticommunists, a critical audience who connected civil rights advocacy with communism. The White Citizens' Council of Montgomery insisted that the film would "give moral support and financial gain to subversive propagandists."[92] *The Defiant Ones* also caught the attention of William C. Sullivan, a high-ranking FBI official and soon to be assistant director of the Domestic Intelligence Division. In a memo written just a few weeks after the film's Chicago premiere, Sullivan issued a warning about the film. He recognized it as "the type of film to be expected in view of [the] racial situation in the country today." But it "is also the type of film communists used in the 1930's to launch their extensive activities in Hollywood. . . . Communist publications undoubtedly will join in the acclaim for the picture." He repeated old information about Kramer teaching at "a communist training school in Los Angeles in 1947" and "being sympathetic to communism" in 1951. Finally, he urged the film was "*Not to Be Ignored,*" as it held the potential to "re-establish the influence" of communists in Hollywood.[93]

These great differences of opinion about *The Defiant Ones'* social message—from anticommunists and reactionary southern segregationists to black and white leftist critics—contrasted with the general endorsement of the film's production and technique. The acting received rave reviews, and Kramer came in for his share of credit as well. "His camera movements and positions have been knowingly chosen, his sense of tempo and dramatic emphasis is sensitive and sure," contended Arthur Knight in a review widely circulated by Kramer's publicity team. *Time* magazine complimented Kramer with an extended cooking metaphor. "For Producer-Director Stanley Kramer, at 44 one of the most skillful chefs in the business, the result of putting such ingredients together is savory cinema, free of froth and sharply seasoned." Even critics of the film, such as Robert Hatch, considered it "first-rate excitement" and "well-photographed," and Pauline Kael of the *New Yorker* later agreed that "the action is exciting; the acting is good."[94] Still, not every aspect of film production and technique received praise. Curtis's "vacillating southern accent" came in for criticism, as did plot inconsistencies and continuity errors. "The men are always sopping around through the rain and falling into mud, yet they always have dry cigarettes to smoke," complained a filmgoer; "what keeps them dry?" And for English critic Peter Cowie, Poitier's blues song "becomes almost unbearably strident by the end of the film."[95]

From his position outside the United States, Cowie noted that *The Defiant Ones* "was a success throughout the world."[96] *The Defiant Ones'* first international screening also constituted its first public release, when it appeared as an official US entry at the Berlin International Film Festival in July 1958. This appearance did not occur without controversy, but Kramer and his colleagues stood firm the face of strong opposition. Given the Cold War context, US officials expressed concern about overseas screenings of films that presented the United States in a negative light. The critical portrayal of American race relations in *The Defiant Ones* made it objectionable. Arnold Picker, at the time in charge of foreign distribution for United Artists, recalled that "enormous pressure was put on us by the State Department and the then Commanding General in Berlin to the effect that this film should not go into that festival." Officials feared audiences would "misinterpret its meaning," and "the film would do us great harm." "We withstood this pressure," Picker added, and it "was a great success."[97] *The Defiant Ones'* world premiere in Berlin led to instant international visibility, with Sidney Poitier winning a prestigious award: the Silver Bear for best actor.

The Berlin Festival began *The Defiant Ones'* appearance on the film festival circuit and subsequent awards. Kramer and his colleagues, especially his publicity team, recognized the prestige and publicity these festivals provided. *The Defiant Ones* received invitations to festivals in Mexico City, San Francisco, Sydney, Valladolid, and Venice. The Valladolid International Film Festival in Spain lauded "the courage and sincerity with which the film exposes a delicate aspect of racial coexistence and for the ethical and fraternal values inherent in the screenplay."[98] Most significant politically was the film's screening in Mexico City, just six months after anti-American violence against Vice President Richard M. Nixon in Venezuela. Journalists reported the "distinctly anti-American atmosphere" at the festival, partly due to Mexican criticisms of racial discrimination in the United States. The right-wing newspaper the *Hollywood Reporter* blamed "commie propaganda." But "the tide was turned instantaneously" with *The Defiant Ones*. Thunderous ovations from an audience of eight thousand replaced "the usual catcalls and derisive whistles that have greeted anything connected to the United States." *The Defiant Ones* was considered "a diplomatic triumph" for the United States and won a Diploma de Honor for its "brilliant theme," "moving story," and "magnificent acting and directing."[99]

Film festivals joined with other entities at home and abroad to provide numerous awards and recognitions for *The Defiant Ones*. The film won a Bodil, the Danish equivalent of the Oscar, for best American film, a Golden Globe for best picture—drama, and a New York Film Critics Award for best picture. In addition to earning best picture awards, Kramer's film received recognition for its social message. Awards came from the United Nations for the "best film illustrating one or more of the principles of the UN Charter" and from the National Conference of Christians and Jews for furthering "tolerant understanding among people of all races, religions, and nationalities." At its convention in November 1958, the National Council of Negro Women both protested the lack of federal action on school desegregation—"The inertia of our Government in this national crisis leaves millions of children stripped of their birthright and unprotected"—and presented Sidney Poitier and Tony Curtis with the Mary McLeod Bethune Human Rights Award for "human relations achievement through the arts." Poitier felt "deeply grateful" and "overwhelmed by this honor" from the most important organization of African American women.[100]

The Defiant Ones also secured nine Academy Award nominations, for best picture, both starring actors, supporting actress and actor, direction, cinematography, film editing, and—most importantly for breaking the blacklist—story and screenplay. In 1957 the Academy of Motion Picture Arts and Sciences (AMPAS) had passed an amendment to its bylaws prohibiting awarding Oscars to anyone admitting or refusing to deny membership in the Communist Party. But, making a mockery of this blacklist mechanism, screenplays written under false names by the blacklisted Dalton Trumbo, Carl Foreman, and Michael Wilson won Oscars. When it became clear to industry insiders that Nedrick Young and Harold Jacob Smith were likely to be nominated and win an Academy Award for their screenplay, negotiations ensued behind the scenes. Trumbo played an important role, seeing Young and Smith's Oscar chances as an opportunity to strike a blow against the blacklist. In a quick succession of events, Young and his supporters forced the issue by revealing his identity in the *New York Times* and on local Los Angeles television in early January 1959.[101] This revelation spurred Ward Bond to state on a January 9 television broadcast, "They're all working now, all these fifth amendment communists. . . . We've just lost the fight." The very next week, "Ban Lifted on Red Candidates for Oscars" headlined the *Los Angeles Times*. The Academy had rescinded the ban as "unworkable and impractical to administer and enforce."[102]

For supporters of the Hollywood blacklist, such as Bond, victims, such as Young and Trumbo, and critics, such as Kramer, the lifting of the ban signaled the beginning of the end of the blacklist. Young was the first beneficiary of the new policy when, in April 1959, he and Smith won their screenwriting Oscar. "I felt it means vindication in a larger sense," Young stated at the time, "not for myself but in relation to all the talent that is not being used because of the blacklist in Hollywood." "Gratifying it was to learn that in Hollywood there is a limit to the length of time a witch hunt can last," wrote Ivan Spear in *Boxoffice* magazine.[103] Yet Young's Oscar citation used his pseudonym, Nathan E. Douglas, and his screenwriting credit for the film was not officially restored to his real name until 1996. So the battle over the Hollywood blacklist was far from over, and Kramer, his colleagues, and his movies remained key figures in the clashes to come. Meanwhile, already at work on his next film, Stanley Kramer turned his attention from the domestic politics of civil rights and liberties to the foreign policy and military strategy of Cold War America.

3 Nuclear War *On the Beach*

With the film awards celebrating *The Defiant Ones* adding up impressively in late 1958 and early 1959, Stanley Kramer decamped to Melbourne, Australia, to make his next movie. The overseas location for *On the Beach* fit with Kramer's international aims and ambitions for a movie about the catastrophic global consequences of nuclear war. He, his production team, and his stars—Gregory Peck, Ava Gardner, and Fred Astaire—spent a long, hot summer in the Southern Hemisphere filming *On the Beach*. An adaptation of Nevil Shute's frightening but fast-selling 1957 novel, the movie is set five years in the future, in 1964. It tells the story of a group of Australians, an American nuclear submarine commander, and his crew awaiting certain death from radioactive fallout following the outbreak of nuclear war in the Northern Hemisphere. Shute, a British expatriate in Australia, drew his title from T. S. Eliot's 1925 poem "The Hollow Men," who were "gathered on this beach." The poem finishes with lines powerfully appropriate for a story about the end of humanity due to nuclear radiation, which Shute used in his epigraph: "This is the way the world ends. Not with a bang but a whimper."

Kramer purchased the film rights within a month of *On the Beach*'s publication as a book—it had first been serialized—after competitive bidding between companies "eager to snag this startling story of what happens to the world after the atomic bombs drop."[1] "This is by far the most important story that I have ever found," Kramer declared. "It is an enormous challenge," he added, "the biggest challenge in my career." The challenges involved in producing and promoting *On the Beach* were many. Filming overseas, keeping the all-star cast happy away from home, and securing the cooperation of the US Navy for military equipment and film footage made Kramer's job difficult. He also needed to transform a grim and depressing story into popular entertainment and to design a promotion campaign to attract a global audience. "I knew

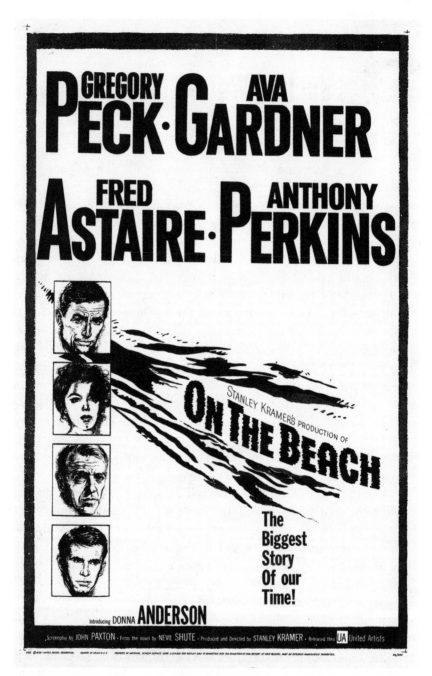

Poster for On the Beach *(1959). Courtesy of Margaret Herrick Library and MGM/UA.*

that it was a story that must reach everybody, so that its message could penetrate every corner of the earth."[2]

Kramer's vision for the film made *On the Beach* an expensive endeavor. His "fabulous offer" of $75,000 cash plus a percentage to Shute for the rights to his novel was only the beginning of what promised to be a "multi-million-dollar production." Casting major Hollywood stars in his pricey picture was "insurance on his investment."[3] "United Artists," he later recalled, "objected strenuously to the project, though I must give the people there credit for their loyalty to me. They did not refuse to finance it." Looking back, Kramer realized the film was "not destined to succeed at the box office." In fact, although the film grossed an estimated $7,189,915 worldwide, the film's high budget and other commitments meant a $700,000 loss in the end. But at the time, Kramer remained confident and committed to the project. "Its subject was as serious and compelling as any ever attempted in a motion picture—the very destruction of mankind and the entire planet."[4]

Taking on this significant subject mattered very much at the time, both within the motion picture industry and as part of American political culture. *On the Beach* signaled a change in Hollywood's approach to the nuclear question. During the 1950s, fewer than 5 percent of films dealt with the subject of nuclear weapons or war. Films about the US military during the Cold War, such as *Strategic Air Command* (1955) and *Bombers B-52* (1957), portrayed nuclear weapons positively, as "benign protectors of democracy," according to historian Tony Shaw.[5] Other nuclear-themed films were low-budget "B" movies in the category of science fiction/horror. Fallout from nuclear testing, for example, sets into motion the plots for *Them!* (1954), about irradiated, giant ants emerging from the New Mexico desert, and *The Incredible Shrinking Man* (1957), about a man dosed with radioactive mist from a strange cloud off the California coast. Although these movies and others like them did have an "anti-atom message," they usually "sugar-coated" the issues or had a happy ending, with the monster contained or the destruction limited.[6] Even nuclear survival films, where a few people continue to live in a postapocalyptic world, had relatively optimistic endings. In *Five* (1951) and *The World, the Flesh, and the Devil* (1959), the survivors confront crisis and conflict but resolve to begin again and build toward the future. The final title for the latter film even replaced "The End" with "The Beginning." As a social problem film, *On the*

Beach, in contrast, bleakly portrayed the complete extinction of life on the planet and adopted a serious, low-key tone. Filmgoers noticed. "The world seemed bent on self-destruction," observed a New York woman. "There was no defense, no escape, no place to run."[7]

The tone of Kramer's film originated with Shute's writing and reflected the critical political moment at the end of the 1950s, due to the latest stage of development of nuclear warfare. After 1954, the advent of hydrogen bombs and missile-delivery systems made the prospect of nuclear war even more destructive and dangerous than the early atomic bombs delivered by airplanes. In recognition of this new, even more chilling situation, pacifists and antinuclear activists formed the National Committee for a Sane Nuclear Policy (SANE) in 1957, the same year Shute's novel came out. SANE at first sought limits on atmospheric testing to protect the population from radioactive fallout and supported international test ban treaty negotiations then ongoing in Geneva, Switzerland. But the committee soon began agitating for nuclear disarmament. Meanwhile, public opinion polls in the United States in 1957 and 1958 showed popular support for a multilateral test ban and an end to the arms race, several years before the 1962 Cuban Missile Crisis raised the nuclear stakes even further. These developments indicated the beginnings of a change in the United States from a culture of nuclear consensus to one of nuclear dissent.[8]

Although Kramer was not an antinuclear activist, he shared a disposition toward dissent. Nuclear war, he felt in 1959, "could happen tomorrow—but must not be permitted to happen, even in a million tomorrows."[9] These feelings, combined with his international ambitions for the film, meant Kramer made a stark, unsparing film with a universal humanitarian message that received worldwide attention. In the process, *On the Beach* provoked great political debate and discussion across the political spectrum, at home and abroad, and from the letters of concerned citizens and editorial pages to Congress and the Oval Office. Many participants boldly questioned the direction of US and Soviet nuclear policy and the claims of political authorities, and they articulated an alternative vision for the future of nuclear weapons. This widespread debate over the message and meaning of Kramer's latest social problem film put government officials and conservative anticommunists very publicly on the defensive for the first time since the start of the Cold War.

Making an International Impact

Every aspect of the production and promotion of *On the Beach* was designed to make the film an international phenomenon, and the reception of the film indicated that Kramer and his colleagues achieved their aims. The script by John Paxton revised several aspects of Nevil Shute's novel and added what was seen at the time as an "American" sensibility to a very British story. The plot involved an international cast of characters, which was reflected in the casting of Americans, Australians, and British expatriates in the film. The overseas location involved significant international cooperation and required Kramer to act as a diplomat in his dealings with his Australian hosts. The cinematic style of an important Italian cinematographer, Giuseppe Rotunno, realized Kramer's vision on screen. A global strategy informed the extensive and expensive promotion for the film. A worldwide, multilingual publicity campaign heralded *On the Beach* as "The First Motion Picture for Everyone All Over the World." Even more unprecedented was the simultaneous global premiere. Screenings were held in eighteen cities on seven continents on December 17, 1959, including behind the Iron Curtain in Moscow. As Kramer put it, "I intended the film to be seen on all continents at the same time, because I wanted to create a film for people in the power of their mass." The intention to address all of humanity with a message "of *importance* on an international scale" was "the dream of the production."[10]

Kramer's aspirations for *On the Beach* were heralded as "remarkably unlike the movie producer's usual endorsement of his product," as were his inspirations.[11] When answering questions about what inspired his latest production, Kramer offered very personal notions, from "self-preservation" to his children. "My nine-year-old son is at school in California," he told one journalist. "One day I received a letter from the school asking, 'In the event of a nuclear attack do you want your child left at school, or will you pick him up afterwards?' When you get a letter like that, there's nothing you can do except make a film like *On the Beach*." He expressed concern and worry about his "two children who will grow up in the world of apprehension and the constant threat of annihilation of the world."[12] "Why, he asked himself, should we accept so dreadful a possibility so matter-of-factly?" Reviewers, commentators, and regular filmgoers commended Kramer for taking on the very subject of *On the Beach*, for making a movie that "dealt dramatically with the hottest global problem—atomic war."[13] "You strike me as a man with the courage to follow through his own convictions," wrote a Massachusetts filmgoer to Kramer, "a rare attribute nowadays." "Stanley Kramer stands alone among Hollywood producers today," Arthur Knight of *Saturday Review* agreed, particularly in "facing up to the problems and issues of our times and our society." Kramer "trains his cameras on what is surely the most important question on earth—survival in the atomic age."[14]

Yet Kramer did not claim or receive sole credit for addressing this "theme, so important for our future," given its well-known origins in Shute's novel. *On the Beach* was a "motion picture version of Nevil Shute's powerful novel," recognized one of many reviewers. For another, less favorable critic, "*On the Beach* was adapted, or rather unceremoniously ripped, from" the original novel. But most respondents felt the film affirmed Shute's aims. The novel's "sense of significance, of social purpose, is apparent in every phase of Mr. Kramer's production," wrote Knight. After all, Knight asked, "How many producers would risk a property in which it is clear from the very outset that everyone must die?"[15] The risk was worth it in Kramer's view, because he believed in the vital importance of Shute's subject. In turn—at least initially—the novelist, whose full name was Nevil Shute Norway, held the producer-director's filmmaking in high regard and felt his book would be handled conscientiously. "I know with your production it will make a magnificent film," he told Kramer. The two men also shared a commitment to creating artistic entertainment with a message that mattered socially and politically. "A popular novelist can often play the part," Shute Norway wrote, "in raising for the first time subjects which ought to be addressed in public." Mutual goals and respect meant their relationship began well. "From the standpoint of the motion picture industry," Kramer stated after purchasing the rights to *On the Beach*, "it is my personal feeling that our future depends on motion pictures of this caliber."[16]

The future of the film also depended on the caliber of the screenplay and, to write the adaptation, Kramer hired John Paxton. Paxton was well known for writing *Crossfire*, an adaptation of a novel directed by Edward Dmytryk and produced by Adrian Scott. Although Paxton avoided organized politics, his association with two of the Hollywood Ten opened him up to red-baiting, as happened when he was writing Kramer's *The Wild One* (1953). Paxton, then, brought to his work on the screenplay for *On the Beach* a familiarity with the process of adaptation, the social problem film genre, collaborating with Kramer, and Red Scare politics.

Paxton knew very well the dilemmas that arise for a writer engaged in transforming a book into a screenplay. "He has considerable power; he is also considerably restricted. . . . In the case of a hit or bestseller such as *On the Beach*, he is acutely aware . . . of the audiences, the millions of readers. And of the author." Paxton considered Shute "a good, solid, story-teller" and hoped to act as "an extension of the author." But he recognized the need to be "aware of what the producer wants." Paxton's first meeting with Kramer revealed the producer-director "to be vigorously convinced that here was a film of potential good and profit. He dismissed—with the fanatic's fortunate talent for self-deception—the evident, enormous difficulties of production." "You got the impression he had already seen the picture," Paxton remembered. The two men agreed to a screenplay in "the spirit of the novel," but they definitely wanted changes.[17]

In the transformation from the page to the screen, the plot of *On the Beach* changed in three significant ways, one of which was the explanation of what caused the nuclear war. In the novel, the war begins not with the United States and the Soviet Union but with attacks and retaliations among smaller countries, which then draw the superpowers into conflict. In the movie, war breaks out unintentionally. Characters call the war an "accident" and a "mistake," and the scientist Julian Osborne (played by Fred Astaire) offers two explanations. Early on he blames "a handful of vacuum tubes and transistors. Probably faulty." But later he surmises, "Somewhere some poor bloke probably looked at a radar screen and thought he saw something." "So he pushed a button . . . and the world went crazy." "In its essentials, his notion is that somebody pulled a boner," the *New Yorker*'s John McCarten noted sardonically, showing "the catastrophic consequences of man's determination to run scientifically and suicidally amuck."[18] Yet this change from the novel made the message of the movie unmistakable. "The devices outgrew us. We couldn't control them," the scientist Osborne states. The proliferation of nuclear weapons in number and across nations created a situation where the world could "shockingly stumble unintentionally along the path to nuclear war." Moreover, the unintentional war "has been shorn of all political implications."[19] The Cold War is mentioned but not as a justification for the war or for the possession of nuclear weapons. Kramer's film presented the nuclear issue as one of humanity and morality rather than geopolitics.

A second, more positively received change from the novel was the inclusion of recurring Salvation Army meetings in a public square in Melbourne. One reviewer considered these scenes to be the "most impact-heightening amendment" made by the filmmakers. As the radiation poisoning relentlessly proceeds, these meetings are attended by fewer and fewer people and have an increasingly despondent and sorrowful mood. Still, the inclusion of these mass prayer meetings sought to provide "good, commercial hope-to-leave-the-theater-with," Paxton recalled, and to lend a measure of religion to Shute's secular story.[20] "Oh Lord, give us the strength, help us to understand the reason for this madness on earth, the reason why we have destroyed ourselves," the minister preaches. In this way, Arthur Knight argued, the film inserted "a note of urgency and hope" to qualify Shute's "stiff-upper-lip pessimism." The backdrop for these religious meetings is a prominent banner reading "THERE IS STILL TIME . . BROTHER." Paxton credited Kramer with the idea for the banner to provide "a legitimate, self-contained statement" that audiences could take away as a message of the film. The banner, flapping in the wind over an empty square, provided the film's final shot. Kramer thought this ending was less depressing than the heroine's suicide that closes Shute's book. Filmgoers and reviewers agreed: "what an inspired final scene!"[21]

The addition of a consummated romance between the two leading characters played by Gregory Peck and Ava Gardner constituted the third major change from the novel. They decided to include "a bigger, more moving love story."[22] In the novel, the romance between the American submarine commander Dwight Towers and the young Australian woman Moira Davidson remains chaste. But Kramer felt "no audience would believe that two such attractive people without filial responsibility and doomed to imminent death with the rest of the world could be content with a mere handshake." "Despite the seriousness of the subject matter, I knew that romance and light moments could not be overlooked." "I wasn't making a documentary film," he argued.[23] Response to this revision was decidedly mixed. Many respondents appreciated the love affair between Peck's and Gardner's characters. "Paxton's script shows great respect for Shute's novel," observed the *Hollywood Reporter*. "But it makes a wise concession to audience preference by having Peck eventually . . . find comfort

in her devotion before the last days." A New York woman, who identified herself as "a fan," praised the "360 degree Gardner-Peck kiss"
that precedes their sexual encounter. "I can only say wow. . . . Was it
inspired by the periscope," she asked Kramer, "and can it be called
a periscopic kiss?" However, other filmgoers and reviewers, as well as
later scholars, criticized the "sentimental sort of radiation romance,"
arguing that it weakened and cheapened *On the Beach*'s social and
political message.[24]

No critic of the changes to *On the Beach* was more vocal or more
vehement than Nevil Shute Norway. At the start, his attitude was very
positive and pragmatic. "Changes are inevitably made when a story is
transferred from the book market to the cinema," he wrote soon after
selling the rights to Kramer, "and these changes are usually distaste-
ful to the author of the book so that he does better to keep out of it."
But his attitude shifted dramatically on reading Paxton's first draft of
a script. In his letters to Kramer over July and August 1958, Shute
Norway became increasingly angry. A letter sent mid-July included a
long list of objections, most of which helpfully corrected mistakes in
the script. A nuclear-powered submarine would not stop at "a refueling
jetty to get gassed up," and no "view of Melbourne can be obtained
from any hill." What distressed the novelist the most, however, was
how the characterization had changed from book to screenplay. He
protested especially the decision "to hot up the love interest"—"that, to
me, is second-rate movie making." Unless Kramer hired a new screenwriter, preferably English, perhaps even Shute Norway himself, "you
will finish up with a bastard picture."[25]

Kramer sought to mollify Shute Norway and seek common ground,
but the conflict only continued and led to a permanent falling-out. After
a private preview, Shute Norway called *On the Beach* "the worst film
that has ever been made of one of my books, without exception," and
he decided to boycott the movie's premiere in December 1959.[26] His
boycott was not overlooked. Gossip columnist Louella Parsons stated
that he had "objected to the sex angle injected in the film." "With or
without sex, Shute is a fine writer," Kramer responded drily. He expressed this sentiment more sincerely when the very next month the
novelist suddenly died from a stroke. "Nevil Shute was a great and fine
writer," Kramer eulogized, whose contribution to "the most important
issue of our day—cannot be overestimated." Although questions arose
over whether the conflicting book and movie versions of *On the Beach*

contributed to Shute's unexpected death, most commentators saw the two versions as very consistent. "Shute did not like the movie," reported the *Chicago Tribune*. "The message of both the book and the movie, however, was the same."[27]

Their similar portrayal of the end of humanity as calm and peaceful struck many spectators as most characteristic of *On the Beach*, whether on the page or on screen. The movie tells its story "unsensationally, toning down its opportunities for violence." "If it horrifies," the *Guardian*'s reviewer contended, it is "not because it has indulged in any virtuosity of gruesomeness. Indeed, one of the main points of this vision of the end is precisely that everything will come with such matter-of-fact calmness."[28] Inevitably, there were filmgoers who wished for more bang. "I think you could have made it more dramatic and impressive," a New York man wrote Kramer, "if you had it open with a picture of an atomic explosion." Others regretted "the concrete images that the film omits," such as "photographs of twisted Japanese cities and people," to realize the full horror of nuclear war on screen. But after *On the Beach* and similar nuclear movies, "the imagery of the deserted metropolis" became part of the "iconography" of science fiction film.[29]

Kramer and Paxton remained faithful to Shute's overall tone as well as his plot, including a plot development about voluntary suicide that very much concerned the PCA. In Shute's novel, the Australian government distributes free suicide pills to anyone who wants to die quickly and painlessly rather than from horrific radiation poisoning. Paxton's screenplay kept this plot development, and PCA officials worried about the immorality of what they called the "problem of eu[t]hanasia." They demanded some new dialogue to indicate that choosing to kill oneself or others—even in the dire situation portrayed in *On the Beach*—was morally wrong.[30] Despite these changes, the Catholic Legion of Decency strongly objected to the finished film for condoning "race suicide." A series of negotiations ensued, because Kramer and his team wanted a Legion A-3 rating, that is, morally unobjectionable for adults. In the end, they convinced Legion director Monsignor Thomas F. Little that the greater sin was the "sin of having permitted the world to reach the state in which it finds itself." Won over, Monsignor Little advised his fellow Catholics that this plot development advanced "the central theme of the film, namely, that nuclear war is race suicide."[31] The "motif of individual suicide" in *On the Beach*, scholar Mick Broderick agrees, "enhanced its grander metaphor of *global* extinction."

The PCA's final analysis of film content categorized this ending—in a marked understatement—as "Unhappy."[32]

Impressively, *On the Beach*'s depressing and distressing storyline did not undercut Kramer's efforts to cast the brightest stars in Hollywood. "There are a surprisingly large number of actors," Kramer observed, who see "a chance to make some contribution to the thought of the body politic, and they gravitate towards it." Gregory Peck was certainly one. Peck was Kramer's first choice for the role of Commander Dwight Towers of the USS *Sawfish*, a nuclear submarine that survives the war submerged and heads to Australia. He "epitomized American values as far as I was concerned," Kramer remembered.[33]

Peck joined the cast enthusiastically. Well known as a Hollywood liberal, he felt strongly about the dangers of nuclear weapons as "a subject which needs airing, which needs dramatizing." Later, he recalled, "I think we all became somewhat imbued with Stanley's mission" to bring attention to "the dangers of nuclear buildup," and "we all wanted to help him do it." Peck also was familiar with the social problem film genre after starring in *Gentleman's Agreement*, and he "scoffed" at the idea that a role in a controversial film could hurt his career.[34] "I have been wanting to work with you for a long time," Peck wrote Kramer, "and have great admiration for the kind of work you do." The actor brought precision and preparation to the role of the straitlaced Towers. In exchanges with Kramer, he sought to refine his character's motivations, particularly regarding the transition between his fidelity to his wife and children, whose deaths he initially denied, and his romance with Moira. Like Shute Norway, Peck later felt that Kramer "was wrong" in adding the love affair, "that he was corrupting my character and Ava's character."[35]

Ava Gardner expressed no such qualms, despite derogatory descriptions of her character, Moira, as "cynical, boozy," "blowsy and unpleasant."[36] Professionally, Gardner was recognized as a bewitching beauty and box-office draw. She was even better known for her private life, especially her tumultuous relationship with singer Frank Sinatra, which began before their wedding in 1951 and lasted beyond their divorce in 1957; Sinatra, in fact, visited her in Australia. Kramer had some idea of their personal turmoil, having dealt with Sinatra on *The Pride and the Passion* (1957).

On the Beach marked an important moment in Gardner's life and career. It was her first film as a free agent after seventeen years under contract to MGM. She drew a salary of $400,000 plus expenses, "happy to finally have the money for my services go to me instead of the damn studio." She also appreciated working with her "old pal Greg Peck," with whom she had made two earlier films, and she cared deeply about *On the Beach*. The script, she recalled, "made me weep. . . . It was a fictional scenario, but my God, everyone in the cast and crew knew it could happen."[37] "Personally, I think it is one hell of a part," Kramer wrote her manager, "and I am looking forward to driving with Ava toward a performance which will be for her the greatest she has done."[38] Reviewers agreed and singled out Gardner's acting as the film's best, a first for an actress in a Kramer production. They also commented on her appearance, notwithstanding the end-of-the-world scenario. "Miss Gardner has never looked worse or been more effective," the actress recalled of one review. "Frankly, I didn't care what the hell they thought. I was proud of being part of this film, proud of what it said."[39]

With Gardner in *On the Beach*, as with Curtis in *The Defiant Ones*, Kramer "sought to create additional excitement by casting against type," a strategy he also employed with Fred Astaire. Gardner "is downright unglamorous as a woman who has lived too hard and drunk too much," Arthur Knight commented. "And Astaire, as the scientist, neither sings a note nor dances a step."[40] "Well, I've always wanted to try and find out just whether I could do that sort of thing," Astaire admitted. "I thought this was the most ideal opportunity." Shute Norway had been thrilled with the casting of dancer Astaire and even offered to write a "charming little 30 second scene" for Astaire's character "where he dances with his mother's Pekinese dog."[41] Reviews of Astaire's performance varied. "In his first straight part, he is devastatingly effective." "Get out of the acting department or I'll take up dancing," Spencer Tracy reportedly wired. But a filmgoer quoted in the *New York Times* complained, "Fred Astaire, heretofore a man of humor and grace, has neither." Kramer's casting of Astaire in a dramatic role was seen to be a great gamble, as was his casting of Anthony Perkins and Donna Anderson as the young married couple, Peter and Mary. They also received mixed reviews. The film was "heavy with a sense of actors acting," according to Knight, until the submarine reconnaissance mission to North America.[42]

For these scenes with the submarine, as had happened with *The Caine Mutiny*, Kramer needed the assistance of the US Navy. "Wanted: one atomic submarine," the *Washington Post* reported on Kramer's

Ava Gardner and Stanley Kramer in a production still for On the Beach
(1959). Courtesy of Margaret Herrick Library and MGM/UA.

August 25, 1958, visit to the Pentagon. There he met with officials
from the Department of Defense and United States Information Agency
(USIA). This high-level meeting came after a rebuff to a request from
Kramer's production designer, Rudolph Sternad. Both the US Navy and
the USIA had objected to aiding *On the Beach*. The film would not "in
any way enhance" or "advance the interests" of the United States or its
military. "Any service cooperation on such a movie would only serve
to dignify the story," stated the navy's response. USIA officials held
nothing back: the "entire theme is negative to say the least, and frankly
there appears to be a tendency to 'blame America' in much of its presentation." Sternad did manage to get some photographs and a promise
of stock footage. This outcome did not satisfy Kramer, who went right
to the top. "I had many meetings with high brass in Washington." At
the August 25 meeting, "all of these people seemed to regard me as
some kind of radical." But the scheduling of a meeting and the size of
the turnout indicated their recognition of Kramer's standing in Hollywood and influence on American culture and politics. It "suggested that
they knew I could not be taken lightly."[43]

These developments also suggested that the US government took seriously from the very start the potential impact of the message of Kramer's film. At that first meeting, Kramer advanced several arguments about the benefits of official cooperation with his movie, and his efforts paid off. According to a Pentagon memo, "Defense would agree to Kramer's outfit making shots of submerging and surfacing of an atomic submarine on practice runs so they could get proper angles of it for *On the Beach.*" In return, Kramer agreed to script changes "to remove the pessimistic slant of novel on 'utter annihilation' which might be unfavorably interpreted." Turner B. Shelton, a former Hollywood producer who directed the USIA's Motion Picture Service, approved of this outcome. Although "he still did not like the story, he felt our cooperation might help to present the whole production in a better light." Subsequently, navy officials requested revisions, large and small. With regard to terminology, "steady on our course" should become "steady as you go" and "take her up" should be "surface." Other mistakes were noted. One navigational bearing in the film, the navy warned, "would place the submarine on land."[44]

Navy recommendations for more substantial revisions indicated Cold War national security concerns and were outlined in a December 1958 memo from the Office of the Chief of Naval Operations. "The principal impact of *On the Beach* on the public will be revulsion against the use of nuclear weapons of any kind and a possible sense of defeatism with respect to the use of armed forces as an instrument of national policy." To moderate this impact, the navy wanted changes in the movie's plot. The United States and its allies should have an "intermediate course of action" rather than total nuclear war and "devastation or capitulation" to the communist enemy. Also, the "nuclear strike forces of the major powers" should be "invulnerable" to attack, and "Communists must bear the principal onus for *On the Beach.*" These discussions of script changes proceeded over several months, and, in the meantime, the navy went back and forth on its commitment to Kramer. He had been promised access to the USS *Sargo* at Pearl Harbor, and he also wanted to film the submarine on location in Australia. But, as he recalled, "since I wouldn't change the script, we didn't get the atomic sub."[45] In the end, Kramer and his team received enough US military assistance, together with invaluable Australian cooperation, to make the movie. The film's opening credits made this clear: "We acknowledge with appreciation the assistance given by the Royal Australian Navy and, in particular, by the officers and men of HMAS *Melbourne* and HMS *Andrew*."

The cooperation of the Royal Australian Navy exemplified the attitude of Australians to the filming of *On the Beach*, although conflicts also arose on location in Australia. The story of Kramer, his production team, and his actors on location is well told by Philip R. Davey in *When Hollywood Came to Melbourne*. In addition to a submarine, an aircraft carrier, and their crews, police assistance was forthcoming. For the final shot of the city, "there is not a soul on the streets—everyone has gone home to die. I was able to get this shot because the people of Melbourne were so cooperative," Kramer noted appreciatively. The disruption to life as usual did provoke some negative press attention, and "huge, ugly headlines," recalled Kramer, were also caused by several incidents involving Gardner.[46] Greeted by reporters on her arrival, she faced a barrage of questions about her personal life, including her complicated relationship with Sinatra. They never let up, and Gardner got fed up. For the rest of the shoot, she did her best to avoid press and public attention. "Ava Gardner Snubbing Fans, Say Australians," headlined the *Los Angeles Times*. Considered even more egregious was a statement attributed to her. "*On the Beach* is a story about the end of the world, and Melbourne sure is the right place to film it." "It was a lie," Gardner insisted. "I would never say anything like it!" And she was telling the truth—even though she "didn't love . . . being on location in Melbourne," where the public bars closed "at 6:00 P.M. sharp." Few knew that a Sydney journalist invented the "notorious non-quote," and Gardner's experience with the Australian press and public only worsened.[47]

There were other challenges to shooting a Hollywood movie overseas. The *Sawfish* mock-up alone took two months and $100,000 to build. Hundreds of extras and some seventy speaking parts needed to be cast there. "And poor Stanley," Gardner remembered, "had to ship a great deal of equipment and props from America." The filmmakers also had to improvise a sound stage, and only the Royal Melbourne Showgrounds were large enough. Because the showgrounds usually held agricultural fairs, the joke around Melbourne was "they moved the pigs out so the hams could move in!"[48] The greatest production difficulties were caused by the Australian summer weather. "Terribly hot," Peck recalled. "There was a spell where the temperature was over one hundred degrees." In fact, as Davey tells, it was the "worst heat wave since

1939," soaring up to 109 degrees. Along with the heat came bushflies. At times, "the air was so thick with flies they almost blackened the skies," described Peck. "There would be thousands of flies crawling on Ava's forehead and in her hair, and the effects men would rush in with a smoke gun and blow smoke in our faces. That would get rid of the flies for a minute or two and allow us to say a few lines before they settled in again." Working in such conditions took its toll. "Everybody here is terrible," Kramer wrote from Australia.[49]

Cinematographer Giuseppe Rotunno had a different perspective. "The heat was excessive and extremely uncomfortable, but . . . it was very helpful in the sense that the actors could physically and psychologically get into their characters." After all, they needed to "feel vulnerable and defenseless against such a catastrophic event." They also needed to appear so, and Rotunno's striking, austere black-and-white photography provided the right look. Working with Kramer for the first time, Rotunno brought experience with neorealism from his native Italy, which fit well with Kramer's visual style. Both used deep focus and long takes. This camerawork allowed "dramatic situations to develop gradually and reach a peak at the end of a scene," with scenes lasting three minutes on average.[50] Davey discusses how Rotunno also innovated by making and using lens filters to transform the "vibrant and vital landscape" of Australia into a "barren and alien-looking atmosphere." In this way, On the Beach conveyed "the progression of radiation in the atmosphere as the movie went on." Gardner attributed additional technical achievements to "the genius of Pepe Rotunno." In one scene where Gardner's and Peck's characters kiss, "the camera circles us from a distance and does a beautiful three-hundred-and-sixty-degree turn that the other technicians kept telling Pepe wasn't possible." In their last scene together, as they are saying goodbye forever, a close-up shot silhouettes the couple against a sunset. Although some critics would consider these to be "middle-brow artistic effects," for Gardner, "some shots will live in your memory forever, and that one always will in mine."[51]

As principal photography in Australia finished up—apart from some scenes shot in California both before and after overseas filming—postproduction and promotion began. Kramer and Rotunno had shot about fifty hours of film, so film editor Fred Knudtson had his work cut out for him—literally. Reporting on Knudtson's task, Australian journalist Ted Madden quipped, "a film editor must be half-artist, half-mechanic and half crazy." Originally planned to run more than three hours with an intermission, *On the Beach* needed to be cut down to 134 minutes. Many, often affecting, scenes had to be deleted. Adding the musical score fell again to Ernest Gold, with the Australian ballad "Waltzing Matilda" as the film's musical motif. Although critical reviews were mixed, Gold's award-winning score presented a song considered Australia's unofficial national anthem in a variety of musical styles and moods. The film's music also played a role in promotion for the film with the release of two albums, the original soundtrack and themes from *On the Beach.*[52]

Promotion for *On the Beach*—from the worldwide publicity to the international premiere—focused on the film's serious subject. Even when he was busy with the production process and dealing with his star actors, Kramer's motivations for making the film were never far from his mind. As a fateful reminder of the critical nature of the nuclear issue, the day he left Los Angeles for Melbourne to start filming, radioactive fallout from nuclear tests in Nevada dispersed to California. As he recalled, a local Los Angeles newspaper reported, "It posed no health problem, however." The producer-director had his doubts.[53] But he, his team, and United Artists expressed no doubts about designing a promotion campaign with an "emphasis on the world-shaking theme over all other box office factors." United Artists ballyhooed their campaign as unprecedented in Hollywood history given its worldwide reach. They also could not resist a bomb-related metaphor. "United Artists officially opens the missile age in motion picture publicity . . . dispersing a message of unmistakably inter-continental significance."[54] Every element of the campaign, every "paratext," was international in orientation: the newspaper display ads, posters, trailers, special screenings, and, especially, the premiere.

Held on December 17, 1959, the global premiere of *On the Beach* "addressed all mankind." "Never Before in the History of the Industry Has the World Been Linked Together by One Motion Picture," blared the publicity.[55] Host cities included Berlin, Caracas, Chicago, Johannesburg, Lima, London, Melbourne, Moscow, New York, Paris, Rome, Stockholm, Tokyo, Toronto, Washington, DC, and Zurich, and even the US naval station in Antarctica premiered the film to ensure coverage of all seven continents. Prominent political figures and dignitaries attended premieres, including the mayors of Berlin and Johannesburg and members of the Swedish and Japanese royal families. International and national charities, such as the Red Cross, sponsored premieres as benefit events.

The Fund for the Republic, an organization dedicated to defending civil rights and liberties, hosted the Hollywood premiere "for the first time anywhere . . . in recognition of the fact that this is no ordinary film."[56] A news conference followed with scientific luminaries and other notable figures, such as Linus Pauling, a winner of the Nobel Prize in Chemistry, and Philip Noel-Baker, who had just won the Nobel Peace Prize. "It may be that someday we can look back and say *On the Beach* is the picture that saved the world," Pauling remarked.[57] With such inspiration, Kramer's team even explored the possibility of winning a Nobel Peace Prize for the producer-director himself. Media coverage of the premieres had a powerful impact. "It is significant that the movie opened simultaneously in so many countries," a Canadian filmgoer wrote to Kramer, as a sign of "international unity" that allowed one "to feel a part of something of value on a worldwide scale."[58]

Just as with *The Defiant Ones*, the reception of *On the Beach* was mostly positive, and most extant audience response concerned the movie's message rather than its artistic or aesthetic qualities. The few responses that concerned *On the Beach* as film art were mixed, with the plot viewed as both "spellbinding" and "plodding" and the acting as both "powerful" and "wooden." A new and noteworthy critical perspective on Kramer's moviemaking emerged with this film, however. Several prominent reviewers, often on the political Left or from overseas, questioned the authenticity of the producer-director's commitment to the genre of social problem films while working within the Hollywood system. The *Guardian*'s film critic believed *On the Beach* reflected a flawed "compromise between a huge brave theme and the star system in Hollywood." A second review in the *Guardian* gave as an example one of the film's titles acknowledging costume design—"Miss Gardner's Gowns: Fontana Sisters, Rome"—as unbefitting "a film about the end of the human race." "No matter if the producer has wanted to make a film with a message," wrote a reviewer from Sweden in 1960, "he has been more interested in making big business." Kramer, the *New Republic*'s Stanley Kauffmann put it bluntly, "doesn't want the world to be blown up; but he doesn't want to lose money saying so."[59] Although only a few critics considered Kramer to be more sensational than sincere, their numbers would grow in time. In 1959 most respondents who endorsed the film extolled Kramer's great courage in combining social conscience and commerce. But not everyone offered their endorsement, sparking a significant political debate about *On the Beach*.

Political Fallout around the World

"Almost everybody in the world, you may have noticed, has had something to say about Stanley Kramer's *On the Beach*," observed one newspaper columnist. Without a doubt, the film's release, with its attendant promotion and publicity, sparked public discussion and debate about the most important issue in the international arena in the late 1950s and early 1960s. British journalist Alistair Cooke called the movie "a political event of the first order." Film reviewers and filmgoers engaged with the film as a political statement more than as a work of art or entertainment. Journalists, other media commentators, politicians, government officials, and scientists recognized the film's content and message as reflecting a "concern with public affairs."[60] As a result, *On the Beach* "aroused comment from Moscow to Melbourne," and "discussion of its theme has found its way off the entertainment pages of newspapers." Kramer related that "the film has met with almost as many editorials as reviews; and sometimes the reviews were not movie reviews, they were political reviews." Political reviews also were issued by members of Congress "blasting or boosting the picture," reported one Los Angeles columnist, "with the result that the film may wind up with as many clippings from the *Congressional Record* as from the daily papers."[61] For Kramer, this controversy was all to the good, for reasons of both commerce and social conscience. Ideally, such widespread interest in his production would increase ticket sales. But Kramer also emphasized the larger political, social, and moral benefits to be gained from all the talk about *On the Beach*.

The value of such talk, in and of itself, became one of Kramer's oft-made points. He felt that in the United States "discussion has been at a low ebb" about nuclear issues. "The world in which we live has come into a position where we must provide a platform for discussion, of which there is not nearly enough."[62] He was not alone in this view. Many observers correctly perceived that too little information about US nuclear policy and programs reached the American public. As historian Lawrence S. Wittner writes, "US officials frequently sought to conduct their operations under a blanket of secrecy." Limiting public knowledge about the extent and effects of nuclear weapons was part of an effort to manage public opinion, mitigate against popular fears, and maintain support for America's Cold War nuclear strategy.[63]

Kramer's hopes for *On the Beach* worked against that effort. He hoped the film would engender a "public discussion on something which we've learned to live with too conveniently and easily, namely the nuclear weapon." "I don't believe we can be too aware of the terrible danger the possibility of a nuclear war presents to the world. And I'm convinced that if we are to control our destiny we must think about it. We must bring the discussion out in the open."[64] Not only did openness counter secrecy; it was necessary for democracy. As Kramer argued, only by "raising these questions and in stimulating discussions" can we "arrive at decisions in a democratic fashion." Even as many began to consider democratic theory less relevant in the era of elite nuclear strategic planning, Kramer advocated for greater participation in decision making.[65]

Many respondents to *On the Beach* agreed with Kramer's commitment to opening up the political discussion of the facts and future of nuclear weapons. The "subject should be discussed," the *Guardian* noted, "in film form as in other forms." Antinuclear activists, scientists, film critics, average filmgoers, and industry insiders weighed in on the film's importance, particularly in stimulating awareness of the possible fate of the world in the age of nuclear weapons. ABC radio dubbed it "<u>the most important motion picture of any kind ever produced</u>," and the *Daily Herald* in London called it "an astonishing and important film." "I urge you to see it," argued its rival newspaper, the *Daily Mirror.* "It is timely and adult." When the National Screen Council chose *On the Beach* as a Blue Ribbon Award winner, a spokeswoman explained that the film tackled "the greatest and most challenging theme of our time."[66] "This is a bold and honest attempt by producer-director Stanley Kramer to awaken us to our peril," asserted Mae Tinee of the *Chicago Tribune.* Admirers of the film hoped raising public consciousness would translate into greater reflection and responsibility on the part of individuals. The *Hollywood Reporter* considered the "thought-provoking" film "worthy of the studious consideration of every member of the public." A "fine film, and an alarming one," one such member of the public wrote Kramer; "it sets the audience to thinking about it for days, and that is what we must do." "They ought to pass a law requiring every American citizen to see this picture," commented comedian Steve Allen.[67]

Even reviewers who criticized the artistic or entertainment value of *On the Beach* endorsed its public value in addressing and raising awareness about the nuclear issue. The film "may not perhaps be entertainment in the usual sense of the word," one critic contended. But it was a film with "high purpose" that "everyone should steel him or herself to see regardless of how great the antipathy toward facing the truth." Another critic who disparaged the film's artistic content still recognized that *On the Beach* dealt "seriously (for the first time in film history?) and very depressingly with the besetting problem of survival in this nuclear-fission age." Letter writers to Kramer answered those who dismissed the movie as grim and depressing. "Of course, the film is devastating but how else can the point be made that there is no alternative to peace?" "You produce not pictures the public wants to see, but pictures you believe the public ought to see," an ABC radio commentator told Kramer. "More power to you!" The mayor of Johannesburg, South Africa, believed *On the Beach* "will give many millions of people food for thought." He hoped "the message will penetrate the consciousness, not only of ordinary people, but of those persons who are in a position to determine whether or not . . . to start the push-button warfare that spells doom for everyone on earth."[68]

On the Beach certainly commanded the attention of political elites in the United States, and, although they condemned the film, they understood its importance.[69] Following on from the navy and USIA's dealings with Kramer, the film's December 1959 release sparked a new round of official concerns. First mentioned by Secretary of State Christian Herter at a cabinet meeting on November 6 as "a tremendous bit of antinuclear propaganda," *On the Beach* became a major topic for discussion and action at a December 11 meeting, chaired by Vice President Richard Nixon because President Eisenhower was overseas.[70] Prominently in attendance and involved with US nuclear policy were Herter, the secretary of defense, and the heads of the Atomic Energy Commission (AEC), the Office of Civil and Defense Mobilization, and the USIA. Karl G. Harr, Jr., a special assistant to the president, "stated that this matter was being raised in Cabinet because of the unprecedented publicity given to this movie." "He recognized that it was not a function of government to attempt to criticize or suppress the movie," but "care should be taken that government officials do not give support" to the film.[71]

This position became the standard response for American political leaders and officials at home and abroad. In what Mick Broderick calls a "concerted negative campaign," various arms of the government provided guidance on how to respond to *On the Beach*.[72] The USIA and the State Department circulated "Information Guidance for Missions Abroad"—an "Infoguide"—and the AEC developed a set of "Possible Questions and Suggested Answers," as did the Defense Department. The content of these documents appeared in the public statements of members of the government and subsequent media reports—especially after being leaked to the press—and became part of the debate over the message and meaning of Kramer's film.[73]

A fundamental point of contention in the public debate over *On the Beach* was whether the film should be viewed as science fiction or as scientifically plausible. US political, military, and civil defense authorities emphasized that the film was "one of science fiction and not science fact." Lt. Gen. Clarence R. Huebner, the director of civil defense for the state of New York, presented this perspective. Huebner called *On the Beach* a "fantasy," lacking a "scientific basis."[74] Senator Wallace F. Bennett of Utah, a Republican member of the Joint Committee on Atomic Energy, repeated this point on the floor of Congress and in the media. The film was "an imaginative piece of science fiction, a fantasy." "In my opinion it paints a distorted picture of what a nuclear war would probably be like." Bennett feared that, even though "the situation, as well as the plot, is fictional . . . millions of people are accepting a fantastic situation as scientific fact."[75] Many print publications reported these official views. "Perhaps the film's vision of universal destruction is not justified by the present and foreseeable scientific facts," the *Guardian*'s film critic mildly noted. Other commentators vehemently endorsed the government's stance. The "book and the film are based on fictional assumptions which are preposterous," contended the head of the *Chicago Daily News* Foreign Service in London.[76]

Kramer and his supporters, including scientific authorities, challenged this official perspective. They admitted that the film fit the genre of science fiction: the events portrayed occur in the future, and they are based on technology not yet in use. But the style and tone of *On the Beach* avoided "the fantasies and extravagances usually associated with 'science fiction.'" Most importantly, the events portrayed were possible and even probable in the near future. Kramer defended the scientific validity of his film. He stated that two years of technical research and "the opinions and predictions of scores of leading scientists" went into the film.[77] Dr. Harold Urey, a Nobel Prize–winning scientist in physical chemistry who worked on the atomic bomb during World War II, confirmed that "the movie *On the Beach* mirrors a dangerous true-life situation." "It is completely within the realm of possibility," he stated after attending a screening. The Federation of American Scientists made *On the Beach* "the first motion picture ever reviewed" in their newsletter and called it "extraordinarily realistic."[78] Even Alistair Cooke, a critic of the film, acknowledged that independent research teams predicted "a nuclear war in the next decade is more likely than not." Defenders of the film also accepted a measure of dramatic license on the part of the filmmakers. "How silly to insist that the picture must be an absolute and exactly documented forecast of what would happen if a nuclear war were touched off in 1964."[79]

The specific scientific issue in contention was the extent and consequences of radioactive fallout following the use of nuclear weapons. For critics, *On the Beach* exaggerated the impact of nuclear radiation. Lieutenant General Huebner specified that the most problematic aspects of the science in the film were "its notions of radioactive phenomena."[80] Senator Bennett denounced as "unscientific, unrealistic and dangerously misleading" the film's premise that "nuclear war has so contaminated the atmosphere that all mankind is being gradually wiped out by fallout." He cited evidence from the so-called fallout hearings held by the Joint Committee on Atomic Energy earlier in 1959. The hearings "clearly demonstrated," he declared, that there would be many survivors after a nuclear attack. Other members of government supported this stance. "Defense brass insists an H-bomb war would not wipe out life on earth as the movie portrays," reported *Newsweek*.[81] Conservative columnist Stewart Alsop, writing in the *Saturday Evening Post*, expounded at length on how *On the Beach* was not "a technically accurate presentation of the radioactive side effects of nuclear warfare." All of his key points can be found in the USIA-State Infoguide on the film. "Radioactivity from fallout dies away very quickly," he pointed out, "a vital fact which is virtually disregarded in *On the Beach*, but which could save millions of lives. . . . As a practical matter, it is simply not true that a nuclear war would mean 'everybody killed in the world and nothing left at all, like in *On the Beach*.'"[82]

These critics did not calm the fallout fears of Kramer and supporters of the film. Kramer contested how Senator Bennett characterized the findings from the fallout hearings, that there would be survivors after a nuclear war, rather than the total devastation shown in the film. "I doubt it," Kramer stated. "I take the view that the results of radiation are untapped as yet . . . terrible, terrible disaster." The *Science News Letter* also referenced the fallout hearings in its coverage of *On the Beach*. "Not complete human extinction from fallout and radiation was forecast in these hearings." But even if "only 50,000,000 American dead, 20,000,000 casualties" resulted, the film "is far from a farce."[83] As a further challenge to Bennett, *On the Beach* received an endorsement from his colleague on the Joint Committee on Atomic Energy, Congressman Chet Holifield, a Democrat from California who chaired the fallout hearings. The film, Holifield believed, "furnishes a graphic and impressive pictorialization of the possible effects of a massive nuclear war on the people of the earth." He had long been a strong advocate for providing more information to the public about nuclear issues. "I feel the public has been informed all too little of the effects of radiation, now and potential," Kramer agreed. For proponents of the film, the objections raised by critics about "how many of us might survive a nuclear war, or the extent of destruction" felt like "interminable hassling and deceptive wishful thinking."[84]

But opponents of *On the Beach* worked to present their position as rational and practical, especially their advocacy of civil defense as protection against nuclear fallout. In keeping with US government policy, official critics backed civil defense measures for the American civilian population, including shelter preparedness. The aim of civil defense policy was to normalize the possibility and survivability of nuclear war, "to make the extraordinariness of nuclear war seem ordinary," as historian Laura McEnaney so aptly puts it.[85] As a result, government officials expressed dismay because the movie's plot did not include any of the main characters preparing to survive radioactive fallout by retreating to an underground shelter. "The assumption that nothing can be done to protect people from fallout is wrong and misleading," the government's Infoguide on the film insisted. "As far away as another hemisphere," the USIA-State Infoguide added, "an ordinary basement would suffice." Publicly, Lieutenant General Huebner picked up on this theme. He criticized the film for neglecting to show any defense against fallout. Such defense, he argued, "is not only possible but relatively simple." Alsop added to this argument. "Dwight and Moira would have survived, if they'd had any sense. All they had to do was to build themselves a cozy little radiation shelter" where they could have "waited it out . . . amusing themselves in any way that might occur to them, while the

radiation died away to sublethal level." "Less dramatic," Alsop concluded, "but more sensible."[86]

These critics of *On the Beach* saw such civil defense as very sensible
on a personal level and absolutely essential for national security. If
American citizens followed the example of the characters in the film,
Senator Bennett warned, they would "be endangering the future of
themselves and their country." At the cabinet meeting on December 11,
1959, Leo Hoegh, former governor of Iowa and the director of the Office of Civil and Defense Mobilization, characterized the film as "very
harmful," because it hindered his office's "efforts to encourage preparedness on the part of all citizens."[87] In this way, *On the Beach* was
understood to be undermining US government policy on civil defense.
"To take this kind of motion picture literally is to invite catastrophe,"
Senator Bennett proclaimed in Congress. "If we assume, as the picture does, that civil defense measures are completely worthless . . . we
will make no effort to take cover, to protect ourselves from fallout, to
resist the attack as best we can." Apart from the personal risks, this
lack of preparedness on America's Cold War home front had military
consequences. According to Bennett, "if an enemy knows we have that
attitude, he will be that much more likely to attack."[88] Edward Teller,
the "father of the hydrogen bomb," also weighed in on this issue. He
believed US civil defense was in "such a tragic state of unpreparedness
that we are practically inviting attack." "Too many Americans," he said,
"have an *On the Beach* attitude" that "all we can do is throw up our
hands, take a suicide pill, and die."[89]

Kramer and his supporters responded to the statements of these
"learned critics" about the science of fallout and the utility of civil
defense. "To me this is beside the point. . . . It may be true," Kramer
admitted, "that atomic fallout could not destroy all human life as rap-
idly as we have shown for dramatic purposes in the film. But I, for one,
never want the question put to a test." "The producer is suggesting that
the best way to avoid the end is to prevent the beginning of the end,"
editorialized the *New York Post*, "and that fall-out shelters should not
be confused with *House Beautiful*."[90] Linus Pauling contended that US
civil defense spending was "too small and a waste of money," when the
"same amount of money spent to avert war would be far more valuable." The *New York Times*'s Bosley Crowther objected to Lieutenant
General Huebner's reassurances "that it is possible to defend against
radioactive fallout—as if that were sufficient to obviate the peril."[91]

Crowther's readers agreed. One reader rejected "defense possibilities" against nuclear weapons, because their destructive power made "completely untenable any hope of defense." "Civil defense officials do not approve of the picture," another reader explained, "because they feel that the shelters and the drills their organizations advocate will seem even more futile in the minds of those who see *On the Beach* than is now the case." This New Yorker recognized the great efforts of US leaders to persuade average citizens to participate in civil defense, as well as how these efforts were met with popular "skepticism and resistance" rather than compliance.[92]

Given this larger context, the film's depiction of characters accepting rather than fighting their doomed fate was all too reminiscent of the civilian population US officials were trying—and failing—to spur into nuclear preparedness. Director Hoegh made this point at the December 11 cabinet meeting. *On the Beach* "produced a feeling of utter hopelessness."[93] Other commentators had the same response, regardless of their ultimate opinion of the film. "And the tragedy is that all these people have done little or nothing to cause their plight and there is nothing they can do to avert it." "Its effect on general audiences, who know they can't do much about it anyway, is so blisteringly miserable that it reduces one to a state of feeling, 'What's the good of anything?'"[94] For civil defense planners, such emotions would only reinforce what they blamed for the lack of citizen participation in their programs: apathy. To counter ostensible civilian apathy, they tried to instill in average Americans "a psychological orientation toward military readiness" and "a survivalist mentality," as McEnaney argues.[95] This attempt carried over into the official reaction to *On the Beach*. The government's Infoguide contended that Kramer's "wholly fatalistic" film "misconstrues the basic nature of man" and "the vitality of the human spirit. . . . It is inconceivable that even in the event of a nuclear war, mankind would not have the strength and ingenuity to take all possible steps toward self-preservation." In his speech to Congress, Senator Bennett offered a similarly inspired view. "I hope—and I believe—that the human race will retain the will to live, the innate courage which keeps us going against seemingly insurmountable odds."[96]

Defenders of Kramer and the film, in contrast, saw hope and political inspiration in *On the Beach*. Many respondents cited the Salvation Army scenes and quoted the banner. "Most of all, we must believe and act on the basic message of *On the Beach*: 'There is still time, brother.'"

Because the film "offers real hope," one English reviewer explained, at "the end I felt cheered and stimulated, not depressed." Even an error in the film—"a very healthy bird wheeling its way through the supposedly lethal radioactive cloud over San Diego"—was "considered a sign of hope" by one reviewer.[97] "There is hope in the picture," wrote a *Denver Post* columnist, "for its very existence means that mankind still has time to avoid atomic disaster." Senator Richard Neuburger, a Democrat from Oregon, affirmed that the film "should help to stir all people everywhere, in and out of Government, to work fervently for peace and understanding among nations." Then, perhaps, a change in nuclear policy could come. "To those of us who work in the so-called 'peace movement' . . . this single film can do more, in terms of effect, than we can possibly hope to accomplish in many months of work." "It alone may be the decisive factor in the fight against the bomb," predicted a California couple.[98]

These positive respondents to *On the Beach* felt political action to change nuclear policy was possible and necessary. One North Hollywood filmgoer and her husband "were so deeply moved by *On the Beach* that we've felt compelled to stir up as much interest in it as we can." They sent out more than a hundred mimeographed letters to family and friends urging them to see the film. Their letter stressed "the importance of this picture to the world in a time when men are busily piling up atom bombs and testing all kinds of screwball atom devices and sprinkling radioactive dust here and there." "I can't say I 'enjoyed' *On the Beach*," admitted another female filmgoer to Kramer. Yet it spurred her "to join the Committee for a Sane Nuclear Policy! Now you know the results of your subversive activities!"[99] "Some may feel an impulse to drink or jump off the George Washington Bridge," envisioned a New York film reviewer after seeing the film. But, he added, referring to the ongoing test ban treaty negotiations, "I suspect most will feel an urge to rush over to the United Nations and shout, 'Keep it up, boys, we're with you!'" In fact, a few months later, in May 1960, thousands did march to the United Nations after a SANE-sponsored rally in New York.[100] And in contrast to Senator Bennett's position, Representative Charles O. Porter, a Democrat from Oregon, used the film to call his congressional colleagues to legislative action to "change the direction of events." "There is time, brother, but not much," he concluded.[101]

The political direction of these responses to *On the Beach* posed a fundamental challenge to US nuclear policy. So, too, did the film. In one of the two key scenes where Fred Astaire's character, the nuclear scientist Julian Osborne, explains the events that led to war and the use of nuclear weapons, he excoriates the strategic logic of the Cold War. "The war started when people accepted the idiotic principle that peace could be maintained by arranging to defend themselves with weapons they couldn't possibly use without committing suicide." Osborne criticizes the commitment to nuclear weapons on both sides of the Iron Curtain, as well as the theory of nuclear deterrence and the arms race that developed. "Everyone had an atomic bomb and counter bombs and counter-counter bombs." With this dialogue, *On the Beach* exposed the illogic and irrationality of the nuclear policy that underpinned military planning and overseas diplomacy for both Cold War adversaries. Osborne uses the word "idiotic" to describe the policy, and commentators on the film used similar vocabulary: "nuclear war has lost its logic," "completely irrational," "the madness of atomic armament."[102] Linus Pauling captured the contradiction at the core of this policy at the press conference following the Hollywood premiere. The idea of using "nuclear weapons as deterrents to war" by creating a "reliable balance of terror"—which would later be called mutually assured destruction, with the alarmingly appropriate acronym MAD—was "to achieve the end of essentially peace." So why not just focus on "giving up war"?[103]

Such antinuclear sentiment was precisely what US officials had feared about Kramer's film. The government's Infoguide had warned of the film's "strong emotional appeal for banning nuclear weapons" and its possible influence on audiences. "It will be unfortunate," the Infoguide continued, if *On the Beach* "drive[s] them to pressure for ban-the-bomb-type solutions to the nuclear weapons problem." For government officials, these antinuclear reactions were "radical solutions to the problem." They failed to take seriously the threat posed by the Soviet Union and, in fact, undermined the entire Cold War project. Instead, "the US and its allies must maintain armed strength to deter aggression and for self-protection if conflict should break out." This strategic commitment to nuclear weapons continued, even as the United States pursued arms control negotiations with the Soviet Union. US officials expressed a measure of optimism that they could channel popular responses to *On the Beach* toward their own ends. According to the Infoguide, the film and the public discussion around it "may offer opportunities to turn this emotional response into intellectual support of our quest."[104] Taking advantage of such opportunities, supporters of US nuclear policy voiced their views in public criticism of Kramer's film, with the loudest voices coming from anticommunist cold warriors. The University of Notre Dame's *Religious Bulletin* condemned the "ban-the-bomb-production" and its "big message—atomic disarmament at any price."[105]

The necessity of maintaining America's nuclear arsenal within the context of the Cold War received support from many respondents critical of *On the Beach*. To forgo or limit nuclear weapons, at the very least, would put US national security at risk. The *New York Daily News* considered *On the Beach* a "would-be shocker" of a film, because arms limitations or disarmament could lead to "scrapping of the H-bomb." Such a move "would strip the West of its best single weapon and leave Russia the world's most powerful nation—with Red China moving up fast."[106] It even could mean conceding defeat to the Soviets in the Cold War. Alistair Cooke drew a historical analogy between *On the Beach* and the British policy of appeasement toward Nazi Germany. "There is no doubt, I think, that the immediate emotional effect of the film could provoke a pandemic of pacifism more threatening to the 'military posture' of the West than the 'peace at any price' campaign of the 1930s." Right-wing historian William Henry Chamberlin agreed that the film was "a hearty plug for appeasement."[107] "People will argue over whether it was politically wise to make a film," offered one commentary, "which may promote a dangerous neutralism." The *Daily News* joined these opinion makers, attacking *On the Beach* as a "defeatist movie" that "plays right up the alley of the Kremlin."[108]

It was true that Cold War justifications of nuclear weapons did not appear in *On the Beach* or in the contributions of Kramer and his supporters to the public debate over the film. In fact, just the opposite occurred. "We had a choice," the scientist Osborne declares in a key scene. "It was build the bombs and risk using them in war—or somehow the Soviet Union and the United States and the people associated with them could live in the world at the same time." In the US media, Kramer did not elaborate on this point much beyond hoping the film would "assist in easing the 'cold war.'" However, in an interview with *Pravda*, he was much bolder. "All of the actors and technicians worked on this film as a crusade," he stated. "We want peace. . . . Our hopes and prayers [are] that our respective leaders will accomplish the machinery of disarmament and peace."[109] Although Kramer did not use the phrase, the content of his comments fit with the Soviet policy of "peaceful coexistence," launched in 1956 under the leadership of Nikita Khrushchev. At the Hollywood postpremiere press conference, Philip Noel-Baker elaborated on the new Soviet policy. "They now want peace and disarmament," he asserted. Gregory Peck made a similar observation after the Moscow premiere. The Soviets "accepted the theme as a dramatic warning . . . that this insanity has got to stop."[110] Supporters of *On the Beach* also noted the commonalities shared between East and West. "It reminds us that the enemy of America is not Russia, the enemy of Russia is not America, but the enemy of both and of everyone is the atomic bomb."[111]

That Kramer's film prompted such statements undermining the basic premise of the Cold War—the eternal enmity between the adversaries—provoked his long-standing anticommunist opposition. A liberal supporter expected as much. "*On the Beach* has struck sharply at a vulnerable spot of vested interests—those who want the lunatic nuclear race to go on to its bitter end." He named as these interests "certain Pentagoners, men connected with the Atomic Energy Commission and get-tough-with-Russia newspapers such as the *Daily News*."[112] In fact, the *Daily News* accused the film's supporters of being "western defeatists and/or traitors." The University of Notre Dame's *Religious Bulletin* charged Kramer with "a long line of leftist hits." His latest "is undoubtedly the greatest psychological warfare movie of the cold war."[113] "*On the Beach* Called Kramer's Christmas Gift to Khrushchev" headlined an editorial in *Hollywood Close-Up*, Jaik Rosenstein's newsletter. And a significant strike on Kramer came from the *American Legion Magazine*. "From the pitch of his film, he has no objection to plugging a line dear to the hearts of communists." "We don't know if the Kremlin issues Oscars or Kikis," the editor added, "but if so an especially big one has been fairly earned by Kramer."[114]

Contrary to the opinion of the American Legion, *On the Beach* did not win any prizes in the Soviet Union, but Kramer's production did receive national and international awards as both film art and message movie. It was nominated for several Golden Globe Awards, including best picture, best director, best supporting actor for Fred Astaire, and for "promoting international understanding." Ernest Gold won for best original score. At the British Academy Awards, Kramer earned an award for best director and Ava Gardner was nominated for best foreign actress. The Newspaper Guild of New York gave *On the Beach* the Page One Award in Movies for "its striking journalistic awareness and dramatic power in treating a subject of tremendous concern in our time." Of course, not everyone appreciated Kramer's film for these very same reasons. It was "a much cussed and discussed motion picture" "damned as emphatically as it has been praised." "The only unanimity in the reactions seems to be that nobody has taken the picture lightly," noted one reviewer.[115] For Kramer, this outcome was an achievement. "I felt it would be provocative . . . at least I wanted it to be. So the fact that the picture is being talked about, by scientists, government officials, religious leaders, and laymen, is gratifying."[116] Although Bosley Crowther criticized "the acerbity with which some authorities have lashed out at this film," Kramer was equanimous. "I think it is healthy for others to disagree with what my movies say," he observed, as he readied himself for his next production. "Thousands have already disagreed with *On the Beach*."[117] And thousands more, including the American Legion, would disagree with the message and those involved in the making of his next film.

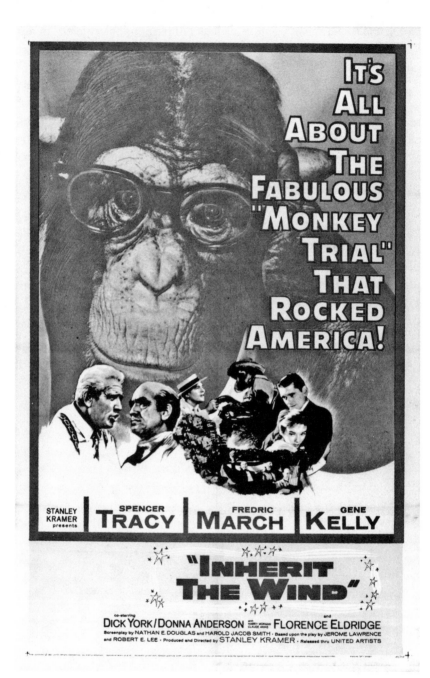

Poster for Inherit the Wind *(1960). Courtesy of Margaret Herrick Library and MGM/UA.*

Inherit the Wind Champions Civil Liberties

As *On the Beach* began its exhibition run in 1959, Stanley Kramer already was well under way with his next film, *Inherit the Wind*, released the very next year. *Newsweek*'s reviewer could not resist noting that the producer-director was turning his attention "from mankind's end to its beginning." "Stanley Kramer's latest exercise in Thinking Big is not on the same physical scale as his last . . . yet the result is more stirring." At the time, Kramer presented his latest film as "the third point in a three-pronged attempt to provide 'provocative' film fare." "In *The Defiant Ones* we dealt with the problem of race." *On the Beach* "concerns the big question, the Bomb. And now I'm dealing with what I consider the third major problem today, freedom of speech and, more important, freedom of thought."[1] Kramer justified his selection of socially important film subjects as an indication of changing audience interest. "These are not the sort of pictures you'd have found able to pay for themselves as recently as five years ago," he argued. "Without intending to hold forth and speak of trends—after all, who can be certain of them?" Kramer felt that "if people start talking about your subject matter or your theme, that's fine. And people these days do talk about serious themes." By 1960, at the start of a new decade, he had earned the title of "the thinking man's producer." But, as *Inherit the Wind* would confirm, "some of the ideas dramatized in his films are not necessarily popular ones."[2]

Kramer's 1960 historical film both recreated and reimagined the famous 1925 Scopes trial, more popularly known as the "Monkey Trial." The trial concerned the violation of Tennessee's state law prohibiting the teaching of evolution in the public schools and pitted two charismatic legal advocates—Clarence Darrow and William Jennings Bryan—in a conflict between evolutionary science and religious fundamentalism. *Inherit the Wind* starred Spencer Tracy and Fredric March as fictional characters based on Darrow and Bryan and was an adaptation of the original hit 1955 play of the same name by Jerome Lawrence and Robert E. Lee. Lawrence and Lee drew the title of their play from the Bible, specifically Proverbs 11:29, "He that troubleth his own house shall inherit the wind." The plot realized this line, because the religious characters set into motion forces that bring about their own various downfalls.

Although a reenactment of the Scopes trial of the 1920s, a decade with its own anticommunist Red Scare, the playwrights were more concerned about their contemporary context of Cold War America. Of particular concern was the stifling and silencing of dissent, but they never made historical claims for their play. "*Inherit the Wind* is not history," they forthrightly stated in their prologue. Instead, the play was a work of fiction "related" to historical events and figures. Once the screen version appeared, they publicly complimented the producer-director. "Stanley Kramer," Lawrence stated, "has done an honest job with our play." "Nothing like integrity and that's Kramer's middle name," Lee added.[3]

Inherit the Wind not only addressed the issues of science versus religion and history on film; it also struck a blow for civil liberties in the context of domestic anticommunism and the Hollywood blacklist. Like the play, the film dealt "with the inherent rights of a schoolteacher to teach freely in the classrooms of this nation," Kramer noted, "however controversial may be his subject matter." Film critic Arthur Knight agreed. "It is a stirring defense of the right to think as a free man, and to obey the dictates of conscience." With its focus on "the courage of a man with firm, if unpopular, convictions," the film was a reminder of the right to hold a minority opinion against that of the majority. Kramer's latest film reflected his political liberalism and commitment to the freedom of conscience and speech. "Knowing the other films of social value that you have produced in the past," the associate director of the American Civil Liberties Union (ACLU) wrote Kramer, "we are confident that *Inherit the Wind* will be another major contribution to public understanding of a controversial social question."[4] Indeed, both during and after production, particularly with the employment of blacklisted screenwriter Nedrick Young, the film provoked discussion about the importance and value of civil liberties in America. As with the debate over *On the Beach*, Kramer and his supporters used this forum to powerfully and profoundly challenge a key component of the Cold War, in this case the domestic suppression of political dissent.

Debating Breaking the Blacklist

With the making of *Inherit the Wind*, Kramer again hired his Oscar-winning screenwriters for *The Defiant Ones* and provoked a clash with anticommunist forces for breaking the blacklist. By the time *Inherit the Wind* began production in 1959, Young had admitted publicly that he had used the pseudonym Nathan E. Douglas for *The Defiant Ones* to circumvent the blacklist. As had happened before HUAC in 1953, he still would not say whether he was a communist, nor would he "recant. "I'm not made that way," Young acknowledged in 1960. "A man has to live with himself." He remained "under political suspicion" and was "supposed to be boycotted by producers," observed the *New York Times*. But Kramer forthrightly justified hiring Young. "It is unfortunate," he argued, that members of the film industry "have at one time or another been censured for past political affiliations." Instead, they deserve "complete freedom of expression," and he asserted his right "to employ anyone of my own choosing."[5] Commentators did not fail to notice that, in coauthoring the screenplay for *Inherit the Wind*, Young helped make a film defending the very freedoms of thought and speech the Hollywood blacklist had denied him.

In early 1960 Kramer's strong stance on hiring Young sparked a public debate in newspapers, on television, and in letters about the necessity and morality of the Hollywood blacklist. Changing circumstances in Hollywood, the nation, and his own career meant that Kramer could take the professional and political risks entailed in publicly breaking the blacklist. This new situation contrasted with that of the early 1950s when Kramer and Carl Foreman parted ways. The FBI had closed their investigation of communist "subversion" in Hollywood in 1958, signaling that agency's belief that members of the film industry no longer posed a threat to American national security. At the same time, Kramer had publicly aired his antiblacklist convictions as a guest on the NBC television show *Youth Wants to Know*. To the surprise of many, including Dalton Trumbo, there was "no press storm, not a word." Developments the following year also boded well for the end of the blacklist. The Motion Picture Industry Council, a "blacklist oversight group," suspended its operations in July 1959, and the Writers Guild of America, West, vowed to fight against the denial of screen credit to those on the blacklist.[6] Young won his Oscar for *The Defiant Ones*, and Hollywood's leading anticommunist, Ward Bond, had admitted defeat. But Red Scare forces across the United States were not yet ready to surrender.

When Kramer's hiring of Young for *Inherit the Wind* became public knowledge, these forces took action. At its 1959 national convention in Minneapolis, the American Legion passed resolutions reaffirming its commitment to the Hollywood blacklist, praising the major studios for adhering to the practice and attacking independent film companies, such as Kramer's, for not.[7] Then in early February 1960, Martin B. McNeally, national commander of the American Legion, issued a statement. The Legion was opening a "war of information" to combat "a renewed invasion of filmdom by Soviet-indoctrinated artists." Kirk Douglas, who had starred in Kramer's *Champion*, had hired and would give screen credit to Trumbo for *Spartacus* (1960)—an event usually considered the first breaking of the blacklist. But McNeally specifically referred to Kramer hiring Young for *Inherit the Wind* and Otto Preminger hiring Trumbo for *Exodus* (1960). Both producer-directors early on explicitly stated their decision to give screen credit to their writers. McNeally called on the "movie-going American public and patriotic motion picture exhibitors" to adhere to the blacklist "as they did ten years ago when they ended the disgrace of a Hollywood then dominated by Red ideology."[8] The Veterans of Foreign Wars later joined the American Legion in criticizing the hiring of Young and Trumbo. They declared that "the unleashing of their 'progressive ideological content' upon the minds of our families and friends, constitutes a grave danger" and protested "this out-right promotion of Communism."[9]

Kramer refused to accept this anticommunist attack and responded. Both he and Preminger issued public statements; Kramer's statement made the front page of the *New York Times*.[10] This exchange of words in print led to a televised debate between Kramer and McNeally on the CBS public affairs program *F.Y.I.* in mid-February. In turn, columnists, industry insiders, academics, professionals, students, military servicemen, members of the clergy, spokesmen for organizations, and concerned individuals weighed in on the issue in print, speeches, and letters to Kramer. These letters represented the views of people from all over the United States. Although most came from California and

New York, letters also arrived from New Hampshire, Pennsylvania, Alabama, Texas, Ohio, Wisconsin, and Nebraska. After film critic Bosley Crowther published an article in the *New York Times* in support of ending the blacklist and advertising the Kramer-McKneally television debate, the newspaper ran a "Blacklist Forum" for readers' letters to the editor.[11]

Perhaps unsurprisingly, the majority of readers' letters published in the *New York Times*, as well as extant letters to Kramer, supported his antiblacklist position. Support also came from most of the media—newspapers and television—the film industry, and liberal organizations, such as the ACLU and the American Veterans Committee, a rival to the American Legion. "Events of the past few weeks in Hollywood, where the voice of the Legion has often been mistaken for the voice of the people, if not the voice of God," the *Nation* editorialized, showed that the "jig might be up for the American Legion's witch hunt."[12] Yet strong criticisms of Kramer and his position also appeared, most prominently from the Hearst press, such as the *New York Daily Mirror* and the *Los Angeles Examiner,* some Hollywood trade papers, and columnists Ed Sullivan, Walter Winchell, and Ward Bond's ally, George Sokolsky. That Kramer's defense against the American Legion's attack provoked such public debate and support indicated that in 1960 the timing was right to reconsider and reassess the Hollywood blacklist.

Kramer's primary argument against the blacklist was a principled one, that the blacklist violated Americans' civil liberties. "This is a nation of laws," he noted in his statement to the *New York Times.* "I think those who disagree with me have as much right to constitutional guarantees as I have." He elaborated on the *F.Y.I.* television program. "I take the position in support of the right of freedom of the individual to work, regardless of previous past political affiliation." "A blacklist," he summed up, "is an anathema to democracy."[13] Kramer's supporters most often and most passionately endorsed this argument. They wrote "to congratulate you for your fine statement defending democracy and individual liberty" and for "the stroke you have made on behalf of free thought and expression." The ACLU believed Kramer "struck an important blow for civil liberties by reminding the public—and the motion-picture industry—that the Constitution and the Bill of Rights are documents of freedom which apply to every American."[14] The Screen Publicists Guild praised Kramer and Preminger for "their refusal to surrender their Constitutional rights and the rights of their writer-employees." And a Philadelphia letter writer asserted that the blacklist did not belong "in this land which guarantees under the Constitution freedom of speech and assembly."[15]

For anticommunists such as McKneally, however, communists did not deserve civil liberties, and the blacklist should remain in place. McKneally argued that "the movie industry must not employ a Communist or anyone who has sought refuge behind the Fifth Amendment when questioned about subversive associations, unless he recants." The *Los Angeles Examiner,* a Hearst newspaper, sided with McKneally and explained why. "A Communist, as most Americans know, is a member of an international conspiracy, controlled and directed by Moscow. The purpose of the conspiracy is to destroy democracy and the very freedoms of conscience and choice upon which Mr. Kramer bases his argument."[16] Other critics of Kramer echoed this anticommunist reasoning. "I would like to protest against your stand," wrote a man from Florida. "There is a growing awareness among patriotic Americans everywhere about the methods and tactics of those who would subvert our democratic republic." Kramer's apparent unawareness of the dangers posed by communists made him, according to the *Examiner,* "politically naïve."[17] "It requires just a modicum of political sophistication to understand that the very nature of Communism," opined columnist Walter Winchell, "demands fanatical dedication from its writers." Letter writers to Kramer made similar charges: "It seems incredible that you should be living in such a vacuum that you do not know the techniques of Communist infiltration." "Come now, Mr. Kramer, we all aren't as gullible as you," wrote a woman from New York.[18]

Over the objections of anticommunists, Kramer asserted his right to hire whom he pleased. "As an individual entrepreneur, I must have the right to hire and fire, according to the dictates of my conscience, those people whom I feel can best do the job for me." He pointed out in his televised debate with McKneally that "the Waldorf Agreement was not an agreement which I as an individual was a party to." As an independent filmmaker, he never promised he would "not knowingly employ a Communist," nor had his and Preminger's *Exodus* financier and distributor, United Artists. Because United Artists was not a production company, its executives never became signatories to the Waldorf Agreement. "Do I fire or hire? There is no law on the books" that deemed "past political or social inclinations" a requirement for employment.[19]

The *Nation's* editors agreed. Hollywood producers should enjoy "the remarkable American privilege of hiring whom they please without concern for the hollow blusterings" of the American Legion. Kramer also held "that a writer's work can be completely divorced from his political views." The ACLU concurred that "an individual should be judged on the basis of his competence not his political beliefs."[20] Similarly, the Society of Magazine Writers emphasized that "private, lawful opinions and activities are considerations not relevant to their employment." These are "external-to-the-job-at-hand criteri[a]," added one letter writer.[21]

But critics of Kramer determinedly disagreed. They found it "incredible that these pseudo-intellectual undesirables are the only writers available." "Would Kramer hire Alger Hiss?" asked the *New York Daily Mirror.* "Would he hire Benedict Arnold?" One letter writer took the analogy even further. Would supporters of Kramer "approve of hiring Adolf Hitler [and his ilk] if they also happened to be competent script writers?"[22] Before being employed in the motion picture industry again, a blacklisted screenwriter "has to do some repentance, you know," maintained McKneally. C. S. Foote, commander of the American Legion Department of California, urged Hollywood to hire "noncontroversial, patriotic writers" rather than "people who don't believe in our way of life." "You can never make me believe that there aren't scores of excellent *loyal* American writers without any Communist stigma who *deserve* employment," exclaimed a Florida woman. But "Stanley Kramer employed non-Reds only when a Red is unavailable," accused Myron Fagan.[23] These correspondents joined McKneally in holding the movie industry—and Kramer as part of it—to its anticommunist commitment. "I strongly object to your employing identified Communist Nedrick Young as script writer in the film *Inherit the Wind!* Please do all you can do to help maintain the 'Waldorf Declaration.'" "Dear Mr. Kramer," wrote a US Navy man, "I'm wondering if you remember the Waldorf Declaration of 1947 which was a promise made by the movie industry to the American people."[24]

McKneally and his supporters believed that the industry's "promise" made at the start of the Cold War needed to be kept, because they saw continuity in domestic and international politics to 1960. Americans were still living "in this day of freedom's darkest peril from the Communists and the communist conspiracy," McKneally stated. He emphasized the continuing threat of communism at home and abroad, arguing that "there remained a hard-core nucleus who had supported the Communist line in Hollywood." The failure to guard against "the complacency of the moment," the *New York Daily Mirror* editorialized, meant "the Commies are back in full swing in Hollywood." "They don't believe in freedom as we believe in it," McKneally told Kramer in their television debate. "They believe in tyranny."[25]

Supporters of McKneally ardently agreed. "To me there is nothing greater than the menace of communism," wrote a Legion member to Kramer. One filmgoer feared "we are being subjected to an overdose of brainwash" and "a conspiracy to undermine our Constitution." "All Americans must stand together to right all forms of insidious Communist penetration," penned another. "Will you do your part?"[26] Ed Sullivan felt similarly, and he believed civil liberties still needed to be sacrificed to fight the ongoing Cold War. "But in the clear and present danger to our country that is posed by Russia," Sullivan declared, "individual rights become subordinate to the common good." This situation was exactly what supporters of Kramer feared. A New York man contended that "there is greater danger to our liberties from within than without."[27]

Instead of continuity, Kramer and his supporters considered the political climate changed since the early days of East-West conflict. A "thaw" in the Cold War beginning in the late 1950s had an impact domestically, "with the Communist Party at lowest ebb, and the Supreme Court rolling back the more extreme legislation of the McCarthy era." The international impact of the thaw included the ongoing Geneva nuclear test ban treaty negotiations and a 1958 cultural agreement between the United States and Soviet Union. Within this new context, Kramer noted that any possible "subversion" could be handled by "legal agencies, the FBI," concerned with national security, with no need for a blacklist. He also commented that "the writers named by the Legion are free and not legally guilty of any treasonable or other unlawful acts."[28] In fact, he reminded his critics, no one ever proved "by the furthest stretch of imagination in the most perilous days of Hollywood that any piece of motion picture film which reached the screen was guilty of propagandizing in a subversive manner." The only evidence offered by anticommunists concerned "past affiliations or suspected affiliations."[29] "Some of these people whose loyalty has been questioned have made a great many mistakes," Kramer argued. "They were guilty of intellectual confusion or whatever you want to call it in times of crisis." But revisiting "those past mistakes" was not necessary.[30]

Differing views of current Cold War conditions fit with how Kramer, McKneally, and their supporters understood what was at stake in Hollywood. "I am in an art form," Kramer proclaimed. "I think the artist must have a freedom of expression." American civil liberties, particularly rights to free speech and artistic freedom, were important not only to the nation but also to the world. Although nuclear weapons dominated the Cold War landscape, as reflected in his last film, *On the Beach*, Kramer felt "the greatest single weapon . . . in America is still personal liberty." Hollywood had a role to play in the Cold War ideological struggle between East and West, specifically projecting American rights and liberties around the globe. But the blacklist compromised the industry's integrity and ability to fulfill that role. Restoring the "freedom to work" for film artists would differentiate the United States from the Soviet Union's "dictatorial system."[31] Kramer's supporters put his stance within this global Cold War context as well. Several argued that the Legion demanded "that Hollywood accept a Soviet-style straitjacket," and would even "foster a monolithic dictatorship analogous to that which controls the U.S.S.R." They instead saw civil liberties as fundamental to US power, arguing that "our Great Country grew strong because it fed on the[se] principles." "Our national greatness is squarely based in freedom for the minority," wrote a military serviceman. And a New York woman thought Kramer's stance would "further the cause of basic human rights anywhere" and "win respect for Americans through the world."[32]

McKneally and others agreed on the cultural and political power of Hollywood but disagreed on how to deploy it. "Hollywood is a vast public interest with a vast impact on the mores of the country," McKneally stated. Yet the film industry chose to "sell to the American people at the box office the works of artists" linked to communism. His California colleague, C. S. Foote, clarified the Legion position. "We feel that any person with a Communist background who reaches so much of the American public should not be given a chance in an industry where his viewpoint might be influential."[33] Anticommunist commentators and letter writers approved of these points. As Martin Quigley, Jr., editorialized in the *Motion Picture Daily*, "the screen possesses enormous powers of influence for good and evil," so "the views—political or otherwise—of picture-makers" mattered very much. "I believe the movie industry should feel they have a grave responsibility in preserving our dear America," insisted an Oregon woman. A New York woman claimed, "We have a right to expect the industry to live up to American ideals and standards, sans foreign ideology." "What it really gets down to," the *Los Angeles Examiner* opined, "is the danger and folly of employing enemies of our society in a particularly susceptible area—the transmission of ideas."[34] Kramer's opponents repeated arguments made by advocates of the blacklist more than a decade earlier, but they gained less traction in 1960.

Instead, Kramer and opponents of the blacklist confidently countered these arguments and worked to change the terms of the debate. They took back the term "American" from the American Legion and other anticommunists and defined their position as patriotic and properly American. Instead of anticommunism being the core of Americanism, this antiblacklist contingent sought to have civil liberties take its place. Mickey Levine, chairman of the liberal American Veterans Committee that opposed the American Legion, expressed "admiration and support" to Kramer "for the patriotic, truly American position you have taken." Other letter writers to Kramer chimed in. "Congratulations upon the American stand you have taken." "I congratulate you on your outspoken American thinking."[35] These correspondents to Kramer also denied any link to communism. "I am not, nor have I ever been a communist. But, as a fellow American, I feel exactly as you do," wrote a Brooklyn woman. Another letter writer emphasized to Kramer, "Believe me I'm 100% American and know nothing about Communism except that it stinks." Like Kramer, these respondents understood respect for civil liberties as consistent with criticism of communism and promotion of Americanism.[36]

With this understanding of Americanism, Kramer and his supporters took aim at the American Legion. They felt it was the lack of respect by the Legion and its allies for freedom of thought and expression—not any communists in Hollywood—that created problems in American society and politics. Students at Bard College assailed the American Legion's "un-American interference in the movie industry," and the Screen Publicists Guild wanted "no tampering, by the Legion or anyone else, with the basic precepts of our democracy."[37] Kramer did not shy away from calling the Legion's position "as totally un-American as anything I can imagine." His supporters agreed, labeling the Legion a "pseudo-patriotic" organization that engaged in "phony flag-waving" and lambasting McKneally's "pretentiously patriotic mouthings." Many felt the American Legion had been allowed, "for far too long, to go largely unchallenged."[38]

Now that Kramer had taken on the challenge, his personal and professional reputation soared. News articles labeled him America's "leading" and "foremost" independent producer, and headlines emphasized his toughness: "Kramer Defies American Legion," "Kramer to Fight Legion Pressure," "Producer Raps Tactics of Legion." In the debate, Kramer exemplified the ideal of American Cold War masculinity, as when he "scoffed at the suggestion that Communist writers could smuggle Communist propaganda into movies without his knowledge." "My films reflect my viewpoint," he stated in the *New York Times*. "I control my pictures—what is said in them, how they are directed and how they are edited."[39] Kramer acted and spoke from a strong, principled position, and his supporters recognized these qualities. "I have never heard anyone in this country speak so courageously publicly." "More power to those who have the guts to speak out!" "It's been too long since any one person of character has had courage enough to stand up and be counted among the *men*."[40] In praising Kramer, supporters referred to his previous films as well as the heroes in his earlier films. "Mr. Kramer's stand took about as much courage as Gary Cooper displayed in *High Noon*," and in defying the Legion he joined "a distinguished list of 'defiant ones.'" As another indication of Kramer's courage and confidence, he offered to address the American Legion at their next national convention and clarify the "concept of freedom of expression in our democracy."[41]

At the height of Kramer's debate with the American Legion in February 1960, it appeared that he, Preminger, Douglas, and others inside and outside the industry had succeeded with a "big breakthrough" that signaled the approaching end of the blacklist. *Variety* reported "the almost complete turnabout of the political climate. . . . It's generally agreed that the actions of Preminger and Kramer have set the stage for the eventual elimination of the blacklists."[42] Never passing up an opportunity to promote Kramer's reputation and career, his company sent out a mass mailing in mid-February 1960 to journalists informing them of the debate and Kramer's role in it. But Kramer did not declare victory yet. As he predicted accurately to a colleague, "So far the writers have been unanimous in support but it's early and they will not continue in that vein."[43] As a result of his prominence in the wake of the debate, Kramer had a new entry in Myron Fagan's latest publication, *Documentations of the Reds and Fellow-Travelers in Hollywood and TV* (1961). Fagan accused Kramer of using his films "as vehicles for the 'comeback efforts' of Red Stars and Directors who had been driven out of Hollywood." Meanwhile, criticisms, including hateful anti-Semitic slurs, mounted. "I take it that you are a Jew," stated an anonymous letter. "Someday we white loyal Americans are going to do something about your kind." "If you do not like the American Legion and what it stands for, why don't you and your big nose go to Israel and stay there," demanded a New Jersey man.[44]

Threats of boycotts against Kramer's films also occurred. Most of these threats were implicit. "Stanley Kramer was very foolish to tangle with Martin B. McKneally of the American Legion over employing commies to write movies," warned Hedda Hopper. "The American Legion is a powerful American organization." The Legion publicized the fact that "Kramer is the fellow who has made it known that he has no objections to hiring communists" and put its membership on alert. If *Inherit the Wind*, along with *Exodus* and *Spartacus*, were to "go over big at the box office the Waldorf Declaration will be broken." Then "Hollywood will be open to a repeat performance of the horrible nightmare of communist infestation of the 1930s and 1940s."[45] Explicit boycott threats also came to Kramer. Most vociferous was Fagan, who practically shouted off the page. "He will continue to make Communist-Loaded films until the American people will boycott every film that bears his name!!!" The editors of the *New York Daily Mirror* put Kramer on notice by recalling anticommunist actions against Hollywood movies in the early 1950s. "If he has forgotten let him be reminded that the motion picture industry was voluntarily and spontaneously boycotted by the American people." Letter writers to Kramer supported these calls for a boycott. A Texas man sent "best wishes for a series of financial flops to you, Mr. Kramer."[46]

With *Inherit the Wind* forthcoming later in 1960, Kramer felt very vulnerable to boycott. This feeling intensified after Frank Sinatra first hired and then, under pressure, fired screenwriter Albert Maltz, one of the Hollywood Ten, that spring. Sinatra, like Kramer, argued that he had the right to hire the best person for the job. But anticommunist

Gene Kelly, Donna Anderson, Dick York, Stanley Kramer, and Spencer Tracy in a production still for Inherit the Wind *(1960). Courtesy of Department of Special Collections, Charles E. Young Research Library, University of California, Los Angeles, with permission from Karen Sharpe-Kramer.*

criticism mounted and even targeted John F. Kennedy, at the time a candidate for the Democratic Party's nomination for president, whom Sinatra supported. In April Sinatra conceded defeat. "Frank Sinatra had knuckled under to the bully-boys of the American Legion," a filmgoer wrote Kramer.[47] "Do I think the American Legion can hurt my picture?" Kramer asked in May. "I think they can make my life miserable." By June, as he turned his attention to completing the production of *Inherit the Wind,* his film company colleagues urged "refraining from engaging in debate" with the "glorious 200% American Legion."[48] Kramer's early 1960 debate with the American Legion did not end the blacklist. But by publicly breaking it and providing a popular forum for questioning its utility and legitimacy, he certainly contributed to its final demise. And by prominently prioritizing civil liberties, he also signaled a political departure for the new decade.

Science versus Religion versus History

Kramer's 1960 film *Inherit the Wind* furthered this discussion and debate about civil liberties in the United States. Freedom of thought and expression were at the center of Kramer's film, the Broadway play on which it was based, and the historical events both the film and play portrayed. The famous 1925 Scopes trial involved the prosecution of John T. Scopes, a young schoolteacher in Dayton, Tennessee, for violating a state law prohibiting the teaching of Darwin's theory of evolution. Scopes considered the law a "threat to freedom," as did his defense team, including the ACLU and celebrity trial lawyer Clarence Darrow. The law, according to the defense, specifically violated freedom of speech and the rights of labor for teachers.[49] These civil liberties issues inspired the playwrights Lawrence and Lee some thirty years later. In crafting their 1955 play, they dramatized and fictionalized historical events to comment on and criticize their historical moment, specifically McCarthyism. Their play debuted only a year after the famous, televised Army-McCarthy hearings, where Senator McCarthy displayed his bullying, belligerent behavior to the nation and drove his political downfall.[50] Kramer picked up on this theme. In promoting his film, he linked its plot about a civil liberties conflict in the past to his recent confrontation with problacklist forces. "Nowadays a motion picture producer engages in a great variety and types of battle," he observed in a trailer for *Inherit the Wind*. "I've been in one or two myself."

Although Kramer's confrontation occurred in the realm of political ideas and ideology, at the Scopes trial and in *Inherit the Wind* the conflict over civil liberties played out between science and religion. In Tennessee in 1925, Protestant Christian fundamentalists built an antievolution movement and succeeded in passing the Butler Act, which made it unlawful "to teach any theory that denies the story of the divine creation of man as taught in the Bible, and to teach instead that man has descended from a lower order of animals."[51] Religious fundamentalists believed in the inerrancy of scripture and thus took literally the Bible's descriptions of God's creation of the earth and the first human beings, Adam and Eve. Darwin's theory of evolution, however, posited natural causes of the origins of species, including humanity, and ignored supernatural explanations. Religious modernists reconciled their old faith with new science, but fundamentalists resisted such reconciliation. Instead, they militantly opposed evolution and pursued legislation such as the Butler Act. Under this law, Scopes was prosecuted and convicted, with the country's most prominent antievolutionist in the lead: three-time Democratic presidential nominee and former secretary of state William Jennings Bryan. "The trial concerned the right of a science teacher to describe Darwin's theory of evolution and the efforts of powerful townspeople to oppose what they considered an attack on the Bible," explained a film reviewer for the *Washington Post*. The Scopes trial, another reviewer wrote, "brought out into the open a bitter conflict between fundamental religion and science."[52]

At the 1925 trial, Clarence Darrow and William Jennings Bryan personified this conflict and, renamed Henry Drummond and Matthew Harrison Brady, were the focus of *Inherit the Wind*'s plot. Kramer recognized the need for compelling actors to capture this dramatic clash, and he sought Spencer Tracy and Fredric March, two of Hollywood's most respected actors and both double Oscar winners. "Stanley Kramer has a mighty good deal cooking," Hedda Hopper reported in 1959, "if he can latch onto [the actors] and boy, is he trying!"[53] Kramer had worked with March in *Death of a Salesman* (1951), and they remained in contact. The actor wrote about seeing *The Defiant Ones*—"we were so very moved"—and *On the Beach*—"simply *great* for my money," and Kramer recalled having "no trouble arousing his interest in the Bryan role." "Tracy, on the other hand, took more convincing."[54] Once cast, the two stars were competitive, and, later, their performances were compared and contrasted. "Fredric March's interpretation of a flamboyant orator," contended the *Chicago Tribune*'s movie critic, "is a broad one," while Spencer Tracy "works hard at being a plain man in search of truth." Kramer's success in casting the leading roles received much praise. The acting "is the triumph of the picture," asserted Bosley Crowther, with "two unsurpassable actors persuaded to play the roles." "Pairing of Tracy and March," *Variety* concluded, "was a stroke of casting genius."[55]

By embodying *Inherit the Wind*'s two main characters, the actors enacted the conflict between science and religion. As Kramer explained, "this is a clash between two giants of law who hold firmly to widely divergent points of view on religious, educational and personal freedom." Although Darrow and the rest of the defense team lost the Scopes case, the film gives them the moral victory. In clarifying the conflict central to the film, reviewers often conflated the actors, the characters, and the historical figures: "March, for the Bible" and "Tracy, for Darwin," summed up one writer.[56] The film's plot pits "Tracy, up against narrow local prejudice toward 'e-volution' as well as up against March," noted Philip K. Scheuer in the *Los Angeles Times*. During the climactic scene where Brady, played by March, is on the stand being questioned by Drummond, played by Tracy, "both heat up that already sweating courtroom with all the fire and brimstone you'd expect from the two great old pros they are." Illustrating their conflict in a quieter scene outside the courthouse, the two men are on a porch talking about earlier days when they were allies, and they are side by side in rocking chairs but rocking out of rhythm. With these actors in these roles, Kramer "wonderfully accomplished," observed Crowther, "a graphic fleshing [out] of his theme."[57]

In discussions of *Inherit the Wind*'s theme, science and religion represented very different ways of thinking about and understanding the world, and most commentators believed science provided the superior approach. The "basic conflict is intellectual," Crowther noted, "freedom of inquiry clashes with the slavery of dogmatic thought." This "contest between Darwin and the Bible," according to *Variety*, opposed "intellectual progress and standpatism."[58] For Kramer, "the true subject of the trial, the play, [and] the film" was the importance of the freedom to explore "ideas and truth." "To me," he recalled, the "Scopes story is important because the pro-religion, antiscience side in this instance refused to examine the ideas of its opponents." In a statement he released with *Inherit the Wind* in 1960, Kramer emphasized that "freedom of enquiry is a living, dramatic process."[59] Crowther agreed. The "crux of his drama" was "the never-settled issue of the freedom of the mind." "It is a fight that men will always have to wage," and, at the end of the film, "you know intellect has won." According to Crowther and other commentators, the film made the "pro-education and pro-enlightenment" case for science; in turn, religion is associated with ignorance "which lead[s] to bigotry and intolerance."[60]

Inherit the Wind's negative association of religion with the forces of reaction and rigidity raised concerns from the very start. The PCA at first deemed the story "unacceptable," because it violated "that portion of the Code which states that 'No film . . . may throw ridicule on any religious faith.'" *Inherit the Wind* contained "an attack on Christian doctrine" and presented "religious thinking people in an extremely unfavorable light." To correct the portrayal of these "near-fanatic, Old Testament fundamentalists" clinging to their "obtuse literal interpretation of the Old Testament," PCA administrators proposed that the film "distinguish this one narrow-minded community from the Christian world as a whole."[61] The PCA's 1959 agreement with Kramer required that the film give "voice to the idea that religion, as practiced in this one community, was not representative of the true Christian faith." In addition, Kramer needed to secure technical advice from the National Council of Churches' Broadcasting and Film Commission located in Hollywood, remove from the screenplay the phrases "hot for Genesis" and "belching beatitudes," and minimize the use of "hell" and "damn." Following these negotiations with the PCA, promotional materials for *Inherit the Wind* were careful to specify "fundamental religion." Film critics did the same. "Kramer's point is that it was not Religion that clashed here with Science, but an articulate segment claiming to represent all Religion."[62]

Kramer, as had playwrights Lawrence and Lee, also portrayed a resolution to the conflict between science and religion with the ending of *Inherit the Wind*. The character of Drummond is in the empty courtroom pondering the two books: the Bible and Darwin's *On the Origin of Species*. He weighs them up and, placing the Bible on top of Darwin's book, leaves the courtroom. Music fills the soundtrack with Leslie Uggams powerfully singing "The Battle Hymn of the Republic." "Mine eyes have seen the glory of the coming of the Lord," she begins, ending with a triumphant "glory, glory, hallelujah." Written by Julia Ward Howe during the Civil War, the song drew on biblical words and images to herald the second coming of Christ and Judgment Day, which would "usher in the Kingdom of God."[63] According to Donald Spoto, the song made "clear that although the film carries no banner for fundamentalism, it is not for all that a nontheistic picture." *Inherit the Wind*'s final gesture toward resolution fit with historical fact, as the Scopes defense team sought to show "how the teaching of the Scriptures and of Darwin were not mutually exclusive nor incompatible." They also made arguments about how Tennessee's Butler Act violated the constitutional separation of church and state, which was designed to protect both. "Religion," as Kramer later stated, "cannot be ignored when it seems to challenge the freedom of our society, just as opposite forces cannot be ignored when they seem to challenge freedom of religion."[64]

Inherit the Wind's effort at resolution had a mixed reception. On the positive side, showing "that the Bible—though it need not always be taken literally—is a book which has offered spiritual solace to people all over the world" meant the PCA could deem the ending of the film "Hopeful." It enabled the Catholic Legion of Decency to classify the film A-3, "Morally Unobjectionable for Adults." Letter writers to Kramer endorsed the film's acceptance of science and religion as different but congruent aspects of human experience. "It gave me, not only pleasure and happiness, but vast knowledge and assurance of the Natural agreement and harmony between Science and Religion." "You have struck a great blow for freedom in all realms," wrote a clergyman from San Francisco.[65] Yet criticism also appeared. "At the very end there is a cryptic scene," *Newsweek* noted, labeling it "back-pedaling." For the *Irish Times*, the film did not have "the full courage of its convictions in the end, the Darrow figure being revealed as a disguised believer." But Kramer defended this ending, which repeated that of the original play and reflected his historical understanding that his old hero Darrow was not "somebody who believed in nothing."[66]

In its reconciliation of science and mainstream religion, *Inherit the Wind* represented both fundamentalism and atheism as extreme and marginal. The film used exaggerated, often egregious stereotypes in the process. The character who gives voice to atheism is not Drummond but the journalist E. K. Hornbeck, based on the historical figure H. L. Mencken and played in the movie by Gene Kelly. His caustic, cynical personality makes him an unpopular and unhappy character and discredits his atheistic standpoint within the film. Protestant Christian fundamentalism was depicted through the characters of Brady, the local minister, and the townspeople of Hillsboro, a "small town in an unidentified southern state, USA" standing in for Dayton, Tennessee.[67] In the *Saturday Review*, Arthur Knight regretted that Fredric March played Brady as "a gross buffoon rather than a once-great man tragically out of touch with his time," a fairer interpretation of William Jennings Bryan at the Scopes trial. Bosley Crowther best translated into words the stereotypes at work in *Inherit the Wind*. From the "fire-snorting fundamentalist minister" and "Bible-thumpers" to the "yokels who hoot . . . and hurl nasty insults," the film showed the "spectacle of dogmatists and bigots at work."[68] The use of the song "Give Me That Old Time Religion" throughout the film reinforced these stereotypes. The song was seen as "too mocking" with the "hymn-singers howling defiantly" and "repeated to the point of some irritation." The overall impression, according to one reviewer, was that the film "holds in ridicule the townspeople of Hillsboro."[69]

This stereotypical representation of religious fundamentalism in the film fit with northern liberal attitudes toward southern conservatives from the time of the Scopes trial to that of *Inherit the Wind*. Newspaper reports out of Dayton in 1925, especially Mencken's articles for the *Baltimore Sun*, were scathing. Mencken called the local townspeople "hill billies" and "morons" with "so-called minds."[70] In the first and most famous history of the 1920s, Frederick Lewis Allen's *Only Yesterday*, published in 1931, the Scopes trial appeared not just as a battle between science and religion but also between modernity and tradition, urban and rural Americans, North and South, knowledge and ignorance, progress and reaction, liberalism and conservatism. This dichotomous framework simplified and stereotyped the fundamentalists and influenced subsequent historians and popular writers. It became part of the "modern Scopes legend" that both structured and was reinforced by Lawrence and Lee's play in 1955 and Kramer's film in 1960.[71] The events associated with the modern civil rights movement intensified this image of the South as underdeveloped and backward. Northern liberals saw the South, not the North, as the site and source of America's racial problems, due to the region's legal segregation and disenfranchisement of African Americans. The violent resistance of white southerners to civil rights activism, as in the school integration crisis in Little Rock, Arkansas, confirmed racial extremism as another negative characteristic of the region. As scholar Neda Atanasoski puts it, "political discourse of the time perceived the South as yet to be fully incorporated into U.S. moral democracy."[72]

As with Kramer's *The Defiant Ones*, the setting and characters in *Inherit the Wind* reflected this popular and political perception of the South. Although there are no black characters and therefore no African American actors in the film, two scenes explicitly refer to the South's unequal and unjust racial system: the arrest and jailing of the character Bertram C. Cates, based on John T. Scopes. The arrest starts like a lynching, with the town's leaders marching to make the arrest. "Old Time Religion" fills the soundtrack, sung by Leslie Uggams, a well-known singer and television star; she provided the "lone and symptomatic black voice" in the movie, as scholar Marjorie Garber notes.[73] Once Cates is in jail, an angry mob gathers by torchlight at night outside and sings, "We'll hang Bert Cates" to the tune of the "Battle Hymn of the Republic." Reviewers commented on these scenes. They showed a "community of generally ignorant, bigoted people supercharged with emotion over the trial," wrote Crowther. This description would have resonated with *New York Times* readers familiar with hostile and biased legal proceedings in the South, such as the Emmett Till murder trial in Mississippi in 1955. "Something is made of mob psychology in this production," noted another film critic, with "religious fervor, even approaching fury." Other reviewers were more critical of these scenes. The opening "seems emptily pretentious and phony-sinister," argued Philip K. Scheuer.[74]

As it turned out, both scenes were invented, furthering stereotypes of fundamentalists and simplifying historical complexity. Scopes was not arrested in this way, nor did he spend any time in jail. Commentators on *Inherit the Wind* and letter writers to Kramer pointed out these "fundamentally important" departures from "the truth." "Scopes was not arrested in the course of persecution by bigots," corrected Julia Howard Griscom in *Films in Review*, "but as the result of volunteering to make a test case" of the law, in answer to a call from the ACLU. These scenes and other similar moments in the film meant the "townsfolk are painted all-black in one-dimensional strokes" and made "every character either black-black or white-white."[75] Brady's characterization as "vociferous" and "bombastic," for example, missed the important connections between antievolution and Bryan's reformist politics. Bryan embraced antievolution on seeing how so-called social Darwinists adapted the theory of natural selection to society and the economy. This adaptation naturalized and justified inequality in social and economic relations as the "survival of the fittest" and, in turn, made them harder to reform.[76] In this case, Bryan's larger political concerns and commitments actually dovetailed with elements of Kramer's liberalism. Such oversimplification may have created a better story. As historian Robert Rosenstone argues, the practice of historical filmmaking requires "strategies of representation"—including omission and condensation—to translate history to the screen. Yet *Inherit the Wind*'s reduction of historical complexity yielded a "fairly crude stacking of cards . . . in favor of good people (people who believe in the inviolable freedom of men's minds) and against bad people (puppets who don't)," the *New Yorker*'s Brendan Gill criticized.[77]

Even as Kramer and his colleagues sacrificed historical complexity in their stereotypical representation of key characters, they sought historical authenticity in their production design to achieve the "look" and "feel" of the past.[78] "A lot of historical research went into every aspect of the production," Kramer recalled. "We built the town square on the lot from scratch because we needed the authenticity of a true Twenties Southern town." The set was "exactly duplicating the Dayton court-room, even to the 1925 floor mike of radio station WGN (Chicago)," an important inclusion, as the Scopes trial was the first to be broadcast live to a national audience. The movie's costumes and makeup aimed to capture the style of the 1920s and the likeness of the historical figures. This aim required the most from March, who donned "face changing make up," a "false wig and stomach stuffing" to perform as "The Great Commoner," as Bryan was known.[79] The aspects of the film dedicated to achieving this "period look" are "reality effects," to borrow literary critic Roland Barthes's concept, descriptive details used to present a historical account as an "unvarnished representation of reality." The reality effects in *Inherit the Wind* drew comment. "Mr. Kramer has certainly succeeded in evoking the period and place of his story," the *Guardian*'s reviewer stated, with the "ancient automobiles and funny sartorial fashions." According to the *Hollywood Reporter*, the film's "production design captures all the charm and all the claustrophobia of the small, steamy Tennessee town." The music, again scored by Ernest Gold, was "carefully chosen and projected to give the period piece the perspective it needs."[80]

Kramer and his filmmaking team also sought historical accuracy in the plot for *Inherit the Wind*. With the screenplay, Kramer charged the writers Young and Smith with "sticking as close as possible to the transcript and descriptions of the trial at the time." Their research folder included *New York Times* articles and efforts to find recordings of the trial proceedings in the Library of Congress. Excitement over 1925 newsreel footage showing "the antics of the crowd in front of the courthouse" turned to disappointment with the discovery that it could not be screened. Not only were the film's "sprockets old-fashioned," but the film itself was "flammable."[81] Given their important role in ini-tiating the trial and defending John Scopes, the ACLU offered to con-tribute to the research. After all, the ACLU's associate director wrote, "it was our interest in testing the Tennessee law barring the teaching of evolution that resulted in this important civil liberties case being brought." Kramer responded that his team had "thoroughly prepared the background of the case" and "were mindful, of course, of the role played by the American Civil Liberties Union." Yet, even as Kramer made claims for historical accuracy, his film completely omitted the role of the ACLU. The movie also left out what the producer-director called "unpleasant elements in the story," perhaps referring to Bryan's refusal to condemn the Ku Klux Klan and Mencken's anti-Semitism. Such facts, he decided, "I will leave to the historians."[82]

Inherit the Wind certainly took dramatic license with the historical record, as with the arrest and jailing of Bertram Cates. In addition, both the play and the film included a romance between Cates and Rachel Brown, the daughter of the fundamentalist minister. Scopes, in fact, did not have a girlfriend, but the filmmakers wanted to "stress the young-love story," with Rachel, played by Donna Anderson, "torn between her love and her duty to her father."[83] Another subplot involved the wife of Brady, played by March's real-life wife, the actress Florence Eldridge. Although the playwrights Lawrence and Lee supported Kramer's "exciting screen translation of our play," they thought "the role of Mrs. Brady has been enlarged beyond its value in the total shape of the play." Film critics felt similarly, observing that her scenes "pad the film unnecessarily."[84] But the prominence of women in *Inherit the Wind*—although largely invented and unintentional—fit the history of the antievolution movement, where women took on a public role as mothers protecting their children from evolutionary teaching. The most melodramatic departure from historical fact moved Bryan's death up five days, so that the character of Brady collapses and dies at the very end of the trial. The *Los Angeles Times* considered this change "only a slight anticipation of history but still a questionably legitimate dramatic footnote to the trial." Taken together, these various inventions were both "true" and "false," in Robert Rosenstone's formulation, both engaging and ignoring the "discourse of history."[85]

This use and misuse of history also appeared in the film's promotion and publicity, "extratextual" efforts to forge a relationship between *Inherit the Wind* and the past. Kramer's team believed it would be far easier to promote this historical film than it had been for *On the Beach*, "as here we have no downbeat theme to fight against." Instead, the campaign guide recommended exploiting the playful, mischievous "monkeyshines" aspects of the "Monkey Trial." Suggestions included a guest appearance by "a local chimp" or the chimpanzee Jerry Ball, who was hired for a three-week tour to promote the movie: "he has cigarettes and will travel," Kramer's publicist assured.[86] "Have him host a screening for other anthropoids," or attend a biology or zoology class "and have a leading professor interviewed on his comparative intelligence to that of humans." Another publicity gimmick involved picketers holding signs with slogans such as "MAN'S RIGHT TO THINK IS NO MONKEY BUSINESS." Several posters for the film also featured chimpanzees, with one ostensibly reading Darwin's book. "In brief," the campaign guide suggested "anything that can tie in the idea of Evolution with fun and monkeyshines." As it turned out, this offbeat approach reflected the historical record. Cartoonists, songwriters, and owners of chimpanzees had exploited the monkey theme at the 1925 Scopes trial. Kramer felt it was important to depict "the carnival atmosphere of the small town at the time of the trial," and his publicist urged "using the monkey and the carnival, circus atmosphere" to sell the film.[87]

The publicity for *Inherit the Wind* drew on history in other ways. The year 1960 marked the thirty-fifth anniversary of the Scopes trial and, together with the film, led to July 21, 1960, being proclaimed "Scopes Trial Day" in Dayton, Tennessee. For that event, John Scopes, who had gone on to study at the University of Chicago and become a successful petroleum engineer, returned to Dayton for the first time. He also toured to promote the film. Although his handlers were warned "not to keep John Scopes up too late [or] force liquor on him," he was effective. "We need to guard those all-important freedoms—of thought and expression—and I thought maybe a picture show might accomplish something."[88] Kramer's publicity team also worked to get major city newspapers to reprint their original coverage of the trial, and Mencken's newspaper, the *Baltimore Sun*, agreed to do so. In the process, they discovered that other prominent figures covered the trial, and they sought endorsements from them for the film. Adlai Stevenson, who had just lost the Democratic Party presidential nomination to John F. Kennedy in July 1960, proved to be "much too busy at that time." But poet Carl Sandburg was available and called *Inherit the Wind* "one of the five greatest pictures ever made." "We should achieve long mileage," wrote Kramer's publicist, with these quotes.[89] In marketing the movie, the filmmakers further engaged with the past by releasing Leslie Uggams's recording of "Give Me That Old Time Religion" as a single and encouraging local restaurants to offer themed fountain drinks at 1925 prices. The proposed menu included Bryan Ale for 10 cents and Scopes Soda for 15 cents.[90]

These engagements with history outside the movie theater augmented the portrayal of the past within *Inherit the Wind*, which received both acceptance and admonition. "From American history," wrote one reviewer, "came the fantastic but factual story." The *Washington Post*'s critic discussed the film's "altered facets" but declared that "in dealing with history license must be taken."[91] Others disagreed and corrected historical inaccuracies and anachronisms, large and small. Philip K. Scheuer complained about the lack of authenticity in the costumes and makeup for the film's two stars. "March looks more like Bryan," he argued, "than Tracy looks like Darrow." A filmgoer questioned Kramer about the costuming of the local fundamentalist minister, who should not have appeared in a clerical collar. A "collar would be considered as too high church," he wrote, wondering "if your research people slipped up on this." A member of a preview audience for the film objected to the character of Hornbeck "eating a Delicious apple," as this "variety was not developed until the 1940s." She recommended "a small round McIntosh" as suitable "of that era." More generally, Brendan Gill complained that, due to "acts of melodramatic license," as spectators "we can never be sure whether we are in history or out of it." In the end, in Gill's opinion, *Inherit the Wind*'s attempt to be both "a valid account of something that actually took place" and "a valid work of artistic creation . . . fails on both counts."[92]

Despite such criticism of *Inherit the Wind*'s filmic representation of the Scopes trial, its historical interpretation of the trial, its significance, and legacy was largely accepted. For the filmmakers and playwrights, as well as popular writers and historians, the Scopes trial—despite a win for the prosecution—constituted a defeat for the fundamentalist antievolution movement and contributed to its decline over time.[93] By 1960, film critics and commentators assumed the issues at stake in the Scopes trial were long settled. For "an enlightened viewer," the subject of *Inherit the Wind* was "pretty much prehistoric water over the intellectual dam," argued Bosley Crowther. "Not many people are bothered by Darwin's theory of evolution today." He did note that "the law against its teaching is still on the books in Tennessee" and that "there are plenty of people who read the Bible literally." But, Crowther asserted, "there are few who have any disposition to try to enforce" either the law or "fundamentalist belief." The "film's issue of fundamentalism vs. science has undoubtedly lost its prime interest in this day and age," contended a *Los Angeles Times* critic. "In today's world," noted another reviewer, "scientific knowledge has become a more demanding requirement in the student curriculum."[94]

As became clear in the years following the 1960 release of *Inherit the Wind,* however, this liberal, secularist understanding of the outcome and impact of the Scopes trial was incorrect. The fundamentalist antievolution movement did not go down to defeat in Dayton in 1925. They succeeded in keeping the Butler Act in Tennessee and passing antievolution legislation in several other southern states. They also influenced high school science textbooks, which largely avoided discussions of evolutionary theory until the late 1950s. In the wake of the 1957 Cold War Sputnik crisis, when the Soviets successfully launched a satellite, the science curriculum in US schools underwent reform. New textbooks put more emphasis on concepts of evolution and reopened the debate between science and religion in America's classrooms. Legal challenges to antievolution legislation such as the Butler Act culminated in *Epperson v. Arkansas* (1968), which declared such laws unconstitutional. At the same time, the antievolution movement transformed itself into an advocate of "creation science," to be taught alongside "evolution science." Kramer later recognized this continuity rather than defeat for antievolution forces. "Even now we have contention between conservative fundamentalists and liberal humanists," he observed in the 1990s.[95] Despite the filmmakers' attention to getting the historical details in *Inherit the Wind* right, they joined other liberal intellectuals in getting the larger interpretation of history wrong.

Inherit the Wind's flawed depiction of antievolutionists and their movement in the past rallied their allies in the present. Kramer remembered "being hounded throughout the filming of the picture" when "religious groups heard rumors that it was going to be an anti-God movie." His publicist expressed an early concern that "the picture would meet with resistance from Fundamentalists or other Southern religious groups." Once the film was out, *Variety*'s reviewer cautioned that it "emphasizes the religion angle to a point that might arouse indignation or resentment among some audiences."[96] They were all right. Fundamentalists as well as conservative evangelicals wrote vehement letters to Kramer, protesting how *Inherit the Wind* "brands Bible-believing evangelicals and popular evangelists as irresponsible, ignorant and disreputable." "You have done us a great disservice," wrote one minister, "unless you are trying to inject venom into the life of our country today." They felt "the picture generally is slanted against Christians" and the film's "plea against bigotry" was contradictory, given the "bigotry" they saw directed against themselves. These religious critics assailed

Hollywood for making *Inherit the Wind* and similar movies, such as *Elmer Gantry* (1960). "How refreshing it would be," telegrammed one man, "to present a story of modern day Christians who are not blustering belching buffoons or wild-eyed fanatics wallowing in the mire of ignorance. The sheer novelty of it would set an all time box office record."[97]

The same could not be said for *Inherit the Wind*, despite being widely and mostly positively reviewed. "The entire town is buzzing about the fabulous reviews," wrote Al Horwits to Kramer. The film was "lively, crackling and stimulating entertainment," "an enthralling film," and "a masterpiece of entertainment." It made the lists of the year's best films in the *New York Times, St. Louis Post-Dispatch, Boston Sunday Herald, Philadelphia Bulletin,* and three Washington, DC, newspapers. It was even chosen by Trans World Airlines to test its new technology for in-flight film screenings.[98] Kramer also received praise for his "assured handling of the story and the people" as director and producer. Many considered *Inherit the Wind* "Stanley Kramer's finest, a film that puts him at the top as a director." *Variety* expected the film "should loom . . . big boxofficewise," and extremely positive responses from preview audiences, even in the South, indicated as much. "Without a doubt, this is the best motion picture I have ever seen," wrote one Houston film-goer. "It held this large theater audience spellbound for two hours." In Nashville the preview audience comments were "overwhelmingly good." But weekly box-office returns ranged from one-quarter to one-half of those of competing films and even Kramer's own, such as *On the Beach.* "I didn't have the heart to write you because business has been so bad on our picture," Kramer's colleague George Schaefer wrote. "Sorry not to be able to give you better news."[99]

Most of the reviews of *Inherit the Wind* "were extravagantly favorable," Kramer recalled, "but that didn't translate into box office success," and this failure "almost broke my heart." He first attributed this failure to his distributor, United Artists, refusing "to spend money on advertising and promotion." But a UA representative disagreed. "Where you get the idea that a $56,000 advance and opening week campaign is skimpy, I can't imagine."[100] Kramer's team soon decided their promotion strategy was problematic. "We know by now we have a top-quality film—if we can't sell it," Kramer wrote a colleague, "it will be our own fault in tactics." But marketing decisions—such as whether to seek intellectual or popular appeal—were difficult to make before Hollywood turned to audience research in the 1970s.[101] The fewer but still prominent negative reviews also contributed to poor box-office returns. "*Inherit the Wind* is a big, strident, broadly acted, fitfully entertaining, and nearly always irritating circus of a picture," Brendan Gill avowed. Arthur Knight felt the film "fails to live up to the size and dignity of its theme." "The fight against bigotry, reaction, and blind conformity continues; and Mr. Kramer must be applauded for his earnest contribution to it. But . . . earnestness is an inadequate substitute for true creativity."[102] Although few in number, these poor reviews appeared in prominent, influential publications.

Looming largest in Kramer's assessment of the film's financial failure, however, were the protests. "At every theater that showed the picture, there were demonstrations against it and against me for being notoriously anti-God."[103] Anticommunists, who understood Christianity as a bulwark against communism, asked, was the film "an effort to undermine one of our great free world institutions?"[104] The American Legion and Catholic War Veterans (CWV) considered Kramer's film to be "Communist propaganda" and "Red-tainted," and they advocated a boycott. An "intelligence briefing" from the CWV about *Inherit the Wind*, as well as *Exodus* and *Spartacus*, circulated among Kramer and his colleagues. It discussed Nedrick Young's appearance before HUAC in 1953 and his refusal "to affirm or deny Communist Party membership." "Members of the Catholic War Veterans and their families can help stop the Communist break-through [in Hollywood] by not patronizing these movies." "Ten years ago, the CWV was in the front line in helping repel the Communists. The 'war' is on again!" As one filmgoer pledged to Kramer, "I, therefore, protest your release of *Inherit the Wind* and refuse to see it, and will do all in my power to keep others from seeing it."[105] Kramer's colleagues tried to make light of these protestors. "Why don't they go after the Dodgers?" Al Horwits exclaimed. "They blew a 6–1 lead last night in Milwaukee and lost 7–6." The various groups opposed to the film certainly had a negative impact on box-office receipts—how much is difficult to ascertain—confirming Kramer's statement that "martyrdom comes hard."[106]

In the end, *Inherit the Wind* grossed only about $2 million worldwide and lost an estimated $1.7 million, but Kramer and his supporters stood by the film. "If profit and loss are the only valid criteria for selecting film subjects, then I made a big mistake, but sometimes there is great value in choosing to take an unpopular stand."[107] Many filmgoers and critics did recognize the intellectual and political value of the film. Whether on stage or on screen, *Inherit the Wind* incorporated content from science, religion, and the law, making it heavy on talk and demanding on audiences.[108] It "offers much that is thought-provoking—a rarity in film fare," concluded the *Chicago Tribune*'s Mae Tinee. At a special MPAA showing before Supreme Court justices and their families, those in attendance sided with the Scopes defense team and endorsed "a man's right to think and to teach." The intellectual content of the film also had political relevance, due to John F. Kennedy's Catholicism. "One impassioned plea by Tracy against pitting Catholics against Protestants, and vice versa, carried a contemporary shock lesson in what could happen in the current presidential campaign."[109] Such respect for the film secured it four Oscar nominations, including best actor for Spencer Tracy, best film editing again for Frederic Knudtson, best black-and-white cinematography for Ernest Laszlo, and best adapted screenplay. Within the context of Kramer's debate with the American Legion, the nomination of Nedrick Young, whose screenwriting credit was officially restored in 1997, and Harold J. Smith constituted another challenge to the Hollywood blacklist.

The most prominent honor for *Inherit the Wind*, however, was its selection as the official US entry for the 1960 Berlin International Film Festival. After the difficult challenge Kramer's company and United Artists faced in getting *The Defiant Ones* into the 1958 Berlin film festival, *Inherit the Wind*'s selection by the Motion Picture Export Association was straightforward. It came with "tacit support" from the USIA, "a sign the U.S. government has softened its opposition to 'controversial films,' especially for entry in international film festivals." Kramer felt that "this [was] a tremendous advance."[110] The festival's location in Berlin, a city divided between East and West and in the midst of ongoing Cold War crisis, lent great political significance to the proceedings. West Berlin mayor Willy Brandt acknowledged this fact in his opening speech: "I welcome all participants in the festival who have proved that Berlin is not an isolated island." The Berlin festival also was associated with serious, social problem films, and *Inherit the Wind* earned recognition as a "striking" example of the festival's preferred genre. Fredric March won a Silver Bear as best actor, as had Sidney Poitier, and the film was named best feature film suitable for young people. For Stanley Kramer, these awards proved he could "strike a responsive chord among Europeans," a success he hoped to repeat with his next historical film and in the very same German city.[111]

Poster for Judgment at Nuremberg *(1961). Courtesy of Margaret Herrick Library and MGM/UA.*

5 Holocaust History in *Judgment at Nuremberg*

A year and a half after *Inherit the Wind* won acclaim at the Berlin International Film Festival, Stanley Kramer's next film, *Judgment at Nuremberg*, based on an original screenplay by Abby Mann, premiered on December 14, 1961, in the very same city. A fictional film based on factual events, *Judgment at Nuremberg* depicted the trial of four judges for their crimes during the Nazi regime. Set in 1948, the film nonetheless related closely to events in 1961, a pivotal moment in both Holocaust remembrance and Cold War hostilities. That year, two major events focused attention on Germany's past and present: the ongoing trial of Nazi war criminal Adolf Eichmann in Israel and the East German Communist authorities building the Berlin Wall in August. In a striking instance of historical simultaneity, the announcement of Eichmann's guilty verdict and death sentence for crimes against the Jewish people coincided with *Judgment at Nuremberg*'s premiere in a city now barricaded between East and West. When Mayor Willy Brandt introduced the film, he thanked "Kramer, whom we know as a good friend of our city and of the Berlin Film Festival." His introduction connected the film's historical subject and current political events. "We cannot deny the fact," he contended, "that the roots of the present situation of our people, our country and our city lie in this fact, that we did not prevent right from being trampled underfoot during the time of Nazi power." "I consider the world premiere of the film *Judgment at Nuremberg* in the Congress Hall in Berlin as an important political event. . . . It will probably be difficult for some of us to watch and hear this film. But we will not shut our eyes to this."[1]

Brandt's introduction pleased and honored Kramer, his company, and United Artists, but the premiere's West German audience did not receive the film well. As Kramer recalled, "An elite crowd of German society sat there nervously but there was no talking, just stunned silence. At the end the audience simply left—no conversation, just utter quiet."[2] Several hundred of the world's press, representing some twenty countries, reported that the German spectators felt "cold outrage" and sat in "stoic silence." Kramer's film was a "grim lesson," a "cinematic blitzkrieg," and a "celluloid time bomb."[3] He and his stars were "cross-examined about their motives in making the film, as if they were politicians rather than artists." Bosley Crowther considered this event "Mr. Kramer's celebrated act of placing his head in the mouth of a lion."[4] "We came to Berlin not expecting total support or enthusiasm," Kramer said at the time. "There are many emotional factors involved for the Germans." This unfavorable reception was unsurprising. Just two months earlier, the German publication of William L. Shirer's *The Rise and Fall of the Third Reich* (1960) had been subject to "withering criticism" in West Germany for reviving anti-German feelings and harming US-German relations.[5] But German reviewers also believed that Kramer crassly exploited the contemporary political situation to further his film's promotion and profitability. It was "bad to premiere the Kramer film 'right in the shadow of the wall,'" they argued, and the film "urgently needed purification of taste." "The film was totally rejected," Kramer recalled. "It never did three cents' business in Germany. It played so many empty houses it just stopped."[6]

Although *Judgment at Nuremberg*'s reception was far more positive in the United States, even enthusiastic, it still did poorly with audiences at the box office and with reviewers equally convinced of Kramer's exploitation of a profound topic. This critique had chased Kramer since the start of his career and arose with his last three films, as he sought to make films on significant social and political subjects for commercial release and popular consumption. But with *Judgment at Nuremberg* the critique became full blown and widely known. Sharp-witted screenwriter and novelist Gavin Lambert labeled the film "an All-Star Concentration Camp Drama, with Special Guest Victim Appearances," a devastating characterization made worse when famed *New Yorker* critic Pauline Kael repeated it in her summation of Kramer's career a few years later.[7] Writing in the British Film Institute's *Sight and Sound*—formerly edited by Lambert—John Gillett called Kramer "the self-appointed conscience of the American cinema." Yet he contended that "Kramer the resourceful showman" always trumped "Kramer the social thinker." For *Time* magazine, the producer-director "arrogantly exceeded his judicial warrant" and "shrewdly timed the release of his movie to coincide with the reading of the judgment in the trial of Adolf Eichmann."[8] That the film's premiere date had been set back in February, before the Eichmann trial had even started, was overlooked in the rush to condemn Kramer for sacrificing good taste and taking unseemly advantage to benefit his movie.

Also overlooked in this condemnation of Kramer and his latest film was the responsibility to history that he and his Oscar-winning screenwriter Abby Mann felt. "I am Jewish," Kramer later stated. "I wanted to film *Judgment at Nuremberg* because those trials said something that I didn't think the world had fully grasped." A wave of neo-Nazi vandalism against synagogues in West Germany in late 1959 reinforced his concerns. The film's portrayal of "past history," he announced at the start of production in 1960, "is especially timely . . . in light of the neo-Nazism now becoming apparent." Also Jewish, Mann felt great compassion for the victims of the Nazis' Final Solution, which motivated his original script for television's *Playhouse 90*, aired in 1959, and on which he based his movie screenplay. "I wanted to pierce the lie; the big lie [in Germany] was, 'we didn't know about it.'"[9] Kramer and Mann shared with their fellow Jewish Americans a commitment to remembrance after the Holocaust, a commitment Kramer showed earlier with *The Juggler*. They also shared a liberal outlook. Mann's scripts for movies and television incorporated his passionate concerns for civil rights and civil liberties, and he joined Kramer in criticizing and challenging the Hollywood blacklist. Their decision to produce *Judgment at Nuremberg* reflected these ongoing personal and political commitments. "I can be more political in the movie than I was on television," Mann felt.[10] As a result, the interplay between the priorities of Hollywood and those of history shaped the production of *Judgment at Nuremberg*, just as it had with *Inherit the Wind*. But unlike the previous film's oversimplification of the past, this latest film yielded a complex portrayal. Within the volatile context of the Eichmann trial and Cold War crisis, Kramer and Mann crafted a historical film that prompted another meaningful public discussion and debate, in this instance about the most significant and tragic events of the twentieth century.

Authenticity and Artifice

Judgment at Nuremberg restaged and reworked an actual historical event: the 1947 Nuremberg trial of judges and legal officials of the Nazi regime, the so-called Justice Case. As Kramer, Mann, and their colleagues confronted the challenges of historical filmmaking, they made choices both toward and against history. The final film reflected the filmmakers' conscious effort toward authenticity and the evocation of the historical mood of immediate postwar Germany, and the casual acceptance of departures from them. The effort to recreate the look and feel of the past involved the use of reality effects, as had happened with *Inherit the Wind*. According to scholar Scott Windham, "a nearly documentary attention to historical detail" characterized *Judgment at Nuremberg* and created the expectation that the film is an "objective and accurate portrayal of past events."[11] Yet the inclusion of reality effects in *Judgment at Nuremberg* was highly selective. At times, such selection lent the film a "false historicity," that is, the appearance rather than the content of history, and drew notice and comment from filmgoers and film reviewers.[12] In choosing the settings, cinematography, and actors—elements of mise-en-scène—Kramer and his colleagues sought historical authenticity and introduced Hollywood artifice into their representation of the past.

By borrowing visual conventions or the look from documentary film, *Judgment at Nuremberg* conveyed a sense of authenticity, even as its characters, events, and dialogue were largely invented. Filmed in black and white and incorporating archival footage, the movie appeared to be an accurate account of the past, rather than a fictionalized representation. For some critics, the black-and-white photography gave the film a "documentary newsreel feel" and an "immediacy," which allowed viewers to relate directly to what they saw as the unmediated content of the film. Similarly, as scholar Judith Doneson emphasizes, *Judgment at Nuremberg* introduced "documentary footage into a fictional context," thus forging a direct relationship to historical discourse.[13] To open the film, the filmmakers used actual newsreel shots of the 1933 Nuremberg rally where Adolf Hitler and his Nazi Party celebrated their rise to power. Later in the movie, they used US Army Signal Corps footage of Nazi concentration camps filmed at the end of the war. As it turned out, the film's "visual mimicry of the documentary form" confused many viewers, who thought they had watched a documentary rather than a dramatic film. New York senator Jacob Javits praised it as "one of the most eloquent documentaries of our time."[14] Audience members at the film's preview in San Francisco in August 1961 expressed a similar misunderstanding, whether they liked the film or not: "Excellent but too documentary," "Too documentary for good entertainment," "I like documentaries and this one is very well done," "Excellent documentary picture." *Judgment at Nuremberg*'s "documentarist properties," as Windham argues, encouraged viewers "to believe that the story, while not 'really real,' is an accurate representation of the real thing."[15]

The film drew on another documentary convention—titles—to establish the film's place and time, aided by the movie's soundscape. In its dramatic opening, an iris shot of a swastika opens up to reveal the Nazi building it adorns, then the hated symbol blows up, accompanied by martial music. Making an aural connection to the past, Ernest Gold's music for *Judgment at Nuremberg* incorporated what one reviewer called "those now terrifying Nazi marching songs." Then a title appears—"Nuremberg, Germany: 1948"—but, in fact, most of the movie was made in Hollywood, California: 1961. "We could film only ten or fifteen percent of the picture in Germany, mostly exteriors," Kramer recalled. "This was a great disappointment to me, since I had hoped to film almost the entire picture there." In the decade and a half since the end of World War II, West Germans had rebuilt much of their war-torn country, making it difficult for the filmmakers to find damaged buildings and rubble-strewn locations. Early on, they even considered filming in East Germany. "But negotiating with the Reds to use their destroyed, damaged areas would undoubtedly be difficult," *Variety* reported in late 1960. The "Commies would probably consider it bad propaganda to show that they had not cleared away the destroyed buildings and rebuilt."[16]

The courtroom setting and its filming also posed a problem. Kramer wanted to film in the actual trial courtroom, but it was still in use every day. "I was allowed, however, to take measurements, descriptions, and photographs so we could construct it on a soundstage in Hollywood." In the process, they discovered that it was very long and wide; the distance between the attorney's box and the witness box was nearly forty feet. "That's a long distance if you try to photograph it!" As a consequence, set designers compressed the distance to twenty-eight feet. For Kramer, changing factual details to accommodate filmmaking did not undermine historical accuracy. "This was a very authentic situation," he contended, and reviewers agreed. "The Nuremberg Court has, of course, been reconstructed with meticulous accuracy."[17] Yet a "courtroom," Kramer noted, "is a very static set." To avoid filming the action in a theatrical manner, as if *Judgment at Nuremberg* were a stage play,

"I learned to move the camera often to achieve a sense of movement for the viewer."[18]

The filmmakers wanted spectators to immerse themselves in the story rather than having their attention drawn to the film's style, but the opposite happened. "Kramer's methods as director make heavy weather of the first half of the film," noted John Gillett, with his "highly mobile camera" gliding "around the speakers (sometimes in 360 degree pans) with an occasional zoom lens shot for emphasis." The camera zooms "backwards and forwards, as if on a piece of elastic," another reviewer observed.[19] Preview spectators felt similarly. "Mr. Kramer's direction and camera work became obtrusive and tricky." "At times the camera movement was distracting." In hindsight, Kramer agreed. "There's too much camera movement," he recalled.[20] Such noticeable cinematography increased viewers' awareness of *Judgment at Nuremberg* as a reconstruction of history rather than the realistic representation the filmmakers sought.

So, too, did the actors. Kramer cast seven major stars in his film: Spencer Tracy as Dan Haywood, the presiding judge; Richard Widmark as Colonel Tad Lawson, the prosecuting attorney; Maximilian Schell as Hans Rolfe, the defense lawyer; Burt Lancaster as Ernst Janning, the lead defendant; Marlene Dietrich as Madame Bertholt, the widow of a German general earlier executed for war crimes; and Judy Garland as Irene Hoffman and Montgomery Clift as Rudolph Petersen, two witnesses for the prosecution. For Kramer, this star power was necessary, as had been the case with *On the Beach*. "Do you think United Artists wanted to make *Judgment at Nuremberg*, the story of a trial?" "You could have heard a pin drop when I proposed it." To convince the company providing financing and distribution, "I studded it with stars to get it made so that I could reach out to a mass audience." Lancaster, for example, had just won a best actor Oscar for *Elmer Gantry*—*Inherit the Wind*'s twin film—and was considered a major box-office draw.[21] And members of the San Francisco preview audience generally loved seeing their favorite, familiar stars. "Judy Garland a rare surprise." "Judy was never better." "Richard Widmark steals the show! He and Clift are superb!"[22]

But those critics who panned the film often blamed the casting. "Director Kramer has stacked seven portentous names," *Time* reported, "above his portentous title—four of them are grossly miscast, but the customers won't realize that until too late." "With a fascinating cast luring me in, I had high hopes for this one," expressed one disappointed filmgoer, proving *Time* magazine correct.[23] Critics of the casting objected most to how these famous stars distracted from the plot and purpose of Kramer's film. According to *Daily Variety*, "in packing his picture with big stars, he has sacrificed some of the desired documentary flavor and authenticity so necessary in a project of this nature." Because "the familiarity intrudes on the spectator's consciousness," it made it difficult "to divorce actor from character."[24] Difficulty divorcing actor from character, given the power of intertextuality, appeared in evaluations of each of the stars' performances. Of course, Kramer's original casting decisions were shaped by the intertextual meanings the actors would bring from earlier films and their star personas to their roles in *Judgment at Nuremberg*.

For Tracy, Schell, and Dietrich and their characters, the casting largely worked. Kramer always wanted Tracy for the role of Judge Haywood. "I knew that if I had him in a picture, it would have a depth and candor that would make people notice." The character of Haywood possessed, in the words of legal scholar Suzanne Shale, "down-home, plain-speaking, salt-of-the-earth, and man-of-the-people American virtues." Those virtues included being fair-minded, impartial, and above political partisanship. That Tracy "fully identified with the principles he enunciates on the screen: The overriding sanctity of justice must prevail at all times under all circumstances," demonstrated consistency between character and actor.[25] In reprising his role from the 1959 televised version of *Judgment at Nuremberg*, the Austrian-Swiss Schell's characterization of defense counsel Rolfe also had integrity, accorded with his larger screen persona, and won him an Oscar for best actor, beating out his costar Tracy. While less uniformly applauded, Dietrich's performance as a "weary, arrogant aristocrat" and military widow appeared consistent with her on- and offscreen personality. She accepted the role after reading the first draft of the script only once, and Kramer considered her "a standard-bearer for us. She knew Germany."[26] The German-born actress had immigrated to the United States before the Nazi regime and was well known for her staunch anti-Nazism and strong support for American soldiers. The film recalls this personal history by including snatches of her signature song, "Lili Marlene," about a soldier's lost love. Even more, Dietrich noted, "I'm not fragile. I'm a daughter of the military." Like Tracy and Schell, Dietrich's "identity resonates beyond the frame."[27]

In contrast, Lancaster, Garland, and Clift were cast against type—Kramer's oft-used strategy—and thus were seen at the time and since as less suitable and less successful in their roles. Scholar Henry Gonshak minces no words: "bluntly put, Lancaster is awful." One reviewer attributed Lancaster's poor performance to the fact that he could not lose his "actor's personality" in the character of German defendant Janning.[28] In fact, Kramer originally wanted Laurence Olivier for the role. "The British," he recalled, "seem to have a knack for portraying Germans well," displaying his comfort with mixing artifice and authenticity. "The off-beat casting of Lancaster," one filmgoer commented, "never really comes off."[29] The casting of Garland and Clift also received criticism. Garland played a German woman who as a young girl figured in a notorious Nazi trial and execution of a Jewish man. She was a "nonrealistic" performer in a "supposedly realistic drama," noted one reviewer, and "sadly misplaced here." "Why, oh why, Garland? I expected her to break into Swanee or something," exclaimed one member of the preview audience. Clift performed as a mentally deficient German man and son of a communist sterilized by the Nazis as part of their eugenics program. "It is one of the most moving roles I've ever read," the actor confessed, but it was also a role seen as incongruous with his matinee idol past.[30]

Yet the star personas and performances of Garland and Clift focused attention on the terrors and traumas suffered by victims of Nazi crimes, an important departure from Hollywood films of the era. The two troubled actors were plagued by problems with drugs, alcohol, accidents, and suicide. Reviewers who saw consistency between their personal lives and their film characters felt the former lent emotional power to the latter. Kramer himself noted that Garland's personal problems "fitted perfectly with the role" of a woman "barely clinging to a semblance of sanity," while "illness had reduced [Clift] almost to the level of the unsound person he was portraying."[31] Many spectators and reviewers found Clift's and Garland's performances overly melodramatic and lacking in the credibility of a "constrained" and "minimalist" style of testifying expected of actual victims of the Third Reich. Historian Carolyn J. Dean has argued that such expectations are highly problematic as they "erase victims' experiences." Instead, Garland's and Clift's painful performances came closer to conveying what Dean believes is necessary: "manifest rather than mastered suffering."[32] The actors played their characters to accentuate, rather than allay, the distress and damage experienced by Nazism's victims. In this way, and contrary to expectations, the star casting in *Judgment at Nuremberg* achieved a measure of historical authenticity out of customary Hollywood artifice.

Historical Accuracy and Dramatic License

With regard to character and plot, Kramer, Mann, and their colleagues also negotiated between the priorities of history and those of Hollywood. At the time, they made different claims about the substance and extent of historical accuracy. In the lead-up to the film's release, the publicity campaign often emphasized *Judgment at Nuremberg* as a true representation. "As a European," stated Maximilian Schell's press release, he believed "Stanley Kramer's picture has the ring of authenticity." According to Richard Widmark's publicity statement, Kramer deserved respect for "producing and directing pictures to which historians of the future will refer and will say, 'That is how it was.'"[33] Yet, in working with Kramer on the screenplay for *Judgment at Nuremberg*, Abby Mann noted that they had two priorities: "One; was it truthful in the ultimate sense? And two; was it dramatic?" By qualifying "truthful" with "in the ultimate sense," Mann understood that the film could not be truthful in every aspect. This understanding compelled the filmmakers to clarify the movie's historical content. "It is based on historical fact, but we have taken the usual dramatic license to juggle dates to some extent and to combine actual characters for better entertainment values." Changing the chronology and using composite characters—as in *Inherit the Wind*—constituted both true and false inventions.[34]

At the time, Mann's screenplay was widely recognized as "scrupulously researched," as was his original script for *Playhouse 90*. "I first saw it live on *Playhouse 90*," Kramer recalled, and soon he had Mann working on a screenplay. "The resulting collaboration turned out to be the happiest I have had," Mann observed a few years later.[35] He read "thousands of pages of trial transcript"; as Suzanne Shale finds, "the screenplay quotes verbatim from American law and jurisprudence, and some of the characters' speeches bear traces of the Nuremberg pleadings." He traveled to West Germany and borrowed books on the Nuremberg trials from the Bavarian State Library in Munich.[36] He also corresponded with and interviewed historical figures from the time, including Abe Pomerantz, who served as a prosecutor at Nuremberg and early on sparked Mann's idea for the script. Meeting General Telford

Taylor, who had served as US chief counsel for war crimes, spurred Mann to focus on the later Justice Case rather than the first, most famous 1945–1946 Nuremberg trial of the major war criminals, such as Hermann Göring and Rudolf Hess. Taylor had provided an introduction on *Playhouse 90*. Mann's work was "a serious attempt to explore the significance of the Nuremberg trials," Shale argues, but "diluted in the process of preparing the commercial presentation."[37] She holds Kramer responsible for this dilution. At the same time, the producer-director sought historical legitimacy for his movie. He oversaw consultation and correspondence with Taylor as well as with Judge James T. Brand, who presided over the original Nuremberg trial; Justice Michael A. Musmanno, another judge at Nuremberg; and Supreme Court justice William O. Douglas, who even took the opportunity to visit the set. All four men augmented Mann's research and raised strong objections to the screenplay's departures from historical fact.

The characters in *Judgment at Nuremberg*, whether based on actual historical figures, composite creations, or wholly invented, became issues of contention. As scholars recognize, compression is almost always a strategy for historical filmmakers, as not every person involved in a historical event can be represented on screen. *Judgment at Nuremberg* was no exception. As Shale notes, the German judges on trial were more "in Nuremberg, but only four by the time they got to Hollywood." Mann based each of the four judges on an individual defendant, but in addition they were composite characters, combining a range of qualities and perspectives. They were also stereotypes, with Janning, the film's real focus, the proud, contradictory Teutonic figure, and the remaining defendants, Emil Hahn, Friedrich Hofstetter, and Werner Lammpe, a brutal Nazi, an obedient bureaucrat, and a broken old man, respectively. Despite being fictional characters, the four "as a group truthfully represent the collection of historical defendants," Windham argues.[38] Nuremberg prosecutor Taylor and Judge Brand did not feel the same about the actions of the characters representing themselves or each other: Lawson and Judge Haywood. Brand specifically objected to Lawson appearing drunk in the film. Taylor, he insisted, was never drunk. In turn, Taylor criticized the fictional Judge Haywood's behavior. "Judge Brand," he argued, "would not conceivably have behaved in such a manner as the script describes."[39] Of most concern was Haywood's friendly relationship with the invented character Madame Bertholt.

Madame Bertholt, the character played by Marlene Dietrich, was a "false invention." Unlike the invented supporting female characters in *Inherit the Wind* who, as it turned out, fit with the factual prominence of women in the US antievolution movement, Bertholt was a fictive element that "ignores the discourse of history."[40] Taylor took issue with any judge, much less Judge Brand, "establishing a friendship with the widow of a convicted and executed war criminal. I find it unthinkable that any of the Nuremberg judges would have established such a connection with anyone so closely affected by the trials." Taylor argued that "such conduct would be highly unjudicial and reprehensible." "It would have given rise to sharp criticism" at the time, and would convey to contemporary moviegoers "an unfounded and derogatory impression of the standards of judicial behavior at Nuremberg."[41] Critics and filmgoers agreed with Taylor. Gavin Lambert denounced the introduction of "a near ludicrous new character," as did audience preview members. "Would prefer omission of most of Marlene Dietrich episode," stated one, calling it "unrealistic" and adding, "no reflection on her acting but character distracts from real interest of the story." Importantly, the Bertholt character did not figure in Mann's initial outline for the movie, and Shale attributes her invention to Kramer.[42] Following Hollywood fashion, the producer-director likely wished to insert a romantic storyline and have a role for the iconic Dietrich in his movie, even if it contravened history.

These exchanges between Hollywood filmmakers and actual historical figures about the characters in *Judgment at Nuremberg* indicate the challenges of historical representation. According to philosopher Hayden White, "verisimilitude . . . is impossible in any medium of representation," and "historical individuals"—whether depicted on screen or page—require some measure of "characterization."[43] The filmmakers shared this understanding. After all, the studio's lawyer, Gunther Schiff, argued, the film's goal is "to depict in a fictionalized manner the essence of what occurred at Nuremberg. Accordingly, Lawson represents not Gen. Taylor but rather a composite picture of a fictional prosecuting officer," and "Haywood is not Judge Brand but is rather a judge who presides at his fictional trial." They were not intended to "depict any actual person." This response provoked a passionate answer from Taylor. "Of course, plays can be written about fictional trials, fictional judges, fictional generals, or anything else," he argued. "But one cannot write a play about a short, bald man in a cocked hat who is

Marlene Dietrich and Stanley Kramer in a production still for Judgment at Nuremberg *(1961). Courtesy of Margaret Herrick Library and MGM/UA.*

commanding the French troops at the Battle of Waterloo and say that this is not a play about Napoleon."[44] This debate about where to draw the line between fact and fiction revealed what for many is the "problem" with historical film: filmmakers viewing history as both essential and dispensable.

Contestation over the filmmakers' inventions in *Judgment at Nuremberg* occurred not only with characters but also with chronology. Mann set the film in 1948, rather than 1947, the year of the actual Justice Case. This date allowed him to connect legal developments at Nuremberg with rising Cold War tensions and conflicts, including the communist takeover of Czechoslovakia and the Berlin blockade and airlift that year. Placing the trial against this changing geopolitical background allowed Mann to introduce a key plot development. US officials are increasingly concerned about strengthening relations with Germany, a former enemy, in the face of deteriorating relations with the Soviet Union, a former ally. Within the context of these shifting alliances, the

Nuremberg trials become a liability as they risk antagonizing the Germans, and the film shows mounting pressure on prosecutor Lawson and Judge Haywood to ease up on the case. "The writing is on the wall," a visiting US senator tells Haywood and another colleague about growing US-Soviet animosity. "We're going to need all the help we can get." As *Variety* summed up, "the cold war is on and the Germans must be wooed."[45]

Mann drew on the views of Abe Pomerantz for this plot line. As he recalled, "Abe Pomerantz, who had participated in the trials, talked about the dilemma of what he felt was the deterioration of the trials because of Cold War politics." Judge Brand objected to the invention of geopolitical "pressures," which "did not exist in the slightest degree," and would have been "improper" and "rejected if they had existed."[46] But Mann and Kramer went with Pomerantz's perspective, and many critics found this plot development to be both effective and brave. Radical journalist I. F. Stone appreciated that the film showed how the "onset of cold war was leading US policy to soft-pedal anti-Nazism in the name of anti-Communism. It's a miracle that a Hollywood team would dare so sensitive an issue." Reviewer Ronald Steel believed that the United States' "sudden embracing of the Germans in the late 1940s, Nazis and all," was an important historical theme deserving even more attention than that given in the film. But "I suppose one should be grateful that Hollywood dared mention it at all."[47]

Not everyone shared this view; vociferous criticism came from anti-communists. "The film again and again, by innuendo and indirection, identifies American-German co-operation in resistance to communist aggression with Nazism," wrote William Henry Chamberlin. He blamed *Judgment at Nuremberg*'s focus on Nazi crimes for reviving "anti-Germanism," which hurt the Western alliance to the benefit of the Eastern bloc. "Some who see the film will question the sense of reopening old wounds now," *Life* magazine noted, "perhaps tending to estrange a free world ally and giving a propaganda wedge to the enemy."[48] One member of the preview audience saw "this movie as one of a series of hate productions. Why not save resentment for the Communist, instead of a party that is no longer in power? Let us live in the present not in the past." Writer Norbert Muhlen faulted the film's false chronology of events for setting up this plot line, noting that "in reality the last international war-crimes trial had been completed a year before the air-lift as much as began." The film "crudely distorts history," he argued.[49]

In defense, Mann asserted this aspect of the plot as a fictional device yet in keeping with a larger historical truth—in effect Rosenstone's concept of "true invention." The truth of this plot invention contrasted with the false inventions in *Inherit the Wind*'s plot that used dramatic license to perpetuate problematic stereotypes. Instead, Mann admitted that Cold War "pressures did not arise until later," after the completion of the 1947 Justice Case, but "they were a dramatic tool" and "had some historical background."[50] Indeed, commentators at the time and historians since supported the screenwriter's assertions. British historian Geoffrey Barraclough writing in the *Nation* in the early 1960s noted that the Cold War "wrought a subtle . . . change in our attitude to Nazi Germany." Telford Taylor prominently made the same point in a *New York Times* article on the Eichmann case in early 1961, just as *Judgment at Nuremberg* went into production. "The [Nuremberg] trials ended . . . and by then the division of Germany and the cold war had wrought a marked change in the international atmosphere. It was all too easy to put aside uncomfortable questions about the past, or even to indulge the thought that although Hitler had gone too far on the Jewish Question, he had certainly been right about the Russians, whose menace the Western Allies were just beginning to realize."[51] Moreover, in the decades since, historians have reinforced the film's interconnections among the Cold War, the US alliance with West Germany, and official American reluctance to confront the Nazi past.

Historians Hasia Diner and Deborah Lipstadt have paid attention to the dilemma this new international situation created for American Jews, a dilemma shared by Kramer and Mann and reflected in *Judgment at Nuremberg*. "Despite American Jewish concerns that Germany had failed to truly confront its unprecedented acts of brutality," Lipstadt argues, "there was little that could be done." Given Germany's, and especially Berlin's, location on the front lines of the Cold War, at the border between East and West, US officials aimed to renew and revitalize them to prove to the Communist bloc the superiority of democratic capitalism. "Their country," according to Diner, "now consorted with and celebrated Germany, the place that in their lexicon embodied the deepest evil."[52] Within this context, the film's "true invention" is not just an example of dramatic license but also a political and historical intervention. If chronology is the foundation for all historical work, then changing chronology can be seen as fundamentally ahistorical or even antihistorical. Yet, with *Judgment at Nuremberg*, Kramer and his team engaged in historical practice despite falsely setting the film in 1948 instead of 1947, because the aim was to show truthfully the impact of Cold War geopolitics on the history and memory of Nazi crimes.

Perpetrators, Witnesses, and Filmic Representation

With *Judgment at Nuremberg*, Kramer, Mann, and colleagues constructed a filmic representation of the Nuremberg trials, Nazi crimes, and the Holocaust that demonstrated their dual commitments to drama and history. The filmmakers drew on conventions associated with the genre of courtroom drama in crafting their story. In courtroom drama, the audience is positioned as an invisible jury, with the filmmakers presenting evidence of guilt or innocence and filmgoers encouraged to render judgment along with the characters in the film.[53] As a result, the filmmakers decided to feature surviving witnesses alongside Nazi perpetrators in *Judgment at Nuremberg's* fictional courtroom. This decision departed from the actual Nuremberg Justice Case and, in fact, was more consistent with the Eichmann trial in Israel, which featured one hundred Holocaust survivors as witnesses for the prosecution. But then, as scholar Pierre Sorlin asserted, "contemporary circumstances" always have shaped historical film—perhaps even more than the past the film depicted.[54] Witnesses as important characters increased *Judgment at Nuremberg's* commercial viability, and, at the same time, aided its larger historical validity. In dramatic terms, witness testimony was more stirring for audiences than having prosecutors read historical documents into the trial transcript, as happened at the original Nuremberg trials. In historical terms, the film's emphasis on witness testimony gave "voice to the victims" and compelled "the world to listen," as Lipstadt demonstrates about the Eichmann trial.[55]

Two witnesses were the characters portrayed by Montgomery Clift and Judy Garland. Clift's Rudolph Petersen is heartbreaking as a victim of Nazi sterilization, and Garland's Irene Hoffman endures testifying and cross-examination about her allegedly sexual and therefore illegal relationship with an older Jewish man. Their testimony provoked the most criticism *Judgment at Nuremberg* received from the PCA. The PCA's Geoffrey Shurlock wrote Kramer, "the subject of sexual sterilization, while used with complete and total validity within the framework of this story, seems to us to be emphasized beyond the point of discretion." He also wanted a change to the dialogue involved in the interrogation of Hoffman. "We ask that you try to find a somewhat softer phrase for 'sexual relations.' Very plain spoken language like this seems to be part of the problem the industry is facing today." The filmmakers ended up removing eleven uses of "sterilization" in the script and changed the mention of a sexual relationship to a "physical" one. "This leaves us the basic minimum references of 'sterilization,'" Kramer argued, "which is, after all, a matter of scientific record, court record, and is a word in common usage. I feel that this will be satisfactory to your needs and I would undertake extreme care and taste in the remaining instances." This conflict with the PCA revealed the conservative moral vision behind its rulings.[56] But it also indicated the impact the emotionally charged testimony of these two witnesses could—and in fact did—have on spectators.

The third prominent witness in the film was prosecutor Lawson, played by Richard Widmark. He provided his own testimony and also introduced, narrated, and verified for the court documentary liberation footage filmed by the US Army Signal Corps. Mann's script describes Lawson's emotions during his testimony: "The horror on his face . . . the astounding revelation of what human beings can do to one another." With US forces in the liberation of Nazi camps at the end of World War II—"a turning point in Western consciousness," in the words of historian Robert H. Abzug—the fictional Lawson witnessed horrific scenes of the aftermath of Nazi killing and torture.[57] He is sworn in to offer firsthand evidence of Nazi crimes, and he brings to his testimony all the "moral righteousness" that came "from the liberating perspective."[58] Supreme Court justice William O. Douglas strongly objected to Lawson taking the stand and urged changes to the screenplay. "This is not proper procedure," he wrote Kramer. "A prosecutor is not supposed to be a witness in the case he prosecutes." Kramer argued that this element reflected the "necessity of building dramatic character," and Lawson remained a witness.[59] For some reviewers at the time and scholars since, his testimony is a "harangue" and "histrionic." Yet actor Richard Widmark conveyed the sense of witnessing as "compelling, necessary, and ultimately redemptive." In this way, he brings the moral authority and urgency of historical eyewitnesses to his trial testimony.[60]

What gave Lawson's testimony such impact was his screening of the documentary liberation footage, making the film itself into a witness. This footage also had appeared in the film *Nazi Concentration Camps* (1945). Produced for the first Nuremberg trial, and then used again with additional footage in the Eichmann trial, *Nazi Concentration Camps* incorporated footage shot by American and British forces when liberating Nazi camps in 1945. The images of the aftermath of Nazi atrocities at Buchenwald and Bergen-Belsen shown in *Judgment at Nuremberg* are now well known, but they remain shocking and traumatic. "This 15-minute sequence is probably the most horrifying and sobering indictment ever shown in a Hollywood film," Ronald Steel declared in his review in the *Christian Century.* "The corpse-strewn trenches, the piles of human hair, the still-smoking crematoriums, the stacks of emaciated bodies serve as a grisly witness to the prosecutor's—and indeed humanity's—case against the Nazis." This film footage alternates with reaction shots from the courtroom audience, which Mann's script pictures. "There are the ones who refuse to see what their eyes tell them. There are the ones who stare incredulously that this nightmare really happened . . . some of them weeping sentimentally," Mann charges. "They weep today and would not raise a finger to do anything different if the same events were to take place tomorrow."[61] Scholars warn against viewing this "highly mediated visual record" as "undirected raw footage" and assuming that these images "speak for themselves." *Judgment at Nuremberg,* however, presents the film as "equivalent to truth," just as it was presented elsewhere. Lawson provides authentication for the footage, testifying that he was an eyewitness to the actual scenes depicted and to the filming of them.[62]

The graphic footage in *Judgment at Nuremberg* garnered much attention, most of it negative, from contemporaries and later from scholars. A few praised the "film within the film." Steel felt "gratified that Kramer has had the courage to show these scenes," although Mann deserves ultimate credit as this footage first appeared in the original television program. Far more commentators offered criticism. Scholars have criticized Kramer's handling of the footage as neither "artistically successful" nor "a satisfactory means of educating the audience about the Holocaust," as Henry Gonshak summarizes.[63] Contemporaries reacted more strongly. For William Henry Chamberlin, its inclusion reinforced anti-Germanism: "how the emotional and propaganda cards are stacked!" *Time* magazine attributed the footage to Kramer's crass exploitation and desire to shock his audience: "to complete his crescendo of sensationalism, Kramer cuts to some film clips of Buchenwald and starts bulldozing piles of corpses toward the horrified customer." In *Commentary,* Jason Epstein thought the images were "so absolutely overpowering in their gigantic obscenity . . . that even the censors in Hollywood should have intervened," as had the censor in London when French filmmaker Alain Resnais's *Night and Fog* (1955) screened.[64]

These negative reactions demonstrated "the act of witnessing for American audiences as unpleasant, shocking, repulsive," as scholar Jeffrey Shandler found with newsreels reporting on the liberation of Nazi camps in 1945. In 1961 members of *Judgment at Nuremberg*'s preview audience confirmed this fact, finding the footage "gruesome" and "dreadful." More recommended cutting this footage than suggested any other change to *Judgment at Nuremberg*. "Eliminate concentration camp films." "Atrocities should not be shown." "The movie scene of the atrocities was in very bad taste—did not belong in this picture." "I think you can omit the prison films. It happened a number of years ago and we are quite aware of what happened."[65] What is evident from this criticism is the absence of the "transformative impact" of witnessing evidenced by the testimony of Widmark's character.[66] Kramer and Mann hoped to have such an impact on their audience. But contemporary spectators of *Judgment at Nuremberg* confirmed what historian Toby Haggith forewarns: the "danger that the viewer becomes hardened and even brutalized" by viewing such horrific images over time, "distancing us from what the Holocaust meant in human terms." Despite this strong negative response from the preview audience, and the scholarly assumption that Hollywood tends "to avoid confronting or offending the public, or even to try and appease the audience when the subject is as disturbing as the Holocaust," Kramer retained the footage. These viewers did not deter the producer-director from fulfilling one of his goals for the film: as he put it, to "convey the horror of what the Nazis did."[67]

Many observers felt the witnesses—whether characters or documentary footage—failed to provide convincing evidence of the perpetrators' guilt. "There is a wide distance between a corrupt judiciary and the concentration camps," noted one reviewer. Judge Brand informed the filmmakers that the evidence provided by witnesses in the screenplay was not enough to convict the perpetrators "under the applicable rules and procedures of Nuremberg." Mann revised the script so that Lawson presents "ample evidence" in documents to support conviction. Even so, the witnesses still provided "the major dramatized evidence." Legal experts similarly criticized the use in the Eichmann trial of witnesses who had no connection to the defendant, but the prosecution's aim, according to Lipstadt, was to "paint the broad picture of the entire destruction process."[68] *Judgment at Nuremberg*'s filmmakers shared this aim and the use of witnesses to achieve it. They also made reactions to witnesses into the crucial moments when perpetrators admitted their guilt. While viewing the film footage during their trial, the defendants, apart from Janning, appear to recognize their personal responsibility for Nazi crimes.

In addition, Kramer and Mann included direct admissions of wrongdoing from the defendants. After viewing the footage in the courtroom, the defendants return to jail and discuss the concentration, or, more accurately, extermination camps with another character, drawn directly from history and a defendant in another trial at Nuremberg, Oswald Pohl. Pohl is linked to Eichmann in the script as having run the camps, and he cold-bloodedly confirms the mass killings perpetrated there. The climax of the film, however, is a confessional outburst from Burt Lancaster's character, Ernst Janning. He later admits that he and every other German knew about the Final Solution. "Maybe we didn't know the details," he admits. "But if we didn't know, it was because we didn't want to know." By including the confession of a Nazi perpetrator in *Judgment at Nuremberg*, Kramer gave audiences the "psychic satisfaction" never provided by the Eichmann trial, which ended without an "unequivocal admission of guilt" from the defendant.[69]

Particularism, Universalism, and Historical Interpretation

Kramer's *Judgment at Nuremberg* not only offered a filmic representation of the Nuremberg Justice Case but also a historical interpretation of those events. The producer-director believed "the story of the War Crimes Trials in which a new standard of international justice is established" held world significance.[70] For its time, the movie offered an innovative interpretation of the meaning of these events. Specifically, the film made cases for what in Holocaust studies has come to be called "particularism" and "universalism" in assessing the causes and consequences of Nazi crimes. Particularism held Germany wholly responsible for Nazi crimes and recognized Jews as the primary targets and victims; with universalism, many people and nations were to blame and persecuted. This interpretation again was less consistent with the actual Justice Case than with the Eichmann trial and shaped by both dramatic and historical factors. Kramer and Mann sought interest and immediacy for audiences and aimed to present a more complex and complete picture of the past. In focusing on the responsibility of Germans and the persecution of Jews, as well as seeing blame and victimhood as widespread, they may have muddled the film's message, as some viewers at the time and since felt. Yet, in offering an interpretative mix of particularism and universalism, *Judgment at Nuremberg* more fully portrayed the complexity of history and the multiple causes and consequences of historical events.

At the climax of the film, Janning's dramatic confession helped make the case for particularism by clearly conveying, as did the Nuremberg and Eichmann trials, the responsibility of German defendants for Nazi crimes. Janning's testimony contradicted the claims of ignorance from German characters earlier in the film. In an emotional exchange with Judge Haywood, Madame Bertholt declares, "We didn't know," and she asserts that only the Nazi leadership "knew what was happening." Haywood's German servants, a married couple, similarly profess their innocence. "Very few Germans knew," Mrs. Halbestadt says, although her husband hints at broader knowledge and guilt: "And if we did know, what could we do?" Some film reviewers criticized the fact that the "German people are on trial." For German filmgoers at the Berlin premiere, "again and again, the accusing finger points and a voice says: 'It was not only Hitler who was to blame, but you, and you, and you.'" William Henry Chamberlin—echoing Mr. Halbestadt—offered a defense: "the average German could not have prevented what a small group of fanatics and sadists did in concentration camps." "People asked how could I, an American, try to rekindle German guilt?" Kramer recalled. "Well, I said that it would indeed have been better if the Germans had made it, but the fact is they didn't. So I did."[71]

For most critics and viewers, however, *Judgment at Nuremberg* made a bold statement about the "most haunting of questions, the degree of involvement of all levels of German society in the awesome criminality of the Nazi regime." "Did they really know nothing? Is such a thing possible?" asked a reviewer for the newspaper of Herut, the Israeli right-wing party. "*Judgment in Nuremberg* rejects these apologetics as absurd." "The direct statement of the picture is the measure of guilt to be assumed by those who 'went along' with Nazism," noted the *Hollywood Reporter*'s critic.[72] Ronald Steel believed the film's message carried even more power "at a time when nearly everyone . . . is eager to bury the Nazi past." The former first lady Eleanor Roosevelt concurred in her regular newspaper column. "It must have taken courage to produce this film at this time—a time when most of us have forgotten what went on in Germany before and during World War II."[73] Preview audiences also agreed. "Thank god no whitewashing of the German people." "The subject matter . . . was very good; pertinent aspects and ideas concerning Germany's guilt were well brought out." "It outlined and detailed the German character perfectly in their denial of knowledge and or responsibility." "Hope producers have the courage to show Germans in their own language."[74] Indeed, at the film's West Berlin premiere in December 1961, the filmmakers did not shy away from this message. Kramer argued that the film "was a challenge to the German body politic," and Widmark "declared that the Germans must accept responsibility for the past." This message rang true for the "French, Belgian and Dutch spectators" at the premiere, who had not forgotten the "German wartime occupation of their countries."[75]

Yet, unlike the Nuremberg and Eichmann trials, *Judgment at Nuremberg* also makes the case for universal responsibility and guilt for the crimes of Nazism. As Judith Doneson contends, the film "simultaneously points the finger of guilt at Germany and universalizes this guilt." The filmmakers aimed to engage and involve viewers personally in the historical events depicted in their film and to demonstrate the relevance of the past for the present. "It is to the conscience of humanity that this film addresses itself," Kramer declared.[76] Following Janning's confessional outburst, defense attorney Rolfe attempts to salvage his case and save his client. "Ernst Janning says he is guilty. If he is, Ernst Janning's guilt is the world's guilt. No more and no less." Rolfe cites damning evidence of international collaboration with Hitler and the Nazi regime, such as the Vatican's 1933 Concordat, the Soviet Union's 1939 nonaggression pact, and American weapons manufacturers, arguing, "The whole world is as responsible for Hitler as Germany." Due to such content, the PCA ruled that the film treated Germany both "sympathetically and unsympathetically."[77] Critics and viewers similarly saw the film as spreading the blame for Nazism. "The focus is on Germany, but in a larger sense it could be on us, too." "Who is responsible?" John Gillett asked. "For Kramer, the answer is: all of us, for Fascism existed because too many people, within Germany and outside, allowed it to flourish." "To a great extent we were all guilty," wrote a member of the preview audience, including "all of us who are too cautious to speak out against evil," added Steel.[78]

The idea of universal guilt—especially the portion borne by the United States—is reinforced at several key moments and contradicts historian Peter Novick's argument that Americans invoked the Holocaust "to celebrate, by showing its negation, the American way of life."[79] When one witness testifies that the Nazis condemned even children to die by hanging, the camera cuts to an African American soldier standing as a guard in the courtroom, reminding the audience of the long history of lynching in the United States. Early on in the film, Rolfe calls into question the right of the former Allied nations to judge Germany; his main target is the United States. While discussing the Nazi sterilization of Rudolph Petersen, for example, he offers an infamous 1927 quote from Supreme Court justice Oliver Wendell Holmes in support of a similar eugenic policy in Virginia: "Three generations of imbeciles are enough." In rejecting US "moral superiority," Rolfe then evokes the tragic consequences of the atomic bombs dropped on Hiroshima and Nagasaki at the end of World War II. "Thousands and thousands of burnt bodies! Women and children!" Bringing even more emotional force to these legal arguments is Maximilian Schell's powerful performance as Rolfe in these scenes; *Time* magazine called his final speech "a pulverizing passage of eloquence."[80]

Kramer and Mann not only made these connections between Nazi Germany and the United States but also posited a "continuum" from World War II to the Cold War. "Mr. Kramer throws a cold, revealing light upon international morality—the morals of nations." *Judgment at Nuremberg* presented "the history of the past thirty years as a single unit held together by the presence of a tendency in the modern world toward mass violence, particularly when national interests are threatened," wrote Jason Epstein in *Commentary*. For critic Hollis Alpert in the *Saturday Review*, "the film tells us, in effect, that we became more concerned with security than with morality and justice" with the Cold War, just as Ernst Janning and his fellow judges did in Nazi Germany.[81] This message was very meaningful to Mann, as he wanted to use the film's story to comment not only on the history and legacy of the Nuremberg trials but also on American anticommunism, including McCarthyism and the Hollywood blacklist. "I tried to put together a movie of ideas," he later stated. "What I was trying to say was that patriotism can be evil." Countries and their citizens must stand up for principles, "particularly in times when it is most difficult to stand for principles. It is the only way one can keep from becoming the enemy." Similarly,

Kramer stated, "I am interested in . . . what we in America stand for. This interest is what attracted me to *Judgment at Nuremberg*." Both men wanted to remind the people of the world, especially Americans, of the importance of standing for "Justice, Truth, and the value of a single human being," in Judge Haywood's words.[82]

Just as *Judgment at Nuremberg* made cases for both particularism and universalism with regard to the causes of Nazi crimes, the film did the same with the consequences by showing Jews both as singled out for Nazi persecution and as one targeted group among many others. Consistent with the Nuremberg trials themselves, which charged the defendants with war crimes and crimes against humanity, Kramer and Mann generally are seen as universalizing the victims of Nazi crimes. "We have penetrated deeply into the souls of people accused of being associated with the most hateful crimes against a large portion of humanity," Kramer argued. As Judith Doneson points out, neither of the two major witnesses for the prosecution—the characters played by Clift and Garland—are Jewish, implying that Jews were not uniquely victimized by Nazi Germany. Lawson's narration of the documentary footage from the Nazi camps repeats much of the original *Nazi Concentration Camps*'s narration and adds to this impression. "Who were the bodies?" he asks. "Members of every occupied country of Europe." "In *Judgment*, the Jew," notes Doneson, "becomes a partner in suffering along with Czechs, Poles, Communists—in other words, with the rest of humanity."[83] In this way, the film weighted more toward universalism than particularism with regard to victims.

Yet *Judgment at Nuremberg* also can be viewed as demonstrating Nazism's specific, devastating impact on European Jews. The Nuremberg trials were remembered as bringing the world's attention to, and documenting, the persecution and murder of European Jews. An article summed up the film's plot as "the trial of the German judges who had condemned countless Jews to death, because of their religion."[84] Also critical was the simultaneity of the Eichmann trial, which convicted the defendant of crimes against the Jewish people specifically, and he is referred to as a Nazi perpetrator in the film. The testimony of Garland's Irene Hoffman focused attention on the racial laws of the Nazi regime, one of "the main stages in the genocide process." Her relationship with an older Jewish man, Lehmann Feldenstein, had led to his trial, conviction, and execution under Nazi *Rassenschande* (race shame) law. Mann used this case—based on an actual one—to show that Nazi laws "were

absolutely repugnant, and should never have been imposed."[85] Moreover, Lawson's narration of the documentary footage, quoted above,
continued. "Two-thirds of the Jews of Europe exterminated," he specified. "More than six million according to reports from the Nazis' own
figures." In naming "the six million," the film used a powerful phrase
in circulation at the time to connote and memorialize the number of
Jewish deaths during World War II. Reviewers and commentators often
used this phrase to refer to Jewish victims. "In a somber courtroom set
in Hollywood, genocide is as current these days as it is . . . in Jerusalem,
where Adolf Eichmann is being tried for responsibility for the deaths
of six million Jews," opened a *New York Times* article on the making
of the film.[86]

The film's case for particularism with regard to Jewish victims was
evident among Jewish American respondents. They understood the
film as representing the Holocaust. At the time, this term was only beginning to be used to refer to the genocide of European Jews by Nazi
Germany, but a filmgoer used the term in a letter to Kramer. "As a Jew
I feel the desire to utter or to shout expressions of gratitude for the ex-
position you have offered," he wrote. "It deals with a holocaust in terms
of the individuals who perpetrated and suffered—and are yet perpetrat-
ing and suffering—the holocaust." As one reviewer stated, "no trial, no
judgment with the punishment that is meted out to the guilty can ever
bring back to life an army of six million men, women, and children."[87]
Organizations such as the American Jewish Congress and the American Association for Jewish Education recognized the film, Kramer, and
Mann for contributing to the Jewish community and the "Jewish Interest." Scholar Alan Mintz, who argues that the film universalizes the
Holocaust, qualifies his argument by recalling how meaningful the film
was to him, his family, and his community as American Jews. "*Judgment at Nuremberg* was the first time in general American mass culture
in which the terrible things that had been done to the Jews of Europe
were being publicly acknowledged."[88] Mintz's personal recollection of
the film's particularistic meanings is as convincing as the evidence he
marshals for universalization.

The film's attention to the "dialectical element within the interpretation of Holocaust" set it apart from most popular representations of
its era and met with a mixed response.[89] Reviews in Israeli newspapers
indicated how the movie's cases for both particularism and universalism provoked a range of opinion. The reviewer for *Herut* conveyed

how both could be integrated into an interpretation of the causes of Nazi crimes. "Stanley Kramer believes that the whole world is guilty of war crimes and is responsible for them, and more than everybody, the German people are to blame." But the left-wing newspaper *Davar* condemned the effort to offer a more complex interpretation as confusing and ineffective. In one review, the critic attributes this interpretation to Kramer's indecision: "He does not acquit and does not convict the German people. He does not make a decision, and thus leaves both sides unsatisfied. Those who think that the entire German people are to blame, because they knew and kept their silence, are not satisfied because of the movie's forgiving tone. And those who object to blaming an entire nation for the crimes of its leaders probably see in it outrageous injustice and an unnecessary condemnation." Another reviewer in *Davar* more damningly accused Kramer of "his beautiful flirt with the Germans in *Judgment in Nuremberg*" and attributed the film's confusion to mercenary motives. "And if Kramer has ever avoided giving a clear answer, it was for commercial reasons."[90] This multiplicity of readings of the film in Israel—apart from the reviewers' tendency to miss Mann's fundamental contribution—and elsewhere demonstrated well the challenges and difficulties of conveying and comprehending such historical complexity through film.

History, Hollywood, and the Holocaust

Even so, Kramer, Mann, and their colleagues crafted a historical film that offered an ultimately truer way to understand the causes and consequences of Nazi crimes that enriched the public dialogue and debate. Contemporary respondents to *Judgment at Nuremberg* engaged with the historical questions it raised. "Besides your magnificent production being fundamentally entertainment, it is, notwithstanding, a most thoughtful, provocative and important historical document," wrote one of Kramer's fellow producers. "Above everything else, it has the authenticity of history, and the impact of great drama," contended a Jewish leader.[91] Most members of the preview audience concurred. "A terrific representation of the Nuremberg trials." "A good historical account." "It was magnificent. It was the truth." "Unfortunately the only bad thing in the movie was the fact that it was true." There were prominent exceptions, such as historical figures General Taylor and Judge Brand and anticommunist commentators, who objected to the film's historical claims. "Many things portrayed are disputable of course," protested one filmgoer at the film's preview.[92] Yet even respondents critical of the film's historical content participated in discussions of the meaning and significance of the important and catastrophic events initiated by it. "But don't let's carp too much," cautioned W. J. Weatherby in the *Guardian*. "We have a rare and timely debate."[93]

Also rare and timely was *Judgment at Nuremberg*'s contribution to Hollywood's engagement with the history of the Holocaust. At the time, Kramer and Mann's film was considered one of a few American motion pictures to take as a subject the crimes and tragedies of the Nazi era. The film was a "political event, a film of courage and artistry." But their early filmmaking efforts cannot be categorized as an example of what has come to be called "the Americanization of the Holocaust."[94] In general, the Americanization of the Holocaust was the process by which a catastrophic European event became an American moral touchstone. Crucial to this process were American cultural representations of the Holocaust, including books, theater, movies, and television.

Hollywood films and popular culture forms about the Holocaust are often characterized as—and criticized for—offering redemptive universal narratives about the Holocaust and avoiding confronting audiences with the grim reality of Nazi genocide and Jewish tragedy.[95] Other films appearing in the same years as *Judgment at Nuremberg* established the optimistic Hollywood approach to the Holocaust. The *Diary of Anne Frank* (1959), for example, ends with her final voiceover, "In spite of everything, I still believe that people are really good at heart." "Anne Frank's book ends in a forgiving tone," stated a review in Israel's most widely read national newspaper, *Maariv*, which then went on to differentiate it from Kramer and Mann's film: "Unlike the movie *Judgment in Nuremberg*, which leaves this cruel time hanging in the air."[96] Their film may have been an American-centric story of the Nuremberg trials. After all, the filmmakers were credited with "dramatizing concepts of American justice" by the American Bar Association, Judge Haywood "was steeped in American traditions of justice," according to Eleanor Roosevelt, and a filmgoer in San Francisco exclaimed that the film "showed the true American ideal of justice!"[97]

But the inclusion of witnesses and perpetrators, universalism and particularism meant *Judgment at Nuremberg* did not deny the "unbearable facts" of the larger history. The filmmakers did not simplify or sanitize this history to satisfy the audience. Robert Hatch of the *Nation* felt the film was constructed "with exemplary bitterness."[98] The film's avoidance of the typical Hollywood "happy ending" reinforced this fact. Instead of finishing with Spencer Tracy's Judge Haywood giving his impassioned speech about truth, justice, and the value of human life, which would be consistent with those films exemplifying the optimism ostensibly central to the Americanization of the Holocaust, the film ends with this pessimistic title: "On July 14, 1949, judgment was rendered in the last of the Nuremberg Trials. Of ninety-nine sentenced to prison, no one is still serving his sentence." Brendan Gill of the *New Yorker* felt "the title not only serves as an integral part of the picture but is its chilling climax." "That final card made me gasp for its truth and courage," Albert Maltz wrote Kramer from Mexico.[99] For Kramer and Mann, as with American Jews generally, the commutation of death sentences against Nazi criminals and pardons for others serving jail sentences that occurred in the early 1950s were devastating. They conveyed "an irrevocable truth," as Mann wrote, "that justice was tempered in the treatment of the Nazis" to foster better US–West German diplomatic relations.[100]

Two historical figures, Judge Brand and Justice Musmanno, strongly if unsuccessfully contested this final statement. Both men pointed out the inaccuracy of the final statement, as it failed to acknowledge the number of Nazi criminals sentenced to death and still in jail. More importantly, they feared the statement "left a feeling of futility for the whole war crimes procedure," even "if some of the defendants were later released." Musmanno felt the filmmakers sought to "derogate what the United States accomplished at Nuremberg" rather than show "how America stepped into the European arena and held high the banner of integrity and of humanity–and of justice."[101] A preview audience member echoed the judges' words. "My only criticism is the notice at end of picture that all prisoners have been released–anti-climactic, frustrating and not necessary." "But the final statement is such an enormously significant one," Mann wrote Kramer, "and as you have stated yourself, we have a responsibility in this picture beyond that of drama."[102] Kramer kept Mann's ending. "This is the dramatist's right to insert a piece of irony which I believe has even greater impact as to the moral principles with which Nuremberg dealt," he answered Musmanno. Filmgoers attending the preview agreed. "The final worth of the picture lies in the comments written at the end." "The fact that all criminals found guilty are now free should be emphasized." "This film is so momentous it shows the utter immorality of what has and *is* happening."[103]

Judgment at Nuremberg's story and message meant viewers did not leave the theater buoyed by a comforting message about human nature or absolved from responsibility. Instead, the film "keeps pounding away at your emotions with the force of a sledgehammer," one critic admitted. "Again and again you get the feeling of self-guilt." In the film, "there is no relief and no forgiveness," *Maariv*'s reviewer argued; "it is not time, yet. *Judgment at Nuremberg* is as much a mirror as it is a history; Mr. Kramer has made a painfully useful film."[104] Members of the preview audience reported similar sentiments. "This is one picture that conveys a message and a feeling which I can't explain. For the present it is a bombshell in a deserted brickyard." As a consequence, even if they rated the film "excellent" or "very good"—which 87 percent of the more than three hundred filmgoers in attendance did—they believed it would not succeed at the box office. "A noble attempt. Will be hard to sell to the public and critics." "Won't make a dime for producer. Will not be popular." "I enjoyed the picture but to its running success I am doubtful. The general public will not go for it."[105] As it turned out, they were right. In the end, *Judgment at Nuremberg* grossed only about $6 million, leading to a loss of $1.5 million. "I was depressed, of course, to see so many near-empty theaters, and I felt like a failure," Kramer recalled.[106]

Negative reviews compounded this failure. As with Kramer's earlier films, some commentators felt the serious message and meaning of *Judgment at Nuremberg* meant it could not be viewed and evaluated in typical Hollywood fashion, as art or entertainment. "Due to the unusual nature of its subject," *Variety* opined, the movie "cannot be gauged by the customary entertainment yardstick."[107] Other reviewers did not hold back from charging Kramer with crimes against cinema, joining those critics and filmgoers who indicted Kramer for crass exploitation of a significant and sensitive topic. "I objected to the obvious sensationalism of the lengthy horror film and the injection of Eichmann's name into the script," expressed a preview audience member.[108] One of the most forthright critics was Stanley Kauffmann in the *New Republic,* who also had condemned *On the Beach.* "Stanley Kramer is one of the rare Hollywood producers interested in social-political subjects," Kauffmann began his review, "and some believe that by tackling such subjects he earns at least partial remission from criticism. (How much? 20 percent off for effort?)" He recalled being "castigated for my review of *On the Beach*, with the implication that anyone who found faults in the film was anti-peace." He was "prepared now to be thought pro-Nazi," as he found the film compromised and concluded that Kramer should "leave serious subjects alone. Better no one in Hollywood dealing with them than glossy, paltering films like this one." Put more concisely, "*Judgment at Nuremberg* is all too easy to sneer at," wrote a British reviewer.[109]

But Kramer, Mann, and their colleagues could take some comfort as the motion picture awards season began. Even before the announcement of the nominations for the Academy Awards, respondents heralded *Judgment at Nuremberg* as eminently Oscar worthy. "I expect a few Oscar winners in the offing," expressed one member of the preview audience. "Maximilian Schell, Spencer Tracy—great! Sure Academy Awards." "By far the most dramatic picture in a long time and is Academy Award material."[110] Kramer's direction was recognized by several commentators, who noted that he had yet to win an Oscar for best director. "After *The Defiant Ones* and *On the Beach*, there is still no Academy Award for him." "I just don't know how they can keep it from you this year."[111] In the end, *Judgment at Nuremberg* earned eleven Oscar nominations, even more than *The Defiant Ones'* nine. Like *The Defiant Ones*, it received nominations for best picture, best director, and four in the acting categories: best actor for both Maximilian Schell and Spencer Tracy, best supporting actress for Judy Garland, and best supporting actor for Montgomery Clift. Frederic Knudtson again picked up a nomination for best film editing, as did Ernest Laszlo for best black-and-white cinematography. On Oscar night, in April 1962, Schell won the best actor award, and Abby Mann won for his screenplay. Mann used his acceptance speech to express his screenwriting philosophy. "A writer worth his salt at all has an obligation not only to entertain but to comment on the world in which he lives."[112]

Kramer did not win the best director or best picture awards, nor did his film win in any other categories. The movie that swept the Oscars that year, winning ten awards and beating *Judgment at Nuremberg* in several categories, was *West Side Story* (1961). But Kramer did receive the very prestigious Irving G. Thalberg Award, considered an honorary Oscar for producers. It recognized Kramer's achievements over his entire career to date as well as what he had accomplished most recently.

Over the previous four years, he had produced and promoted a major film every single year. In the process, he and his films provoked public debates about the most significant social and political issues in Cold War America. He participated prominently in these debates, offering a vital liberal perspective on civil rights and civil liberties, nuclear weapons and the Holocaust. Just prior to the premiere of *Judgment at Nuremberg*, Bosley Crowther labeled Kramer "Hollywood's Producer of Controversy," a label that stuck. "Mr. Kramer is an unusual producer," rare among a "breed not particularly noted for its contentiousness and audacity." By 1962, Kramer had gained professional and political prominence in the United States. These developments also made his international reputation. In Israel he was lauded as having "a unique prestige in the American and international film industry."[113] This prestige even extended behind the Iron Curtain. As it turned out, Stanley Kramer's global stature would take him, his movies, and his liberal internationalism to Moscow the very next year.

6 Cinematic Diplomacy in Cold War Moscow

The timing of Stanley Kramer's *The Defiant Ones, On the Beach, Inherit the Wind,* and *Judgment at Nuremberg* between 1958 and 1961 and his achievement of the Thalberg Award in 1962 overlapped with significant years in the Cold War. The message and meaning of these four films and his professional prominence contributed to Kramer's emergence as an important cultural and political figure on the international stage, just as a "thaw" began in relations between the United States and the Soviet Union. The death of Joseph Stalin in 1953 made possible the rise of Nikita S. Khrushchev to the position of Soviet premier, and he initiated a process of liberalization at home and easing icy tensions abroad. This process was real but also "slow and contradictory," and it occurred simultaneously with major Cold War conflicts, including the Berlin and the Cuban Missile crises. As a series of dynamic developments rather than a static standoff, the Cold War was "made and remade in various moments."[1] These years provided such moments, which intersected in myriad ways with Kramer's film productions and public persona.

In 1958, the same year as the release of *The Defiant Ones,* the US and Soviet governments signed a historic cultural agreement that allowed for reciprocal exchanges of people and cultural products with the aim of increasing contact and building ties, of "raising the Iron Curtain." Kramer's films were among the first American films to be screened in the Soviet Union following the agreement, and Moscow was one of the world cities in which *On the Beach* premiered in December 1959. While the Soviets purchased annually only four or five Hollywood films during the years of the cultural agreement, they purchased seven of Kramer's—the most of any US filmmaker.[2] Kramer became quite well known and well liked in the Soviet Union among government officials,

Stanley Kramer and Maximilian Schell backstage at the 34th Academy Awards ceremony, after winning the Irving G. Thalberg Award and best actor Oscar for 1961. Copyright © Academy of Motion Picture Arts and Sciences.

filmmakers, critics, and audiences. The Soviets invited Kramer to visit in 1960, but he could not accept until 1963 when he came as a member of the jury for the third biennial Moscow International Film Festival. Kramer's participation in the festival, which included a range of activities and public statements, solidified his reputation with the Soviets as well as the US Department of State.

Over the rest of the 1960s and after, Kramer and his films were a prominent presence in the Soviet Union and can be viewed as a crucial aspect of US cultural diplomacy at a new stage of Cold War international relations. His international profile and presence helped make the Moscow film festival an important site for Cold War political maneuvering, as well as for artistic and commercial exchanges. In all his dealings with Moscow, Kramer expressed a commitment to liberal internationalism and uncompromisingly acted on his liberal, universal ideals. The "Cold War trope of freedom" was real and not rhetoric to him.[3] Although the reception of his words and actions in the Soviet Union varied, his importance as an independent, liberal, and social problem filmmaker was widely recognized and respected. Esteem for Kramer in the United States also rose as part of his cultural diplomatic dealings behind the Iron Curtain. Like other cultural diplomats, he contributed to the ideological and symbolic struggle that was as much a part of US Cold War strategy as military, diplomatic, and economic aspects. After all, Kramer had often said the Cold War was as much a "war of ideas" as anything else, and ideas were his stock-in-trade.[4]

Stanley Kramer as a Cinematic Diplomat

Stanley Kramer had long believed in cultural diplomacy. Pursued by governments and private entities, cultural diplomacy uses expression in the arts and the media and exchanges of ideas and people to foster international relations and mutual understanding. "The more we exchange the less prone we are to misunderstand and resent," Kramer argued, echoing prominent advocates of the US-USSR cultural agreement. Former senator and State Department official William Benton felt "the Iron Curtain of misunderstanding" could be lifted through exchanges and was "the best hope of each for avoiding total destruction."[5]

As a filmmaker, Kramer focused on expression and exchanges around film and saw the power of what can be called "cinematic" diplomacy. He felt the film medium "represents the heart and humanity" that can connect people of different nations. The right kind of films "know no national boundaries or national distinctions." They show "the filmgoer of Paris or Leningrad, New York or Buenos Aires . . . that his spiritual or emotional problems are, after all, little different from those which affect all the races of mankind."[6] Kramer wanted to build international ties around the world, but he particularly sought exchanges with the

Soviet Union. "I am very much interested in the cultural exchanges of our respective nations," he wrote a Soviet embassy officer in Washington in 1960, "and would welcome the opportunity to see and talk to your artists and creators." Kramer advocated both the "fast" media of mass communication and the "slow" media of people-to-people exchanges—using both film and filmmakers—to improve US-USSR relations. "We are curious, we know too little, we want to know so much about the Soviet Union," he told *Pravda* that same year.[7]

Kramer's commitment to cultural diplomacy once again put him at odds with the political Right. Anticommunist Americans did not like the 1958 US-USSR cultural agreement. They feared it would make the United States even more vulnerable to communist subversion. "The Russia-firsters among us, plus a great many well-intentioned Americans, are currently whooping it up for a greater 'cultural exchange' between the United States and the happy homeland of bolshevism," editorialized the *American Legion Magazine* in 1959. But what would be exchanged? Perhaps, as in the past, "subversion, sabotage, and espionage" from Russian visitors, but most certainly communist propaganda would result. "Since our State Department is pressuring the movie industry to show red films in American movie theaters," soon moviegoers would be watching films made by "Soviet film propagandists . . . designed to advance the red tide."[8] The American Legion also believed the cultural agreement "would serve as the excuse for the re-employment of alleged Communist or Communist-indoctrinated individuals in Hollywood," reported *Variety*. "Hollywood producers would use the argument that if it's okay to show films made by Russian Communists, why should the domestic variety be prevented from working?" And, in fact, this argument was used by opponents of the Hollywood blacklist. "It would appear that we sanction having 'Exchange Students,' i.e., communists from Russia," pointed out an industry insider to Kramer. "But to hire a writer, who is, by the way, an American citizen, is taboo. Who makes these 'cockeyed' rules, one must wonder."[9]

Of course, Kramer favored free expression and exchange on both sides of the Iron Curtain, which, combined with his filmmaking prominence, made him a much sought-after commentator in the Soviet Union. In interviews and in writing, Soviet journalists asked for his opinions on films, filmmakers, and film industries around the world, but they also requested his views on Cold War international politics and policy generally. In late 1959 a magazine editor asked Kramer for his viewpoint on Soviet premier Khrushchev's recent, historic tour of the United States. This first-ever American visit by a Soviet leader reflected the warming of superpower relations and included talks at Camp David with President Eisenhower and stops at Hollywood production studios. Khrushchev's visit was politically controversial in the United States. "Letters, telegrams, and petitions flooded Congress opposing the visit," historian Donald T. Critchlow writes, "while conservative periodicals lashed out against the visit of Stalin's former lieutenant."[10] The liberal Kramer responded very differently when asked, did Khrushchev's visit signal a relaxing of "international tension"? "From my point of view," Kramer argued,

> nothing but good can result from this kind of friendly exchange. . . . As an individual who works in the world of films, I value the importance of communications. The most basic kind of communication is, of course, people speaking to people. Chairman Khrushchev and President Eisenhower's visits are a first step. If there is to be a free exchange of music, films, books, and, eventually it is hoped, people, then world tensions must ease.

He concluded, "As an American living in the atom age, I can never lose hope that ultimately all tensions must be eased to the point where they no longer exist."[11]

Through such statements and his film *On the Beach*, Kramer expressed his commitment to the idea of peaceful coexistence between the East and West blocs, although he avoided the phrase itself, given its origins with Khrushchev. The promotion campaign for *On the Beach* provided several opportunities for Kramer to express his support for better relations with communist nations. "I do not believe the Soviet Union personally wants war," he asserted at the press conference following the Hollywood premiere. All of these developments strengthened Kramer's reputation in the Soviet Union as a "progressive" and permitted his films to be imported. But Kramer's popularity was even more widespread. As one American newspaper noted, "the Russians" had "long revered Mr. Kramer as something of a folk hero."[12]

Soviet admiration for Kramer had many sources, yet he never understood the complexity of his appeal or his audience. He believed they heralded him "as a hero" because he "made anti-American films. . . . They assumed that because I dealt with some of the flaws in the fabric of American life, I must be anti-American. They were as wrong as the witch-hunters in America had been."[13] It was true that conservative anticommunists, such as those in the American Legion, often made this assumption. In 1962 right-wing historian William Henry Chamberlin deemed several of Kramer's films "to fit in neatly with the Moscow outlook on world affairs." Chamberlin focused on *Judgment at Nuremberg*. But he also named *Death of a Salesman* "an admirable object lesson in the heartlessness and degeneration of American capitalism, and *On the Beach*, where the audience is shown the gloomy picture of life on this planet totally destroyed by a nuclear war." He expected "a warm reception behind the Iron Curtain" for Kramer's latest film.[14] Yet neither Chamberlin nor Kramer fully explained the filmmaker's popularity in the Soviet Union at the time. In fact, different groups within Soviet society emphasized different aspects of Kramer's life, work, and politics.

Filmmakers greatly respected his successful career as an independent filmmaker in Hollywood. Vladich Alekseevich Nedelin, a Soviet screenwriter and biographer of Kramer, called him a "legendary figure within modern American cinema." Kramer brought "a new force . . . in absolute and obvious defiance of the fully-developed norms and traditions of American film." He was "energetic and charismatic," and he took risks. The early years of his career were "a great gamble." His filmmaking was "more direct and manly, more forceful and sharply polemical" than that of most Hollywood filmmakers. Nedelin's gendered and emotive language revealed a Soviet version of Kramer's masculine image as robust. Nedelin also endorsed Kramer's conviction that "real art should always prove something and always fight for something." Principles should be prioritized over profit in moviemaking.[15] As one prominent political newspaper, *Sovietskaya Rossia*, asked, "So the question is, which is most important, rubles or human souls?" They believed Kramer answered the latter. Such emotive praise fit with what scholar George Faraday calls the "heroic artist paradigm of cultural politics under state socialism," which Soviet cultural producers valued highly and government officials endorsed but also prevented. Kramer's achievement of relative independence and creative autonomy within the US motion picture industry was much admired in the Soviet Union. Soviet filmmakers had long looked to independent film producers in the United States for inspiration. They especially sought out those they understood to have more "leftist and pro-Soviet sympathies" than most of Hollywood, which is how they saw Kramer.[16]

Similarly, Kramer's liberal politics, especially his criticism of the Hollywood blacklist, were recognized in the Soviet Union. They knew Kramer was not a communist. As Nedelin stated, "Stanley Kramer is not just not a communist, but a person who is far from the 'left' in general." Even so, the liberal Kramer was part of what Nedelin admiringly called the "American Resistance" against anticommunism in the United States. The political attacks and protests directed at Kramer and his films over the years were known in the Soviet Union. "They knew that there had been numerous demonstrations against me in America," Kramer recalled. Nedelin believed that Kramer had barely escaped the blacklist in the early 1950s. Throughout "the serious ordeal" with HUAC and other anticommunist forces, such as the Wage Earners Committee and the American Legion, "the sword of Damocles would constantly be hanging above Kramer." Yet Nedelin noted that Kramer was not always on "the heroic side of this Resistance," like Carl Foreman or Arthur Miller. Early on he was "with the majority of intimidated and lost American democratic intelligentsia." Still, Kramer's association with Foreman and Miller, as the producer of *High Noon* and *Death of a Salesman*, garnered him some political credibility among the Soviets. Nedelin explained that Foreman's screenplay had indicted "McCarthyism's wave of investigations and mass repressions," and, over the late 1950s, "Kramer's creativity grew with anti-McCarthyism." By the 1960s, Kramer's politics and "future path" were firmly with the "American Resistance."[17]

The Soviets also welcomed the content and style of Kramer's filmmaking. His social problem films, in particular, corresponded to key elements of the socialist realism and antiformalism dictated by Soviet officials. As a goal for cultural production in the Soviet Union, socialist realism was expected to contribute to the construction of socialism and communism. In contrast to social realism, or a critical depiction of reality, socialist realist plots were simplistic and formulaic. The hero endures injustice and oppression and struggles always optimistically toward building the "bright socialist future."[18] Kramer's films shared similar ideological commitments, strong heroes and plots, and messages of universalism and social justice, if not the goal of socialism or consistent optimism. "The films of Stanley Kramer, evidently cultivated Russia's favorite Western film-maker," wrote a British critic, "were constantly put forward as models: in his films you always know where you were and whose side you were supposed to be on." "Kramer's appeal to the emotions and his didactic tendencies please the Russians," reported an American journalist.[19] "For many years I was the only one in Hollywood making pictures with any social commentary," he said as explanation of his popularity in the USSR. "They see me as a [filmmaker] who manages to capture their humanist aspirations on film." His conventional filmmaking style further fit with Soviet demands for clarity and accessibility for audiences and denunciations of the avant-garde or experimentation.[20] When they screened in the Soviet Union, Kramer's films were judged as meeting or deviating from these aesthetic and ideological requirements.

The Defiant Ones, for example, received extremely positive reviews from Soviet respondents. When a group of Soviet film directors, cameramen, and actors traveled to the United States in the wake of the new 1958 US-USSR cultural agreement, they saw *The Defiant Ones* and "were very impressed." According to Soviet director Vladimir Shneiderov, the film "exposed the problems of racism and social inequality in the capitalist American society." "This movie witnessed the great possibilities of American cinema," Shneiderov declared, "when it worked with progressive themes in realistic spirit."[21] Also recognized was how the film's message and making challenged both American racism and the Hollywood blacklist. In 1961 Raisa Orlova, a literary critic and expert on American literature, credited the film's screenplay to Harold Jacob Smith and Nedrick Young, rather than his pseudonym Nathan Douglas, demonstrating awareness of Young's real identity despite the blacklist. She wrote passionately about the character of Noah Cullen, "It is he who teaches the laws of humanity to the white man chained to his side, and he who emerges triumphant from the grim struggle. . . . Thinking about him," Orlova exclaimed, "you feel the fighting motto of the struggling American Negroes: full equality of rights in this generation." Nedelin felt that the movie "built the road for this Negro mass movement" and was where "Kramer—the renowned producer— revealed himself as a major director." It was "his personal coat-of-arms in today's cinema."[22]

On the Beach did not meet with the same acclaim in the Soviet Union. When the prominent film director Sergei Gerasimov reviewed *On the Beach* in 1959, he complimented "the sincerity of the anti-war theme" and the "general technique," but he criticized "the dominant and unrealistic fatalism of the film." Filmmaking should be "used to brighten, not threaten life."[23] Alexander Chakovskii, a reviewer for

Pravda, raised related objections. He indicted the movie's dystopic vision of the future, which contradicted the Soviet utopian vision of progress toward communism. The film's theme reflected "atomic psychosis." These arguments fit with the official Soviet perspective on science fiction as, according to historian Patrick Major, a genre of the West and "dystopianism as a decadent Western import." Chakovskii expressed particular concern that a movie would show "the destruction of life on earth" just as the negotiations over a test ban treaty proceeded in Geneva, "a time when mankind is on the point of breaking through to new worlds."[24] Kramer recalled that the Soviets "wanted the answer to saving the world from nuclear destruction." "Pal, if I'd had a solution," Kramer told one Soviet filmmaker, "I'd have provided it." The film's pessimistic ending was one reason why Soviet officials chose not to put the film in general release. When officials reconsidered this decision six years later, in 1965, they again opted out of public screenings. *On the Beach* was "too intimidating for a normal Soviet viewer with the graphic results of nuclear war."[25]

Soviet responses to *Inherit the Wind* and *Judgment at Nuremberg,* as well as Kramer's later films, were far more favorable overall. With *Inherit the Wind,* Kramer expressed certainty that the Soviets "missed the point" about civil liberties and simply "saw it as antireligionist." Instead, the producer-director missed something himself. When a stage production of the play appeared later in the 1960s, it was very popular with Soviet audiences. One American critic concluded that the story in *Inherit the Wind* appealed because it depicted with clarity and morality "clashes between individuals (good guys) and the group (bad guys)." For Nedelin, Kramer's film showed the injustice of the American justice system. US courts "made it possible in the name of justice," he argued, "to lynch anyone and anytime." Echoing communist legal critiques, Nedelin contended that the movie exposed the way American law functioned behind a façade of fairness to the benefit of the powerful in society. *Inherit the Wind* further showed "struggle and resistance" against this functioning.[26] Kramer also perceived a mixed Soviet reception for *Judgment at Nuremberg.* They "liked the idea that the Germans couldn't use the excuse of orders from above to clear themselves of war crimes," he believed. "But they didn't like the argument by Maximilian Schell that the Russians were also guilty for entering a pact with the Nazis." As it turned out, even as their focus remained on German fascism, Soviet respondents connected with the film's "question of personal responsibility." "This powerful antifascist film," Nedelin concluded, "shakes not only yesterday's but today's world."[27]

For all these reasons—his career an independent filmmaker, his liberal and *anti*-anticommunist politics, and his social problem films—the Soviets began inviting Kramer to visit their country. The normal practice was to invite an American filmmaker to the Soviet Union as a way to facilitate film exchanges and justify the future purchase of their films. Kramer received invitations every year in the early 1960s. Even after his negative review of *On the Beach*, Sergei Gerasimov himself, in his position as president of the Cinema Division of the Association of Soviet Societies for Friendship and Cultural Bonds with Foreign Countries, invited Kramer. The Association of Film Makers of the Soviet Union asked him to visit two years in a row. The correspondence between Kramer and his potential Soviet hosts was warm and sincere, and they considered him a "guest of honor." "Realizing the extreme importance of personal contacts between creative film workers we would be very pleased to offer you a large possibility to get acquainted with the Soviet cinema," wrote officers of the Association of Film Makers. In turn, they hoped to screen some of Kramer's films for their members. When Kramer met with the Soviet delegation to a film festival in San Francisco in 1962, he made a strong impression and prompted another invitation. The delegation "brought back many pleasant memories and, particularly, about their meeting with you."[28] Kramer wanted to build on these contacts and connections in the Soviet Union. But before he could act as a cinematic diplomat with the Soviets, he had to establish his credibility and credentials with his own State Department.

This situation posed a challenge for Kramer, because the Moscow screening of *On the Beach* as part of the movie's world premiere in December 1959 had not made US government officials happy. The State Department and the USIA had rejected *On the Beach* for inclusion under the 1958 cultural agreement. "Government has no wish to censor but cannot endorse this film," Kramer's assistant, publicist Myer P. Beck, reported. "They would not show it in Moscow. . . . U.S. has certain policy with reference to A-bombs," but *On the Beach* says "in effect there is no alternative but peace at any price." But Kramer's company and United Artists, including president Arthur B. Krim, still sought to secure a Moscow screening. They were supported by media commentators who saw the world premiere as "an imagination-baiting event."[29] In her gossip column, Louella Parsons pointed out the benefits of a Moscow screening for both Hollywood and humanity. "It is an opening 'wedge' for Hollywood produced films outside the 'cultural exchange' plan. . . . But far more important," she emphasized, is "the theme of the story," which "can do more against the cold (or hot) war in Russia than a dozen meetings of diplomats."[30] When Kramer and UA's strategy of direct engagement with the USSR succeeded, the Hollywood trade press heralded "the Moscow coup." Nedelin strongly believed Moscow's participation in the world premiere constituted a significant international event. "The premiere that was screened at the same time, the same day and the same hour, in Moscow, New York, Paris, Tokyo and London fell from the screen on the viewers and the media like a storm."[31]

But US government officials did not join in the celebrations of *On the Beach*'s Moscow premiere. They considered the maneuver by Kramer's company and UA an "end-run" and "expressed displeasure" about this circumvention of official channels. State Department and USIA officials in the United States sought urgent information about the premiere from the US embassy in Moscow. The premiere did not take place before a general audience—to the relief of US officials—but before a capacity crowd at Dom Kino, the "House of Cinema" and the club of the Union of Film Workers. Gregory Peck and his wife attended, as did the US ambassador and other embassy officers. A representative of the film workers' union introduced and thanked Peck and spent time "lauding Stanley Kramer." Peck then made "a brief, effective, and well received speech on the role of films in developing better international relations."[32] Media coverage of the premiere also was positive. "An audience of about 1,000 persons, made up primarily of Soviet film artists, producers and cultural officials, warmly applauded," reported the *New York Times*. They clapped for Peck, the film, and even US ambassador Llewellyn Thompson—"something unprecedented in Moscow," according to *Variety*. "They loved us in Moscow," Peck related. "They laughed in all the right places, and applauded after many dramatic sequences."[33]

In the end, US officials in the Moscow embassy concluded that the impact of the premiere was mostly positive. They included a measured review of *On the Beach* in their communication to the State Department. Acting as much like film critics as diplomatic staff, they were "unanimous as to the film's dramatic quality and the high professional skill of production, photography and acting." They agreed that the "film had a powerful impact on Soviets and Americans alike." Moreover, contrary to assumptions in Washington, the Moscow embassy saw the film as sending messages that advanced US interests. The film showed that the United States was "deeply concerned about the dangers of possible nuclear war." It also undermined the idea of "an invincibly strong" Soviet Union, because their country is destroyed in the course of the film. Fred Astaire's character, the scientist Julian Osborne, explains the war's escalation by referring to the Soviets. "They didn't think we'd fight no matter what they did. We fought. We expunged them and we didn't do such a bad job on ourselves." This key dialogue, it turned out, had been omitted from the Russian subtitles. Finally, in presenting Kramer's long-standing message about "the universality of the human situation," the film "reduced to complete foolishness" the Soviets' "interminable polemics regarding differences between the two camps." In the end, the embassy argued, *On the Beach* "cuts deeply both ways."[34]

Despite the more favorable perspective of the US embassy toward *On the Beach*'s Moscow premiere, opinions of Kramer remained mixed at the State Department, USIA, and FBI. It did not help that the Union of Film Workers representative revealed in his introductory remarks at the premiere that *The Defiant Ones* also had been shown in Dom Kino, "a fact [of] which the Embassy was unaware."[35] This revelation added to official mistrust of Kramer and his actions in Moscow. This situation continued even as presidential administrations shifted in 1961 from the Republican Eisenhower to the Democrat John F. Kennedy. Kramer recognized that cultural diplomacy was a joint effort by public officials and private actors and that his relationships with US officials affected his pursuit of cinematic diplomacy.[36] Along with the rest of the motion picture industry, he understood the need to work with and secure approval from the US government. At this point in the Cold War, American filmmakers agreed to "be wholly guided by the attitude of the State Department" and accepted "U.S. State Dept. guidance when it comes to dealings with the Russians." As a result, in April 1961 Kramer wrote the renowned journalist Edward R. Murrow, who had just become the director of the USIA in the new Kennedy administration, about a possible visit and article for the Soviets. "Does your Department have any viewpoint, advice or negations with which I should be familiar?" Murrow responded cautiously. He endorsed an article "on the use of motion pictures as an art form" but expressed concern about how to avoid "any possible misunderstanding or any danger of distortion" by the Soviets.

About both the article and a possible visit, Murrow referred Kramer on to other officials for consultation.[37]

Kramer's subsequent correspondence with Turner B. Shelton, who continued as director of the USIA's Motion Picture Service into the first year of the Kennedy administration, indicated the public-private nature and negotiation involved in cultural diplomacy. Kramer had dealt with Shelton in the past, during the production of *On the Beach*. To ensure all was "in order," Kramer sent Turner a draft of an interview for publication in *Iskusstvo Kino* (The Art of the Cinema). The editor of this Soviet journal sought Kramer's "view on some fundamental problems of the modern art of cinema." Kramer began by citing "Aristotle's definition of pure drama as that which purges the emotions," then he listed recent films from around the world "which fulfill the requirements of this definition." He included films from the Soviet Union, Japan, and Greece. *Hiroshima, Mon Amour* (1959), directed by France's Alain Resnais, and *La Dolce Vita* (1960), directed by Italy's Federico Fellini, were "the kind of films which stir people's emotions." Although Shelton accepted Kramer's premise about the relationship among film, emotion, and empathy—"I certainly agree with you 100%"—he felt the article needed to name two or three American films. The films by Resnais and Fellini, Shelton also argued, "have given the West some misgivings." Resnais's antinuclear war film showed graphic, devastating images of Hiroshima after the US dropping of the atomic bomb, and Fellini's film indicted licentious, Western celebrity culture. Shelton worried about "the effect of these films on anti-Western audiences" and urged "this slight change."[38] Kramer did add two US films, but he did not remove *Hiroshima, Mon Amour* and *La Dolce Vita* from his interview.

This move reflected Kramer's strong commitment to freedom of expression in art and politics, but it also reinforced the wariness of US officials about a Kramer visit to the Soviet Union. Yet his public arguments that his films "could never have been made in a controlled economy" and that "the idea of freedom of the individual, freedom of the artistic concept, freedom . . . to criticize" underpinned his career began to find an audience among US officials.[39] Shelton eventually approved a trip in 1961 and that year even invited Kramer—"as an outstanding figure in the American motion picture industry"—to be part of the first US delegation to a Moscow film festival. "Your presence would mak[e] known . . . the tremendous cultural and artistic achievements that have come about as a result of the free and unfettered society in which we live." Shelton also agreed that a possible solo visit by Kramer in 1962 fell within the exchanges allowed by the 1958 US-USSR cultural agreement. At the same time, he discouraged Kramer from appearances "on any public means of communication—such as radio or television—where you might be embarrassed by having any statement you might make used out of context." Kramer also should do nothing "outside of the context of either the spirit or the letter of the Exchange Agreement" and must "consult with us prior to issuing any invitation to a Soviet citizen to visit the United States." As Kramer fielded these various requests, he sought to reassure Shelton. "You know very well I would not make a move without meeting with the State Department people involved under any circumstances."[40] This series of negotiations finally resulted in Kramer being invited, accepting, and attending the Moscow film festival in July 1963.

The 1963 Moscow International Film Festival, with its motto "For Humanism in Cinema Art, for Peace and Friendship among Nations," was an auspicious event for Kramer. He had attended and won prizes at other international film festivals, but never had he had such influence and impact. Film festivals served a "valuable purpose," he believed, "by bringing together film makers from all over the world to judge each other's contributions to the screen and to exchange ideas." Invited again by Sergei Gerasimov, Kramer this time had the distinction and status of attending the festival as a member of the jury, which would decide and award the festival prizes. "We beg of you in this letter in hope that you . . . support the success of this Festival and its ideas of world-wide friendship," Gerasimov wrote.[41] Kramer also had earned the approval of the State Department, a necessary condition for attending the Moscow film festival. Most importantly, Kramer won the enthusiastic endorsement of George Stevens, Jr., who had replaced Shelton as the director of the USIA Motion Picture Service in 1962 and would head up the US delegation to Moscow. The son of a respected Hollywood director, Stevens was an ideal choice for this position. He knew the film industry intimately and was an energetic administrator during what historian Tony Shaw calls "the USIA's golden age of Cold War filmmaking." At the time, recognition was widespread that "the United States has been laggard on the film festival front" and needed leadership. "In this area, USIA's Stevens has been playing a powerful role," noted the *Los Angeles Times*.[42]

Stevens decided to take advantage of the opportunity provided by Kramer's attendance at the 1963 Moscow festival. "I proposed a small Kramer retrospective that would show the seriousness in American film production to the Russian cinema community," Stevens recalled. But the State Department strongly objected. The US government continued to oversee American film festival participation, including the selection and exhibition of specific films, to fit the foreign policy priorities at the time. Just as when State Department officials raised objections to *The Defiant Ones* screening at the 1958 Berlin film festival, some believed Kramer's "proposed films would work against U.S. interests" in 1963: "*The Defiant Ones*, because the Tony Curtis chain-gang prisoner was a racist; *Judgment at Nuremberg*, because the film had a negative portrayal of the Germans, who were our allies in the struggle against international Communism; and *On the Beach*, because it dealt with the specter of nuclear war." "The dispute rose to the highest levels of the department," Stevens noted, "with Averell Harriman, our wartime ambassador to Russia, and Llewellyn Thompson, the most recent past ambassador, taking opposing sides." Resolution finally came "because the films were to be shown primarily to members of the Soviet film unions" rather than to the public. Even the Central Committee of the Communist Party of the Soviet Union took note of this disagreement, concluding that Kramer's films "would be shown only in closed session" due to high-level "pressure."[43]

This type of dispute over the controversial nature of his films always angered Kramer. "The cardinal sin of twenty years of motion picture export by this country is that films have been censored to project a certain 'American Image,'" he told a journalist later in 1963. He recognized that US policymakers were waging a "cultural offensive" during the Cold War, deploying American cultural products, such as movies, to achieve geopolitical goals. Hollywood movies played a powerful role in projecting, or propagandizing, the "American way of life." Yet Kramer disapproved of how this fact limited the export of social problem films. "Any sore spots or problems of our society received a blanket—no export! And this attitude . . . is sheer idiocy."[44] For years, he had cited the diplomatic triumph of screening *The Defiant Ones* at the 1958 Mexico City film festival, despite official pressures. Instead of fearing that a US social problem film creates "a bad impression overseas," Americans should feel confident that it demonstrates US freedoms as it "could not have been made in a totalitarian society. This in itself is a great propaganda weapon." The approval of Kramer's retrospective by the Democratic Kennedy administration signaled a positive change. "For years our State Department's watchword on film export was 'neutrality'—nothing critical or controversial. Under the present administration, the policy has been relaxed." This relaxation was no doubt aided by Murrow's decision to "display the United States 'warts and all.'" Even so, the State Department requested cuts to *Judgment at Nuremberg*, including Rolfe's references to Hiroshima and Nagasaki and the film's final title about the release of former Nazis. Kramer wanted the film to stay intact. But he prioritized its Soviet screening over any censorship concerns, hoping to demonstrate the diplomatic benefits of bolder, more realistic portrayals of the United States.[45]

Kramer's plans for Moscow proceeded together with those of the entire US delegation, under the guidance of State Department and USIA officials. The newlywed Stevens decided to make the Moscow trip into a honeymoon, and Abby Mann planned to accompany Kramer. In Moscow they expected time for "free discussion" among Soviet and American filmmakers and tours of Soviet studios to see "more of the life of the Soviet people," as stated in the film festival program. To prepare, Kramer secured a copy of Khrushchev's recent speech, "High Ideological Content and Artistic Mastery Constitute the Great Strength of Soviet Literature and Art." This speech heralded a clampdown on Soviet artists despite the cultural "thaw." In implementing this new cultural policy, Ivan A. Pyryev, a film director and chairman of the Union of Film Workers, reminded film workers that the "development of motion pictures in our country . . . is a very important part of our national, party-oriented business of government." He declared that there was "no place" in Soviet motion pictures "for formalistic affectations and for imitation of the bourgeois West." In response, some Westerners expressed concern about the "possible effect of an ideological upheaval in the Soviet Union" on the Moscow festival. Within this changing situation, Kramer hoped his contribution would be "productive of a little more understanding among artists."[46]

Stanley Kramer's Mission to Moscow

Under the leadership of George Stevens, Jr., the United States for the first time made "an all-out affirmative effort" at a Moscow film festival, and Kramer emerged as a key figure in this effort.[47] His importance followed from his membership on the festival jury and the planned retrospective of his film work for Soviet filmmakers. Kramer also introduced screenings of *West Side Story* (1961), a film shown out of competition at the festival. The irony of offering the introduction to a movie musical that swept the 1962 Academy Awards with ten awards—beating *Judgment at Nuremberg* in several categories, including best picture and best director—was not lost on Kramer and his colleagues. Hastily arranged public screenings of Kramer's own films—not just the planned screenings for Soviet filmmakers—later followed. These public screenings of *The Defiant Ones* and *Judgment at Nuremberg* drew audiences in the thousands and received standing ovations and positive comments in the Soviet press. What made Kramer's festival contributions so significant was how they incorporated and reflected his liberal politics. He used every opportunity in Moscow to take public and controversial stances, explaining and endorsing the American values and rights to free speech and artistic freedom he so respected and appreciated. In contrast to what some State Department officials initially had feared, Kramer's liberalism went over very well both in the USSR and back in the United States. With his films, actions, and public statements, Kramer's participation at the Moscow film festival showed the potential and power of US cinematic diplomacy in the Cold War context.

The 1963 festival Kramer attended provided only the third biennial opportunity for US participation. The United States declined to participate in the inaugural Moscow festival in August 1959 but had sponsored the first American National Exhibition in Moscow just the month before. The site of the famous "kitchen debate" between Vice President Richard Nixon and Khrushchev, the exhibition was an outcome of the 1958 cultural agreement and a landmark event for US cultural display in the Soviet capital. Despite official nonparticipation in the festival, Hollywood films were permitted to screen out of competition "to show representative examples of American film production before people in the Soviet Union." When *The Diary of Anne Frank* (1959) screened, 20th Century-Fox's Spyros Skouras introduced it, joking that "the Soviets' seven-year plan would benefit if the Russians bought more 20th films."[48] In 1961 the new Kennedy administration changed policy and decided to take part in the second Moscow film festival, despite the ongoing conflict over Berlin. But a tense political moment occurred when the Soviet audience walked out on the US entry at the festival,

Sunrise at Campobello (1960), a film about Franklin Roosevelt's early struggle with polio and paralysis. Although the *Guardian* concluded that the film simply "bored" the audience, theories and accusations flew on the American side about this "sensational" and "contemptuous" reaction. Canadian film reviewer and broadcaster Gerald Pratley put it bluntly: "the Americans retired in disgrace from the 2nd film festival in Moscow."[49]

These earlier experiences made the 1963 Moscow film festival a high-stakes event for the United States, a fact Kramer and his colleagues well understood.[50] The US government and Hollywood participated to promote American interests and worked hard to ensure that American films and delegates were positively received by the Soviet film festival organizers, audiences, and government officials. The timing was good. The festival occurred in the middle of July, at the very same time that US and Soviet officials were also in Moscow negotiating the first nuclear test ban treaty. Spurred by how dangerously close the two adversaries came to nuclear war during the Cuban Missile Crisis in October the year before, these negotiations ended in success. This historic diplomatic initiative signaled the likelihood of a good reception for Americans in Moscow.

Stevens brought to Moscow "one of the largest and most impressive delegations from America to appear at any international film event," and the delegates came ready to participate in a range of artistic, commercial, and political exchanges. Film festivals intermingled art, commerce, and politics, although each festival was known for having a different emphasis, or "identity marker": Venice for artistic innovations, Cannes for commercial relations, Berlin for political and intellectual contributions.[51] "They're all different," Kramer said. "Cannes has starlets" and "Venice has a canal. . . . Berlin has a surface of great solemnity and intellectuality. But deep down they're all politics and deal-making and girl-chasing." The Moscow festival "is usually quite an official, ceremonial event," he noted, and it "brings out all the creative people, not just the film people . . . poets, writers, painters." Kramer anticipated talking and toasting into the "wee hours" with the other participants.[52]

Kramer, Stevens, and the rest of the American delegation publicized that they "came to Moscow with a new approach." Instead of playing it safe and "presenting politically non-controversial pictures as it had in the past," they would be screening "three outspoken features"—Kramer's two films and *West Side Story*—out of competition. As Kramer put it, these movies were "commenting on flaws in the American fabric."[53] The US film officially entered into competition, however, was *The Great Escape* (1963). Starring Steve McQueen, the film was based on a true story, but it blended fact and fiction to depict British and American prisoners of war making a bold escape from a German POW camp during World War II. The Soviets had not been in favor of this selection and had delayed announcing the US official entry, hoping for a change. They resented the "light and humorous treatment" of the camp, including "the cowboy, adventure film atmosphere." McQueen's motorcycle escape, which the actor—an avid motorcyclist—had insisted on, certainly defied reality and contravened history.[54] Particularly egregious for the Soviets as well as participants from other European countries was how the "horrors of the occupation and the Nazi torture chambers" were glossed over and the "antagonism of the enemies is intentionally smoothed down." This representation of the POW camp "perplexed" Soviet reviewers, even if the film "was shot flawlessly technically and the acting is excellent." The film festival committee had expressed this point of view months earlier. They were "not happy," the American embassy in Moscow reported to the State Department, "because theme [of] German POW camp, even in comedy film, not funny here."[55]

Unlike *The Great Escape*, Kramer's seriousness was never doubted by the Soviets, nor was his popularity. "Kramer was a great success in Moscow," Stevens recalled. "Filmmakers applauded his films, often shouting 'Kraaaamer, Kraaaamer, Kraaaamer' at their conclusion." In fact, "continuous," "enthusiastic," and even "shocking" applause greeted Kramer everywhere. For Kramer, this response was "strange and embarrassing," and he feared the rest of "the American delegation was looking at me as though I was the leader of the American Communist Party."[56] The "respect he enjoyed," according to Stevens, "became a kind of wonderful asset to the American delegation." As a sign of this high regard, Soviet filmmakers gave Kramer an award for his "outstanding treatment" of "major themes of today" in his films shown at the festival. "This award came as a total surprise," and "he was not aware it was being made until nudged by his interpreter."[57] Kramer's popular reputation matched his professional one, and American journalists often expressed surprise at this fact. "Incidentally, each time the U.S. delegation has been presented on the stage, the biggest ovation has gone to Kramer and not to the stars," reported *Variety*. "His record as a distinguished film maker is obviously more familiar to Muscovites than that of the performers." Given that Kramer shared the stage with actors such as Danny Kaye, Tony Curtis, and Susan Strasberg, such positive audience response was considered noteworthy by the US press.[58]

Even more newsworthy was Kramer's prominent role in a controversy between the American delegation and their Soviet hosts over the screening of *West Side Story.* The popular Oscar-winning film, codirected by Jerome Robbins and Robert Wise, recreated the "bold and daring" musical play from 1957.[59] The play and the film innovatively integrated the work of some of the best-known and most accomplished figures in American musical theater. With a book by Arthur Laurents—playwright of the original *Home of the Brave*—music by Leonard Bernstein, lyrics by a young Stephen Sondheim, and choreography by Robbins, *West Side Story* updated William Shakespeare's *Romeo and Juliet* to contemporary New York. This modern love story across racial and ethnic differences occurred against the backdrop of juvenile gang rivalry in, coincidentally, Kramer's old neighborhood of Hell's Kitchen. As "a favorite Soviet propaganda subject" happened to be "American street gangs," some commentators surmised that the Soviets wanted the movie musical showing in the festival for just this reason. "This must be because the Russian people want to see U.S. films—or perhaps because [Soviet authorities] like to distribute U.S. films—that emphasize the less admirable aspects of American life."[60] The main characters in *West Side Story* were working-class, white, ethnic Americans and Puerto Rican immigrants, "outsiders . . . disenfranchised from society." The film also criticized racial prejudice and questioned the American Dream, most explicitly with the song "America." This number pitted those Puerto Rican characters who believed in the United States as a "land of opportunity" against those who did not and made their case through satirical, even cynical lyrics. "Its message," declares Marc Bauch, "is a parody on pro-USA propaganda."[61]

The film's challenging content made *West Side Story* a significant choice as one of the US films to show out of competition in Moscow, which Kramer acknowledged when he had the honor of introducing the film at several early screenings. "Today we do not come shouting virtue. Here is a film about one of our faults. We have a few."[62] As he saw it, the film reflected "social problems in America today," specifically juvenile delinquency and "the assimilation of Puerto Ricans." He reminded the Soviet audience that the film portrayed only one side of life in an American city and asked to "see the forest as well as the trees."[63] "Now," he continued, "here is the secret of one of the strengths of our society. You will see in this film that we are able to criticize and satirize ourselves as well—or better—than anyone else might have done it." Asserting the value of artistic freedom from censorship, Kramer added, "We have always had a freedom from fear in this regard."[64] His speech went over well, and American officials asked him to repeat it at later screenings. "Applause at right places indicated audience clearly understood message of speech," reported the US ambassador to the Soviet Union, Foy D. Kohler, to the State Department. After forwarding on Kramer's "effective" speech for "possible media exploitation," stories appeared in the US press. "I suppose you had to sit through *West Side Story* again for the sake of American prestige, even though you weren't too enthusiastic about it the first time," wrote his colleague Myer P. Beck jokingly. "Anyway, you made a very nice speech, as reported in the . . . *New York Times*.[65]

Kramer's speeches and attendance at these early screenings did not end his involvement with *West Side Story*. The American delegation quickly discovered that the Russian translation, broadcast over loudspeaker, ruined the effect of the musical numbers. In fact, US officials had raised this problematic possibility before the start of the festival. "Sov[iet]s intend [to] have Russian version read over English track," reported the Moscow embassy, "clearly damaging audibility and understanding of film." The State Department agreed. "Since Leonard Bernstein score related to Jerome Robbins dances most important value of *West Side Story*, imperative any voicing over be kept to absolute minimum." When Kramer, along with the rest of the American delegation and the film's exhibitors, insisted on this change at a screening, the Soviet government newspaper *Izvestia* accused the United States specifically of censoring the song "America" for its "criticism of life in America."[66] "Was it only for purely aesthetic considerations that the Americans did not want such a text should be broadcast in the Russian language?" asked *Izvestia*, according to US media reports. "Not likely." *Izvestia* proceeded to publish a Russian translation of the lyrics. Given the popularity of *West Side Story*, members of the American delegation were quite aware that the "sardonic lyrics" of "the show-stopping, bouncy song contrast realities of certain aspects of Puerto Rican life in New York with the ideals of material abundance and democracy," noted the *Los Angeles Times*. "The article (falsely) accused the American delegation of insisting on deletion of the number's text," reported the US embassy, "implying that the lyrics are too anti-American."[67]

Kramer answered *Izvestia*'s accusation at the next screening of *West Side Story*. He read aloud the lyrics for "America" and asserted that aesthetic, not political, considerations motivated the decision not to "interfere with Bernstein's music. . . . The record is now clear," Kramer declared. His strong stance received compliments from the Hollywood trade press. "Stanley Kramer took the opportunity of rebutting allegations," *Variety* reported. "Hitting back at *Izvestia*," he "made it clear that they had nothing to conceal." Concerned about Kramer's impact, the head of the KGB, the Soviet security agency, urged "discontinu[ing] the practice of speechmaking outside competition."[68] But, in the end, Kramer helped quell the controversy. "In presenting this film we are dedicated to the search for mutual understanding by airing our problems," he added to his introductory speech. "We hope to see some of your films on your problems. Thus we will get to know and, perhaps, like each other." In what Americans considered a retraction, *Izvestia* noted, "One cannot help but welcome the words of Mr. Kramer that American cultural figures hope for friendly feelings between the American and Soviet peoples." The newspaper also opined that "Mr. Kramer answered the film critique in a completely suitable manner." "In long run," reported the US embassy, "article probably more in our favor than against us." What began as "an international incident, but ended up being a master stroke in free world diplomacy," was due in no small part to Kramer.[69] His efforts in Moscow mattered, but so did his credibility as a cultural producer who had long sought to make real America's rhetoric of freedom, rather than accepting its contradictory Cold War limits.

The excitement and interest in Kramer generated by his role in the *West Side Story* controversy and his commitment to artistic freedom persisted throughout the two-week film festival. Public screenings of his films *The Defiant Ones* and *Judgment at Nuremberg* were quickly scheduled. The Soviets, American officials, and the US press closely followed his activities. In all his public statements and actions, Kramer expressed his core beliefs about the social and political functions of art. The Moscow film festival provided an international stage and audience for his long-standing ideas about how art should confront social problems, could only flourish in an environment free from censorship, and would increase understanding across cultural differences and national borders. At a press conference midway through the festival, Kramer again stressed the value of free "artistic endeavor," a point Abby Mann also made. "I must say in all candor, an artist . . . must be free to assail any institution, any status quo, any sacred cow, and let the chips fall as they may." Although Mann believed both American and Soviet filmmakers "have followed the dictates of our countries," Kramer contrasted the freedom and independence he enjoyed as an American filmmaker with the restrictions and control under which his Soviet colleagues operated. As a "free creative artist," Kramer noted that he had the "right to search out and develop anything he considers worthwhile, without being forced to adhere to any predetermin[ed] line." In this way, he advanced one of the key arguments that appeared in US propaganda for the superiority of the American political and social system over that of the Soviets. Needless to say, US embassy officials felt Kramer "acquitted himself admirably."[70]

Kramer continued to speak and act on his principles and impress American government officials in his role as a member of the festival jury. His service on the jury meant watching thirty-four films in twelve days—"it was an excruciating experience"—but having a voice in determining the festival prizewinners provided an opportunity to advance US interests.[71] The Moscow film festival and its sister Karlovy-Vary festival in Czechoslovakia were well known for consistently awarding films from their own and other communist countries. American officials and filmmakers often complained about the lack of fair play and the fact that political criteria trumped artistic merit in the competition. "It's No Surprise: Home Film Wins in Moscow Fest" and "Soviet (Natch!) Film Wins Fest Staged in Moscow" headlined Hollywood newspapers after an earlier festival.[72] This history meant the 1963 jury deliberations were tense.

Just as the stakes were high for the American delegation, they were for the Soviet hosts as well, especially following the recent implementation of their new cultural policy. One impact of the cultural clampdown was the Soviet Union's official festival entry, *Meet Baluyev*. "A trite and highly conventional story of a Soviet pipeline builder's triumph over adversity, it was an example of 'socialist realism' at its worst." Mark Frankland, the Moscow correspondent for the British newspaper the *Observer*, summarized the Soviet situation. "Western art which is not 'progressive' must be energetically attacked," and "the cultural superiority of Socialism" must be demonstrated.[73] As a result, the Soviets tried to direct the jury toward selecting an Eastern bloc film to receive the Grand Prix as the best film.

But Kramer, along with a majority of the other jury members from the West, believed *8½* (1963) should win. Federico Fellini's semiauto-biographical film concerned a director's emotional turmoil while struggling to make a movie. One review pronounced it an "extravagantly bold movie, in parts surrealistic, which draws on Freud for its concept and on Picasso for its photography." In short, the film was "the very antithesis of Socialist realism." Kramer felt the movie "deeply stirred young Russian intellectuals with its innovations in film technique." Conflict ensued, with the relationship between art and politics at stake for both sides. The Czech jury member later confessed, "I was ordered by my government not to vote for *8½*."[74] The conflict reached a crisis point when the jury members from the West, including Kramer, refused to participate in a decision that did not award the Grand Prix to *8½*. They walked out of a meeting and forced the issue.

US officials gave much of the credit to Kramer, using language that projected a persona of commanding masculinity for the producer-director. "Stanley Kramer led the fight within jury, lasting three days, drawn on ideological grounds." "It was only by boldly walking out . . . that Stanley Kramer saw justice done to the Italian entry *8½*, the outstanding film at the Festival."[75] News reports presented the walkout differently, as a collective decision by the Western jurors, and did not single out Kramer. "What really happened was an artists' plot against the politicians." But everyone agreed the walkout was effective. Soon after, the jurors were recalled. Stevens expressed dismay when Soviet officials came to get Kramer. "I was a little worried for Kramer," Stevens reported, as "he was taken away! He was taken away, and taken back to the Jury meeting."[76]

The jury reconvened, voted, and awarded the Grand Prix to *8½*, citing Fellini's "outstanding creative directing which reflects the inner struggle of an artist in quest of truth." It was a "reasonable compromise," Soviet authorities proclaimed. According to Stevens and news reports, the Soviet minister of culture, Ekaterina Furtseva, later pulled Kramer aside. "I hear you were a naughty boy today." "Perhaps Soviet officials, knowing about his 'problem films,' felt that they had selected a 'pushover' as the American jury member," speculated the US embassy. "If so, the officials were disappointed." The embassy also reported on Eastern bloc members congratulating Kramer "on his 'struggle for truth,' and his victory." On accepting the award, Fellini said "the prize would help artists in their search for truth the whole world over." Western journalists hailed the outcome as striking "a blow in favor of liberty of the arts in the Soviet Union."[77] But Aleksei V. Romanov, head of the USSR State Committee on Cinematography and charged with enforcing the new cultural policy for cinema, held a press conference to refute this interpretation. The win for *8½* was not a "'concession' to Western ideology" or a rejection of "the basic principles of Soviet art." Romanov denounced the film as "contradictory and confused, the world of its images is troubled and morbid, and the form is unusually complicated." "Stick to socialist realism, boys," the *New York Times*'s Bosley Crowther summarized. The Soviets did not withdraw the prize, however. It was a denunciation, not a repudiation, and Western commentators believed this development represented a positive step. "I think it was more of a moment and it meant more to people," Stevens claimed, "than can be refuted in one statement" by Romanov.[78]

For Kramer, these events reinforced that "movie makers have a right to . . . strive for self-expression," as did the public screening of *The Defiant Ones*. Despite the late scheduling, odd times, and changes of venue, the film drew audiences in the thousands. To introduce the film, Kramer repeated the points he made with *West Side Story*. He conceded America's faults and recognized the rights to free speech that allowed Americans to call attention to them. But he also brought something new to his discussions of *The Defiant Ones*: his claim that the United States was correcting its social problems in the area of race relations. Responding to "unrelenting Soviet attacks on American racial problems," Kramer told the Soviet press that "the U.S. Constitution provides equal rights for all and [the] American Negro [is] now in [a] culminating phase of achieving guaranteed rights," according to embassy reports, with the "American Constitution an ideal being strived toward." Kramer's message of racial progress was precisely what US officials sought to convey.[79]

Kramer believed *The Defiant Ones* challenged the Soviet assumption that "most Americans subscribe to racial inequality." Instead, the audience saw a film about the issue "made by Americans in America" and came "to realize we are aware [of] and desire to change the injustices." He also explained the violent resistance of those Americans who did not—as in Little Rock, Arkansas, a Soviet propaganda subject—as "the last-ditch struggle of the dwindling number of die-hards who would preserve the status quo." Kramer's introductory comments were "applauded after each sentence." After the screening, some "8,000 spectators in Moscow's Sports Palace jumped to their feet" and offered "an extraordinary display of emotion," reported the *New York Times*. "Many wiped tears from their eyes as others cheered and clapped. They refused to leave for many minutes."[80]

What also made the screening of *The Defiant Ones* so powerful was the presence of Sidney Poitier. Although at first Poitier had not planned to be at the Moscow film festival, once the public screenings of the film were scheduled, he traveled from London. Stevens advocated the actor's attendance, as he felt that "if Sidney Poitier attended the showing, the positive aspects of the film would outweigh any negative impression" made by the film's critique of American race relations. Poitier's status as "Hollywood's beacon of racial democracy" had international reach, and he presented *The Defiant Ones* as an example of artistic freedom. "Such a picture could only be made in a free country, unafraid of self-criticism," he said, joining Kramer on this point.[81] Poitier also enjoyed great popularity in the Soviet Union, as did other African American artists. *The Defiant Ones*, Nedelin noted, showcased "the rare talent of the exceptionally promising Sidney Poitier who became in this picture one of the greatest actors of the American screen." For the Soviets, Poitier represented the struggle to overcome oppression. When his character in the film states fatalistically, "You live all your life and you never utter a word till you die," the Soviet audience roared with applause. Kramer saw the response as an "excess of emotion. . . . It was," he said, "one of those rare meetings of people, minus politicians," fostering international understanding.[82]

Kramer felt such "people-to-people" interactions demonstrated the positive impact of cinematic diplomacy, which continued with the public screening of *Judgment at Nuremberg*. A capacity audience filled the six-thousand-seat Palace of Congresses the day after the festival's close and received the film with "stunned silence." Kramer remembered "excited and audible—if somewhat shocked—response on two occasions." The first occasion was when the Soviet Union's role in the 1948 communist takeover of Czechoslovakia is invoked with "the Russians making their move." The second occasion occurred when Maximilian Schell's defense lawyer, Hans Rolfe, mentions the Soviets' 1939 nonaggression pact with Nazi Germany as evidence of universal responsibility and shared guilt for Nazi crimes, as the pact "gave the Germans time to launch a war in the West."[83] "A murmur of understanding and, one felt, agreement, or at least self-doubt, swept the audience when Schell specifically mentioned the Soviet-Nazi Pact," reported the Moscow embassy. Moreover, embassy officials felt the film's message about individual guilt and responsibility for atrocities and wrongdoing "fell on rich soil among persons whose memories of the Stalin period are still fresh." After the screening, "a prominent young director told Kramer that the Soviet people love Kramer because 'you look at truth in the eye, even when it concerns us and you must cuss us out.'"[84] Although some viewers considered the film "anti-Soviet," others felt it "is generally fair to us" and "passionately indicts fascism from general humanist positions." Many praised Kramer and Mann's work. The "struggle against the fascist danger" has "been presented acutely psychologically, emotionally and deeply in Stanley Kramer's film *Judgment at Nuremberg.*"[85]

Yet the decision of the American delegation and embassy to allow Kramer's two films to be seen publicly in Moscow provoked conflict with State Department and USIA officials back in the United States.

> Department notes with some surprise that US delegation, contrary to understanding achieved in Washington, supported Kramer in arranging showing to large audience of *Judgment at Nuremburg* and *Defiant Ones*. Despite excellent positive reaction to these films by audience under festival circumstances (including eloquent introduction by Kramer), Department and USIA continue [to] regard these films unsuitable. . . . We feel these films would only serve [to] support uninterrupted Soviet propaganda themes depicting US democracy as hoax and Federal Republic as creature of Nazi war criminals.[86]

The Moscow embassy strongly disagreed. "Admiration for US courage in looking problems squarely in eye is most prevalent reaction." "Showing these films," the embassy concluded, "has resulted in pro-American, not anti, impact."[87] Soviet officials may have intended with Kramer's attendance and films what Washington feared: to provoke anti-Americanism. But this is not what happened on the ground in Moscow. "Judging by audience reaction to these films, by the great respect the Soviet creative intelligentsia obviously feels for Kramer, and by comments which have been expressed to us here at the embassy," Ambassador Kohler wrote, "the Kramer message was not lost."[88] These developments indicated the difficulty officials faced in anticipating or controlling the reception of US cinematic diplomacy, whether positive or negative.

The success of US cinematic diplomacy at the 1963 Moscow film festival and Kramer's contributions were well recognized at the time. "Outstanding personage [at] Festival undoubtedly Stanley Kramer who gave freedom of creative arts big boost in capital of dictatorship of the arts," telegrammed Kohler from Moscow. Kramer "personifie[d]" artistic freedom and pursued "mutual understanding through creative criticism." "It is obvious that he was burning with an idea which he felt it was necessary to get across here," Kohler later wrote USIA director Murrow. "It is seldom one has the privilege of seeing a man imbued with an idea, who is working so selflessly, courageously, and so effectively."[89] Murrow, in turn, thanked and complimented Kramer for his participation in the Moscow film festival, which "reflects great credit upon the film community and the country, as well as upon you personally." The USIA also awarded Kramer a certificate of merit that year for "outstanding service in advancing international understanding." Meanwhile, the US media cheered when Steve McQueen received the Silver Prize for his acting in *The Great Escape*–the first time the United States won a prize at a film festival in a communist country. The Union of Sports Societies also awarded McQueen a diploma for his motorcycle riding in the movie, despite derision coming from other Soviet circles. Abby Mann received another award for his *Judgment of Nuremberg* screenplay, this time from the cinematic journal *Iskusstvo Kino*. Canadian critic Gerald Pratley sent his kudos to the US festival delegation. "This year, as a result of intelligent planning and execution, the Americans scored a resounding, happy and impressive triumph." He credited Stevens, primarily, and then Kramer.[90]

Back home, Kramer and Stevens together and separately made public and media appearances to promote their accomplishments at the Moscow film festival. Stevens saw the festival as "a distinguished success for the United States, American films, and the free world in general." He believed that "the appearance of the impressive U.S. delegation at the festival made a deep impact." Kramer restated his festival messages about motion pictures as an important method of international communication, which can foster mutual understanding.[91] But he also directed his comments to an American audience. "Our power—our one great power—is in the full demonstration of real freedom in film-making," even if, or better yet when, it leads to social and self-criticism. "What better propaganda can you use," he asked, "than to show the Russian people a film we made about our problems, when they know they can't be critical of their own society? You can't do any better than to show the truth of what you are, and the strength to examine what you are."[92] Kramer, along with many American liberals, was "convinced that there existed a natural affinity between intellectual freedom and their democratic society," and the promotion of one contributed to the promotion of the other. "We have made a dent for the first time," he asserted, in the Cold War conflict. "Well, mebbe," the *Los Angeles Times*'s Philip K. Scheuer hedged. But the film critic noted, "All this would have been unthinkable even a year ago."[93]

"Stanley's visit to Moscow," recalled George Stevens, Jr., "marked a high point in the cultural exchange between the two countries during those long years of estrangement."[94] Stevens's recollections indicated how Kramer's participation in the Moscow film festival dovetailed with US Cold War policy and politics in 1963. In this way, the liberal Kramer finally found his fit during the Democratic Kennedy administration and in the new decade of the 1960s. His professional reputation and political credibility made him an appealing and convincing cultural diplomat. His experience with selling messages through the production and promotion of his many movies contributed to his ability to transmit American liberal ideals abroad. At that historical moment, he exemplified how cultural diplomats could engage in representing or "performing the nation."[95] Even as he criticized the United States, and, in fact, because he did so—and used his freedom of expression to do so—Kramer helped legitimize US political values and leadership in a world dominated by the Cold War. Official acclaim for Kramer's performance in Moscow also garnered him positive media attention and popular acceptance back in the United States. That Kramer's social problem films and liberal politics came to be seen as mainstream after 1963 indicated a changing American culture, politics, and society as the Cold War thawed. In turn, Stanley Kramer's filmmaking priorities and political perspectives allowed him to contribute to further change as the decade of the 1960s continued.

Stanley Kramer during production of It's a Mad, Mad, Mad, Mad World
(1963). Courtesy of Margaret Herrick Library and MGM/UA.

7 An Old Liberal in New Hollywood

The year of Stanley Kramer's remarkable achievement and acclaim at the 1963 Moscow film festival also marked significant developments relating to the issues addressed in his recent films. The historic March on Washington took place in August 1963 and is considered the high point of the modern, interracial civil rights movement, a phase of the movement reflected in *The Defiant Ones*. The march demonstrated support for civil rights legislation outlawing racial segregation and disenfranchisement, which passed in the next two years. Also in August 1963, the Limited Nuclear Test Ban Treaty was signed by the Cold War superpowers, propelled by the Cuban Missile Crisis in October 1962. Although truly a "limited" and not comprehensive ban, it did prevent atmospheric tests of nuclear weapons to limit the dangers of radioactive fallout so powerfully conveyed in *On the Beach*. Challenges to assaults on civil liberties as seen in *Inherit the Wind* mounted in the early 1960s, with organized protest against HUAC. In early 1963, HUAC was recuperating from a first-of-its-kind confrontation with representatives of Women Strike for Peace, who had refused to "cower" before the committee and instead mocked the proceedings at recent hearings. Also in 1963, philosopher and writer Hannah Arendt published her book *Eichmann in Jerusalem*. In the wake of the Eichmann trial, "an array of intellectuals began to grapple seriously with the issues raised by the Holocaust," as had *Judgment at Nuremberg*.[1] The liberal political perspective expressed in Kramer's filmmaking now seemed less controversial than conventional. As a sign of his respected and renowned stature, the New York premiere of his 1963 film was a fundraiser for two Kennedy family charities, with the president's brothers, Robert and Edward, in attendance.

Soon, the cutting edge of controversy in Hollywood movies and American politics would be pursued by a younger generation more radical than the middle-aged Kramer. The decade of the 1960s is known as a time of transition and change in the United States and worldwide. A critique of the politics, society, and culture of Cold War America slowly developed and then swiftly dominated the American scene. A "kaleidoscope of movements"—the Black Power phase of the civil rights movement, the American Indian and Chicano movements, the student and anti–Vietnam War movements, the women's and gay liberation movements, and the environmental movement—propelled social and cultural change, personal and political transformation. Hollywood filmmakers picked up on the changing mood of the sixties, just as the Old Hollywood system transformed into the so-called New Hollywood. Instead of a few major studios controlling the production, distribution, and exhibition of motion pictures, by the 1960s a less integrated, more fluid motion picture industry emerged—for a time. The increasing prestige and influence of European art films also encouraged experimentation. In New Hollywood—an era he helped establish through his independent career—Kramer would come to be seen as old-fashioned in his film themes and technique. Yet he also would enjoy the biggest financial successes of his career. Mainstream acceptance had its benefits at the box office, even as film reviewers became more strident in their criticisms, and Kramer's liberal politics continued to be challenged from both the Right and Left.

Steering a Career's Course

As Stanley Kramer pursued his career as an independent producer-director in the new decade, the US motion picture industry faced challenging times. By 1960, average weekly attendance at the movies had dropped to 40 million, half of what it had been in the 1940s when Kramer began producing. By 1970, weekly attendance had fallen to less than 20 million. One major studio, RKO, went out of business; MGM closed its production studios and quit making movies; and the other surviving film companies were purchased by big corporate conglomerates. The number of films made also declined. In 1963 only 143 films were produced, an "all-time low."[2] One of the great movie successes of that year, released just a few months after his mission to Moscow, was Kramer's *It's a Mad, Mad, Mad, Mad World* (1963). A madcap comedy, the film was a new genre for Kramer and a significant departure for a producer-director who had made his name with serious social problem films. Another departure—as well as a return—for Kramer during the decade involved moving several projects from United Artists to Columbia Pictures, including *Ship of Fools* (1965). He also returned to producing movies directed by others. Kramer recognized that the "generation gap" said to be dividing older and younger Americans during the 1960s existed in Hollywood, and he decided to produce films with younger directors. The decade brought big changes to Kramer's personal life as well, with his divorce from Anne Pearce Kramer in 1963 and his remarriage to actress Karen Sharpe in 1966. That Kramer managed to steer a course for his career through such difficult times revealed his ability to survive and succeed in the New Hollywood.

Given Kramer's prominence in the industry, his views on the state of the US motion picture industry and what could be done to improve it were sought out in the early 1960s. One change advocated by many inside and outside Hollywood concerned the censorship regime run by the PCA. Under attack from filmmakers and civil libertarians motivated by a changing American society and culture, combined with the need to attract audiences, the Production Code had been significantly revised in 1956. Further revisions were demanded to provide for freer expression, but Kramer did not think censorship was "the big issue at all." "I have never been prevented by censorship from doing any piece of material that I wanted to do," he contended in 1962.[3] In fact, Kramer still fondly remembered "Hollywood's censor," Joseph Breen, who had retired from the PCA in 1955, and arranged a private screening of *Judgment at Nuremberg* for him. Kramer's comfort with the Production Code set him apart from his colleagues, however. In 1968 the Motion Picture Association of America replaced the code with the current ratings system, which limits the age of the audience for a film rather than regulating film content. After experiencing this new system, Kramer felt "it works," giving the filmmaker "maximum freedom of the screen" and the filmgoing audience "responsibility for choosing what it wants to see."[4]

Other industry-related issues drew comment from Kramer, such as innovations in film technique and the cost of distribution. On different occasions, he discussed various color techniques, widescreen and 3-D cinema, and even an "experiment with the olfactory nerves known as 'Smellovision.'" While other directors experimented with narrative form and editing and cinematography, Kramer felt none of these could "compete with the essential business of motion pictures which is the telling of a good story within the framework of cinematic terms. . . .

Innovations for the sake of innovations become pointless and eventually self-defeating," he argued. From some commentators, he received criticism for continuing with traditional filmmaking; from others came compliments for avoiding new elements such as "endings-that-you-have-to-figure-out-for-yourself."[5]

The producer-director also addressed problems with the distribution system. "Distribution of a film now costs far too much money." He named high distribution fees and the involvement of too many companies "all over the world, charging desperately in each instance against every picture." They "are getting too much of the gross dollar," he felt.[6] In these comments, Kramer identified the most significant continuity between Old and New Hollywood. Even as production diversified, the major studios maintained control of distribution. "Distribution," according to scholar Geoff King, "has become the key strategic source of control over the industry," especially "control of international distribution networks." The revenues generated from distribution meant the major studios still dominated Hollywood.[7] Kramer observed and objected to this development, as a hindrance to independent production and profits.

As another hindrance, Kramer identified star salaries as a problematic factor in the New Hollywood. With the major film studios in decline, movie stars had greater freedom, independence, and negotiating power. In contrast to the old system of studio contracts and control, they could more easily set the terms of their employment and demand higher salaries from producers. "It's our own fault," Kramer admitted. "We've gone into competitive bidding for established stars and built their salaries up and up." But he also knew he "had paid what I had to pay to get what I wanted," given the centrality of the cast to the success of a motion picture. For this reason, he very much valued his actors. "Actors are my strongest weapon for communication." He became known as "an actors' director" by the early 1960s.[8] Not every actor Kramer hired worked well with him. Some called him "a perfectionist," and Anthony Perkins felt he had been "gruff, short, sarcastic" while filming *On the Beach*. Yet many actors—prominent and not—reported good experiences under Kramer's direction. He sought to relax nervous performers with quips, cigarette breaks, and compliments. "Cut! That was a beaut!" he would say. "Kramer takes the view that an actor thinks, reflects, reacts and has a feeling about the part he's playing,"

Spencer Tracy stated after starring in *Judgment at Nuremberg*. "That's all for the good."[9]

As the 1960s continued, one hurdle that Kramer had faced from the start of his producing career was no longer one he needed to clear: the Hollywood blacklist. The blacklist was certainly not over for everyone in Hollywood, and for some filmmakers it never would be. Kramer was more fortunate. For the rest of his career, he never confronted another controversy over his business associates, as he had with Carl Foreman, or his hiring decisions, as he had with Nedrick Young. Foreman's filmmaking career continued, and he was cleared, off the blacklist, and back at Columbia Pictures by 1957. Young had gone on to write and also act in a few films after working with Kramer. But his opportunities for employment remained limited. Despite his Oscar win for *The Defiant Ones* and his nomination for *Inherit the Wind*, he continued to battle the blacklist. In December 1960, after the release of *Inherit the Wind*, he became the lead plaintiff of twelve blacklisted filmmakers in a lawsuit against the Motion Picture Association of America and the major studios. *Nedrick Young, et al. v. Motion Picture Association of America, Inc., et al.* claimed that the motion picture industry had violated the Sherman Antitrust Act by conspiring to institute and maintain the Hollywood blacklist. They sought an injunction to end the industry practice of blacklisting and $7.5 million in damages to compensate the plaintiffs.[10] Not everyone on the blacklist supported the *Young* lawsuit. Dalton Trumbo, for example, "refused to participate in such a suit." He "feared it would have the effect of closing the door to reemployment that he had pried open," along with Young and others. With the breakthrough of 1960, due to *Exodus*, *Spartacus*, and *Inherit the Wind*, Trumbo believed "the blacklist was doomed because of ethical and economic reasons."[11]

Young and his fellow plaintiffs disagreed. A legal injunction would have ended the Hollywood blacklist immediately and for everyone, rather than chipping away through the slow, often individualized process advocated by Trumbo. At an event at New York's Carnegie Hall in September 1961, Young offered a speech in support of the lawsuit. He spoke spiritedly about the American freedoms of speech, assembly, and political affiliation. "From whom have these liberties been stolen? Not from the few victims of the blacklist, but from the whole nation." The anticommunist opposition sought to "still our voices," "to try and almost kill our spirits." But these forces had not won over the past thirteen years of the blacklist, and now a new decade dawned. "The time has come to un-silence ourselves," he argued. "The time has come to fight back."[12] Unfortunately, victory was not quick in coming. Instead, the injunction was denied, and the case for damages dragged on until 1965, when it was settled for less than $100,000. That year, a legal review of the *Young* case provided a victory of sorts, determining that "the Hollywood blacklist seems clearly illegal." Also that same year, Peter Bart observed in the *New York Times*, "the residue of political fear seems to have been almost completely erased" in the movie industry. Nedrick Young had too few years left to live, however, and he died in 1968 at the age of only fifty-four. His obituary in the *New York Times* did not mention the lawsuit to which he gave his name, but it did recall his political principles and screenwriting successes. "Nedrick Young, 54, Defied the Blacklist: Writer Who Won Oscar for *Defiant Ones* Dies."[13]

Contributing to the waning of the blacklist was a new generation of filmmakers in Hollywood, unscathed by old political conflicts and welcomed by Kramer. "With the Old Guard passing from the scene and younger people coming in," he observed in 1962, "the challenges are all to the good." He considered "the entrenched managements of the large film companies" to be "obstructive" to "the forward progress of motion pictures," including cinematic influences from overseas. "Just look at what has been happening in the past few years. The exciting things that have stimulated people into coming into theaters—such as the French 'new wave,' the new Italian neo-realists, and Britain's 'angry young men'—are scornfully resisted by the 'control factors' in the American industry. In fact, they are not even dreamed of, much less understood, by the heads of our big companies."[14] "I've always been frustrated," he said, "that the mood and approach of young directors all over the world has so far outdistanced, artistically, the American approach." But he anticipated a change in the near future. He began participating in a pioneering example of "university-industry collaboration" to train student filmmakers through a film production course at the University of California, Los Angeles. Kramer also believed that "many young people are now finding greater freedom on the American scene . . . since the demise of the large studio operation." More creative control for filmmakers in Hollywood was not only "encouraging, it's rather revolutionary for us."[15]

Kramer looked to this younger generation when he needed directors for several movies he wanted to make in the early 1960s. "I felt an urgency to make these films" but was busy with *It's a Mad, Mad, Mad, Mad World*. The "scripts were completed—I wanted to go ahead." One director he hired was Hubert Cornfield for *Pressure Point* (1962). Some fifteen years younger than Kramer, Cornfield grew up in France, where he became acquainted with French New Wave directors and their innovations with narrative form and technique. Kramer promised him autonomy and authority as the director. "Now that's a terribly rare attitude in this industry," Cornfield felt.[16] Cornfield also collaborated on the screenplay, adapted from psychologist Robert Lindner's collection of case histories, *The Fifty-Minute Hour* (1955). The screenplay tells the story—in flashback—of a prison psychiatrist treating a sociopathic American Nazi convict, while the contemporary frame involves another psychoanalytic case. The psychotherapy brings less than successful results: the patient remains evil but understands himself better. This outcome fit with the end of the "golden age" of propsychology films that occurred in the 1960s, with the "public recognition that psychotherapy offered no instant cures," a change since Kramer's 1949 film, *Home of the Brave*. Cornfield expressed *Pressure Point*'s therapeutic theme through hallucinations, dreams, and memories portrayed with new film techniques, and his experimentation received mixed reviews, as did the film. Kramer did not blame Cornfield but himself. "When a producer doesn't give a film the time it is due, it should be no surprise when the project doesn't work as planned."[17]

What Kramer and his contemporaries felt worked at the time—although scholars since offer a different analysis—was the casting of Sidney Poitier in the role of the psychiatrist.[18] As with *Home of the Brave*, this casting involved substituting a black character for a Jewish one, in this case the actual Jewish psychologist, Robert Lindner. Kramer made this substitution because "in the contemporary sense it seemed more pointed, valid and dramatic. Also I was anxious to show the Negro in a different position to that of the subservient, noneducated one," he added. This character, together with the American Nazi patient played by Bobby Darin, made *Pressure Point*, according to the *Los Angeles Times*'s Philip K. Scheuer, "something of a cross between his *The Defiant Ones* and *Judgment at Nuremberg*."[19] But Poitier publicly praised this decision, most prominently when he testified at

congressional hearings on racial discrimination prior to the film's release in late 1962. Within the context of the civil rights movement,
Poitier discussed the "fight being waged for equality of opportunity" in
Hollywood. He named Kramer as one who "has recognized the Negro's
aspirations in this direction. . . . What particularly impressed me was his
willingness to have a key role rewritten so that it could be played by a
Negro actor," Poitier commented. As it turned out, Poitier's role as the
prison psychiatrist was the only leading role for an African American
in a Hollywood film that year. The next year, the NAACP protested this
lack of black representation in Hollywood and cited Kramer's films,
particularly *The Defiant Ones*, as exceptions for providing "serious approaches to Negro life in the United States."[20]

More contemporary racial content and film technique did not translate into success at the box office for *Pressure Point*, so Kramer hoped to
do better with his next production, *A Child Is Waiting* (1963), directed
by John Cassavetes. An actor as well as a director—he had costarred
with Poitier in *Edge of the City* (1957)—Cassavetes had a reputation as
"a member of the New York cinematic avant-garde." His jazz-inflected
independent production, *Shadows* (1959), won a critics' award at the
Venice International Film Festival. Coincidentally, he was born in the
same year as Kramer's previous director, Hubert Cornfield. "I thought I
would put all the eggs in one basket and let John Cassavetes (who represented a younger school of directors) express himself in a more modern
vein," Kramer explained in 1964.[21] Abby Mann wrote the screenplay,
based on an earlier television drama of his, just as had happened with
Judgment at Nuremberg. A Child Is Waiting, another social problem
film, concerns social attitudes and discrimination toward children with
learning and developmental problems. Kramer not only engaged again
his screenwriter from *Judgment at Nuremberg* but also two of the stars,
Judy Garland and Burt Lancaster. The genre, writer, and actors of *A
Child Is Waiting* were, thus, familiar to Kramer.

Not so the filmmaking approach of the director Cassavetes, and, although that new, unconventional quality was precisely why Kramer
hired him, it led to conflict. The young filmmaker pursued a realistic,
documentary aesthetic with an improvisational directorial style. "John
Cassavetes belongs to the 'let it happen' school of directing," Kramer
recalled, the antithesis of his own method. At the time, Cassavetes complained "that Kramer interfered too much." Cassavetes's biographers
offer more dramatic stories. One details "a violent dispute" between the

two men as the editing process began. Cassavetes later commented that he disagreed with Kramer's approach to the social problem film, which he characterized as editorializing. "An editorial doesn't *do* anything. An editorial only makes you feel guilty. And I don't think that is what a film is about."[22] Another biographer, Raymond Carney, tells how this conflict between "two enormous egos" led Kramer to fire Cassavetes and take over postproduction. According to Kramer, the clash came because "I had to order a recut because the director's cut just wasn't going to bring audiences in. And there were headlines and it turned ugly for a bit. So I went back to directing."[23] Kramer's recollection about the conflict with Cassavetes returning him to directing overlooked another less than successful film he produced at the time with Richard Wilson, a director his own age: *Invitation to a Gunfighter* (1964).

Taken together, these three films produced by Kramer under the direction of others lost nearly $4 million, but he made up for these losses with *It's a Mad, Mad, Mad, Mad World*, released in 1963. The film was a blockbuster bonanza at the box office, grossing $26 million, which equaled about $450 million in 2014 dollars. Although production costs also were high, United Artists "came out ahead" in their financial relationship with Kramer due to this film.[24] *It's a Mad, Mad, Mad, Mad World* not only signaled a change in the producer-director's profit and loss statement but also in film genre. "I'm tired of controversy," Kramer told *Newsweek* in 1960. "I'm making the biggest comedy in the history of the business—'Something a Little Less Serious.' It's a long, Keystone Cops comedy. Somebody said to me, 'You should do something a little less serious,' and so we used that as the title." "The action revolves around a mass automobile chase for buried gold," he summarized for the *New York Times*. The movie was a "comedy involving greed and chase."[25] As the release date got closer, Kramer shied away from identifying the movie's message, or even admitting that it had a message. "It's a film without a message," he asserted in 1962, the year before the film came out, "except that everybody, under certain conditions, is possessed of a touch of larceny." "The picture says that, one way or another, greed leads to no good," Kramer recalled. "But I didn't say anything like this when the picture was released."[26] The irony of a movie about greed becoming a great financial success was not lost at the time or since.

Nor was the apparent contradiction of Kramer, the producer of controversy, producing a comedy. "Stanley Kramer Turns to Humor," headlined the *New York Times*. "When Stanley Kramer does a comedy, it's news," Hedda Hopper reported as the lede in her gossip column, "because he's the daddy of those soul-searching, somber movies." "There was a growing presumption in the industry that I couldn't do comedy," Kramer later stated. "I was determined, in a burst of modesty, to produce and direct the funniest comedy anyone had ever seen."[27]

The film was an extravaganza and an expensive one. If the budget had been $600,000, Philip Scheuer contended, Kramer "would have been content to call it 'It's a Mad World.' But with a $6-million investment he feels he has to add three more 'Mads.'" Scheuer catalogued the film's extravagances: a 135-day shoot, an original script by William and Tania Rose twice the usual 150 pages, and a theatrical running time of three and a half hours.[28] It was not just the longest slapstick comedy ever made. It was also the "widest-screened (Cinerama)"—a process involving shooting with three cameras and screening with three projectors in a simultaneous and synchronized fashion—"and the most many-starred (over thirty—count them—Buster Keaton to Jerry Lewis)." The cast was a "who's who" of the contemporary comedy world, and included Milton Berle, Sid Caesar, Buddy Hackett, ZaSu Pitts, Mickey Rooney, Phil Silvers, Jonathan Winters, and Ethel Merman. The spectacle of the "endless indignities" suffered by Merman's character and played for sexist laughs by the male comedians confirmed 1963 as a prefeminist moment, even if, as Kramer stated, she "managed to hold her own."[29] As a police officer, Spencer Tracy played the straight man.

For respondents, their opinion of the size of Kramer's enterprise translated into their opinion of the film overall. This "big, big, big, big, long, long, long, long film," asserted one review, was more "exhausting than exhilarating" and "sad proof that the saying 'the bigger the better' just isn't often true." The title of the *New Yorker*'s review said it all. "Why, Why, Why, Why?"[30] Critics who indicted the magnitude of the movie often condemned the development of the theme. "Everyone in this immense cast is motivated by self-seeking, meaningless greed," Hollis Alpert argued in the *Saturday Review*. The film was "a vicious portrait of people dominated by nothing but the insatiable, nagging urge to get hold of a big pile of dough." "The basic idea, a comedy of greed in the land of the almighty dollar, was a good one," wrote another reviewer. Nevertheless it "collapsed under ton upon ton of excess flab." But *Film Daily* believed the movie "is the blockbuster that should revitalize movie-going for sheer fun."[31] Audiences loved the film—and nowhere more than in the Soviet Union. The popularity of Kramer's "funny and dynamic" film revealed not only Soviet moviegoers' enjoyment of the plot but also their engagement with the message about greed. *Izvestia* asked, "Is this not a snapshot of the very essence of Americanism?" One teenage filmgoer wrote, "the capitalist West is mad about money," and "in America a human greed and lust for money is the most important driving force." "Stanley Kramer demonstrated this," he concluded.[32] Such responses reinforced Kramer's reputation there as a courageous social critic. At home, Hollywood recognized the film with five Oscar nominations and a win for best sound effects, the first-ever award in that category.

Kramer's next film as a producer-director, *Ship of Fools* (1965), returned him to Columbia Pictures and to the subject of the Nazi Holocaust. Abby Mann's screenplay adapted Katherine Anne Porter's best-selling 1962 novel of the same name. When Kramer secured the film rights, Porter considered it "very happy news." She had been "tremendously . . . impressed" with *Judgment at Nuremberg*'s "terrible boldness and beauty." "Bless you," she wrote Kramer, "you don't make it easy for anybody."[33] The challenge to condense a book, which Mann called "monumental" but other commentators called "massive" and "interminable," took a year and was deemed "enormously skillful." The resulting movie told nine separate but interlocking stories. The many major characters made the film "a sea-going *Grand Hotel*," quipped Scheuer. Like the famous 1932 film, it "throws together a motley crew and passengers for a crucial period in their lives and then parts them."[34] The time is 1933, and the trip is from Veracruz, Mexico, to Bremerhaven, Germany. Mann and Kramer moved the date of Porter's novel up two years to correspond to Adolf Hitler's rise to power in Germany. The conflicts among the characters "foreshadow the world holocaust that is soon to come," Mann explained. The passengers and crew stand in for humankind's lack of foresight and resistance in confronting the evils of Nazism. The most famous lines in the film belonged to a Jewish character, who responds to the anti-Semitic slurs of a Nazi on board. "There are nearly a million Jews in Germany. What are they going to do—kill us all?" *Ship of Fools* "touched upon . . . the darker realities of World War II," film scholar Annette Insdorf observes.[35]

The French actress Simone Signoret, who starred in the film along with Vivien Leigh, Lee Marvin, and José Ferrer, later criticized Kramer for the film's interpretation of Nazi crimes. She did not see in *Ship of Fools* the interpretative mix of particularism and universalism that *Judgment at Nuremberg* had offered. Instead, Signoret expressed anger over the film's particular focus on the Nazi persecution of Jews rather than a more universal approach that included other persecuted groups. "Americans have a blind spot," she argued after the release of *Ship of Fools* in 1965, "when it comes to the crimes of the Nazis. They immediately think of the Jews, only the Jews." Although of Jewish heritage herself, Signoret also was a leftist, along with her husband, actor Yves Montand. In the 1950s they had been the target of anticommunist attacks and refused visas to travel to the United States. When Signoret won the Oscar for her performance in *Room at the Top* (1959), she believed that her victory was Hollywood's vote both for her and against Cold War anticommunism. To her mind, *Ship of Fools* should have mentioned Nazi Germany's persecution of communists, and she put the blame on Kramer. A "man like you does not have the right to make a film on Nazism and omit the communists." She saw "in that omission" by the liberal Kramer "a lot of malice and a lot of hypocrisy" toward the Left.[36] In her indictment of Kramer, the actress indicated how conventional and compromised Hollywood liberalism appeared to more politically radical commentators by the mid-1960s.

Just as Kramer's political reputation was outflanked from the Left in 1965, his critical reputation drew fire with the reception of *Ship of Fools*. Kramer promoted the film as very current, recognizing the changes under way in the audience and approach for Hollywood movies. It was closer to the "European than the American school of filmmaking," he argued, with an "episodic, even disjointed" narrative. He also "brought two young people more into the foreground to represent modern young people to a greater extent."[37] And *Ship of Fools* garnered many positive reviews. Most notable was Scheuer's review, which included rare praise for Kramer's direction. "Kramer," Scheuer wrote, "convinced me that his dependability as a director (not free from certain camera-conscious pretensions in the past) has caught up with his shrewd managerial stewardship of some 15 years." Arthur Knight agreed. "This is a new Stanley Kramer, not hitting each scene head-on or underscoring every significant statement."[38]

But critical reviews were forthcoming from influential sources. *Time* continued its scathing stance against Kramer and Mann seen earlier with *Judgment at Nuremberg*. Kramer "seldom resorts to nuance when an overstatement will do," and due to "Abby Mannerisms" the characters are "spouting Meaningful Dialogue." The reviewer for the Israeli newspaper *Herut* felt *Ship of Fools* played it safe. He bemoaned the loss of "Kramer's fighting spirit. But, like other artists, the American director grew old. Grew old and rich. He still wants to make controversial films, just not too controversial." In contrast to Kramer's claim of currency, the *Herut* reviewer argued that the film was instead "distant and historic."[39]

A number of these critiques went beyond the specific movie *Ship of Fools* to attack Kramer's entire career and approach to filmmaking. "Daring? Provocative? Not in the least," stated Midge Decter in *Commentary*. "Fashionable, rather, and cheap." She derided Kramer's overall style as "middlebrow seriousness." *Middlebrow* was not an inaccurate description to apply to Kramer, as so-called middlebrow culture occupied a place between high and popular culture and combined artistic and commercial aims. But as to his messages about serious subjects, Decter considered them "facile" and "smugly offered." Although elements of this critique had appeared before with earlier films, these critical voices grew louder as the 1960s continued. To "treat problem subjects" early in Kramer's career "was daring," but "to exploit them now is much less original," wrote the English critic Peter Cowie.[40] For the *New Republic*'s Stanley Kauffmann, Kramer's films seem "designed to make the liberal feel satisfied with his enlightened state." In contrast, "a true film of social comment is one that fills a conscientious viewer with shame—for things left undone." In accusing Kramer of failing to fulfill a fundamental function of the social problem film—to express a "combination of idealism and guilt over the state of the world"—Kauffmann undermined Kramer's credibility in his trademark genre.[41]

The most withering and influential critic of Kramer in the 1960s was Pauline Kael, soon to be hired as a film critic for the *New Yorker*. She used her review of *Ship of Fools* to survey and scorn Kramer's entire career, and she issued her famous, contemptuous summary statement that Kramer's reputation was "based on a series of errors: he is widely assumed to be the director" of movies he had produced with more accomplished directors, such as Fred Zinnemann and Edward Dmytryk. Instead, the movies Kramer actually directed himself were safe and smug, "shallow" and "opportunistic." "In Kramer's work the artist's accuracy is missing," she contended. Critics had rewarded the producer-director for his good intentions rather than recognizing the bad outcomes of his filmmaking. Even though Kael thought *The Defiant Ones* was Kramer's best movie, "the singleness of purpose behind it all is a little offensive." *On the Beach* was "a lousy movie," *Inherit the Wind* "continued the formula of using 'controversial' subjects in noncontroversial ways," and in *Judgment at Nuremberg* "the large issues were dramatized in ludicrous terms." Kael then introduced what she came to call "the Kramer syndrome," the main symptom of which was making self-important and self-indulgent movies. He became a negative reference for Kael from then on. She criticized a screenplay by saying "Stanley Kramer has returned to us, lugging leftover dialogue from *On the Beach*," and deemed another director "as wrong-headed as a Stanley Kramer."[42] Kael's crushing critique would shape the reception of the rest of Kramer's career and films.

Stanley Kramer and the Politics of the Sixties

From the mid-1960s on, Kramer confronted a changing political scene as he continued to make movies that reflected his liberal politics. Political events and developments increasingly discredited American liberalism as having the answers to social problems. The achievement of historic civil rights legislation in 1964 and 1965 did not rectify racial inequalities in income, housing, or education, and African American neighborhoods, including Watts in Los Angeles, erupted in riots. Liberals also were held responsible for the Vietnam War. The escalation of American involvement in Vietnam occurred during the liberal Democratic administrations of President Kennedy and, after his assassination in 1963, President Lyndon B. Johnson. As a result, a younger generation of activists defined their radical politics in opposition to the liberal tradition represented by Kramer. The reception of his next film, *Guess Who's Coming to Dinner* (1967), and the film he responded with, *R.P.M.* (1970), revealed as much. Even so, the producer-director felt caught in the middle. "I agreed with the college students in some of what they were demanding from the world—a more liberated society, an end to the Vietnam War and to racism, less hypocrisy and dishonesty in their parents' generation, less corruption in the establishment." In 1965, for example, he donated $1,000 to the Student Nonviolent Coordinating Committee, "considered to be the most radical and controversial of all major civil rights organizations." Despite this common ground, "the kids saw me as the establishment, and that bothered me," Kramer recalled. "I wanted to be more than a discarded liberal."[43] In the late

1960s and early 1970s, Kramer's liberal filmmaking and politics met with challenges from new audiences on the political Left and Right.

Kramer's 1967 film *Guess Who's Coming to Dinner* was the most popular, profitable, and pummeled of all his films, as well documented and analyzed by writer Mark Harris and scholar Susan Courtney.[44] The story covers a liberal, middle-aged, white couple in San Francisco coming to terms with their daughter's marriage to a black man in the course of one day. For many filmgoers, the movie provided enjoyable entertainment. It undoubtedly helped that Spencer Tracy and Katharine Hepburn starred as the married couple. Their ninth film together, *Guess Who's Coming to Dinner* recalled their old romantic "battle-of-the-sexes" comedies, such as *Woman of the Year* (1942) and *Pat and Mike* (1952). Their long-standing partnership on screen was matched off screen. Although the Catholic Tracy remained married to his wife, his relationship with Hepburn was an open secret by 1967. Audiences brought this knowledge into theaters, as well as the fact that Tracy had died only weeks after finishing the movie. In ill health throughout filming, he appreciated that "it's Stanley who puts me to work." "I tell him my life expectancy is about seven and a half minutes and he says, 'Action!'" To ensure Tracy's performance, Kramer negotiated salary deferrals and shorter workdays. The intertextual meaning of the stars' scenes together gave them unique poignancy. Also contributing to the film's great success was the star power of Sidney Poitier in the role of the fiancé. That year's top star, Poitier appeared in two other major movies in 1967, *To Sir, with Love* and *In the Heat of the Night*, which won the best picture Oscar. "I loaded the deck, of course," Kramer stated, referring to his stellar cast.[45]

With a script by William Rose and funding from Columbia Pictures, Kramer produced a film hailed as one of the year's best by mainstream film reviewers, filmgoers, and the film industry. Bosley Crowther deemed it "delightfully acted and gracefully entertaining." He even promised filmgoers "euphoria and likely enjoyment of this witty and glistening film." Charles Champlin considered *Guess Who's Coming to Dinner* "must-viewing for anyone who has ever cared about movies." It "is a deeply-moving film, guaranteed to leave no eye undamp."[46] The film was extremely popular and broke many box-office records. "Anytime people brave freezing weather, and stand in an almost endless line to see a movie, it must be extraordinary! This interracial love story is really rocking the boat," contended one columnist.[47] At the Oscars,

Guess Who's Coming to Dinner tied with *Bonnie and Clyde* for the most nominations, with ten each. These honors included best picture, director, screenplay, editing, and four acting nominations. Tracy received a posthumous nomination—only the second time this event occurred in the Academy's history—and Hepburn and Rose won in their categories. Awards also were forthcoming from outside the industry. Kramer and his film were praised for challenging "where the real prejudice is felt" and for contributing "to a better understanding of the problems all peoples face."[48]

Despite such effusive praise, Kramer's laudable and lucrative film was also lambasted as unrealistic and old-fashioned within the context of the transformations and turmoil of the late 1960s. For Kramer, the film's message advocating the acceptance of interracial marriage continued to be very current in 1967. Despite recent revisions to the Production Code, "the film industry taboo against even the implication of sex between blacks and whites was still in force," he recalled. And, unlike most earlier films, *Guess Who's Coming to Dinner* provided a happy ending for the interracial couple. Moreover, only six months earlier, the US Supreme Court had struck down as unconstitutional laws prohibiting interracial marriage in *Loving v. Virginia* (1967). At the time of the court's ruling, sixteen states still had antimiscegenation laws, a fact mentioned in Rose's screenplay. "Why, in 16 or 17 states you'd be breaking the law. You'd be criminals," the father of Poitier's character warns his son. Laws against interracial marriage had buttressed the separate and hierarchical racial order in private life just as segregation laws had in public life, and the right to marry regardless of race was considered a civil rights victory.[49] Kramer's film supported this right and showed the characters opposed to interracial marriage as in the wrong.

The mainstream black press enthusiastically endorsed the film as a result, but other Americans on the liberal-left did not. In the *Los Angeles Sentinel*, A. S. Doc Young wrote about this "Hollywood breakthrough. . . . Guess what Stanley Kramer has done? Defying the 'greatest' of all American bugaboos—and, hence, the most awesome of Hollywood bugaboos—he has produced a motion picture which picks us up and carries us one giant step closer to the realization of our age-old dream of equality among the human beings of this nation." "*Guess Who's Coming to Dinner* will prove to be a solid blockbuster in race relations," argued Young's colleague Bill Lane. "I strongly believe this happy-ending movie can do more for the cause of brotherhood than a Civil Rights demonstration," Roland Forte opined in Cleveland's *Call and Post*.[50] For many liberal and leftist critics and commentators, however, the film's message about interracial marriage was long outdated. "The film was famously known, as one critic-wag put it, as 'the best film of 1957.'" When Kramer screened and discussed *Guess Who's Coming to Dinner* during a tour of college campuses in early 1968, he discovered their "objection: that I made a film about a problem the university student maintains does not exist."[51] The high-profile interracial marriage of Secretary of State Dean Rusk's daughter in the fall of 1967 indicated as much.

But responses from racist Americans belied the assumption that Kramer and his colleagues were playing it safe with the film's racial theme. White supremacist protests and pickets still occurred at theaters exhibiting the film, as had happened with *The Defiant Ones* nearly a decade earlier. And not just in the South. The Ku Klux Klan protested in Hamilton, Ohio, for example. Numerous, hostile letters to Kramer from filmgoers condemned the film. They came from all over the United States, including Florida, Georgia, Kansas, New Jersey, and Pennsylvania. Women and men wrote, and many letters were anonymous or signed with a pseudonym, such as "Disgusted Citizen." "I could not believe anyone would make such an inflammatory picture in these racially troubled times." Some letters were anti-Semitic, and one addressed Kramer as "White Nigger." It was an "immoral and filthy movie" and advocated "mongrelisation of the races," wrote an Alabama man. "I felt like throwing-up every time that *black* Poitier touched the little white girl," a Pennsylvania letter writer seethed. "It was disgusting," fumed two California women, "and we wondered how much the NAACP paid you to push THAT." Other letter writers advanced arguments in defense of their racist reactions to the film. One woman explained why interracial marriage was against the will of God, and an anonymous letter opposed biracial offspring. These letter writers were not alone. Public opinion polls at the time showed widespread opposition to interracial marriage, with only 20 to 25 percent of Americans surveyed approving.[52]

For these reasons, Sidney Poitier believed that "*Guess Who's Coming to Dinner* is a totally revolutionary movie" and that this racially reactionary response was "what so many critics failed to see" when reviewing the film. This failure occurred especially when critics decried the role he played in the film, the esteemed Dr. John Prentice, as out of step with changing ideas about race in America.[53] The characterization of Prentice reflected Kramer and his colleagues' liberal integrationist or assimilationist stance on race. In this view, race was inseparable from racism and could only signify stigma. When racism was eliminated as a social problem, race as a category or concept would also disappear, leaving a supposed "colorblind" society. As Poitier's Prentice tells his father, "you think of yourself as a colored man. I think of myself as a man." But the prominence of Black Power by 1967 challenged that view. Race came to be seen as a source of pride for African Americans and other groups, not just a source of discrimination. This perspective appeared in criticisms of Poitier and his film roles and countered the actor's positive assessment of his recent movies.

One of the most prominent and provocative critiques appeared in the *New York Times* a few months before the release of *Guess Who's Coming to Dinner*. Playwright and drama critic Clifford Mason's "Why Does White America Love Sidney Poitier So?" answered his own question. The actor's roles made him "a showcase nigger." In "flight" from black "identity and historical fact," Poitier played "a good guy in a totally white world," where he is "helping the white man solve the white man's problem." In keeping with the priorities of the black arts movement, Mason called for movies concerned with "the dignity, the manhood, the thinking of the Negro in his world." Without that change, "there can be no true portrait of the Negro and no true art." Mason's attack set the context for the reception of Poitier's latest role in a Kramer film and exposed the gap between Poitier's film portrayals and contemporary culture and politics.[54]

This gap widened further with critical reviews of *Guess Who's Coming to Dinner*. Renata Adler, a member of a new, younger generation of film critics, replaced Bosley Crowther on his retirement at the *New York Times*. She observed that Poitier played "a kind of deliberate, type-cast, reverse racial stereotype." Even if this new stereotype was less egregiously racist than the old Hollywood caricatures of African Americans, it was still a black stereotype created by and for white Americans rather than a realistic representation.[55] "Surely more and more Negroes today reject this washing-out of color," noted Stanley Kauffmann, "and insist on thinking of themselves as Negroes." A growing mood of black separatism also discouraged interracial marriage. During his tour of college campuses, Kramer visited Stanford, where he was asked, "Why did you make Poitier so white?" Revealing his lack of understanding of the new politics of race, Kramer responded, "I don't know exactly what white means."[56] James Baldwin would soon tell him. "Baldwin Blasts Poitier's Hit Role," headlined one newspaper. As Baldwin had done with *The Defiant Ones*, he challenged the characterization of Poitier's character. Prentice was one of "those who think of themselves as white" and "has had to become a living freak" to succeed in a white racist society. "James Baldwin has been very critical of me," Kramer recalled, "and though it hurt, what he said is true. . . . He said I had not completely captured on film the soul of the black man, and that no white man could do that." Baldwin went easy compared to critic Maxine Hall Elliston, who called the film "warmed over white shit."[57]

The class status of Poitier's role also catalyzed criticism. Prentice was a medical doctor with impeccable credentials. "He is not simply a doctor," one reviewer noted, "he is a magna cum laude from Johns Hopkins, a Yale professor, and assistant director of the World Health Organization," and a published author. "He's an important guy," observes one character in the film. "No wonder he doesn't have much to say about himself," Tracy's character, Matt Drayton, comments condescendingly. "Who the hell would believe him?"[58] For many critics, such as Baldwin, Prentice's exceptionalism reflected racism on the part of the filmmakers: to be even considered a potential husband for a white woman, he had to be extraordinary. "Why isn't the character Poitier acts just an average Negro," asked a University of Maryland student of Kramer, and "not the exceptionally successful one he plays?" "That he's not in an inferior position to the girl and her family is the point," Kramer asserted, "making race the only impediment to the marriage."[59] Yet, despite his extensive accomplishments and prominence, Prentice defers to the Draytons, submitting to their decision on whether he will marry their daughter. He is also embarrassingly reprimanded—while shirtless—by the Drayton family housekeeper, Tillie, the stock stereotype of the mammy. She is loyal to the white family, a civil rights conservative, and speaks in Hollywood's false black dialect. "You're one of those smooth-talkin' smart-ass niggers just out for all you can get with your black power and all your other troublemaking nonsense." Prentice does not even respond, prompting one reviewer to wonder about "a Black Power interpretation" of the scene.[60]

Such deference and passivity from Poitier's Prentice led to objections from critics, especially in the realm of sexuality. Despite the 1960s' sexual revolution, which encouraged freer and more open sexual expression, John Prentice and the Draytons' daughter, Joey, have not yet had sex. Some commentators still believed that the interracial intimacy shown in *Guess Who's Coming to Dinner* was a great advance on earlier movies. Remarked one reviewer, "We see a mixed couple hug and kiss—in Technicolor!—for the first time in a Hollywood picture." Yet the couple only kiss once, quickly in the back of a taxicab, which spectators see in the rearview mirror from the cabdriver's disapproving point of view. Some southern exhibitors deleted this shot. Kramer later blamed such censorship concerns and Columbia Pictures for so little public display of affection. He also claimed "a very difficult time getting them into bed," given the movie's one-day timeframe.[61] "Kramer has sidestepped anything as embarrassing as an integrated love scene," noted *Time*'s reviewer. Young filmgoers lambasted this decision. "OK, so if they're in love, why don't they kiss? This is another cop-out," wrote a reviewer for *Glamour*, a young women's magazine. "Also, if they love each other, why haven't they slept together?" Later in the film, Joey tells her mother that, although she would have happily slept with John, it was he who refused. "It's pretty old-fashioned to make the character of the Negro so pure and simple," a college student told Kramer. Baldwin's analysis was more damning. Even "in this day of so many liberations," he bitingly commented, interracial sexual relationships remained "inadmissible fantasies."[62]

Women's liberation also was absent from the film, and, although the modern feminist movement was just gaining ground, commentators did question the representation of women in the film. Tillie, the black housekeeper, is not the only caricatured female role in *Guess Who's Coming to Dinner*. Joey Drayton is, too. Kramer cast Katharine Houghton, Hepburn's niece, in the role of the daughter and fiancée. In his acerbic review in *Life* magazine, Richard Schickel called her "the imbecile daughter," because she is surprised when her parents do not immediately approve of her imminent interracial marriage. "Such unworldliness, such lack of elementary knowledge of her own class and family's nature is totally unbelievable," he scolded.[63] Renata Adler expressed the same point and similarly bluntly. "For the plot to work, the girl has to be tactless, shrill, insensitive and obtuse, which she is." "Why," Kramer was asked by a female student at Stanford, "was the girl in the picture so naïve?" "Maybe it could have been better," Kramer admitted.[64] In fact, Houghton's role was better in the screenplay. One scene included Joey telling her father, "I don't understand what's wrong with you—you brought me up to believe that a person's worth is not based on the color of their skin, but on what they are intrinsically. If anything, I'm not worthy of *him*, because he's a world-famous doctor and I'm young and haven't done anything!" "For me, that scene *saved* me as a character," Houghton believed. But that scene did not appear in the final film, making yet another female character in a Kramer film less than credible or convincing.[65]

The generation gap constituted another aspect of the 1960s political scene portrayed unconvincingly in *Guess Who's Coming to Dinner*. Kramer posited and promoted the difference between the generations—more so than race relations—as the main theme of his movie. "It's about young and old viewpoints, and in this case the bone of contention happens to be the acceptance of interracial marriage. But this film says that the new generation won't live like the last generation simply because that's the way it's supposed to be. Life has moved on," he concluded.[66] In the film, the younger generation, represented by John Prentice and Joey Drayton, as well as a white delivery boy and a young black maid, are shown to have accepted cultural and social change. The older generation, represented by both sets of parents, the taxicab driver, Tillie, and Mrs. Drayton's assistant, have not. The genial Catholic priest and friend of the Drayton family is the one tolerant exception among the mature characters at the start of the film. It is Poitier's Prentice who most angrily articulates the generation gap in a harsh confrontation with his father. "You and your whole lousy generation believes the way it was for you is the way it's got to be! And not until your whole generation has lain down and died will the deadweight of you be off our backs!" Baldwin identified this scene as where the film was the most untrue to the black American experience, where it came "unglued," and he implied that generational difference in the 1960s was greater among white than black Americans.[67]

Young Americans joined Baldwin in criticizing the movie's portrayal of the generation gap, especially their side of the divide. "The film in fact asks us to 'relate,'" declared *Glamour*'s reviewer, but *Guess Who's Coming to Dinner* barely hints at the ever-evolving youth culture and politics of that tumultuous time.[68] The year of the film's release, 1967, also marked the famous "Summer of Love" in San Francisco, when the city became the capital of the so-called hippie counterculture. Yet the only indication that the story was set in the same time and place is when Joey puts a flower behind John's ear, while sitting on the Draytons' sunny patio with the cityscape as a (painted) backdrop. This scene called to mind the lyric of the popular hit song that summer: "If you're going to San Francisco, be sure to wear some flowers in your hair." The Draytons' maid and the delivery boy also dance to the sound of contemporary rock music. Conspicuously absent from the movie is the highly politicized atmosphere and activism in the city and in Berkeley and Oakland across the San Francisco Bay. The civil rights, Black Panther, student, and anti–Vietnam War movements have no impact on the interpersonal dynamics in the Drayton home. "We are on the heights of San Francisco," Baldwin noted. "The difficult and terrified city, where the niggers are, lives far beneath the heights." Kramer heard complaints about this missing context while on his tour of college campuses. "Why doesn't Hollywood make pictures that deal more really with our life?"[69]

What became unmistakable—and unsettling—to Kramer was that the younger generation perceived him as a member of the liberal establishment. In an oft-told and pointed anecdote, Kramer said, "I told the students I had been fighting the establishment all my life," but they immediately responded, "you're a part of it." That the plot of his latest movie pivoted on the character development of a liberal, middle-aged, white male—Spencer Tracy's Matt Drayton—reinforced this perception.[70] Drayton is a crusading newspaper editor and a good liberal, with a photo of Franklin Delano Roosevelt featured prominently on his desk. Given patriarchal customs, as the father of the bride-to-be, he has the final decision on the marriage. His thoughts, actions, and conflicts drive the plot, and the priest calls him "a broken-down, old, phony liberal come face-to-face with his principles." Revealing Kramer's conception of who came to watch his films, as well as his own subjectivity, he believed "the audience was able to identify with Tracy" because "he expressed all the things the armchair liberals were thinking." Thus, when Drayton eventually approves of the marriage in a moving monologue at the film's end, "the audience believed, just as he believed."[71] "There'll be a hundred million people right here in this country who will be shocked and offended and appalled by the two of you," he told the young couple. In the face of such "prejudices and bigotry . . . the two of you will just have to ride that out." Tracy's last speech was reminiscent of those he gave reiterating the value of liberal, universal ideals at the end of *Inherit the Wind* and *Judgment at Nuremberg*. Tracy, it was said, became Kramer's "mouthpiece."[72]

Karen Sharpe-Kramer and Stanley Kramer at his induction into the Hall of Fame at New York University, his alma mater, 1968. Courtesy of Karen Sharpe-Kramer.

Such liberal sentiment went over very well with mainstream audiences but not with the students Kramer encountered during his college tour. Recognizing "the width of the Generation Gap," he sought to "narrow the Communication Gap." It was an improbably timed tour early in 1968, just a few months before the student strike at Columbia University in April set off an explosion of student protests across the United States, which were matched by uprisings around the globe, including Mexico, France, and Czechoslovakia. In Kramer's discussions with students, the topics ranged beyond their responses to *Guess Who's Coming to Dinner* to film, culture, and politics generally, and he discovered how very differently they thought. "Of one thing I am sure: the Generation Gap is very real. . . . This new unsmiling generation," as he labeled them, "blame us for the whole Goddamn mess," referring to the Vietnam War and social conflicts of the sixties. "I can understand that— and I felt guilty enough for myself and my contemporaries," he wrote in an article for the Directors Guild. He recognized their "bitterness" and "the desire of youth to divorce itself" from the older generation or "through student power to exert control themselves." But at the same time, he lamented their refusal to listen to his perspective and the loss of "sentiment—oh, sentiment, the whipping boy of the film buff, 1968 version."[73] Other filmmakers in New Hollywood also recognized this new audience as "difficult," demanding movies to express their disillusionment and cynicism. With *Guess Who's Coming to Dinner*, Kramer said he wanted "a gentle catharsis. They demand a purge." "Those students draw blood," he added.[74]

Kramer's experience of his campus visits and the critical reception of *Guess Who's Coming to Dinner* made 1968 a turning point for him, just as it was considered for the sixties as a whole. Despite the film's spectacular success—it was the second-highest-grossing film that year and made three times the amount of *It's a Mad, Mad, Mad, Mad World*—Kramer began a period of self-reflection. "It's a changing society and I subscribe to change," he stated. "But I can't arrive at a complete understanding."[75] He realized that his formative experiences of the Great Depression, the Roosevelt administration, and New Deal liberalism were no longer recognized as relevant. When he tried to make the case on his college tour that the Depression years of 1929–1933 were "as big a crisis for us as 1964–1968 has been for them," the students scoffed. "Now when I react," he confessed, "I must ask myself why? Damn it, am I not with it? Am I not dealing with the right ideas?" He started to refer to himself as a "tired" or "discarded" liberal, at just the historical moment when the liberal consensus in the United States fractured.[76] The terrible assassinations of Martin Luther King, Jr., and Robert Kennedy, the Tet Offensive in the Vietnam War, and violent antiwar, student, and racial protests at home—particularly at the Democratic National Convention in Chicago—all occurred in 1968. Together, these events helped deliver white southern and northern working-class votes and, thus, the White House to a Republican president, Richard Nixon, that fall. The New Deal coalition to which Kramer had belonged for decades ended.

Such political developments and personal doubts translated into Kramer's moviemaking. "Everything was happening fast in the '60s," he remembered. "Too fast for me, it seemed." At the time, he felt the "social revolution has become so accelerated that I may have said my piece on racial discrimination." In fact, *Guess Who's Coming to Dinner* was his fourth and last film on American race relations and, according to historian Donald Bogle, "proved one of the last of the explicitly inte-grationist message pictures" made in Hollywood.[77] Kramer considered making a movie about the Vietnam War. He bought the rights to a book called *Search and Destroy*, but "I can't satisfy myself on just what Viet Nam is all about." He recognized that it "isn't an official war," without a declaration of war by Congress, and "so shocking" that "I am now thinking in terms of antiwar films."[78] But he never made it. Instead, he made for United Artists *The Secret of Santa Vittoria* (1969), based on a best-selling novel by Robert Crichton about an Italian village occu-pied at the end of World War II by Germans. "I envisioned the picture as a celebration of principle and resistance," Kramer remembered, as the villagers successfully hide a huge hoard of wine from the German occupiers. It also was "a comedy, an attempt to entertain, to make a shot right down the middle." Starring Anthony Quinn and Anna Mag-nani, the film won the Golden Globe for best comedy. But the film—"so energetically gross"—and Kramer—"with confident bad taste"—became again a target of Pauline Kael's stinging criticism.[79]

The film Kramer made to convey his experience of the end of the sixties was his 1970 film *R.P.M.*, with the poster adding an asterisk help-fully referring to "Revolutions Per Minute." This story of a student rebellion at the fictional Hudson University featured his leading man from *The Secret of Santa Vittoria*. Anthony Quinn played the role of the acting university president, F. W. J. "Paco" Perez. Erich Segal, who had a best-selling novel and a movie in progress, *Love Story* (1970), wrote the screenplay, but the character of Paco Perez was Kramer's alter ego. "Quinn will play it from my viewpoint. His character will be that of a discarded liberal."[80] The character Perez is a well-known sociologist, raised in a working-class Puerto Rican family in New York, with strong liberal, even radical, credentials. In his youth, he supported labor strikes, fought for the Republicans in the Spanish Civil War, and opposed McCarthyism. He is also cool, rides a motorcycle, and sleeps with students; Ann-Margret costarred in the movie as his current lover. As a result, Perez has political credibility with the student radicals. He is their third choice—after Che Guevara (dead) and Eldridge Cleaver (unavailable)—for university president after they force the resignation of the last one. Conflicts soon ensue due to student intransigence and unwillingness to compromise. Perez is caught in the middle, between the students and the university's board of trustees, and he faces a moral and political dilemma. In the end, he sides with the trustees—the establishment—and decides to call in the police to forcibly remove the students from an occupied administration building for the film's finale.

R.P.M. was one of several movies about the student rebellion to be released in 1970, and none in the cycle was wholly successful. "In the standard Hollywood vulgarizing tradition, the theme of student revolution was turned into a riot-movie fad," Kael wrote, "polished off now by Stanley Kramer's grandstanding liberalism."[81] Critics called *R.P.M.* "phony" and a "pre-fabricated cop-out." The dialogue was embarrassingly clichéd and passé. "Hey, man, we thought your head was on straight," says a student. "But you don't know where it's at." Reviewers mocked the film as another entry in Kramer's "cinematic history of the Great Issues of Our Time" and as "F.W.M. (Fraught With Meaning)." More meaningful critiques demonstrated that the superficial story in *R.P.M.* slighted the very real issues American students faced in higher education and offered a distinctly conservative message. For example, curriculum reform was one of the demands on which the Hudson University students refused to compromise. As it turned out, such reform in the 1960s and 1970s opened up the academic world to new groups and perspectives, including women and African Americans.[82] Commentators also recognized the film as "the most personal film Kramer has made." The producer-director's "own career parallels that of the professor," and both represent the "once all-too-liberal, now-a-bit-baffled man in the middle." "The trouble with *R.P.M.* was that I was trapped because I was looking for myself," Kramer recalled. "I was looking for something in which to believe." Yet, in contrast to the other films in the cycle, Charles Champlin credited him with capturing "a more honest—and sobering—picture of the real failure of protestors and protested-against to communicate."[83]

R.P.M. expressed Kramer's pessimism about bridging "the Communication Gap," but with his next two films he still sought to communicate with new audiences. *Bless the Beasts and the Children* (1971) told the story of a group of six "misfit" adolescent boys at a summer camp in Arizona, who decide to save a herd of buffalo from being killed for sport and succeed, although at the cost of one boy's life. "I had imagined it as a saga of constructive youthful rebellion," Kramer remembered. The movie made a strong case for animal rights and the protection of endangered species, and Kramer linked the status of the penned animals to that of the boys: "in freeing the buffalo, they free themselves." "Barbs are also thrown at the cult of violence and the gun," *Variety* pointed out. Respondents connected the film to the My Lai massacre in the Vietnam War and the National Guard shootings of antiwar protestors at Kent State University. "You name it, it's there."[84]

With *Oklahoma Crude* (1973), Kramer made a historical film set in 1913 about wildcatters in the Oklahoma oilfields fighting against the oil corporations. "It is also the story of a strong, brave woman, played by Faye Dunaway," who "prevails against the all-devouring big boys," Kramer recapped. "It isn't hard to see Kramer's eyes lighting up [as] here are two filmable causes rolled into one: the cause of Women's Lib and the cause of the little man against the monopolies," a critic noted drily. Prominently featuring a female character was a departure for Kramer, but the film still fails to offer a convincing portrayal. Dunaway's character, Lena Doyle, "is a feminist who can't hack it," declared one reviewer, because her independence is wholly compromised in the end.[85]

Neither film earned great revenues or reviews in the United States, but both played extremely well and had an important cultural and political impact behind the Iron Curtain. Throughout the 1960s and early 1970s, Kramer's films screened at international film festivals, including the Moscow festival. His movies, such as *It's a Mad, Mad, Mad, Mad World* and *Ship of Fools*, continued to circulate and win fans in the Soviet Union. He remained prominent even as a change in leadership displaced Nikita Khrushchev from power, and the era of the more conservative Leonid Brezhnev began. "Stanley Kramer is one of the most popular American film directors with Soviet audiences," claimed the *Hollywood Reporter* in 1971. He also enjoyed greater critical respect there than he did in the United States. In a 1967 review in *Izvestia*, one Soviet critic discussed films "by major artists such as Fellini, Antonioni and Kramer."[86] These three directors were never grouped together elsewhere. Kramer's continuing commitment to a conventional Hollywood filmmaking style set him apart from such cutting-edge European art cinema. "Stanley Kramer says he's self-styled, old-fashioned and counter-revolutionary about picture-making. He's not overly impressed by the new waves," a stance Soviet officialdom appreciated. Official acceptance, critical approval, and popular appeal made Kramer "an exception" among foreign filmmakers in the Soviet Union. His films were "acclaimed by many famous Soviet directors, actors and writers" and "delighted ordinary viewers" alike.[87]

When Kramer returned in person as part of the US delegation to the 1967 Moscow film festival, he was again greeted with exceptional acclaim. "All received generous applause until Stanley Kramer, the American director, was presented," stated the official delegation report. "On hearing his name the audience rose at once to its feet and applauded and waved for a minute and a half."[88] His attendance in 1967 was not uncontroversial, however. Several Hollywood celebrities, including Elizabeth Taylor, her husband Richard Burton, and *The Defiant Ones* star Tony Curtis, canceled their trips that year. Fallout from the Arab-Israeli Six-Day War, with the Soviet Union and the United States supporting opposite sides, contributed. "Curtis, who is Jewish, spelled out that Soviet Israel policy was his reason for dropping his plans to go to the festival," reported the *Los Angeles Times*. "Soviet attacks on Israel in the United Nations and Soviet aid to Arab nations" were objectionable. An MPAA representative quickly backpedaled, stating "not one of the withdrawals was for 'ideological or political reasons.'"[89] But the Soviets were not appeased, and the initial official reception for the US delegation made "for instant ice cubes and chilblains." Within the context of this international crisis, Kramer's decision to attend the 1967 Moscow festival and his warm welcome mattered very much. "The point is that the cultural exchanges have had some small leavening effects, there and here," he argued. "And it's damned important to keep those channels of communication open. . . . I understand exactly how the people felt who dropped out of the delegation," Kramer added. "But what's important is to keep talking."[90]

The producer-director took a similar position on the occasion of his next visit to the Moscow film festival in 1971, but it meant launching a liberal challenge to the conservative Nixon administration. After 1968, Kramer and the US government began to have differing political perspectives and festival agendas. The continuation of the Vietnam War and the change in presidential administration from Democrat to Republican clashed with Kramer's embattled liberalism. In 1971 the US government declined to participate in the Moscow film festival, citing the screening of films critical of the US war in Vietnam and, thus, "anti-American" at previous festivals. Kramer criticized this decision as "very foolish." He still strongly believed in cinematic diplomacy. Films "get through one nation to the other, one people to the other." Demonstrating his ideological independence from the prowar, Republican administration, Kramer brought *Bless the Beasts and the Children* to screen out of competition in Moscow. Kramer's film played to a cheering crowd of six thousand spectators. "Your film teaches all of us kindness and the humanity inside humanity," responded the prominent Soviet poet Yevgeny Yevtushenko.[91]

Further enhancing Kramer's reputation with the Soviets was how his films and politics continued to reflect his liberal, universal ideals. This commitment culminated in a Golden Prize for Direction for *Oklahoma Crude* at the 1973 Moscow film festival. Unlike the previous festival, this one occurred within the context of a détente in US-Soviet relations, a lessening of tensions between the superpower rivals long advanced by Kramer. He was cited for his "humanist contribution to the development of world cinema." "I am hated and loved unduly," Kramer stated, reflecting on his career and the reception of his films and his politics at home and abroad. Over the preceding decades, he had confronted social problems and advocated social change. In the process, his liberal views and values had moved from the margins to the mainstream of American society and found an international audience. Yet, as a producer-director and a public figure, he remained a target of film and political critics. As a sign of social progress, although an ironic one, attacks now came more frequently and fervently from the Left than the Right. "Our world today is a better world than 25 years ago because it's more truthful," Kramer observed, "but it isn't any easier to live in."[92]

Stanley Kramer on location, early 1970s. Courtesy of Department of Special Collections, Charles E. Young Research Library, University of California, Los Angeles, with permission from Karen Sharpe-Kramer.

Conclusion:
Legacies of a Hollywood Liberal

In January 2015, when actor Kevin Spacey won a Golden Globe for his performance in the television drama series *House of Cards*, he took the audience by surprise and used his acceptance speech to laud Stanley Kramer, who died in 2001. Spacey told the story of his last visit with Kramer, "one of the great filmmakers of all time," who was quite ill at the time and living in the Motion Picture and Television Fund Home. "I realized that I had never told him what I had thought about his work, about how much his work had meant to me." Spacey had long respected Kramer as a filmmaker. "You go back and look at film after film, where he tackled stuff before anybody else had the nerve to bring it up in Hollywood—racism, nuclear proliferation, you name it." So Spacey decided to tell him. "The films you made, the subjects you tackled, the performances you got out of some of the greatest actors who ever walked the earth, the Oscars you won. Your films will stand the test of time and will influence filmmakers for all time." Given Kramer's failing health, Spacey "didn't know whether he had really retained what I said or not." "But, as I stood up to leave, he grabbed my hand. . . . And he said as clear to me as anything he had ever said, 'Thank you so much for saying that. That means so much to me. I just wish my films could have been better.'"[1] The audience of fellow filmmakers responded with muted ahhing, conveying their recognition of Kramer's poor critical reputation and their sympathy for the producer-director at the end of his life.

Spacey's tribute served as an appreciation of Kramer's filmmaking career but also inadvertently sparked a firestorm about Kramer's political reputation. After the Golden Globe Awards ceremony, Richard Johnson, a columnist for the *New York Post*, wrote about Kramer's actions during the Cold War Red Scare. He argued that Kramer should be "remembered for his cowardice during the blacklist era," in how he dealt with his conflict with Carl Foreman in 1951.[2] Johnson based his column on a 2002 documentary, titled *Darkness at High Noon: The Carl Foreman Documents* and directed by a politically conservative filmmaker, Lionel Chetwynd. Epitomizing the old saying that "politics makes strange bedfellows," the right-wing Chetwynd presented the former communist Foreman's side of the story as "a tale of betrayal and destruction" and "an indictment of Stanley Kramer."[3] Swift rebuttals to Chetwynd's documentary in 2002 and Johnson's column in 2015 came from Kramer's widow, Karen Sharpe-Kramer, as well as media commentators. To assess these opposing perspectives, historian Larry Ceplair offered a definitive account of the Kramer-Foreman conflict. He concluded that both men's actions at the time "resulted from conflicting, but not dishonorable, loyalties and principles." Kramer and Foreman were "decent men, confronted with indecent circumstances over which they had little control." Writer Glenn Frankel recently cited and confirmed Ceplair's conclusions as well.[4]

Remembering the hostile political environment of Cold War America reminds us of how anticommunist forces created untenable, "no-win" situations for both liberals and leftists during the Hollywood blacklist. Indeed, even as Kramer and Foreman took conflicting actions that led to their relationship's end in 1951, they were both criticized by the Hollywood Left and Right alike. In the face of the Hollywood blacklist, they each struck a balance between their political ideals and pragmatic concerns. The outcome for Kramer was the preservation of his career and his company, and both outlasted the blacklist and the Red Scare. Few of the post–World War II independent producers on the liberal-left survived the Cold War, according to historian Michael Denning; Kramer was one of them.[5] By surviving, he went on to fight the Wage Earners Committee and the American Legion, to hire blacklisted screenwriters who went on to win Academy Awards, and to make motion pictures and public pronouncements that challenged Cold War orthodoxies. Despite his conflict with Foreman, he did not believe, as revisionist scholar Jennifer Delton recently argued about liberals in Cold War Hollywood, that "liberal principles were more effectively promoted by purging Communists than by defending their rights."[6] Quite the opposite.

The responses to Spacey's speech at the Golden Globes and after served as reminder that Kramer was—and in the twenty-first century still mattered as—both a cultural and political figure. As his late career continued in the 1970s, he reflected on his role in both arenas.

Politically, he still sought a middle path between the Left and the Right, even as the political landscape changed. "What happened to my revolutionary critics?" he asked in 1973. "We still have the war, pollution, the ghettos." Moreover, these ongoing, terrible tragedies at home and abroad were only made worse by the conservative "Nixon's sweeping victory" to a second term in the 1972 presidential election. But Kramer still maintained his political principles. "I feel the necessity for making a commitment, for establishing hope in what in many ways is a shoddy society." He also reflected on his cultural contributions. "Without exhibiting any mock humility, I think there's something wrong with all my films," he observed. "I think back to each, and there isn't one about which I can't say, 'I wish I had cut that sequence or I wish I hadn't used that actor or I wish it had been paced better.'" In a comment that presaged his exchange with Spacey more than two decades later, he added, "That feeling of incompleteness about every film I make is going to go on forever."[7]

After Kramer made that observation, he made only two more motion pictures. *The Domino Principle* (1977) was a political thriller about an assassination plot, starring Gene Hackman and Candice Bergen. *The Runner Stumbles* (1979) was a courtroom drama about a defrocked Catholic priest's trial for the murder of a nun, his former lover, with Dick Van Dyke and Kathleen Quinlan. Neither film did anything to recuperate Kramer's mixed critical, popular, and industry reputation. "When you work two years on a piece of material, and then are rejected by the public first, and only secondarily by the critics, it's very painful." Newspaper coverage of Kramer's career noted how "the barbs of those critics," such as Pauline Kael, "had left their scars."[8] Although Kramer completed several television programs in his late career, including remakes of several of his films, he never made another motion picture.

Reflecting his disillusionment with the direction of his career and politics, Kramer left Hollywood in 1978. At the age of sixty-five and after forty-five years in the movie capital, colleagues still considered him "a thoughtful, zestful, engaging man." But he was ready for a change. "I have been wanting to get out of Hollywood for a long time, but I never had the courage to pick up and go."[9] He and his wife, Karen, had two young daughters: Katharine, whom they named after Katharine Hepburn, and Jennifer. They decided to move to Bellevue, Washington, because "I wanted my kids to grow up and be educated away from the insanity of Beverly Hills." "Also I felt that after being reasonably progressive for many years, maybe I had fallen half a step behind in Hollywood. I thought that by getting out I could find some answers."[10] He made his last film, *The Runner Stumbles*, in Washington. He began writing a regular newspaper column for the *Seattle Times*, fulfilling Italian critic Tino Ranieri's early characterization of him as, at heart, a journalist and critic. He wrote "on everything from abortion to nuclear war—trying to be provocative, elicit comment, and bring myself up to date." Elicit comment he did, and his "controversial" column "brought in a lot of mail." He kept busy hosting a television program showing classic films and teaching at the local college and university. And he continued to explore filmmaking opportunities. His creative "juices had begun to flow again. And with them came new ideas."[11]

Kramer remained committed to the social problem film genre and concerned about contemporary issues. He deeply felt that the problems addressed in his earlier films had not yet been solved. In the twenty years since *On the Beach*, "we've become blasé about the whole question" of nuclear weapons, which he still considered the world's most critical issue. As the Cold War heated up again in the 1980s, he became active in the resurgent antinuclear movement. As to his racially themed movies, such as *The Defiant Ones*, "Americans think racism has been eliminated. They're dead wrong." He also pointed out that thirty-five years after *Inherit the Wind* was first released, "the next generation of believers stood in front of theaters and intimidated those who wanted to see the film," interfering with freedom of speech. "Since the 1950s, human nature hasn't changed that much," he believed. "We haven't really progressed with our morality in this country, sometimes I feel that we have *regressed*." Kramer did appreciate the changes in international relations begun by Mikhail Gorbachev that eventually brought the Cold War to a peaceful end. "I just returned from a visit to the Soviet Union and I think that glasnost is real," he reported in the mid-1980s. "Now, isn't it amazing that all of the writers and directors and poets and painters who talked with me so intimately twenty-five years ago about what they dreamed of and what they wanted have got it in some part now?"[12] Still believing in building ties through cinematic diplomacy, he sought to make films about Lech Walesa, the leader of the Polish Solidarity union movement, and the Chernobyl nuclear disaster. In 1986, at the age of seventy-three, he returned to Hollywood to do so.

Kramer did not succeed in making these films, but the last two decades of his life brought him much attention and many accolades. The publication of Donald Spoto's 1978 biography, which included oral interviews with Kramer, began the process. Continuing throughout the 1980s and 1990s, retrospectives of his career occurred in television documentaries and at museums, universities, and film festivals both at home and abroad. In 1983, twenty years after his prominent participation in the Moscow International Film Festival, he was honored there with a screening of seven of his films, including three never seen in the Soviet Union. The same year he was feted at the relatively new Montreal World Film Festival. Kramer received appreciations from inside and outside the US motion picture industry as well. He earned a Producers Guild of America Lifetime Achievement Award in 1991 and in 1998 won the very first NAACP Vanguard Award, designed to recognize a "person whose groundbreaking work increases understanding and awareness of racial and social issues."[13] In 2002, after his death, the Producers Guild introduced a new award in his name. The Stanley Kramer Award aptly recognizes films that "illuminate provocative social issues." The winners include many of the most important documentary and dramatic films about social problems in recent years, such as *An Inconvenient Truth* (2006), about catastrophic climate change, and *Hunting Ground* (2015), about sexual assaults on college campuses. Films about police shootings, the AIDS crisis, and bullying have won the Kramer Award as well, indicating that Kramer's legacy is alive and well in the twenty-first century.

Today, Kramer is more celebrated for his commitment to socially conscious filmmaking and for confronting the commercial challenges entailed in working as a Hollywood independent than condemned for the compromises he made or the contradictions that emerged in the process. Both before and after his death, Kramer's filmmaking colleagues offered testimony about his influence and impact on their own careers, as Kevin Spacey did. "I could *never* have made *Schindler's List*," producer-director Steven Spielberg stated, "if it weren't for *Judgment at Nuremberg*. You paved the way for me."[14] For Spoto's biography, actor Sidney Poitier commended Kramer. "He made one hell of a commitment to things when commitment was difficult for everyone. People have short memories: in the days he started making films about important social issues, there were powerful Hollywood columnists who could break careers. He knew this, and he said to himself, 'What the hell—I either do it or I can't live with myself.' For that attitude we're all in Stanley Kramer's debt." Kramer so valued this praise that he repeated it word for word in his own 1997 memoirs. Poitier also penned a foreword for those memoirs and continues to comment on Kramer's contributions. "I have to acknowledge Stanley as probably the most important element in my career," Poitier recently remarked. "He was a remarkable, extraordinary and very principled man who was pivotal to moving me forward in my craft."[15]

Such sympathetic statements multiplied after Kramer's death from pneumonia in 2001, but his critics participated in the rush of reminiscences as well. Obituaries complimented the producer-director for his "socially groundbreaking films" and "bold movies [that] challenged his audiences' perceptions of racial prejudice, Nazism, and the bomb." Yet they also conveyed criticisms of his work—as "sentimental and simplistic"—and of his politics—as "wishy-washy liberal." Film critic David Thomson considered it the "greatest oddity" that Kramer received a two-page obituary in the *New York Times*, after "such critical pasting and so many box-office failures."[16]

The mix of positive and negative evaluations of Kramer's filmmaking prompted socialist film critic David Walsh to ask the very pertinent question, "Why was Stanley Kramer so unfashionable at the time of his death?" Walsh attributed this development to two factors. First, "Kramer's technique and approach [fell] out of favor" with critics, audiences, and fellow Hollywood filmmakers. Walsh also identified "a shift in the social mood" in the United States.[17] Indeed, emerging out of the 1960s was a cultural mood of cynicism and irony. As the basis for cultural critique, cynicism and irony can reveal political lies and social hypocrisies but also can reinforce disillusionment and disengagement. At the same time, the electoral victories of conservative Republicans, especially with President Ronald Reagan in the 1980s, signaled a period of social reaction. These developments contributed to the decline of Kramer's trademark genre, at least for a while. Historically, social problem films emerge in the context of social idealism and reform. "If social change is impossible," scholars Peter Roffman and Jim Purdy conclude, "then problem films are irrelevant."[18]

Stanley Kramer never came to believe that. He held onto his sincere belief in the possibilities for liberal reform and the positive function of the social problem film, regardless of whether he was out of step with the new age of irony. The "forthright earnestness of Stanley Kramer's pictures has gone out of fashion," noted one writer after his death. "Stanley Kramer was nothing if not honest and thoughtful," asserted another. "He had honest and thoughtful to burn." Back in 1968, critic Andrew Sarris, too, acknowledged Kramer's sincerity: "He will never be a natural, but time has proven that he is not a fake."[19] Making sense of Kramer's significance requires recognizing what his sincerity as a social problem filmmaker and Hollywood liberal meant, especially at the height of his career at the turn of the 1960s. "What I learned about the evils of racism, the threat of nuclear war and the danger of religious intolerance I learned in theaters watching Kramer movies with a box of popcorn in my lap," Hollywood reporter David Robb recalled. Scholar Terry Christensen agreed. "Kramer's movies surely contributed to the development of the social consciousness of the sixties activists, a generation of Americans who were teenagers when Kramer was most prolific."[20]

"Our mistake was that we regarded Kramer's social conscience as his artistic albatross. Actually, it was his badge of honor," admitted film critic Michael Wilmington. By participating in the public sphere with his productions and pronouncements during the Cold War, Kramer shaped an era and an ethos, and he advanced liberal reform in the 1960s. He also shared its defeats dealt by both the Left and Right at the end of the decade. But in the intervening years, Kramer undoubtedly achieved his aim "to be recognized as someone who knew how to use film as a real weapon against discrimination, hatred, prejudice, and excessive power." "I hope I did alright."[21]

NOTES

List of Abbreviations

Institutions
Herrick Library: Margaret Herrick Library, Beverly Hills, California

Archival Collections
Eisenhower Papers: Papers of Dwight D. Eisenhower as President, 1953–
1961, Dwight D. Eisenhower Presidential Library, Abilene, Kansas
Kramer Papers: Stanley Kramer Papers, 1945–1984, Department of Special
Collections, Charles E. Young Research Library, University of California,
Los Angeles, California
Sokolsky Papers: George E. Sokolsky Papers, 1916–1962, Hoover Institution
Archives, Stanford University, Stanford, California

Other Records and Files
1959 Moscow Festival Clippings file: Moscow Film Festival, 1959 Clippings
File, Herrick Library
1963 Moscow Festival Clippings file: Moscow Film Festival, 1963 Clippings
File, Herrick Library
AEC Questions and Answers: AEC Possible Questions and Suggested
Answers on the Film, *On the Beach* (Copy), 8 December 1959, Cabinet
Meeting of 11 December 1959, box 15, Cabinet Series (Ann Whitman
File), Eisenhower Papers
American Legion Clippings folder: American Legion—Newspaper Clippings
folder, box 115, Kramer Papers
American Legion Correspondence folder: American Legion—
Correspondence re: Comments folder, box 115, Kramer Papers
American Legion Trade Clippings folder: American Legion—Trade Paper
Clippings folder, box 115, Kramer Papers
AMPTP Records: Association of Motion Picture and Television Producers
Records, Herrick Library
BBC Moscow festival folder: *Bless the Beasts and the Children*, Film Festival
Moscow folder, box 138, Kramer Papers
Beck Publicity folder: Publicity—"ITW" Myer P. Beck folder, box 32,
Kramer Papers

Blowitz-Maskel Publicity folder: Publicity—Blowitz-Maskel, "The Defiant Ones" folder, box 18, Kramer Papers

Brand folder: Judge James T. Brand—"JAN" folder, box 36, Kramer Papers

F.Y.I. television transcript: *F.Y.I.*, television transcript, American Legion—CBS-TV, 14 February 1960 folder, box 115, Kramer Papers

Horwits Publicity folder: Publicity—"ITW" Al Horwits folder, box 32, Kramer Papers

ITW Campaign Guide: Campaign Guide for Stanley Kramer's *Inherit the Wind*, box 32, Kramer Papers

ITW Clippings file: *Inherit the Wind* Clippings file, Herrick Library

ITW Comments folder: Comments, Congratulations, Wires, and Quotes—"ITW," box 30, Kramer Papers

JAN Clippings file: *Judgment at Nuremberg* Clippings File, Herrick Library

JAN Comments folder: Comments, Congratulations, Wires, and Quotes—"JAN" folder, box 36, Kramer Papers

Kramer Clippings file: Stanley Kramer Clippings file, Herrick Library

Mann Contract folder: Abby Mann—Contract—"JAN" folder, box 37, Kramer Papers

Music folder: Music—Song "Long Gone" folder, box 18, Kramer Papers

Musmanno folder: Justice Michael A. Musmanno—"JAN" folder, box 38, Kramer Papers

OTB Clippings file: *On the Beach* Clippings file, Herrick Library

OTB Comments folder: Comments, Congratulations, Wires and Letters and Quotes folder, box 24, Kramer Papers

OTB promotion pamphlet: *On the Beach* promotional exhibition pamphlet, Publicity folder, box 25, Kramer Papers

Paxton Publicity folder: *On the Beach*—Publicity folder, John Paxton Papers, Herrick Library

Paxton Reviews folder: *On the Beach*—Reviews folder, John Paxton Papers, Herrick Library

PCA Records: Motion Picture Association of America Production Code Administration Records, Herrick Library

Research folder: Research—"ITW" folder, box 33, Kramer Papers

Russia Correspondence folder: Russia—Correspondence folder, box 109, Kramer Papers

Shute folder: Nevil Shute folder, box 26, Kramer Papers

State Department Moscow Festival file: File Education & Culture USSR (MO) EDU 14–1 FILM, Box 2186, Record Group 59, National Archives, College Park, Maryland

State Department *OTB* Premiere file: File 511.615/1–359, Box 2186, Record Group 59, National Archives, College Park, Maryland

State Department Post–Moscow Festival file: Box 3275, MP–Motion
Pictures N, Subject-Numeric Files, 1963, Record Group 59, National
Archives, College Park, Maryland
Taylor folder: Telford Taylor–"JAN" folder, box 39, Kramer Papers
TDO Awards folder: Awards–"The Defiant Ones," folder, box 17, Kramer
Papers
TDO Clippings file: *The Defiant Ones* Clippings file, Herrick Library
Thomas Publicity folder: Publicity–Thomas George, "The Defiant Ones"
folder, box 18, Kramer Papers
UA Publicity folder: Publicity–United Artists Releases–"The Defiant Ones,"
box 18, Kramer Papers
USIA Moscow 1963 Festival file: Subfile "Moscow-1963," File USSR EUR
Moscow 2 of 4 Reports Film, Box 3 Moscow Film Festival, entry 166,
RG 306, National Archives, College Park, Maryland
USIA-State Infoguide: Cabinet Paper, USIA-State Infoguide 60–24, 4
December 1959, Cabinet Meeting of 11 December 1959, box 15, Cabinet
Series (Ann Whitman File), Eisenhower Papers

Interviews and Presentations
Overs interview: Knud Overs interview, Publicity–*Judgment at Nuremberg*
Al Horwits–Releases folder, box 38, Kramer Papers
Pravda interview: *Pravda* interview, [1960], Russia–Correspondence folder,
box 109, Kramer Papers
Stevens presentation: George Stevens, Jr.'s Presentation on US Participation
in the 1963 Moscow Film Festival, State Department Auditorium, 12
August 1963, 11–12, USIA Moscow 1963 Festival file

Other Abbreviations and Acronyms

ACLU   American Civil Liberties Union
AMPAS   Academy of Motion Picture Arts and Sciences
CWV   Catholic War Veterans
FBI   Federal Bureau of Investigation
MPAA   Motion Picture Association of America
NAACP   National Association for the Advancement of Colored People
PCA   Production Code Administration
SANE   National Committee for a Sane Nuclear Policy
SK   Stanley Kramer

Introduction: "The Thinking Man's Producer"

1. Stanley Kramer with Thomas M. Coffey, *A Mad, Mad, Mad, Mad World: A Life in Hollywood* (New York: Harcourt Brace, 1997), 187.

2. Ronald Steel, "Kramer's Nuremberg," *Christian Century*, 14 March 1962, 32; Hollis Alpert, "Haunting Question," *Saturday Review*, 2 December 1961, 43–44; "Cinema: The New Pictures," *Time*, 17 October 1960, 67; "Cinema: Show Trial," *Time*, 15 December 1961, 87.

3. Philip K. Scheuer, "*Inherit the Wind* Erupts in Hot Shower of Sparks," *Los Angeles Times*, 2 October 1960, B3; Steel, "Kramer's Nuremberg"; Arthur Knight, "The Importance of Being Earnest," *Saturday Review*, 8 October 1960, 30.

4. Gene Siskel, "The Movies," *Chicago Tribune*, 11 November 1971, B12.

5. Pauline Kael, "The Intentions of Stanley Kramer," in *Kiss Kiss Bang Bang* (London: Calder & Boyars, 1970), 203, 206.

6. Andrew Sarris, "Movie Journal," *Village Voice*, 10 November 1960, 11, and *The American Cinema: Directors and Directions, 1929–1968* (New York: E. P. Dutton, 1968), 260, 107; Phillip Lopate, *Totally, Tenderly, Tragically: Essays and Criticism from a Lifelong Love Affair with the Movies* (New York: Anchor, 1998), 11.

7. Thomas Doherty, "HomeVideo: *Judgment at Nuremberg*," *Cineaste*, Spring 2005, 59.

8. "Kramer, Columbia Sign $25,000,000 Film Deal," *Los Angeles Times*, 19 March 1951, 1, 4; Yannis Tzioumakis, *American Independent Cinema: An Introduction* (Edinburgh: Edinburgh University Press, 2006), 115.

9. Rabbi Balfour Brickner, "Study Guide," Publicity–*Judgment at Nuremberg* Myer P. Beck–Correspondence folder, box 38, Kramer Papers.

10. Jonathan Bell and Timothy Stanley, eds., *Making Sense of American Liberalism* (Urbana: University of Illinois Press, 2012), 4.

11. The term is Kirsten Fermaglich's in *American Dreams and Nazi Nightmares: Early Holocaust Consciousness and Liberal America, 1937–1965* (Waltham, Mass.: Brandeis University Press, 2006), 4.

12. Bosley Crowther, "Hollywood's Producer of Controversy," *New York Times*, 10 December 1961, SM76–85; Steven J. Ross, "Introduction: Why Movies Matter," in Ross, ed., *Movies and American Society* (Malden, Mass.: Blackwell, 2002), 9.

13. Velma West Sykes, "*On the Beach* (UA) Is the Choice for February Blue Ribbon Award," *Boxoffice*, 14 March 1960, news clipping, Paxton Reviews folder; John T. Harcourt, "Plea for Peace," *New York Times*, 24 January 1960, X7.

14. IFL to SK, 24 December 1959, and to Editor of *Science*, 24 December 1959, *OTB* Comments; Michael Wall, "The Defiant One," *Guardian*, 8 July

1960, 7; GM, Hollywood, Calif., to SK, 26 January 1960, American Legion Correspondence folder. Initials have been used for correspondence from filmgoers in the interest of privacy.

15. Text of proposed advertisement included in SK to Mr. HFS, 29 February 1960, American Legion Correspondence folder. On this Cold War contradiction, see Andrea Friedman, *Citizenship in Cold War America: The National Security State and the Possibilities of Dissent* (Amherst: University of Massachusetts Press, 2014).

16. Richard L. Coe, "Stanley Kramer Speaks His Mind," *Washington Post,* 12 September 1950, B7; Bosley Crowther, "'A' Movies on 'B' Budgets," *New York Times,* 12 November 1950, [23]; Thomas Schatz, *Boom and Bust: American Cinema in the 1940s,* vol. 6, *History of the American Cinema,* ed. Charles Harpole (Berkeley: University of California, 1997).

17. Kramer, "The Independent Producer," *Films in Review,* March 1951, 1, 2.

18. Kael, "Intentions of Stanley Kramer," 204.

19. Mark Harris, *Pictures at a Revolution: Five Movies and the Birth of the New Hollywood* (New York: Penguin, 2008), 297.

20. Meg Jacobs, "The Uncertain Future of American Politics, 1940 to 1973," in Eric Foner and Lisa McGirr, eds., *American History Now* (Philadelphia: Temple University Press, 2011), 151–174.

21. Aram Goudsouzian, *Sidney Poitier: Man, Actor, Icon* (Chapel Hill: University of North Carolina Press, 2004), 150; Kramer with Coffey, *Mad, Mad, Mad, Mad World,* 21.

22. For a careful delineation of the different strains of liberal anticommunism, see Larry Ceplair, *Anti-Communism in Twentieth-Century America: A Critical History* (Santa Barbara, Calif.: ABC-CLIO, 2011), 153–154.

23. Andrew Paul, "Reassessing Blacklist Era Television: Civil Libertarianism in *You Are There, The Adventures of Robin Hood,* and *The Buccaneers,*" *American Studies* 54, no. 1 (2015): 30.

24. Fermaglich, *American Dreams and Nazi Nightmares,* 9.

25. Kramer statement, television episode of NBC's *Youth Wants to Know,* 3 August 1958, UCLA Film and Television Archives.

26. Kramer, quoted in Donald Spoto, *Stanley Kramer, Film Maker* (Hollywood, Calif.: Samuel French, 1978), 16–17; Kramer, quoted in George Stevens, Jr., *Conversations with the Great Moviemakers of Hollywood's Golden Age* (New York: Knopf, 2006), 563.

27. Kevin Brownlow, *Behind the Mask of Innocence* (New York: Knopf, 1990), xix, xxi.

28. Peter Roffman and Jim Purdy, *The Hollywood Social Problem Film: Madness, Despair and Politics from the Depression to the Fifties* (Bloomington:

Indiana University Press, 1981), viii, 11; Steve Neale, *Genre and Hollywood* (New York: Routledge, 2000), 108.

29. Roffman and Purdy, *Hollywood Social Problem Film*, viii.

30. Kramer, quoted in Overs interview; Arthur Knight, "The Producer-Director at Work," *Saturday Review*, 2 December 1961, 45.

31. Kramer, quoted in Joseph Wershba, "Daily Closeup: Stanley Kramer, Movie Maker," *New York Post*, 28 January 1960, news clipping, American Legion folder, box 115, Kramer Papers; Noël Carroll, *Interpreting the Moving Image* (Cambridge: Cambridge University Press, 1998), 260–261.

32. Matthew Bernstein, *Walter Wanger: Hollywood Independent* (Berkeley: University of California Press, 1994), 394.

33. *Judgment at Nuremberg* review, *Cue*, 23 December 1961, *JAN* Clippings file; "AJ Citing Kramer," *Variety*, 26 April 1967, Stanley Kramer Clippings File, Herrick Library.

34. Rob Roy, "Roy 'Draws Bead' on Problem Pics: Finds Pro, Con Debates Justify Beefs, Bravos," *Chicago Defender*, 9 August 1958, 19; R. V., "*On the Beach*, U.S.A., 1959," *Monthly Film Bulletin*, [1960], *OTB* Clippings file.

35. Steel, "Kramer's Nuremberg"; David Thomson, *The New Biographical Dictionary of Film*, 5th ed. (New York: Knopf, 2010), 534.

36. Wershba, "Daily Closeup"; Knight, "Producer-Director at Work."

37. John Howard Lawson, *Film in the Battle of Ideas* (New York: Garland, 1953), 19.

38. John Howard Lawson, *Film: The Creative Process* (New York: Hill & Wang, 1964), 160–161. See also Paul Thomas Atkinson, "Relations of Production: Marxist Filmmakers in Hollywood, 1933–1953," MA thesis, University of Auckland, 2015; Kramer, quoted in SMU Collection of Ronald L. Davis: Oral Histories on the Performing Arts, Herrick Library.

39. Kramer, quoted in *On the Beach* interview, UCLA Film and Television Archives, and in Overs interview.

40. Knight, "Importance of Being Earnest," 30; Myron C. Fagan, quoted in John E. Fitzgerald, "The Responsible Movie Maker," *St. Jude: A National Catholic Monthly*, September 1962, 9, *JAN* Comments folder; Daniel Stoffman, "*Bless the Beasts and Children* Takes Aim and Misses Cause," *Toronto Daily Star*, 27 September 1971, 64.

41. Kramer, quoted in "Soviets React to US Candor," *Los Angeles Times*, 18 August 1963, L3.

42. Kramer, quoted in Spoto, *Stanley Kramer*, 223; "*Anne Frank* No *Nuremberg* Parallel," *Variety*, 8 March 1961, Kramer Clippings file; James Meade, "*Inherit the Wind*: Film Is Rated 'Excellent,'" *San Diego Union*, 1 September 1960, news clipping, Beck Publicity folder.

43. Dick Williams, "Stanley Kramer Gives His Films Adult Stature," *Los Angeles Mirror*, 8 November 1960, Kramer Clippings file; BJ, Huntington, W.Va., to SK, 3 December 1960, n.a., Pacific Palisades, to SK, 30 August 1960, and WWM, CBS Radio, to SK, 21 October 1960, *ITW* Comments folder.

44. Kramer, quoted in Dave McIntyre, "Front Row," *Evening Tribune*, news clipping, Paxton Publicity folder; Kramer, quoted in Ed Lukas, "Kramer Defends Hiring Purged Writers before Beverly Hills Club Group," *Beverly Hills Citizen*, American Legion Clippings folder; Kramer, quoted in Stevens, *Conversations with the Great Moviemakers*, 561.

45. Robert C. Allen and Douglas Gomery use this concept for movie reviews in *Film History: Theory and Practice* (New York: Knopf, 1985), 90.

46. Tino Ranieri, review of *Judgment at Nuremberg*, *Gazzettino* (Trieste), 28 December 1961, *JAN* Comments folder.

47. Jackie Stacey, *Star Gazing: Hollywood Cinema and Female Spectatorship* (London: Routledge, 1994), 49–79; MAP, Bellrose, N.Y., to SK, 14 February 1960, and LS, Brooklyn, N.Y., to SK, 8 February 1960, American Legion Correspondence folder; Janet Staiger, *Perverse Spectators: The Practices of Film Reception* (New York: New York University Press, 2000), 30–31.

48. Spoto, *Stanley Kramer;* Vladich Alekseevich Nedelin, *Stanley Kramer* (Moscow: Iskusstvo, 1969); Kramer with Coffey, *Mad, Mad, Mad, Mad World*; Jason Mittell, "A Cultural Approach to Television Genre Theory," *Cinema Journal* 40 (Spring 2001): 3–24; Rick Altman, *Film/Genre* (London: British Film Institute, 1999); Jonathan Stubbs, *Historical Film: A Critical Introduction* (New York: Bloomsbury, 2013).

49. Saul Austerlitz, "Rethinking Stanley Kramer," *Moving Image Source*, 25 August 2010, http://www.movingimagesource.us/articles/rethinking-stanley-kramer-20100825.

50. Jeremy Byman, *Showdown at High Noon: Witch-Hunts, Critics, and the End of the Western* (Lanham, Md.: Scarecrow Press, 2004); Glenn Frankel, *High Noon: The Hollywood Blacklist and the Making of an American Classic* (New York: Bloomsbury, 2017); Harris, *Pictures at a Revolution*.

51. Kramer, quoted in "Guess Who's Coming to New Film Concept," *Los Angeles Times*, 7 January 1973, 1.

52. Kramer with Coffey, *Mad, Mad, Mad, Mad World*, 9–10; Kramer, quoted in Walter Wagner, *You Must Remember This: Oral Reminiscences of the Real Hollywood* (New York: G. P. Putnam's Sons, 1975), 284.

53. Kramer with Coffey, *Mad, Mad, Mad, Mad World*, 9–10; social worker, quoted in Joseph J. Varga, *Hell's Kitchen and the Battle for Urban Space:*

Class Struggle and Progressive Reform in New York City, 1894–1914 (New York: Monthly Review Press, 2013), 19–20; Russell Sage Foundation study, quoted in Richard O'Connor, *Hell's Kitchen: The Riotous Days of New York's West Side* (1958; reprint, New York: Old Town Books, 1986), 179.

54. Kramer with Coffey, *Mad, Mad, Mad, Mad World*, 11–12.

55. Ibid., 10, 21; Kramer, quoted in Spoto, *Stanley Kramer*, 23.

56. Irwin S. Guernsey, DeWitt Clinton High School, to SK, 24 February 1960, American Legion Correspondence folder; Kramer, quoted in Wagner, *You Must Remember This*, 284.

57. Kramer with Coffey, *Mad, Mad, Mad, Mad World*, 20.

58. Ibid., 10, 20–21.

59. Kramer, quoted in Stevens, *Conversations with the Great Moviemakers*, 56; Kramer, quoted in Kenneth Turan, "Movie Message Maker," *Washington Post*, 5 July 1971, D2. On Jewish Americans and the New Deal, see Deborah Dash Moore, *To the Golden Cities: Pursuing the American Jewish Dream in Miami and L.A.* (Cambridge, Mass.: Harvard University Press, 1994), 8.

60. Kramer, quoted in Wagner, *You Must Remember This*, 284.

61. "All Quiet on the Western Front" and "City Lights," *New York University Medley*, May 1930, 14, 25, and February 1931, 16, 26, NYU Archives.

62. Kramer, quoted in Wagner, *You Must Remember This*, 284; Kramer, quoted in Norma Lee Browning, "Too Much Emphasis Placed on Oscars, Kramer Believes," *Chicago Tribune*, 6 April 1969, F13.

63. Saverio Giovacchini, *Hollywood Modernism: Film and Politics in the Age of the New Deal* (Philadelphia: Temple University Press, 2001).

64. Lary May, *The Big Tomorrow: Hollywood and the Politics of the American Way* (Chicago: University of Chicago Press, 2000), 180–182.

65. Giovacchini, *Hollywood Modernism*, 2; Nick Smedley, *A Divided World: Hollywood Cinema and Émigré Directors in the Era of Roosevelt and Hitler, 1933–1948* (Bristol, UK: Intellect, 2011), 8.

66. Kramer, quoted in Wagner, *You Must Remember This*, 284–285.

67. Kramer with Coffey, *Mad, Mad, Mad, Mad World*, 6; Kramer, quoted in Overs interview.

68. Kramer, quoted in Spoto, *Stanley Kramer*, 23.

69. Kramer, quoted in James Bawden, "Stanley Kramer: Hollywood Liberal," *Classic Images*, February 2011, 10; Jeffrey Geiger, *American Documentary Film* (Edinburgh: Edinburgh University Press, 2011), 135; Richard Koszarski, "Subway Commandos: Hollywood Filmmakers at the Signal Corps Photographic Center," *Film History* 14, no. 3/4 (2002): 296–315.

70. Kramer with Coffey, *Mad, Mad, Mad, Mad World*, 7; Kramer, quoted in "Kramer on Use of Film 'As Weapon,'" *Variety*, 31 July 1963, Kramer

Clippings file; Jerry D. Lewis, Pacific Palisades, Calif., to SK, 1 March 1960, American Legion Correspondence folder.

Chapter 1. A Hollywood Independent

1. Kramer, quoted in Joseph McBride, "Kramer: 'Never Good Spokesman for Blacks Because I Was White,'" *Variety*, 29 October 1975, news clipping, Kramer Clippings file; Denise Mann, *Hollywood Independents: The Postwar Talent Takeover* (Minneapolis: University of Minnesota Press, 2008), 23.

2. Bosley Crowther, "'A' Movies on 'B' Budgets," *New York Times*, 12 November 1950, [23].

3. Anticommunist activists, quoted in Brian Neve, "HUAC, the Blacklist, and the Decline of Social Cinema," in Peter Lev, *The Fifties: Transforming the Screen, 1950–1959*, vol. 7, *History of the American Cinema*, ed. Charles Harpole (New York: Scribner's, 2003), 71.

4. Mann, *Hollywood Independents*, 71.

5. Stanley Kramer with Thomas M. Coffey, *A Mad, Mad, Mad, Mad World: A Life in Hollywood* (New York: Harcourt Brace, 1997), 8.

6. Janet Staiger, "The Package-Unit System," in David Bordwell, Janet Staiger, and Kristin Thompson, eds., *The Classical Hollywood Cinema: Film Style and Mode of Production to 1960* (New York: Columbia University Press, 1985), 330–331.

7. Kramer with Coffey, *Mad, Mad, Mad, Mad World*, 9; Kramer, quoted in Donald Spoto, *Stanley Kramer, Film Maker* (Hollywood, Calif.: Samuel French, 1978), 25.

8. Crowther, "'A' Movies on 'B' Budgets," [38]; Eric Rhode, *A History of the Cinema: From Its Origins to 1970* (London: Allen Lane, 1976), 478.

9. Kramer, quoted in Walter Wagner, *You Must Remember This: Oral Reminiscences of the Real Hollywood* (New York: G. P. Putnam's Sons, 1975), 287–288; Kramer, "Of Financing and Independent Producing," *New York Times*, 8 May 1949, X5.

10. Kramer, quoted in Wagner, *You Must Remember This*, 286–287; Kramer, quoted in Crowther, "'A' Movies on 'B' Budgets," [38].

11. Philip K. Scheuer, "Stanley Kramer's Smash Hits Prove His Fitness to Survive," *Los Angeles Times*, 17 July 1949, D1.

12. Kramer, quoted in Rick Setlowe, "Modern Youth Takes Itself Big," *Variety*, 10 January 1968, news clipping, Kramer Clippings file; Kramer, quoted in Ezra Goodman, "Champion Producer," *New York Times*, 10 April 1949, X4.

13. Kramer, quoted in Spoto, *Stanley Kramer*, 36; Mark Harris, *Pictures at a Revolution: Five Movies and the Birth of the New Hollywood* (New York: Penguin, 2008), 228.

14. "Stanley Kramer," in Anna Rothe, ed., *Current Biography, 1951* (New York: H. W. Wilson, 1952), 365.

15. Kramer, quoted in Crowther, "'A' Movies on 'B' Budgets," [23]; Kramer, "The Independent Producer," *Films in Review*, March 1951, 4.

16. Crowther, "'A' Movies on 'B' Budgets," [23].

17. Glass, quoted in Crowther, "'A' Movies on 'B' Budgets," [38].

18. Kramer, quoted in Scheuer, "Kramer's Smash Hits," D1; Hedda Hopper, "Looking at Hollywood," *Chicago Tribune*, 20 May 1947, 24.

19. "An Oral History with Daniel Taradash," interviewed by Barbara Hall, Oral History Program, Herrick Library, 197.

20. Kramer, quoted in Scheuer, "Kramer's Smash Hits," D1; Mann, *Hollywood Independents*, 23.

21. Kramer, "Independent Producer," 4; Kramer, "Of Financing and Independent Producing," X5.

22. Kramer, quoted in Scheuer, "Kramer's Smash Hits," D4; Kramer, quoted in Ray Oviatt, "Provocative Movie Producer: Stanley Kramer Simply Thrives on Controversy," *Toledo Blade*, 14 February 1960, sec. 4, p. 3.

23. Peter Roffman and Jim Purdy, *The Hollywood Social Problem Film: Madness, Despair and Politics from the Depression to the Fifties* (Bloomington: Indiana University Press, 1981), viii; Brian Neve, *Film and Politics in America: A Social Tradition* (London: Routledge, 1992), 83; Steve Neale, *Genre and Hollywood* (New York: Routledge, 2000), 45.

24. Kramer with Coffey, *Mad, Mad, Mad, Mad World*, 9.

25. Ibid., 19–20; Foreman, quoted in Neve, *Film and Politics in America*, 112.

26. Kramer with Coffey, *Mad, Mad, Mad, Mad World*, 23–24.

27. Leger Grindon, *Knockout: Boxers and Boxing in American Cinema* (Jackson: University Press of Mississippi, 2011), 79; Philip K. Scheuer, "Douglas 'Champion' in Sock Saga of Heel," *Los Angeles Times*, 2 May 1949, B5.

28. Kramer with Coffey, *Mad, Mad, Mad, Mad World*, 35; Laurents, quoted in Judith E. Smith, *Visions of Belonging: Family Stories, Popular Culture, and Postwar Democracy, 1940–1960* (New York: Columbia University Press, 2004), 376n6.

29. *Variety*, quoted in John Nickel, "Disabling African American Men: Liberalism and Race Message Films," *Cinema Journal* 44 (Autumn 2004): 25; Thomas F. Brady, "Crusade in Hollywood," *New York Times*, 6 March 1949, X5.

30. Donald Bogle, *Primetime Blues: African Americans on Network Television* (New York: Farrar, Straus & Giroux, 2001), 19–20; Edwards, quoted in Pamala S. Deane, *James Edwards: African American Hollywood Icon* (Jefferson, N.C.: McFarland, 2009), 28; Stephen Vaughn, "Ronald Reagan and the Struggle for Black Dignity in Cinema, 1937–1953," *Journal of Negro History* 77 (Winter 1992): 1–16, reprinted in *Journal of African American History* (Winter 2002).

31. Thomas Cripps, *Making Movies Black: The Hollywood Message Movie from World War II to the Civil Rights Era* (New York: Oxford University Press, 1993), 291; Mark A. Reid, *Redefining Black Film* (Berkeley: University of California Press, 1993), 2, 78; Michael Rogin, *Blackface, White Noise: Jewish Immigrants in the Hollywood Melting Pot* (Berkeley: University of California Press, 1996), 239.

32. Several articles in *New York Amsterdam News*, quoted in Smith, *Visions of Belonging*, 173, 377n18; Chase, quoted in Deane, *James Edwards*, 28; Lillian Scott, "A Hollywood Independent Shows Big Studios How It's Done," *Chicago Defender*, 14 May 1949, 16; *Chicago Defender*, quoted in Deane, *James Edwards*, 30.

33. Reviewer, quoted in Thomas R. Cripps, "The Death of Rastus: Negroes in American Films since 1945," *Phylon* 28, no. 3 (1967): 268; Kramer with Coffey, *Mad, Mad, Mad, Mad World*, 40.

34. Lorraine Hansberry, "The Case of the Invisible Force: Images of the Negro in Hollywood Films," reprinted in David Platt, ed., *Celluloid Power: Social Film Criticism from* The Birth of a Nation *to* Judgment at Nuremberg (Methuchen, N.J.: Scarecrow, 1992), 459–460.

35. Reviews in *Nation* and *Time*, quoted in Deane, *James Edwards*, 23–24.

36. Kramer, quoted in Spoto, *Stanley Kramer*, 55.

37. Fred Zinnemann, "On Using Non-Actors in Pictures," *New York Times*, 8 January 1950, 87; Kramer with Coffey, *Mad, Mad, Mad, Mad World*, 47; Susan L. Mizruchi, *Brando's Smile: His Life, Thought, and Work* (New York: W. W. Norton, 2014), 83.

38. Kramer, quoted in Leo Verswijver, *"Movies Were Always Magical": Interviews with 19 Actors, Directors and Producers from the Hollywood of the 1930s through the 1950s* (Jefferson, N.C.: McFarland, 2003), 77; Bosley Crowther, "The Screen: Four Newcomers on Local Scene," *New York Times*, 21 July 1950, 15.

39. Janet Staiger, *Perverse Spectators: The Practices of Film Reception* (New York: New York University Press, 2000), 30–31.

40. James Gilbert, *Men in the Middle: Searching for Masculinity in the 1950s* (Chicago: University of Chicago Press, 2005).

41. Kramer with Coffey, *Mad, Mad, Mad, Mad World*, 52; Bosley Crowther, "What Price Glory?" *New York Times*, 30 June 1950, X1.

42. Kramer, "Independent Producer," 4.

43. Kramer, quoted in Crowther, "'A' Movies on 'B' Budgets," [38]; Preminger, quoted in Pam Cook, ed., *The Cinema Book* (London: British Film Institute, 1985), 154; Blaustein, quoted in Larry Ceplair, "Julian Blaustein: An Unusual Movie Producer in Cold War Hollywood," *Film History* 21, no. 3 (2009): 263.

44. Kramer, quoted in Overs interview and in Alberto Shatowsky interview, Publicity–*JAN* Al Horwits–Releases folder, box 38, Kramer Papers; Kramer, quoted in Oviatt, "Provocative Movie Producer," and in *Stage and Screen: Interviews by Donald McDonald with Walter Kerr and Stanley Kramer* (Nashville, Tenn.: Center for the Study of Democratic Institutions, 1962), 46.

45. Kramer, quoted in Overs interview and in "Odyssey of a Former Film Editor," *Cinemediator*, Spring 1968, 23.

46. Tino T. Balio, *United Artists*, vol. 1, *1919–1950: The Company Built by the Stars* (Madison: University of Wisconsin Press, 2009), 202.

47. Mae Tinee, "Kramer Takes Bold Film Approach," *Chicago Daily Tribune*, 13 November 1960, G14.

48. Kramer, quoted in "Big Global Puff for Kramer's *Wind*," *Variety*, 1 June 1960, *Inherit the Wind* Clippings file, Herrick Library; Mann, *Hollywood Independents*, 126.

49. Campaign Guide for Stanley Kramer's *Inherit the Wind* and Al Horwits to SK, 30 June 1960, 8 August 1960, and 16 August 1960, Horwits Publicity folder.

50. *Champion* and *The Men* advertisements, *Los Angeles Times*, 29 April 1949, A6, and 29 September 1950, 17.

51. Kramer, quoted in Hollis Alpert, "The Movies and the Critics," *Saturday Review*, 26 December 1964, 11; Kramer, quoted in Richard L. Coe, "Film Producer in Solemn Vein," *Washington Post*, 11 October 1960, B14; Hubbard Keavy, "Stanley Kramer Gambles with Film Fortunes," news clipping, Paxton Publicity folder.

52. *Judgment at Nuremberg* audience preview cards, San Francisco, August 1961, box 40, Kramer Papers.

53. Joshua Gamson, *Claims to Fame: Celebrity in Contemporary America* (Berkeley: University of California Press, 1994); Charles L. Ponce de Leon, *Self-Exposure: Human-Interest Journalism and the Emergence of Celebrity in America, 1890–1940* (Chapel Hill: University of North Carolina Press, 2002).

54. "Cinema: New Horizon," *Time*, 13 November 1950, 100; "Talk with the Director," *Newsweek*, 17 October 60, 114; Ezra Goodman, "Champion

Producer," *New York Times,* 10 April 1949, X4; Crowther, "'A' Movies on 'B' Budgets," [40].

55. Kramer, quoted in Joseph Wershba, "Daily Closeup: Stanley Kramer, Movie Maker," *New York Post,* 28 January 1960, news clipping, American Legion folder, box 115, Kramer Papers; Keavy, "Kramer Gambles with Film Fortunes."

56. Daniel J. Boorstin, *The Image: A Guide to Pseudo-Events in America,* 50th anniversary ed. (New York: Vintage, 2012), 57.

57. Edwin Schallert, "Kramer Packages Dick, Brodie and Other Stars," *Los Angeles Times,* 19 April 1949, A7; Richard Dyer MacCann, "Independence, with a Vengeance," *Film Quarterly* 15 (Summer 1962): 20; "Cinema: New Horizon," *Time,* 13 November 1950, 100.

58. "Kramer, Columbia Sign $25,000,000 Film Deal," *Los Angeles Times,* 19 March 1951, 1, 4; Penelope Houston, "Kramer and Company," *Sight and Sound,* July/September 1952, 20.

59. The Waldorf Statement, reprinted in Larry Ceplair and Steven Englund, *The Inquisition in Hollywood: Politics in the Film Community, 1930–60,* reprint (Urbana: University of Illinois Press, 2003), 455.

60. Scott, "Hollywood Independent," 16; "An Oral History with Daniel Taradash," 148; Kramer, quoted in Verswijver, *"Movies Were Always Magical,"* 79.

61. Lary May, *The Big Tomorrow: Hollywood and the Politics of the American Way* (Chicago: University of Chicago Press, 2000), 181–182.

62. Kramer, quoted in A. William Bluem and Jason E. Squire, eds., *The Movie Business: American Film Industry Practice* (New York: Hastings House, 1972), 163.

63. Kramer with Coffey, *Mad, Mad, Mad, Mad World,* 20–21.

64. "Kramer to Do Life of F. D. Roosevelt," *New York Times,* 5 October 1951, 38; JH, New York, to SK [March 1960], American Legion Correspondence folder.

65. Paul Buhle and Dave Wagner, *Radical Hollywood: The Untold Story behind America's Favorite Movies* (New York: New Press, 2002), 86.

66. Ferrer, quoted in "Ferrer Denies Link to Reds," *Motion Picture Herald,* 26 May 1951, 36, José Ferrer Clippings File, Herrick Library.

67. Neve, *Film and Politics in America,* 123.

68. Victor S. Navasky, *Naming Names* (New York: Viking, 1980), 89.

69. M. J. Heale, *American Anticommunism: Combating the Enemy Within, 1830–1970* (Baltimore: Johns Hopkins University Press, 1990), 159.

70. John Sbardellati, *J. Edgar Hoover Goes to the Movies: The FBI and the Origins of Hollywood's Cold War* (Ithaca, N.Y.: Cornell University Press, 2012), 3.

71. FBI summary reports on Stanley Kramer, 29 February 1960 and 1 August 1960; Memo, Special Agent in Charge, Los Angeles, to Director, FBI, 29 December 1960, 100–433715–4.

72. Kramer with Coffey, *Mad, Mad, Mad, Mad World*, 85.

73. Letters to Stanley Kramer Company, Sokolsky Papers.

74. Irving Reis to Stanley Kramer Company, 1 June 1951, box 26, and Kirk Douglas to Stanley Kramer Company, 23 September 1952, box 29, Sokolsky Papers; John Cogley, *Report on Blacklisting*, vol. 1, *Movies* (New York: Fund for the Republic, 1956), 152–153; J. Hoberman, *An Army of Phantoms: American Movies and the Making of the Cold War* (New York: New Press, 2011), 173–174.

75. Foreman, quoted in Navasky, *Naming Names*, 157.

76. Kramer with Coffey, *Mad, Mad, Mad, Mad World*, 85–86.

77. Foreman, quoted in Navasky, *Naming Names*, 158.

78. Kramer, quoted in ibid., 160; Larry Ceplair, "Shedding Light on *Darkness at High Noon*," *Cineaste*, Fall 2002, 21; Kramer with Coffey, *Mad, Mad, Mad, Mad World*, 86–87.

79. Thomas M. Pryor, "Kramer Splitting with Film Partner," *New York Times*, 26 September 1951, 36; "Partner Turns on Reluctant Film Quiz Witness," *Washington Post*, 27 September 1951, 8; "Kramer, Foreman Sever Relations," *New York Times*, 23 October 1951, 35.

80. Kramer with Coffey, *Mad, Mad, Mad, Mad World*, 87.

81. Bosley Crowther, "A Western Legend," *New York Times*, 3 August 1952, X1.

82. Cooper, quoted in Jeffrey Meyers, *Gary Cooper: American Hero* (New York: Cooper Square, 1998), 239; Foreman, quoted in Hoberman, *Army of Phantoms*, 176.

83. Jeremy Byman, *Showdown at High Noon: Witch-Hunts, Critics, and the End of the Western* (Lanham, Md.: Scarecrow, 2004); Luraschi, quoted in David N. Eldridge, "'Dear Owen': The CIA, Luigi Luraschi and Hollywood, 1953," *Historical Journal of Film, Radio and Television* 20, no. 2 (2000): 174–175.

84. Foreman, quoted in Byman, *Showdown at High Noon*, 83; Wayne, quoted in Randy Roberts and James S. Olson, *John Wayne: American* (Lincoln: University of Nebraska Press, 1995), 349; Luraschi, quoted in Eldridge, "'Dear Owen,'" 174; Kramer with Coffey, *Mad, Mad, Mad, Mad World*, 73.

85. Ceplair, "Shedding Light," 22; Glenn Frankel, *High Noon: The Hollywood Blacklist and the Making of an American Classic* (New York: Bloomsbury, 2017), 187–188.

86. Kramer, quoted in James Bawden, "Stanley Kramer: Hollywood Liberal," *Classic Images*, February 2011, 11; unnamed colleague, quoted in Hollis Alpert, "Postwar Generation: The Movies," *Saturday Review*, 14 March 1953, 63.

87. This is an indictment of Kramer made in Lionel Chetwynd's documentary *Darkness at High Noon: The Carl Foreman Documents* (2002) and discussed in the conclusion. On the settlement agreement, see Ceplair, "Shedding Light," 22, and Frankel, *High Noon*, 210.

88. Tom Stempel, *Framework: A History of Screenwriting in the American Film*, 3rd ed. (Syracuse, N.Y.: Syracuse University Press, 2000), 171.

89. George Eells, *Hedda and Louella* (New York: G. P. Putnam's Sons, 1972), 225; Ellen Schrecker, *Many Are the Crimes: McCarthyism in America* (New York: Little, Brown, 1998), 62; David Caute, *The Great Fear: The Anti-Communist Purge under Truman and Eisenhower* (New York: Simon & Schuster, 1978), 503.

90. J. B. Matthews, "Did the Movies Really Clean House?" *American Legion Magazine*, December 1951, 12–13, 49–56.

91. "Editor's Corner," *American Legion Magazine*, May 1960, 6.

92. "Editor's Corner," *American Legion Magazine*, December 1959, 6.

93. Fagan, quoted in John E. Fitzgerald, "The Responsible Movie Maker," *St. Jude: A National Catholic Monthly*, September 1962, 9, *JAN* Comments folder.

94. See my *Hedda Hopper's Hollywood: Celebrity Gossip and American Conservatism* (New York: New York University Press, 2011); Hedda Hopper and SK interview, 17 October 1961, Stanley Kramer folder, Hedda Hopper Papers, Herrick Library.

95. Jaik Rosenstein, "On the Beach Called Kramer's Christmas Gift to Khrushchev," *Hollywood Close-Up*, 17 December 1959, American Legion Clippings folder.

96. Bond to Sokolsky, 10 August 1951, 6 October 1951, 19 January 1952, and 12 May 1952, box 26, Sokolsky Papers.

97. Bond to Sokolsky, 19 January 1952, box 26, Sokolsky Papers; John A. Noakes, "Official Frames in Social Movement Theory: The FBI, HUAC, and the Communist Threat in Hollywood," *Sociological Quarterly* 41, no. 4 (2000): 657–680.

98. W. C. Sullivan to A. H. Belmont, FBI memo, 4 September 1958 [file number illegible]; Hedda Hopper column, *Los Angeles Times*, 21 May 1951, B8.

99. Laslo Benedek, "Transferring *Death of a Salesman* to Film," *New York Times*, 9 December 1951, 131; Edwin Schallert, "Kramer Enlarges Operation Methods," *Los Angeles Times*, 15 July 1951, D3.

100. Mae Tinee, "March Misses, but *Salesman* Is Potent Film," *Chicago Daily Tribune*, 30 January 1952, A2; Edwin Schallert, "Drama," *Los Angeles Times*, 21 December 1951, B5.

101. Kramer, quoted in Ed Lukas, "Kramer Defends Hiring Purged Writers before Beverly Hills Club Group," American Legion Clippings folder.

102. Bond to Sokolsky, 10 August 1951 and 19 January 1952, box 26, Sokolsky Papers; Fagan, quoted in Fitzgerald, "Responsible Movie Maker," 9.

103. Nathan Abrams, "An Unofficial Cultural Ambassador: Arthur Miller and the Cultural Cold War," in Peter Romijn, Giles Scott-Smith, and Joes Segal, eds., *Divided Dreamworlds? The Cultural Cold War in East and West* (Amsterdam: Amsterdam University Press, 2012), 15, 24.

104. Ibid., 15.

105. "Am. Legion Pickets *Salesman* in D.C.," *Variety*, 7 March 1952, and "Am. Legion Pressure Causes Exhibs Seek *Salesman* Out," *Variety*, 23 April 1952, news clippings, *Death of a Salesman* Clippings file, Herrick Library; Ceplair and Englund, *Inquisition in Hollywood*, 386; Caute, *Great Fear*, 503.

106. Cogley, *Report on Blacklisting*, 1:113–114.

107. "Producer Kramer Sues for Million," *Los Angeles Times*, 8 January 1952, 5; lawsuit, quoted in "Kramer Files Suit for $1,000,000 Libel," *New York Times*, 8 January 1952, 22; Kramer, quoted in "Stanley Kramer to Fight to Clear His 'Good Name,'" *Film Daily*, news clipping, AMPTP Records.

108. Thomas M. Pryor, "Hollywood's Militant Stand," *New York Times*, 13 January 1952, X5; "Aroused Filmdom to Fight Attacks," *New York Times*, 9 January 1952, 24; Bond to Sokolsky, 19 January 1952, box 26, Sokolsky Papers.

109. Jimmie Fidler, "Views of Hollywood," news clipping, 14 January 1952, folder 665, AMPTP Records; Kramer, quoted in Spoto, *Stanley Kramer*, 75.

110. Edward Dmytryk, *Odd Man Out: A Memoir of the Hollywood Ten* (Carbondale: Southern Illinois University Press, 1996), 186, 175. The *Daily Worker* is quoted on 176.

111. Michael Blankfort, 20th Century-Fox Film Corporation, 25 September 1961, to SK, *JAN* Comments folder.

112. Bond to Sokolsky, handwritten note, 20 March 1952, box 26, Sokolsky Papers.

113. Bernard F. Dick, ed., *Columbia Pictures: Portrait of a Studio* (Lexington, Ky.: University Press of Kentucky, 1992), 15.

114. Kramer, quoted in Thomas M. Pryor, "Hollywood Giant," *New York Times*, 23 June 1957, 93; Kramer, quoted in Roy Newquist, *A Special Kind of Magic* (New York: Rand McNally, 1967), 47.

115. Kramer, quoted in Arthur Knight, "Not with a Bang or a Whimper," *Saturday Review*, 24 October 1959, 33; Kramer with Coffey, *Mad, Mad, Mad, Mad World*, 124.

116. Yannis Tzioumakis, *American Independent Cinema: An Introduction* (Edinburgh: Edinburgh University Press, 2006), 112, 118. Tzioumakis details the UA-Kramer 1957 contract on 114–119.

117. Tzioumakis, *American Independent Cinema*, 115; Kramer, quoted in Arthur Knight, "Shop Talk in Hollywood," *Saturday Review*, 23 December 1961, 36; Kramer, quoted in Pryor, "Hollywood Giant," 93.

118. Kramer, quoted in Spoto, *Stanley Kramer*, 185.

119. Thomas M. Pryor, "Hollywood Giant," 93, and "Hollywood Plan," *New York Times*, 2 February 1958, X7.

120. Young, quoted in *The Defiant One*, written and directed by Jan Johnson and Pat Wright (Fayetteville, N.C.: GroundSwell Pictures, 2014), DVD.

Chapter 2. Civil Rights Meets *The Defiant Ones*

1. Kramer, quoted in Philip K. Scheuer, "Kramer Revivifies Style of Early Hits," *Los Angeles Times*, 2 June 1958, C9.

2. Peter Cowie, "The Defiant One," *Films and Filming*, March 1963, 15–19.

3. Mae Tinee, "Kramer Has High Hope re *Defiant Ones*," *Chicago Daily Tribune*, 17 August 1958, E13.

4. Stanley Kramer, "Soviets React to US Candor," *Los Angeles Times*, 18 August 1963, L3; Kramer statement, television episode of NBC's *Youth Wants to Know*, 3 August 1958.

5. Young, quoted in Bob Thomas, "Nedrick Young Writes Again after Being on Blacklist," *Ocala Star-Banner*, 13 April 1960, 9; Young, quoted in *The Defiant One*, written and directed by Jan Johnson and Pat Wright (Fayetteville, N.C.: GroundSwell Pictures, 2014), DVD.

6. Mae Tinee, "Here's What Movie World Has in Offing," *Chicago Daily Tribune*, 27 July 1958, E9; "*Defiant* in Oct. 1 Debut," *Los Angeles Times*, 20 September 1958, B2.

7. Aram Goudsouzian, *Sidney Poitier: Man, Actor, Icon* (Chapel Hill: University of North Carolina Press, 2004), 153; Gordon Hitchens, "The Defiance in *The Defiant Ones*," *Film Culture*, Fall/Winter 1970, reprinted in David Platt, ed., *Celluloid Power: Social Film Criticism from* The Birth of a Nation *to* Judgment at Nuremberg (Methuchen, N.J.: Scarecrow, 1992), 519; Fagan, quoted in John E. Fitzgerald, "The Responsible Movie Maker," *St. Jude: A National Catholic Monthly*, September 1962, 9, *JAN* Comments folder.

8. John Nickel, "Disabling African American Men: Liberalism and Race Message Films," *Cinema Journal* 44 (Autumn 2004): 26.

9. My discussion here owes much to Peter Roffman and Jim Purdy, *The Hollywood Social Problem Film: Madness, Despair and Politics from the Depression to the Fifties* (Bloomington: Indiana University Press, 1981), and [Nedrick Young and] Harold Jacob Smith to the Screen Editor, *New York Times*, 8 February 1959, X7. Young's name was redacted when the letter was published, likely explained by his being on the blacklist at the time. See also Hitchens, "Defiance in *The Defiant Ones*," 520.

10. Ernest Giglio, *Here's Looking at You: Hollywood, Film and Politics*, 3rd ed. (New York: Peter Lang, 2010), 282n21; Peter Roffman and Beverly Simpson, "Stanley Kramer," in Gary Crowdus, ed., *The Political Companion to American Film* (Chicago: Lakeview, 1994), 235–236.

11. Roffman and Purdy, *Hollywood Social Problem Film*, viii; [Young and] Smith to the Screen Editor, X7.

12. Larry Ceplair, "The Base and Superstructure Debate in the Hollywood Communist Party," *Science and Society* 72 (July 2008): 319–348; Judith E. Smith, *Visions of Belonging: Family Stories, Popular Culture, and Postwar Democracy, 1940–1960* (New York: Columbia University Press, 2004), 325.

13. Emma Hamilton and Troy Saxby, "'Draggin' the Chain': Linking Civil Rights and African American Representation in *The Defiant Ones* and *In the Heat of the Night*," in Ian Gregory Strachan and Mia Mask, eds., *Poitier Revisited: Reconsidering a Black Icon in the Obama Age* (New York: Bloomsbury, 2015), 73–96, quotation on 77.

14. [Young and] Smith to the Screen Editor, X7; Stanley Kauffmann, "Together and Alone," *New Republic*, 1 September 1958, 23.

15. Bosley Crowther, "Ambiguous Finales," *New York Times*, 1 February 1959, X1; [Young and] Smith to the Screen Editor, X7.

16. Young as "Douglas" and Smith, paraphrased in Thomas M. Pryor, "Hollywood Views," *Los Angeles Times*, 9 March 1958, X7.

17. Thomas, "Nedrick Young Writes Again," 9.

18. Kramer, quoted in Philip K. Scheuer, "Tyro Writers Break Chains," *Los Angeles Times*, 19 March 1958, C11; Ben Irwin to Cy Endfield, quoted in Brian Neve, *The Many Lives of Cy Endfield: Film Noir, the Blacklist, and Zulu* (Madison: University of Wisconsin Press, 2015), 118; Tom Stempel, *Framework: A History of Screenwriting in the American Film*, 3rd ed. (Syracuse, N.Y.: Syracuse University Press, 2000), 171.

19. Sidney Poitier, *The Measure of a Man: A Spiritual Autobiography* (New York: HarperCollins, 2000), 102.

20. Dalton Trumbo, quoted in Helen Manfull, ed., *Additional Dialogue: Letters of Dalton Trumbo, 1942–1962* (New York: M. Evans, 1970), 407.

21. Josh Smith, quoted in Larry Ceplair and Christopher Trumbo, *Dalton Trumbo: Blacklisted Hollywood Radical* (Lexington: University Press of Kentucky, 2014), 348; Tony Curtis with Peter Golenbock, *American Prince: A Memoir* (New York: Harmony, 2008), 193.

22. Kramer statement, television episode of NBC's *Youth Wants to Know,* 3 August 1958.

23. Analysis of Film Content, 14 May 1958, *The Defiant Ones* file, PCA Records.

24. Geoffrey M. Shurlock to SK, 6 February 1958, *The Defiant Ones* file, PCA Records.

25. Kramer, quoted in Thomas M. Pryor, "Hollywood Urged to Stage TV Show–*Defiant Ones* Cast," *New York Times,* 10 January 1958, 20, and in Blowitz-Maskel press release [January 1958], Blowitz-Maskel Publicity folder; Kramer, quoted in Scheuer, "Kramer Revivifies Style," C9.

26. "*Defiant Ones,*" *New York Times,* 17 August 1958, SM70; Scheuer, "Kramer Revivifies Style," C9.

27. Kramer, quoted in Bosley Crowther, "Hollywood's Producer of Controversy," *New York Times,* 10 December 1961, SM84; Poitier, quoted in "From the Army Archerd Archive," *Daily Variety,* 8 June 2007, Kramer Clippings file; Goudsouzian, *Sidney Poitier,* 3; Curtis with Golenbock, *American Prince,* 194.

28. Nora Sayre, "The Man Who Came to Dinner," *New York Times Book Review,* 28 May 2000; Donald Bogle, quoted in Gladstone L. Yearwood, "The Hero in Black Film: An Analysis of the Film Industry and Problems in Black Cinema," *Wide Angle* 5, no. 2 (1982): 46.

29. Stanley Kramer with Thomas M. Coffey, *A Mad, Mad, Mad, Mad World: A Life in Hollywood* (New York: Harcourt Brace, 1997), 150; Poitier, quoted in Tony Curtis and Barry Paris, *Tony Curtis: The Autobiography* (London: Heinemann, 1993), 146; Sidney Poitier, *This Life* (New York: Knopf, 1980), 212.

30. Andrea Slane, "Pressure Points: Political Psychology, Screen Adaptation, and the Management of Racism in the Case-History Genre," *Camera Obscura* 15, no. 3 (2001): 77; Harry M. Benshoff and Sean Griffin, *America on Film: Representing Race, Class, Gender, and Sexuality at the Movies* (Malden, Mass.: Blackwell, 2004), 85.

31. Kramer, quoted in Thomas M. Pryor, "A *Defiant One* Becomes a Star," *New York Times,* 25 January 1959, SM27; Poitier, paraphrased by Kramer with Coffey, *Mad, Mad, Mad, Mad World,* 151; Roland Leander Williams, Jr., *Black Male Frames: African Americans in a Century of Hollywood Cinema, 1903–2003* (Syracuse, N.Y.: Syracuse University Press, 2015), 107.

32. Nickel, "Disabling African American Men," 27; Hernán Vera and Andrew M. Gordon, *Screen Saviors: Hollywood Fictions of Whiteness* (Lanham, Md.: Rowman & Littlefield, 2003), 154; Poitier, quoted in "Sidney Poitier: Negro Actor with a Full Work Schedule," *Look*, 28 October 1958, *TDO* Clippings file.

33. Curtis with Golenbock, *American Prince*, 192–193; Curtis, paraphrased in Kramer with Coffey, *Mad, Mad, Mad, Mad World*, 149; Curtis and Paris, *Tony Curtis*, 141.

34. Allison Graham, *Framing the South: Hollywood, Television, and Race during the Civil Rights Struggle* (Baltimore, Md.: Johns Hopkins University Press, 2001), 143, 13; Neda Atanasoski, "Cold War Carmen in US Racial Modernity," *Cinema Journal* 54 (Fall 2014): 88–111.

35. Curtis with Golenbock, *American Prince*, 192–194; "Kramer Film Stars Equal," *Los Angeles Times*, 27 September 1958, B2.

36. Theodore Bikel, *Theo: An Autobiography* (Madison: University of Wisconsin Press, 2002), 198.

37. Synopsis, *The Defiant Ones* file, PCA Records; Hamilton and Saxby, "'Draggin' the Chain,'" 90.

38. [Young and Smith] to the Screen Editor, X7.

39. Young, quoted in Thomas, "Nedrick Young Writes Again," 9.

40. Hamilton and Saxby, "'Draggin' the Chain,'" 85.

41. The earliest and most famous example of such black feminist analysis was Michele Wallace, *Black Macho and the Myth of the Superwoman* (New York: Dial, 1978). See also Hamilton and Saxby, "'Draggin' the Chain,'" 85; Robyn Wiegman, *American Anatomies: Theorizing Race and Gender* (Durham, N.C.: Duke University Press, 1995), 118–119.

42. Tino T. Balio, *United Artists*, vol. 2, *1951–1978: The Company That Changed the Film Industry* (Madison: University of Wisconsin Press, 2009), 143; Bikel, *Theo*, 199.

43. Ad and Kramer, quoted in Blowitz-Maskel press release [January 1958], Blowitz-Maskel Publicity folder.

44. Curtis with Golenbock, *American Prince*, 192; Albert Johnson, "*The Defiant Ones*," *Sight and Sound*, Autumn 1958, 316, *TDO* Clippings file; "Poitier, Curtis Find Pleasure in 'Fights' in Pix *Defiant Ones*," *Chicago Defender*, 9 August 1958, 19.

45. George Thomas, Jr., "Rich Film Lode in Old Kernville," *New York Times*, 6 July 1958, X5; Bikel, *Theo*, 198.

46. See correspondence in Music folder; Imogen Sara Smith, *In Lonely Places: Film Noir beyond the City* (Jefferson, N.C.: McFarland, 2011), 114.

47. [Young and] Smith to the Screen Editor, X7; Abbe Niles, NYC, to the Screen Editor, *New York Times*, 8 February 1959, X7.

48. David Wallerstein, paraphrased in Thomas to SK, Bill Blowitz, Mike Beck, 18 July 1958, Thomas Publicity folder.

49. Lisa Kernan, *Coming Attractions: Reading American Movie Trailers* (Austin: University of Texas Press, 2004), 7, 2.

50. Wallerstein (see n. 48); Thomas Doherty, *Teenagers and Teenpics: The Juvenilization of American Movies in the 1950s* (Philadelphia: Temple University Press, 2002), 2–9.

51. "Winners: Editorial Writing," http://www.pulitzer.org/awards/1958.

52. SK to Harry S. Ashmore, *Arkansas Gazette*, Little Rock, 28 February 1958, Thomas Publicity folder.

53. George Thomas, Jr., to William F. Blowitz, 31 March 1958, Thomas Publicity folder.

54. "*The Defiant Ones*," *Motion Picture Herald*, 26 July 1958, *TDO* Clippings file.

55. Blowitz-Maskel press releases, n.d., Blowitz-Maskel Publicity folder.

56. Anthony Holden, *The Oscars: The Secret History of Hollywood's Academy Awards* (Boston: Little, Brown, 1993), 210; "Chain Plays Role [in] Poitier's Latest," *Chicago Defender*, 6 August 1958, 18; "A Story of Hate Enchanted," *Life*, 11 August 1958, *TDO* Clippings file.

57. *The Defiant Ones* advertisements, *New York Times*, 24 September 1958, 23, and *Chicago Tribune*, 11 August 1958, A10.

58. The work of feminist film scholar Laura Mulvey is perhaps the most influential. See her "Visual Pleasure and Narrative Cinema," *Screen*, Autumn 1975, 6–18.

59. Blowitz-Maskel Campaign Slants, n.d., and Blowitz-Maskel Memo, 19 March 1958, Blowitz-Maskel Publicity folder; Curtis and Paris, *Tony Curtis*, 142.

60. Gunther H. Schiff to Harold Stern, 1 May 1959, and Poitier, paraphrased in Harold H. Stern to Gunther H. Schiff, 20 April 1959, Music folder; Tinee, "Kramer Has High Hope," E13.

61. James Naremore, "Uptown Folk: Blackness and Entertainment in Cabin in the Sky," *Arizona Quarterly* 48 (Winter 1992): 99–124, quotation on 100.

62. Gunther H. Schiff to I. B. Kornblum, 1 May 1959, Music folder.

63. Tinee, "Here's What Movie World Has," E9.

64. George Thomas, Jr., to SK, 5 August 1958, Thomas Publicity folder; "Movie of the Week," *Jet*, 21 August 1958, 65; "Is Poitier Hollywood's Best Actor?" *Jet*, 5 February 1959, 58–61.

65. Outline of Campaign for "TDO," UA Publicity folder.

66. George Thomas, Jr., to SK, Bill Blowitz, Mike Beck, 4 August 1958, Thomas Publicity folder; Wallerstein, paraphrased in "Big Campaign for Loop Pix," *Chicago Defender*, 5 August 1958, 18.

67. George Thomas, Jr., to SK, telegram, 9 August 1958, Thomas Publicity folder.

68. Outline of Campaign for "TDO," UA Publicity folder.

69. Lee Blackwell, "Off the Record," *Chicago Defender*, 6 August 1958, 10.

70. Outline of Campaign for "TDO," UA Publicity folder; George Thomas, Jr., to Bill Blowitz, Mike Beck, SK, 15 August 1958, Thomas Publicity folder.

71. "Record-breaker" press release, n.d., and George Thomas, Jr., to Myer P. Beck, telegram, 25 August 1958, Thomas Publicity folder.

72. Myer P. Beck to SK, 29 September 1958, *TDO* Awards folder; Jackie Robinson, quoted in *The Defiant Ones* ad, *Jet*, 20 October 1959, 29.

73. Mae Tinee, "Prison Film Is a Classic of Its Kind," *Chicago Daily Tribune*, 14 August 1958, C18; Roi Ottley, "New Hollywood Movie Has Sensitive Racial Plot," *Chicago Daily Tribune*, 10 August 1958, SW15.

74. Summary of audience preview cards from Dallas, Texas, October 1958, George Thomas, Jr., to SK, etc., 11 October 1958, Thomas Publicity folder.

75. Philip K. Scheuer, "Film Hits Hard at Race Hate," *Los Angeles Times*, 17 August 1958, E1; Kauffmann, "Together and Alone," 22–23; Bosley Crowther, "A Season Come to Life," *New York Times*, 5 October 1958, X1.

76. "A Story of Hate Enchanted"; Donald Spoto, *Stanley Kramer, Film Maker* (Hollywood, Calif.: Samuel French, 1978), 204. Michael Rogin pointed out Kramer's use of this image in two of his films in *Blackface, White Noise: Jewish Immigrants in the Hollywood Melting Pot* (Berkeley: University of California Press, 1996), 239.

77. Morton I. Moskowitz, Brooklyn, N.Y., to Screen Editor, "Freudian Slant," *New York Times*, 8 February 1959, X7; Goudsouzian, *Sidney Poitier*, 154; Williams, *Black Male Frames*, 108.

78. "Hail Poitier as Top Negro Actor," *Chicago Defender*, 26 August 1958, A6; "Poitier, Tony Curtis Brave Mob in New Film," *Afro-American*, 2 August 1958, 7; Kauffmann, "Together and Alone," 22–23.

79. R. P., "Essay in Tolerance: *The Defiant Ones*," *Manchester Guardian*, 4 November 1958, 5; "Hollywood at Its Best," *Newsweek*, 25 August 1958, *TDO* Clippings file; Kramer, quoted in Pryor, "*Defiant One* Becomes a Star," SM27; "Hail Poitier as Top Negro Actor," A6.

80. Robert Hatch, "Films," *Nation*, 11 October 1958, 219.

81. Lenny Bruce, quoted in Graham, *Framing the South*, 138; David E. Kaufman, *Jewhooing the Sixties: American Celebrity and Jewish Identity—Sandy Koufax, Lenny Bruce, Bob Dylan, and Barbra Streisand* (Waltham, Mass.: Brandeis University Press, 2012), 105–106.

82. James Baldwin, *The Devil Finds Work* (London: Michael Joseph, 1976), 61–62.

83. Dick Gregory, quoted in Vera and Gordon, *Screen Saviors*, 157; Mark A. Reid, "The Black Action Film: The End of the Patiently Enduring Black Hero," *Film History* 2, no. 1 (1988): 27; Baldwin, *Devil Finds Work*, 66; Giglio, *Here's Looking at You*, 264.

84. "*Defiant Ones* Roosevelt Pix Still on Top," *Chicago Defender*, 22 September 1958, 19; Crowther, "Hollywood's Producer of Controversy," SM76; Hilda See, "*The Defiant Ones* Sidney Poitier's Best: Looms a Natural for 'Oscar' Award Critics Predict," *Chicago Defender*, 26 July 1958, 19; John L. Scott, "*The Defiant Ones* Forceful, Exciting," *Los Angeles Times*, 2 October 1958, C13.

85. Melissa Ooten, "Censorship in Black and White: *The Burning Cross* (1947), *Band of Angels* (1957), and the Politics of Film Censorship in the American South after World War II," *Historical Journal of Film, Radio and Television* 33, no. 1 (2013): 89–90.

86. Montgomery White Citizens' Council, quoted in "Alabama Bans *Defiant Ones*," *Afro-American*, 2 May 1959, 2; "Movie Banned," *Mirror-News*, 10 April 1959, *TDO* Clippings file.

87. "Southern Censorship Bars All Films with 'Interracial Flavor,'" *Afro-American*, 11 April 1959, 15.

88. Summary of audience preview cards from Dallas, Texas, October 1958, George Thomas, Jr., to SK, etc., 11 October 1958, Thomas Publicity folder; Mrs. W. J. H., Texarkana, Arkansas, n.d., Protests–"The Defiant Ones" folder, box 18, Kramer Papers.

89. "Integrated Showings for *Defiant Ones*," *Hollywood Reporter*, 7 February 1961, *TDO* Clippings file.

90. Summary of audience preview cards from Dallas, Texas, October 1958, George Thomas, Jr., to SK, etc., 11 October 1958, Thomas Publicity folder; Lily May Caldwell, *Birmingham News*, to Mort Nathanson, Publicity Manager, UA, [May 1859], Protests–"The Defiant Ones" folder, box 18, Kramer Papers.

91. Hazel A. Washington, "This is Hollywood," *Chicago Defender*, 16 August 1958, 19; Kauffmann, "Together and Alone," 23.

92. Montgomery White Citizens' Council, quoted in "*Defiant Ones* Run Canceled," *Los Angeles Times*, 11 April 1959, 7.

93. W. C. Sullivan to A. H. Belmont, FBI Office Memorandum, 4 September 1958 [file number illegible].

94. Arthur Knight, "Links in the Human Chain," *Saturday Review*, 26 July 1958, 23; "Cinema: The New Pictures," *Time*, 25 August 1958, 80; Hatch, "Films," 219; Pauline Kael, "The Intentions of Stanley Kramer," in *Kiss Kiss Bang Bang* (London: Calder & Boyars, 1970), 205.

95. Scott, "*Defiant Ones* Forceful, Exciting," C13; Charles B. Wheeler to Screen Editor, *New York Times*, 15 March 1959, X8; Cowie, "Defiant One," 18.

96. Cowie, "Defiant One," 18.

97. Kenneth Osgood, *Total Cold War: Eisenhower's Secret Propaganda Battle at Home and Abroad* (Lawrence: University Press of Kansas, 2006), 225; Arnold M. Picker to George Stevens, Jr., Motion Picture Service, United States Information Agency, 31 July 1963, Russia–Correspondence folder, box 109, Kramer Papers.

98. City of Valladolid prize, quoted in "Pix, *The Defiant Ones* Hailed Abroad," *Chicago Defender*, 2 May 1959, 18.

99. "*Defiant Ones* Dispels Anti-American, Pro-Soviet Aura at Mex Film Fest," *Hollywood Reporter*, 21 October 1958, *TDO* Clippings file; Paul P. Kennedy, "Film on Racial Amity Overcomes Hatred of U.S. at Mexican Fete," *New York Times*, 20 October 1958, 31; Mexico Film Festival 1958 Diploma de Honor, *TDO* Awards folder.

100. UA press release, 24 March 1959, *TDO* Awards folder; "Negro Group Fails in Bid to See Ike," *Washington Post*, 16 November 1958, B6; "NCNW Picks Poitier, Curtis for Human Relations Award," *Chicago Defender*, 15 November 1958, 18.

101. Ceplair and Trumbo, *Dalton Trumbo*, 355–356, 364; Thomas M. Pryor, "Coast Scenarist Reveals Identity," *New York Times*, 1 January 1959, 38.

102. Bond, quoted in Stempel, *Framework*, 173; "Ban Lifted on Red Candidates for Oscars," *Los Angeles Times*, 15 January 1959, B1.

103. Young, quoted in "Ex-Blacklist Writer Wins," *Chicago Defender*, 8 April 1959, 2; Ivan Spear, "Spearheads," *Boxoffice*, 9 February 1959, *TDO* Clippings file.

Chapter 3. Nuclear War *On the Beach*

1. Louella Parsons, "Stanley Kramer Buys *On the Beach*," *Washington Post*, 10 September 1957, B7.

2. Kramer, quoted in "Film to Be Made of *On the Beach*," *New York Times*, 9 September 1957, 21, and in *OTB* promotion pamphlet.

3. Parsons, "Kramer Buys *On the Beach*," B7; Kramer, quoted in "Film to Be Made of *On the Beach*," 21; Hubbard Keavy, "Stanley Kramer Gambles with Film Fortunes," news clipping, Paxton Publicity folder.

4. Stanley Kramer with Thomas M. Coffey, *A Mad, Mad, Mad, Mad World: A Life in Hollywood* (New York: Harcourt Brace, 1997), 158; Yannis Tzioumakis, *American Independent Cinema: An Introduction* (Edinburgh: Edinburgh University Press, 2006), 129.

5. Bryan Fruth et al., "The Atomic Age: Facts and Films from 1945–1965," *Journal of Popular Film and Television* 23 (Winter 1996): 154; Tony Shaw, *Hollywood's Cold War* (Amherst: University of Massachusetts Press, 2007), 152.

6. Lawrence H. Suid, *Guts and Glory: The Making of the American Military Image in Film*, rev. ed. (Bowling Green: University Press of Kentucky, 2002), 223; Michael J. Strada, "Kaleidoscopic Nuclear Images of the Fifties," *Journal of Popular Culture* 20 (Winter 1986): 190.

7. MH, New York, to SK, 5 December 1959, *OTB* Comments folder.

8. Shaw, *Hollywood's Cold War*, 153; Scott C. Zeman and Michael A. Amundson, *Atomic Culture: How We Learned to Stop Worrying and Love the Bomb* (Boulder: University Press of Colorado, 2004), 2–6.

9. Kramer, quoted in *"On the Beach* Film Adapted from Shute Tale," *Los Angeles Times*, 22 December 1959, A7.

10. Kramer, quoted in Alistair Cooke, "First Night for Doomsday," 17 December 1959, *Guardian*, 8; *OTB* promotion pamphlet.

11. Cooke, "First Night for Doomsday," 8.

12. Kramer, quoted in *Pravda* interview; Kramer, quoted in Peter Cowie, "The Defiant One," *Films and Filming*, March 1963, 18–19.

13. Kramer, paraphrased in Dave McIntyre, "Front Row," *Evening Tribune*, news clipping, Paxton Publicity folder; Dick Williams, *"On the Beach* Stirs Disputes," news clipping, Paxton Publicity folder.

14. WG, Holyoke, Massachusetts, to SK, 4 March 1960, American Legion Correspondence folder; Arthur Knight, "Not with a Bang or a Whimper," *Saturday Review*, 24 October 1959, 32.

15. McIntyre, "Front Row"; Cowie, "Defiant One," 18; Knight, "Not with a Bang or a Whimper," 32.

16. Shute, quoted in Philip R. Davey, *When Hollywood Came to Melbourne: The Story of the Making of Stanley Kramer's* On the Beach (Melbourne: P. R. Davey, 2005), 9, 2; Kramer, quoted in "Film to Be Made of *On the Beach*," 21.

17. John Paxton, "Scripting *On Beach*," *Dallas Times Herald*, 17 January 1960, 3, 14, Paxton Publicity folder.

18. John McCarten, "The Current Cinema: Goners," *New Yorker*, 2 January 1960, 47.

19. Our Film Critic, "A Look at the End of the World," *Guardian*, 14 December 1959, 5; Williams, *"On the Beach* Stirs Disputes"; John Beaufort, "Fantasy Affirms Human Values under a Nuclear Cloud," *Christian Science Monitor*, 22 December 1959, news clipping, Paxton Reviews folder.

20. Beaufort, "Fantasy Affirms Human Values"; Paxton, "Scripting *On Beach*," 14.

21. Knight, "Not with a Bang or a Whimper," 32; Paxton, "Scripting *On Beach*," 14; Warwick M. Tompkins, *Camera and Crane*, Los Angeles, to SK, 21 December 1959, *OTB* Comments folder.

22. Paxton, "Scripting *On Beach*," 14.

23. Kramer, paraphrased in Leonard Lyons, "Lyons Den," *Chicago Defender*, 6 April 1959, 5, and 19 January 1960, 5; Kramer, quoted in *OTB* promotion pamphlet; Stanley Kramer, "Politics, Social Comment and My Emotions," *Films and Filming*, June 1960, 8.

24. "Controversial *On Beach* Brilliantly Executed Pic," *Hollywood Reporter*, 2 December 1959, Paxton Reviews folder; MvS, New York, to SK, 19 August 1959, *OTB* Comments folder; "Cinema: New Picture," *Time*, 28 December 1959, 44; Giglio, *Here's Looking at You*, 234.

25. Norway, quoted in Davey, *When Hollywood Came to Melbourne*, 9; Nevil Shute Norway to SK, 14 July 1958, Shute folder.

26. Norway, quoted in Davey, *When Hollywood Came to Melbourne*, 16, and cited from Julian Smith, *The Biography of Nevil Shute Norway* (1976).

27. Louella Parsons, "Hollywood Is Talking About," *Washington Post*, 27 December 1959, H7; Kramer, quoted in Davey, *When Hollywood Came to Melbourne*, 210; "Nevil Shute, Best Seller Author, Dies," *Chicago Tribune*, 13 January 1960, B3.

28. R.V., "*On the Beach*, U.S.A., 1959," *Monthly Film Bulletin*, [1960], *OTB* Clippings file; Our Film Critic, "A Look at the End of the World," 5.

29. VM, Flushing, New York, to SK, 14 February 1960, American Legion Correspondence folder; Ernest Callenbach, "*On the Beach*," *Film Quarterly* 13 (Winter 1959): 56; Mick Broderick, *Nuclear Movies* (Jefferson, N.C.: McFarland, 1991), 22.

30. Geoffrey M. Shurlock to SK, 28 October 1958, and Memo for Files, 28 October 1958, *On the Beach* file, PCA Records.

31. Little and Kramer, quoted in G. Tom Poe, "Historical Spectatorship around and about Stanley Kramer's *On the Beach*," in Melvyn Stokes and Richard Maltby, eds., *Hollywood Spectatorship: Changing Perceptions of Cinema Audiences* (London: British Film Institute, 2001), 94; Msgr. Little, quoted in George J. Schaefer to Reverend Sebastiano Baggio, 4 December 1959, *OTB* Comments folder.

32. Broderick, *Nuclear Movies*, 23; Analysis of Film Content, *On the Beach* file, PCA Records.

33. Kramer, "Politics, Social Comment and My Emotions," 8, and quoted in James Bawden, "Stanley Kramer: Hollywood Liberal," *Classic Images*, February 2011, 70.

34. Peck, quoted in Murray Schumach, "*On the Beach* Includes Moscow in 18-City Premiere on Dec. 17," *New York Times*, 30 November 1959, 27, and in Ava Gardner, *Ava: My Story* (London: Bantam, 1990), 244.

35. See exchange of letters between Gregory Peck and Kramer, December 1958, *On the Beach*–Correspondence folder, box 48, Gregory Peck Papers, Herrick Library; Peck, quoted in Gardner, *Ava: My Story*, 245.

36. Gardner, *Ava: My Story*, 238; Hazel Flynn, "*On the Beach* Premiere Has World Theme," *Beverly Hills Citizen*, 18 December 1959, *OTB* Clippings file.

37. Gardner, *Ava: My Story*, 237.

38. Kramer, quoted in Davey, *When Hollywood Came to Melbourne*, 31.

39. Gardner, *Ava: My Story*, 240.

40. Knight, "Not with a Bang or a Whimper," 33.

41. Astaire, quoted in Davey, *When Hollywood Came to Melbourne*, 35; Nevil Shute Norway to SK, 9 July 1958, Shute folder.

42. Leonard Mosley, "First View of a Shattering Film: Why I Had to Fly the Atlantic Just to See It," *Daily Express*, 21 October 1959, Paxton Reviews folder; Tracy, quoted in First Selection of quotes on *OTB* from Harold J. Salemson to SK, 2 December 1959, *OTB* Comments folder; Albert L. Weeks, "Inglorious Failure," *New York Times*, 24 January 1960, X7; Knight, "Not with a Bang or a Whimper," 33.

43. Richard L. Coe, "Kramer Trods Off-Beat Path," *Washington Post*, 26 August 1958, B8; Navy and USIA responses, quoted in Suid, *Guts and Glory*, 224; Kramer with Coffey, *Mad, Mad, Mad, Mad World*, 160.

44. Bertram Kalish, "Memo for the Record: *OTB*–Stanley Kramer Cooperation," 27 August 1958, and C. C. Kirkpatrick, Navy Chief of Information, to Assistant Secretary of Defense for Public Affairs, 10 November 1958, Navy folder, box 25, Kramer Papers.

45. Chief of Naval Operations, Memo, 5 December 1958, and Kirkpatrick to Chief, Production Branch, Audio-Vision Division, Department of Defense, 20 October 1958, Navy 2 folder, box 25, Kramer Papers; Donald E. Baruch, Office of News Services, Office of the Assistant Secretary of Defense, Public Affairs, to SK, 4 November 1958, and SK to Admiral Arleigh Burke, Chief of Naval Operations, USA, 27 October 1958, Navy folder, box 25, Kramer Papers; Kramer, quoted in Donald Spoto, *Stanley Kramer, Film Maker* (Hollywood, Calif.: Samuel French, 1978), 211.

46. Kramer with Coffey, *Mad, Mad, Mad, Mad World*, 165; Kramer, quoted in Bawden, "Stanley Kramer," 70.

47. "Ava Gardner Snubbing Fans, Say Australians," *Los Angeles Times*, 21 March 1959, 4; Gardner, quoted in Peer J. Oppenheimer, [article on Ava

Gardner], Paxton Publicity folder; Gardner, *Ava: My Story*, 238. Neil Jillett was the journalist. See Davey, *When Hollywood Came to Melbourne*, 56.

48. Davey, *When Hollywood Came to Melbourne*, 41–42, 46–47; Gardner, *Ava: My Story*, 238–239.

49. Peck, quoted in Gardner, *Ava: My Story*, 244–245; Davey, *When Hollywood Came to Melbourne*, 63; SK to Bill Blowitz, 10 December 1958, Blowitz-Maskel Publicity folder.

50. Rotunno, quoted in Davey, *When Hollywood Came to Melbourne*, 184; Tzioumakis, *American Independent Cinema*, 130–131.

51. Davey, *When Hollywood Came to Melbourne*, 45; Gardner, *Ava: My Story*, 239; Stanley Kauffman, "Waiting for the End," *New Republic*, 14 December 1959, 22.

52. Davey, *When Hollywood Came to Melbourne*, 143, 155–157, 191, 194, Madden quotation on 157.

53. Kramer, quoted in John Rosenfield, "Kramer Prefers an Argument to Academy Prizes," *Dallas Morning News*, 7 February 1960, Paxton Publicity folder.

54. *OTB* promotion pamphlet.

55. Henry B. Maloney, "Two Outstanding Movies," *Clearing House*, March 1960, 442; *OTB* promotion pamphlet.

56. Philip K. Scheuer, "Chilling *On the Beach* Premieres in 18 Nations," *Los Angeles Times*, 18 December 1959, 2.

57. Pauling, quoted in Scheuer, "Chilling *On the Beach* Premieres," 2.

58. Myer P. Beck to George Thomas, Jr., 31 August 1959, and MB, Toronto, to SK, 5 January 1960, *OTB* Comments folder.

59. Our Film Critic, "A Look at the End of the World," 5; "From the Hideously Convincing to the Bathetic: Strange Mixture of *On the Beach*," *Guardian*, 10 March 1960, 19; Sven G. Winquist, "Swedes on *Beach* Per Editors' Bias," *Variety*, 30 December 1959, *OTB* Clippings file; Kauffman, "Waiting for the End," 22.

60. McIntyre, "Front Row"; Cooke, "First Night for Doomsday," 8; Richard Dyer MacCann, "Hollywood Letter: The Film Year in Quick Review," *Christian Science Monitor*, 12 January 1960, Paxton Reviews folder.

61. Hy Hollinger, "*Beach* Is Controversial Hit with Raps and Raves on Preems: N.Y. and Overseas," *Variety*, 21 December 1959, Paxton Publicity folder; Kramer, "Politics, Social Comment and My Emotions," 8; Williams, "*On the Beach* Stirs Disputes."

62. Kramer, quoted in Samuel D. Berns, "The 'Controversial' Film Is Defended by Kramer," *Motion Picture Daily*, 3 May 1960, American Legion Trade Clippings folder.

63. Lawrence S. Wittner, *Resisting the Bomb: A History of the World Nuclear Disarmament Movement, 1954–1970*, vol. 2, *The Struggle against the*

Bomb (Stanford, Calif.: Stanford University Press, 1997), 149. See also Allan M. Winkler, *Life under a Cloud: American Anxiety about the Atom* (Urbana: University of Illinois Press, 1999), 104–105.

64. Kramer, "Politics, Social Comment and My Emotions," 8; Kramer, quoted in McIntyre, "Front Row."

65. Kramer, quoted in "Kramer Criticizes American Legion's 'Un-American' Means," *Independent Film Journal*, 13 February 1960, 15, American Legion Trade Clippings folder; Paul Boyer, *Fallout: A Historian Reflects on America's Half-Century Encounter with Nuclear Weapons* (Columbus: Ohio State University Press, 1998), 118.

66. Our Film Critic, "A Look at the End of the World," 5; William Winter, broadcast on ABC Radio Network, 24 November 1959; reviews, quoted in George Thomas, Jr., to Lionel Hogg, *Melbourne Herald*, 19 December 1959, *OTB* Comments folder; Mrs. Shirley H. Gunnels, quoted in Velma West Sykes, "*On the Beach* (UA) Is the Choice for February Blue Ribbon Award," *Boxoffice*, 14 March 1960, Paxton Reviews folder.

67. Mae Tinee, "Atomic War Film Shows Dying Earth," *Chicago Tribune*, 18 December 1959, B6; "Controversial *On Beach* Brilliantly Executed Pic"; WG, Holyoke, Massachusetts, to SK, 4 March 1960, American Legion Correspondence folder; Allen, quoted in Harold J. Salemson to SK, 2 December 1959, First Selection of *OTB* Quotes, *OTB* Comments folder.

68. Hazel Flynn, "*On the Beach* Premiere Has World Theme," *Beverly Hills Citizen*, 18 December 1959, *OTB* Clippings file; Our Film Critic, "A Look at the End of the World," 5; Sidney Harmon to SK, 9 September 1959, Walter Winter to SK, 21 October 1959, and Mayor of Johannesburg to Walter Boxer, UA, 24 December 1959, *OTB* Comments folder.

69. The response of the US government to *On the Beach* has received attention from many scholars, most recently and comprehensively by Mick Broderick, "Fallout *On the Beach*," *Screening the Past*, 17 June 2013, http://www.screeningthepast.com/2013/06/fallout-on-the-beach/; Daniel J. Pearson, "'Possible Questions and Suggested Answers': *On the Beach*, the Eisenhower Administration, 'The Bomb,'" *Binghamton Journal of History*, Spring 2010, https://www.binghamton.edu/history/resources/journal-of-history/daniel-pearson.html; Poe, "Historical Spectatorship," 95–98. See also Boyer, *Fallout*, 110; Shaw, *Hollywood's Cold War*, 156–157; Winkler, *Life under a Cloud*, 105.

70. Herter, paraphrased in Cabinet Meeting Minutes, 6 November 1959, box 14, Cabinet Series (Ann Whitman File), Eisenhower Papers.

71. Harr, paraphrased in Cabinet Paper, 16 December 1959, Record of Action, Cabinet Meeting of 11 December 1959, box 15, Cabinet Series (Ann Whitman File), Eisenhower Papers.

72. Broderick, "Fallout *On the Beach*." See also Winkler, *Life under a Cloud*, 6.

73. Cabinet Paper, USIA-State Infoguide and AEC Questions and Answers; Memorandum for Assistant to the Secretary of Defense (Atomic Energy), 15 December 1959, Nuclear Energy Matters (8) [September 1959–March 1960], box 5, White House Office, Office of the Special Assistant for National Security Affairs: Records, 1952–1961, OCB Series, Subject Subseries, Dwight D. Eisenhower Presidential Library; Poe, "Historical Spectatorship," 96; Shaw, *Hollywood's Cold War*, 157.

74. Reply to a Question, addendum to AEC Questions and Answers; Huebner, quoted in "*On the Beach* Scored by Civil Defense Head," *New York Times*, 18 December 1959, 34.

75. Bennett, *Congressional Record*, 11 January 1960, 208–209, *OTB* Comments folder; Bennett, quoted in "*On the Beach* Scored," *New York Times*, 6 January 1960, 24.

76. Our Film Critic, "A Look at the End of the World," 5; *Chicago Daily News* head, quoted in Williams, "*On the Beach* Stirs Disputes."

77. "Controversial *On Beach* Brilliantly Executed Pic"; Kramer, quoted in "More Fallout *On the Beach* in Kramer Rebuttal to Solon," *Variety*, 2 January 1960, 3, Kramer Clippings file.

78. Urey, quoted in "Is It Preview? Urey Wonders," news clipping, Paxton Publicity folder; Michael Amrine, Federation of American Scientists Newsletter, quoted in third selection of quotes on *OTB* from Harold J. Salemson to SK, 7 December 1959, *OTB* Comments folder.

79. Cooke, "First Night for Doomsday," 8; Williams, "*On the Beach* Stirs Disputes."

80. Huebner, quoted in "*On the Beach* Scored," 34.

81. Bennett, quoted in "*On the Beach* Scored," 24; *Newsweek*, quoted in Williams, "*On the Beach* Stirs Disputes."

82. Stewart Alsop, "Let's Stop Talking Nonsense about Fallout," *Saturday Evening Post*, 23 July 1960, *OTB* Clippings file.

83. Kramer, quoted in "More Fallout *On the Beach*," 3; Kramer, "Politics, Social Comment and My Emotions," 33; Watson Davis, "Show Radiation Death in Motion Picture," *Science News Letter*, 5 December 1959, 390.

84. Holifield, quoted in "More Fallout *On the Beach*," 3; Richard G. Hewlett and Jack M. Holl, *Atoms for Peace and War, 1953–1961: Eisenhower and the Atomic Energy Commission* (Berkeley: University of California Press, 1989), 272, 454–455; Williams, "*On the Beach* Stirs Disputes."

85. Laura McEnaney, *Civil Defense Begins at Home: Militarization Meets Everyday Life in the Fifties* (Princeton, N.J.: Princeton University Press, 2000), 10.

86. USIA-State Infoguide; Huebner, quoted in *"On the Beach* Scored," 34; Alsop, "Let's Stop Talking Nonsense."

87. Bennett, quoted in *"On the Beach* Scored," 24; Hoegh, paraphrased in Cabinet Paper, 16 December 1959, Record of Action, Cabinet Meeting of 11 December 1959, box 15, Cabinet Series (Ann Whitman File), Eisenhower Papers.

88. Bennett, *Congressional Record*, 11 January 1960, 208–209, in *OTB* Comments folder.

89. Teller, quoted in "Civil Defense 'Invites' War, Teller Says," *Chicago Tribune*, 7 November 1960, B10.

90. Kramer, quoted in McIntyre, "Front Row"; Williams, *"On the Beach* Stirs Disputes."

91. Pauling, quoted in *OTB* Press Conference transcript, 17 December 1959, *OTB* Comments folder; Bosley Crowther, "Liable to Fallout: *On the Beach* Rouses Ire of Specialists," *New York Times*, 17 January 1960, X1.

92. John T. Harcourt, "Plea for Peace," and Allen Klein, "On Viewing a *Beach,*" *New York Times*, 24 January 1960, X7; McEnaney, *Civil Defense Begins at Home*, 38.

93. Hoegh, paraphrased in Cabinet Paper, 16 December 1959, Record of Action, Cabinet Meeting of 11 December 1959, box 15, Cabinet Series (Ann Whitman File), Eisenhower Papers.

94. Harold Whitehead, "The Screen," *Montreal Gazette*, 6 February 1960, 22; C. A. Lejeune, "At the Films: The Chariots and the General," *Observer*, 20 December 1959, news clipping, Paxton Reviews folder.

95. McEnaney convincingly argues that "apathy" does not capture the complexity of civilian responses to early Cold War civil defense. McEnaney, *Civil Defense Begins at Home*, 65–66, 34, 38.

96. USIA-State Infoguide; Bennett, *Congressional Record*, 11 January 1960, 208–209, in *OTB* Comments folder.

97. Marion Bacon, Toronto, to SK, 5 January 1960, *OTB* Comments folder; Knight, "Not with a Bang or a Whimper," 33; "At the Pictures," *Punch*, 30 December 1959, Paxton Reviews folder; Albert L. Weeks, "Inglorious Failure," *New York Times*, 24 January 1960, X7; Tinee, "Atomic War Film Shows Dying Earth," B6.

98. Larry Tajiri, "The Spectator: Kramer Poses the Question of Man's Fate and the Atom," *Denver Post*, 20 October 1959, Paxton Reviews folder; First Selection of quotes on *OTB* from Harold J. Salemson to SK, 2 December 1959, Jack C. Voelpel, Committee for World Development and World Disarmament, 17 November 1959, and Jacquey and Eddie Aurault, Beverly Hills, to SK, 18 December 1959, *OTB* Comments folder.

99. JB, North Hollywood, to SK, 4 November 1959, *OTB* Comments

folder; LH, New York, to SK, 10 February 1960, American Legion Correspondence folder.

100. New York reviewer, quoted in Richard Griffith, *"On Beach* Impresses New York Reviewers," *Los Angeles Times*, 2 January 1960, A11; Boyer, *Fallout*, 109.

101. Porter, quoted in *Congressional Record*, 12 January 1960, 312.

102. *OTB* Press Conference transcript, 17 December 1959, and quotes from screenings in Berlin and Munich, *OTB* Comments folder.

103. *OTB* Press Conference transcript, 17 December 1959, *OTB* Comments folder. Michael Kimmage addresses the irrational rationality of nuclear strategy in "Atomic Historiography," *Reviews in American History* 38 (2010): 146.

104. USIA-State Infoguide.

105. Review of *OTB*, *Religious Bulletin*, University of Notre Dame, 2 March 1960, news clipping, *OTB* Comments folder.

106. *Daily News*, quoted in Hollinger, *"Beach* Is Controversial."

107. Cooke, "First Night for Doomsday," 8; William Henry Chamberlin, "The Revival of Anti-Germanism," *Modern Age* 6 (Summer 1962): 280.

108. "Dire Drama on the Death of the World," news clipping, Paxton Publicity folder; *Daily News*, quoted in Hollinger, *"Beach* Is Controversial."

109. Schumach, *"On the Beach* Includes Moscow," 27; Kramer, quoted in *Pravda* interview.

110. *OTB* Press Conference transcript, 17 December 1959, *OTB* Comments folder; Peck, quoted in Army Archerd, *"Beach* Is Controversial Hit with Raps and Raves on Preems: Peck at Moscow Bow," *Variety*, 21 December 1959, Paxton Publicity folder.

111. William Winter, broadcast on ABC Radio Network, 24 November 1959, *OTB* Comments folder.

112. Allen Klein, "On Viewing a *Beach*," *New York Times*, 24 January 1960, X7.

113. *Daily News*, quoted in Williams, *"On the Beach* Stirs Disputes"; Review of *On the Beach*, *Religious Bulletin*, University of Notre Dame, 2 March 1960, news clipping, *OTB* Comments folder.

114. Rosenstein, *"On the Beach* Called Kramer's Christmas Gift to Khrushchev," *Hollywood Close-Up*, 17 December 1959, American Legion Clippings folder; "Editor's Corner: A Movie," *American Legion Magazine*, March 1960, 6.

115. Meade, *"On the Beach* Creates Hassle"; McIntyre, "Front Row."

116. Kramer, quoted in McIntyre, "Front Row."

117. Crowther, "Liable to Fallout," X1; Kramer, quoted in "Kramer Criticizes American Legion's 'Un-American' Means."

Chapter 4. *Inherit the Wind* Champions Civil Liberties

1. "The Monkey Trial," *Newsweek*, 17 October 1960, 114; Kramer, quoted in Thomas McDonald, "Hollywood 'Trial,'" *New York Times*, 1 November 1959, X7.

2. Kramer, quoted in Richard L. Coe, "Film Producer in Solemn Vein," *Washington Post*, 11 October 1960, B14; James Meade, "*Inherit the Wind*: Film Is Rated 'Excellent,'" *San Diego Union*, 1 September 1960, news clipping, Beck Publicity folder.

3. Albert Wertheim, "The McCarthy Era and the American Theatre," *Theatre Journal* 34 (May 1982): 221; Jerome Lawrence and Robert E. Lee, *Inherit the Wind*, reprint (New York: Bantam, 2003); Lawrence and Lee, quoted in Kaspar Monahan, "Screen Version of Broadway Hit Pleases Authors," *Pittsburgh Press*, 19 August 1960, 12.

4. Kramer, quoted in *Pravda* interview; Arthur Knight, "The Importance of Being Earnest," *Saturday Review*, 8 October 1960, 30; Alan Reitman to SK, 1 December 1959, and SK to Alan Reitman, 9 December 1959, Research folder.

5. Thomas M. Pryor, "Coast Scenarist Reveals Identity," *New York Times*, 1 January 1959, 38; Young, quoted in Bob Thomas, "Nedrick Young Writes Again after Being on Blacklist," *Ocala Star-Banner*, 13 April 1960, 9; Bosley Crowther, "Hollywood's Producer of Controversy," *New York Times*, 10 December 1961, SM76; Kramer, quoted in Overs interview.

6. Kramer statement, television episode of NBC's *Youth Wants to Know*, 3 August 1958; Trumbo, quoted in Helen Manfull, ed., *Additional Dialogue: Letters of Dalton Trumbo, 1942–1962* (New York: M. Evans, 1970), 470; Larry Ceplair and Christopher Trumbo, *Dalton Trumbo: Blacklisted Hollywood Radical* (Lexington: University Press of Kentucky, 2014), 364.

7. Murray Schumach, "Attacks by Legion Confuse Film Men," *New York Times*, 3 September 1959, 30.

8. McKneally, quoted in "American Legion Drive on 'Invasion' by Reds to Begin in March Magazine," *Motion Picture Daily*, 5 February 1960, 7, American Legion Trade Clippings folder.

9. Milwaukee County Council, VFW, Resolution "Communism and the Motion Picture Industry," n.d., Horwits Publicity folder.

10. Murray Schumach, "Kramer Defies American Legion over Hiring of Movie Writers," *New York Times*, 8 February 1960, 1.

11. See 214 letters to SK, American Legion Correspondence folder, and "Blacklist Forum," *New York Times*, 21 February 1960, X7.

12. "Buster's Bluster," *Nation*, 20 February 1960, 158.

13. Kramer, quoted in Schumach, "Kramer Defies American Legion," 35;

Kramer, quoted in *F.Y.I.* television transcript; SK to JF, Jamaica, N.Y., 16 March 1960, American Legion Correspondence folder.

14. DNM, Chairman, Student Representative Party, University of Chicago, to SK, 8 February 1960, RWG, Cambridge, Massachusetts, to SK, 15 February 1960, and Patrick Murphy Malin, Executive Director, ACLU, New York, to SK, 9 February 1960, American Legion Correspondence folder; Malin, quoted in Murray Schumach, "A.V.C. Hits Legion in Film Dispute," *New York Times*, 16 February 1960, 31.

15. Screen Publicists Guild, quoted in "Kramer Debates with Legion Head," *Independent Film Journal*, 27 February 1960, American Legion Correspondence folder; DP, Philadelphia, Letter to the Editor, *New York Times*, 21 February 1960, X7.

16. McKneally, paraphrased in Murray Schumach, "Kramer Debates with Legion Head," *New York Times*, 15 February 1960, 22; "The Real Issue," *Los Angeles Examiner*, 17 February 1960, American Legion Clippings folder.

17. AB, Sarasota, Florida, to SK, 23 February 1960, American Legion Correspondence folder; "Real Issue."

18. Walter Winchell of New York, American Legion Clippings folder; JF, Jamaica, New York, to SK, 28 March 1960, and ECW, Jamestown, New York, to SK, 15 February 1960, American Legion Correspondence folder.

19. Kramer, quoted in *F.Y.I.* television transcript, 3, 4; Ceplair and Trumbo, *Dalton Trumbo*, 405; Kramer, quoted in Ray Oviatt, "Provocative Movie Producer: Stanley Kramer Simply Thrives on Controversy," *Toledo Blade*, 14 February 1960, sec. 4, 3; Kramer, quoted in Schumach, "Kramer Defies American Legion," 35.

20. "Buster's Bluster," *Nation*, 20 February 1960, 158; Kramer, quoted in *F.Y.I.* television transcript, 7; Schumach, "A.V.C. Hits Legion in Film Dispute," 31.

21. Murray Teigh Bloom, President, Society of Magazine Writers, to SK, 20 February 1960, and AF, Hanover, New Hampshire, to SK, 4 May 1960, American Legion Correspondence folder.

22. ECW, Jamestown, New York, to SK, 15 February 1960, American Legion Correspondence folder; "The Commies Are Back," *New York Daily Mirror*, typescript, 9 February 1960, American Legion Clippings folder; RM, Manhasset, Long Island, Letter to the Editor, *New York Times*, 21 February 1960, X7.

23. McKneally, quoted in "Legion's Film Stand Defended," *Los Angeles Mirror-News*, 15 February 1960, American Legion Clippings folder; Foote, quoted in "Producer Raps Tactics of Legion," *Los Angeles Times*, 9 February

1960, 3; Fagan, quoted in John E. Fitzgerald, "The Responsible Movie Maker," *St. Jude: A National Catholic Monthly*, September 1962, 9, *JAN* Comments folder; FH, Fort Lauderdale, Florida, to SK, 19 February 1960, American Legion Correspondence folder.

24. RHB, Skokie, Illinois, to SK, 30 December 1961, *ITW* Comments folder; McKneally, paraphrased in Schumach, "Kramer Debates with Legion Head," 22; WTB, USS Coral Sea Navy, to SK, 25 June 1960, American Legion Correspondence folder.

25. McKneally, quoted in "Debate Right of Ex-Reds to Write Movies," *Chicago Daily Tribune*, 15 February 1960, B10, and in "Legion Head Says Red Alert Will Continue," *Los Angeles Times*, 10 February 1960, 6; "The Commies Are Back"; McKneally, quoted in Schumach, "Kramer Debates with Legion Head," 22.

26. WO, Toledo, Ohio, American Legion, 1st Vice Commander, to SK, 13 March 1960, and JK, Jamaica, New York, to SK, 28 March 1960, American Legion Correspondence folder; RHB, Skokie, Illinois, to SK, 30 December 1961, *ITW* Comments folder.

27. Ed Sullivan, "For the Record," reprinted from *New York Daily News* in *Hollywood Reporter*, 23 February 1960, American Legion Trade Clippings folder; MAP, Bellrose, New York, to SK, 14 February 1960, American Legion Correspondence folder.

28. Walter Fitzmaurice, "Washington . . . Newsreel," *Film Daily*, 16 February 1960, 1, American Legion Trade Clippings folder; Kramer, quoted in *F.Y.I.* television transcript, 3, 6.

29. Kramer, quoted in "Kramer Firm on Resisting Pressure," *Film Daily*, 3 May 1960, American Legion Trade Clippings folder; Kramer, quoted in Schumach, "Kramer Defies American Legion," 1.

30. Kramer, quoted in Oviatt, "Provocative Movie Producer," 3.

31. Kramer, quoted in *F.Y.I.* television transcript, 3, 12.

32. "Hollywood's Commissars," *New York Post*, 9 February 1960, American Legion Clippings folder; MAF, New York, New York, to SK [11 March 1960], LHK, Legacy TV show, Philadelphia, to SK, 14 February 1960, Lt. PV, Long Beach, California, to SK, 2 March 1960, and ER, Forest Hills, New York, to SK, 29 February 1960, American Legion Correspondence folder.

33. McKneally and Foote, quoted in "Producer Raps Tactics of Legion," 3; McKneally, quoted in "Legion Head Says Red Alert Will Continue," *Los Angeles Times*, 10 February 1960, 6.

34. Martin Quigley, Jr., "Editorial: Rights and Risks," *Motion Picture Daily*, 11 February 1960, 1, American Legion Trade Clippings folder; Mrs. CB, Forest Grove, Oregon, to SK, 9 June 1960, and JK, Jamaica, New York,

to SK, 28 March 1960, American Legion Correspondence folder; "The Real Issue," editorial, *Los Angeles Examiner*, 17 February 1960, American Legion Clippings folder.

35. Mickey Levine to SK, 8 February 1960, American Legion Correspondence folder and quoted in Schumach, "A.V.C. Hits Legion in Film Dispute," 31; LHK, Legacy TV show, Philadelphia, to SK, 14 February 1960, and LG, Philadelphia, to SK, 16 February 1960, American Legion Correspondence folder.

36. Mrs. SF, Brooklyn, New York, to SK, 14 February 1960, and VP to SK, 14 February 1960, American Legion Correspondence folder.

37. The Student Body of Bard College, Annandale-on-Hudson, New York, to SK, 9 February 1960, American Legion Correspondence folder; Screen Publicists Guild, quoted in "American Legion Hit," *New York Times*, 19 February 1960, 23.

38. Kramer, quoted in Schumach, "Kramer Defies American Legion," 1; LM, New York, New York, to SK, 10 February 1960, JHG, New York, New York, to SK, 22 February 1960, and MM, Montclair, New Jersey, to SK, 14 February 1960, American Legion Correspondence folder; DAB, Upper Montclair, New Jersey, Letter to the Editor, *New York Times*, 20 February 1960, 22.

39. K. A. Cuordileone, *Manhood and American Political Culture in the Cold War* (New York: Routledge, 2015); Kramer, paraphrased and quoted in Schumach, "Kramer Defies American Legion," 35.

40. Maurice Ghnassia, *Stage and Screen Avenues*, newsletter [1960], American Legion Clippings folder; JWH, Hollywood, Florida, to SK, 9 February 1960 and MC, New York, New York, to SK, 14 February 1960, American Legion Correspondence folder.

41. "More Hollywood Defiance," *St. Louis Post-Dispatch*, 14 February 1960, American Legion Clippings folder; AF, Hanover, New Hampshire, to SK, 4 May 1960, American Legion Correspondence folder; SK to American Legion, n.d., American Legion–CBS-TV, 14 February 1960 folder, box 115, Kramer Papers.

42. Murray Schumach, "Hollywood Reviewed: Profits, TV Sales, Realistic Views Marked Confident Industry's Year," *New York Times*, 25 December 1960, X9; Hy Hollinger, "Mixed Emotions of a Disunited Industry Facing Renewed Slurs on Commie-Angled Scripters," *Variety*, n.d., American Legion Clippings folder.

43. SK to Bud [Burdick], 15 February 1960, American Legion Correspondence folder.

44. Fagan, quoted in Fitzgerald, "Responsible Movie Maker," 9; Anonymous, Los Angeles, to SK, 23 February 1960, and JEB, Montclair, New Jersey, to SK, 15 February 1960, American Legion Correspondence folder.

45. Hedda Hopper, "Looking at Hollywood," *Chicago Daily Tribune*, 11 February 1960, D5; "Editor's Corner: A Movie," *American Legion Magazine*, March 1960, 6; "Will the Public Support Re-Entry of Reds in Films?" *American Legion Magazine*, April 1960, 29–32; McKneally, quoted in "American Legion Magazine Sees Test Under Way on Film Work for 'Reds,'" *Motion Picture Daily*, 21 March 1960, 6, American Legion Trade Clippings folder.

46. Fagan, quoted in Fitzgerald, "Responsible Movie Maker," 9; "Commies Are Back"; JLKT, Austin, TX, to SK, 16 February 1960, American Legion Correspondence folder.

47. Scott Allen Nollen, *The Cinema of Sinatra: The Actor, on Screen and in Song* (Baltimore, Md.: Luminary, 2003), 214–216; BB, New York, New York, to SK, 29 April 1960, American Legion Correspondence folder.

48. Kramer, quoted in Samuel D. Berns, "The 'Controversial' Film Is Defended by Kramer," *Motion Picture Daily*, 3 May 1960, American Legion Trade Clippings folder; Al Horwits to SK, 23 June 1960, Horwits Publicity folder.

49. Jeffrey P. Moran, *The Scopes Trial: A Brief History with Documents* (New York: Palgrave, 2002), 24–25.

50. Marjorie Garber, "Cinema Scopes: Evolution, Media, and the Law," in Austin Sarat and Thomas R. Kearns, eds., *Law in the Domains of Culture* (Ann Arbor: University of Michigan Press, 2000), 141–142.

51. Moran, *Scopes Trial*, 75; Michael Lienesch, *In the Beginning: Fundamentalism, the Scopes Trial, and the Making of the Antievolution Movement* (Chapel Hill: University of North Carolina Press, 2007), 2.

52. Richard L. Coe, "Keith's *Wind* Is a Cracker," *Washington Post*, 9 November 1960, C10; John L. Scott, "*Inherit the Wind* Stirring Film Play," *Los Angeles Times*, 3 November 1960, B13.

53. Hedda Hopper, "Odets Directs Own 'Story on Page One,'" *Los Angeles Times*, 12 June 1959, A9.

54. Fredric March to SK, 6 October 1958 and 3 September 1959, Fredric March—"ITW" folder, box 31, Kramer Papers; Kramer with Thomas M. Coffey, *A Mad, Mad, Mad, Mad World: A Life in Hollywood* (New York: Harcourt Brace, 1997), 170, 173.

55. Mae Tinee, "Film Based on Trial Is Fascinating," *Chicago Daily Tribune*, 4 November 1960, B18; Bosley Crowther, "Screen: Triumphant Version of *Inherit the Wind*," *New York Times*, 13 October 1960, 41; "Film Review: *Inherit the Wind*," *Variety*, 29 June 1960, *ITW* Clippings file.

56. Kramer, quoted in Mae Tinee, "Kramer Takes Bold Film Approach," *Chicago Daily Tribune*, 13 November 1960, G14; C. A. Lejeune, "Parade of Veterans," *Observer*, 10 July 1960, 24.

57. Philip K. Scheuer, "*Inherit the Wind* Erupts in Hot Shower of Sparks,"

Los Angeles Times, 2 October 1960, B3; Crowther, "Screen: Triumphant Version of *Inherit the Wind*," 41.

58. Crowther, "Screen: Triumphant Version of *Inherit the Wind*," 41; "Film Review: Inherit the Wind," *Variety*, 29 June 1960, *ITW* Clippings files.

59. Donald Spoto, *Stanley Kramer, Film Maker* (Hollywood, Calif.: Samuel French, 1978), 222–223; Kramer with Coffey, *Mad, Mad, Mad, Mad World*, 174.

60. Bosley Crowther, "Intellect in Films," *New York Times*, 16 October 1960, X1; Crowther, "Hollywood's Producer of Controversy," SM79; Samuel D. Berns, "*Inherit the Wind*," *Motion Picture Herald*, 9 July 1960, *ITW* Clippings file. See also Kirsten Shepherd-Barr, *Science on Stage: From Doctor Faustus to Copenhagen* (Princeton, N.J.: Princeton University Press, 2006), 113.

61. Geoffrey M. Shurlock to Frank McCarthy, 20th-Fox, 24 March 1955, and Albert Van Schmus, Memo for the Files Re: *Inherit the Wind*, 10 June 1955, *Inherit the Wind* file, PCA Records.

62. Geoffrey M. Shurlock to SK, 15 October 1959, *Inherit the Wind* file, PCA Records; *Inherit the Wind* Preview Program and James Powers, "Kramer Production Has Humor, Drama," *Hollywood Reporter*, 28 June 1960, *ITW* Clippings file.

63. John Stauffer and Benjamin Soskis, *The Battle Hymn of the Republic: A Biography of the Song That Marches On* (New York: Oxford University Press, 2013), 15.

64. Spoto, *Stanley Kramer, Film Maker*, 220, 218; Moran, *Scopes Trial*, 33–34; Kramer with Coffey, *Mad, Mad, Mad, Mad World*, 174.

65. Synopsis and Analysis of Film Content, 1 April 1960, *Inherit the Wind* file, PCA Records; Asfaw Tessema, Addis Ababa, to SK, 29 October 1962, and Bishop James A. Pike, San Francisco, to SK, 9 November 1960, *ITW* Comments folder.

66. "Monkey Trial," 114; Our Film Correspondent, "Film Notes," *Irish Times*, 31 October 1960, 8; Kramer, quoted in "Talk with the Director," *Newsweek*, 17 October 1960, 117.

67. Synopsis and Analysis of Film Content.

68. Knight, "Importance of Being Earnest," 30; Crowther, "Screen: Triumphant Version of *Inherit the Wind*," 41; Crowther, "Intellect in Films," X1.

69. Julia Howard Griscom, "*Inherit the Wind*," *Films in Review*, August–September 1960, *ITW* Clippings file; Crowther, "Intellect in Films," X1; Scott, "*Inherit the Wind* Stirring Film Play," B13; Berns, "*Inherit the Wind*."

70. H. L. Mencken, "Darrow's Speech Great but Futile," *Baltimore Evening Sun*, 14 July 1925, 1, reprinted in Moran, *Scopes Trial*, 93.

71. Frederick Lewis Allen, *Only Yesterday: An Informal History of the 1920s* (New York: Harper & Row, 1931); Edward J. Larson, *Summer for the Gods: The Scopes Trial and America's Continuing Debate over Science and Religion* (New York: Basic Books, 1997), 225.

72. Neda Atanasoski, "Cold War Carmen in US Racial Modernity," *Cinema Journal* 54 (Fall 2014): 99.

73. Garber, "Cinema Scopes," 134–135.

74. Crowther, "Screen: Triumphant Version of *Inherit the Wind*," 41; Scott, "*Inherit the Wind* Stirring Film Play," B13; Scheuer, "*Inherit the Wind* Erupts," B3. Margery Fernald reinforces this analysis in "*Inherit the Wind*: The Remaking of American History" (PhD diss., University of Colorado, 1999), 123–124.

75. Griscom, "*Inherit the Wind*"; Scheuer, "*Inherit the Wind* Erupts," B3; Knight, "Importance of Being Earnest," 30.

76. Kramer with Coffey, *Mad, Mad, Mad, Mad World*, 173; Edward J. Larson, *Trial and Error: The American Controversy over Creation and Evolution* (New York: Oxford University Press, 1985), 47; Edward B. Davis, "Science and Religious Fundamentalism in the 1920s," *American Scientist* 93 (May–June 2005): 254.

77. Robert A. Rosenstone, ed., *Revisioning History: Film and the Construction of a New Past* (Princeton, N.J.: Princeton University Press, 1995), 208; Brendan Gill, "The Current Cinema: Talkers," *New Yorker*, 22 October 1960, 98.

78. Robert A. Rosenstone, *Visions of the Past: The Challenge of Film to Our Idea of History* (Cambridge, Mass.: Harvard University Press, 1995), 59; Ronald L. Numbers, "*Inherit the Wind* Film Review," *Isis* 84, no. 4 (1993): 764.

79. Kramer, quoted in James Bawden, "Stanley Kramer: Hollywood Liberal," *Classic Images*, February 2011, 13; *Inherit the Wind* Program, and "Film Review: Inherit the Wind," *Variety*, 29 June 1960, *ITW* Clippings files; Moran, *Scopes Trial*, 42; Knight, "Importance of Being Earnest," 30.

80. F. R. Ankersmit, *The Reality Effect in the Writing of History: The Dynamics of Historiographical Topology* (Amsterdam: Noord-Hollandsche, 1989), 139–140; Our Film Critic, "A Case of Bigotry," *Guardian*, 9 July 1960, 3; Powers, "Kramer Production Has Humor, Drama."

81. Kramer with Coffey, *Mad, Mad, Mad, Mad World*, 170, 172; Myer P. Beck to Earl Kramer, 2 October 1957, Beck Publicity folder.

82. Alan Reitman to SK, 1 December 1959, and SK to Alan Reitman, 9 December 1959, Research folder; John T. Aquino, *Truth and Lives on Film: The Legal Problems of Depicting Real Persons and Events in a Fictional Medium*

(Jefferson, N.C.: McFarland, 2005), 117; Kramer with Coffey, *Mad, Mad, Mad, Mad World*, 172.

83. *ITW* Campaign Guide; Numbers, "*Inherit the Wind* Film Review," 764.

84. Jerome Lawrence and Robert E. Lee to SK, 14 October 1959, Jerome Lawrence and Robert E. Lee–Agreement *ITW* folder, box 31, Kramer papers; Tinee, "Film Based on Trial Is Fascinating," B18. In fact, Bryan's wife was a semi-invalid who needed his care; see Aquino, *Truth and Lives on Film*, 117.

85. Jeffrey P. Moran, *American Genesis: The Evolution Controversies from Scopes to Creation Science* (Oxford: Oxford University Press, 2012), 40; Scheuer, "*Inherit the Wind* Erupts," B3; Rosenstone, *Visions of the Past*, 72–73.

86. *ITW* Campaign Guide; Al Horwits to Myer P. Beck, 16 September 1960, Horwits Publicity folder; Jonathan Stubbs, *Historical Film: A Critical Introduction* (New York: Bloomsbury, 2013), 35.

87. *ITW* Campaign Guide; Kramer, quoted in McDonald, "Hollywood 'Trial,'" X7; Al Horwits to SK, 3 August 1960, Horwits Publicity folder.

88. Karen L. Riley, Jennifer A. Brown, and Ray Braswell, "Historical Truth and Film: *Inherit the Wind* as an Appraisal of the American Teacher," *American Educational History Journal* 34 (Fall 2007): 271; Myer P. Beck to Selma Holstein, 12 October 1960, Beck Publicity folder; Scopes, quoted in news clipping, *Newsweek*, 24 October 1960, *ITW* Clippings file.

89. Myer P. Beck to George Thomas, 21 July 1960, Al Horwits to Jack Kofoed, *Miami Herald*, 19 August 1960, Al Horwits to Myer P. Beck, 4 May 1960, Al Horwits to Allan Widdem, *Hartford (Conn.) Times*, 23 August 1960, and Al Horwits to SK, Cannes, 19 August 1960, Horwits Publicity folder; Myer P. Beck to George Thomas, Jr., 16 September 1960, Beck Publicity folder.

90. Al Horwits to Myer P. Beck, 19 August 1960, Horwits Publicity folder; *ITW* Campaign Guide.

91. Kay Proctor, "*Inherit the Wind* Notably Adapted," *Los Angeles Examiner*, 3 November 1960, *ITW* Clippings file; Coe, "Keith's *Wind* Is a Cracker," C10.

92. Scheuer, "*Inherit the Wind* Erupts," B3; Kenneth S. Cohen, New York, New York, to SK, 16 October 1960, and George Thomas, Jr., to Mike Beck, Earl Kramer, and Al Horwits, summary of comment cards, Hollywood preview, 29 August 1960, *ITW* Comments folder; Gill, "Current Cinema: Talkers," 98.

93. Larson, *Summer for the Gods*, 246.

94. Crowther, "Intellect in Films," X1; Scott, "*Inherit the Wind* Stirring Film Play," B13; Berns, "*Inherit the Wind*."

95. Larson, *Trial and Error*, 3, 4, 92; Lienesch, *In the Beginning*, 205; Kramer with Coffey, *Mad, Mad, Mad, Mad World*, 168.

96. Kramer with Coffey, *Mad, Mad, Mad, Mad World*, 174; Al Horwits to SK, 18 July 1960, Horwits Publicity folder; "Film Review: Inherit the Wind," *Variety*, 29 June 60, *ITW* Clippings file.

97. James DeForest Murch, Chairman Evangelical Action Commission, Washington, DC, to SK, 21 October 1960, Rev. Joseph C. Holbrook, Jr., to SK, 28 October 1960, Joseph D. Easter, "Greatest Picture of 1960," *Lake Elsinore Daily Sun*, news clipping, 29 December 1960, and Joel Allen to SK, August 1960 telegram, *ITW* Comments folder.

98. Al Horwits to SK, 30 June 1960, Horwits Publicity folder; Coe, "Keith's *Wind* Is a Cracker," C10; Our Film Critic, "A Case of Bigotry," *Guardian*, 9 July 1960, 3; Berns, *"Inherit the Wind"*; Correspondence, Beck Publicity folder.

99. "Film Review: *Inherit the Wind*," *Variety*, 29 June 1960, *ITW* Clippings file; Mrs. HPS, Houston, Texas, to SK, [August 1960], *ITW* Comments folder; B. Cranch to Mori Krushen, UA, New York, 3 August 1960, Beck Publicity folder; George J. Schaefer to SK, 9 November 1960 and 22 November 1960, George Schaefer–"ITW" folder, box 33, Kramer Papers.

100. Kramer with Coffey, *Mad, Mad, Mad, Mad World*, 175; "Stanley Kramer on Film," *Daily Variety*, 5 November 1982, Kramer Clippings file; Roger H. Lewis, UA, to Myer P. Beck, 16 September 1960, Beck Publicity folder.

101. Kramer, quoted in Tino T. Balio, *United Artists: The Company That Changed the Film Industry*, vol. 2, *1951–1978* (Madison: University of Wisconsin Press, 2009), 203–204.

102. Gill, "Current Cinema: Talkers," 98; Knight, "Importance of Being Earnest," 30.

103. Kramer with Coffey, *Mad, Mad, Mad, Mad World*, 175.

104. Easter, "Greatest Picture of 1960."

105. "Alert–Condition Red," Catholic War Veterans communiqué, Nathan E. Douglas and Harold Jacob Smith–"ITW" folder, box 31, Kramer papers; WTB, USS Coral Sea Navy, to SK, 25 June 1960, American Legion Correspondence folder.

106. Al Horwits to SK, 19 August 1960, Horwits Publicity folder; Kramer, quoted in Berns, "'Controversial' Film Is Defended by Kramer."

107. Balio, *United Artists*, 2:144; Kramer with Coffey, *Mad, Mad, Mad, Mad World*, 175.

108. Shepherd-Barr, *Science on Stage*, 9.

109. Tinee, "Film Based on Trial Is Fascinating," B18; "Darrow Won This Round," *Washington Post*, 11 October 1960, B6.

110. "U.S. Film for Berlin Picked," *Los Angeles Times*, 22 June 1960, 12;

Kramer, quoted in Michael Wall, "The Defiant One," *Guardian Observer*, 8 July 1960, 7.

111. Brandt, quoted in Ellen Lentz, "Drama-Dominated Screen Festival in Berlin," *New York Times*, 10 July 1960, X7; "Big Global Puff for Kramer's *Wind*," *Variety*, 1 June 1960, *ITW* Clippings File.

Chapter 5. Holocaust History in *Judgment at Nuremberg*

1. Willy Brandt, translated introductory speech at premiere, 14 December 1961, Congress Hall, Berlin, Publicity–"JAN" Al Horwits–Correspondence folder, box 38, Kramer Papers.

2. Kramer, quoted in James Bawden, "Stanley Kramer: Hollywood Liberal," *Classic Images*, February 2011, 72.

3. Martin Quigley, Jr., "'An Important Political Event,'" *Motion Picture Herald*, 27 December 1961, Nathan Broch, "Film *Judgment at Nuremberg* Time Bomb for Both Germanys" and "*Nuremberg* Premiere in Berlin Was Grim Lesson for Germans," *Los Angeles Mirror*, 20 December 1961 and 25 December 1961, and Leonard Mosely, "The Face in the Film That Will Make a Nation Cringe," *London Express*, 14 December 1961, *JAN* Clippings file.

4. W. J. Weatherby, "Cinema Gossip Entrances the Walled-In Egghead," *Guardian*, 16 December 1961, 4; Bosley Crowther, "Hollywood's Producer of Controversy," *New York Times*, 10 December 1961, SM76.

5. Kramer, quoted in Quigley, "'Important Political Event'"; Gavriel D. Rosenfeld, "The Reception of William L. Shirer's *The Rise and Fall of the Third Reich* in the United States and West Germany, 1960–62," *Journal of Contemporary History* 29 (January 1994): 96.

6. Broch, "*Nuremberg* Premiere"; Erik C. Eil, translated review from *Welt on Sonntag*, 24 September 1961, in folder Publicity–"JAN" Myer P. Beck–Correspondence, box 38, Kramer Papers; Kramer, quoted in Donald Spoto, *Stanley Kramer, Film Maker* (Hollywood, Calif.: Samuel French, 1978), 229.

7. Gavin Lambert, "*Judgment at Nuremberg* Review," *Film Quarterly* 15 (Winter 1961–1962): 51; Pauline Kael, "The Intentions of Stanley Kramer," in *Kiss Kiss Bang Bang* (London: Calder & Boyars, 1970), 208.

8. John Gillett, "*Judgment at Nuremberg*," *Sight and Sound* 31 (Winter 1961/1962): 41; "Cinema: Show Trial," *Time*, 15 December 1961, 87.

9. Kramer with Thomas M. Coffey, *A Mad, Mad, Mad, Mad World: A Life in Hollywood* (New York: Harcourt Brace, 1997), 178; Kramer, quoted in A. H. Weiler, "Passing Picture Scene: *Judgment at Nuremberg* to Be Made by Stanley Kramer," *New York Times*, 31 January 1960, X7; Mann, quoted in Suzanne Shale, "The Conflicts of Law and the Character of Men: Writing

Reversal of Fortune and *Judgment at Nuremberg*," *University of San Francisco Law Review* 30 (Summer 1996): 1007.

10. Hasia R. Diner, *We Remember with Reverence and Love: American Jews and the Myth of Silence after the Holocaust* (New York: New York University Press, 2009); Shale, "Conflicts of Law," 1006–1007; Mann, quoted in Murray Schumach, "Hollywood Trial," *New York Times*, 30 April 1961, X9.

11. Scott A. Windham, "The Trials of Representation: Critical and Aesthetic Reflections of Holocaust Perpetrator Trials, 1960–65" (PhD diss., University of North Carolina–Chapel Hill, 2002), 80.

12. Robert A. Rosenstone, *Visions of the Past: The Challenge of Film to Our Idea of History* (Cambridge, Mass.: Harvard University Press, 1995), 59–60; F. R. Ankersmit, *The Reality Effect in the Writing of History: The Dynamics of Historiographical Topology* (Amsterdam: Noord-Hollandsche, 1989), 139–140.

13. Harris Dienstfrey, in Dienstfrey and Jason Epstein, "Two Views of *Judgment at Nuremberg*," *Commentary* 33 (January 1962): 57; Judith E. Doneson, *The Holocaust in American Film*, 2nd ed. (Syracuse, N.Y.: Syracuse University Press, 2002), 10.

14. Caroline Joan (Kay) S. Picart and David A. Frank, *Frames of Evil: The Holocaust as Horror in American Film* (Carbondale: Southern Illinois University Press, 2006), 66; Senator Jacob K. Javits to SK, 25 April 1962, *JAN* Comments folder.

15. Audience preview cards, San Francisco, August 1961, box 40, Kramer Papers; Windham, "Trials of Representation," 92.

16. Isabel Quigly, "Salutary Clangers," *Spectator*, 22 December 1961, 928; Kramer with Coffey, *Mad, Mad, Mad, Mad World*, 185; "Postwar Germany So Well De-Rubbled Kramer May Seek 'Ruins' in H'wood," *Weekly Variety*, 5 October 1960, *JAN* Clippings file.

17. Kramer with Coffey, *Mad, Mad, Mad, Mad World*, 185; Robert Hatch, "Films," *Nation*, 6 June 1962, 20; Kramer, quoted in Spoto, *Stanley Kramer*, 230; James Powers, "*Judgment at Nuremberg* Moving, Important," *Hollywood Reporter*, 18 October 1961, *JAN* Clippings file.

18. Kramer with Coffey, *Mad, Mad, Mad, Mad World*, 186.

19. Gillett, "*Judgment at Nuremberg*," 41; Quigly, "Salutary Clangers," 928.

20. Audience preview cards, San Francisco, August 1961, box 40, Kramer Papers; Kramer, quoted in Spoto, *Stanley Kramer*, 230.

21. Kramer, quoted in George Stevens, Jr., *Conversations with the Great Moviemakers of Hollywood's Golden Age* (New York: Knopf, 2006), 564, and in Bawden, "Stanley Kramer," 70.

22. Audience preview cards, San Francisco, August 1961, box 40, Kramer Papers.

23. "Cinema: Show Trial," *Time*, 15 December 1961, 87; audience preview cards, San Francisco, August 1961, box 40, Kramer Papers.

24. "*Judgment at Nuremberg*," *Daily Variety*, 18 December 1961, *JAN* Clippings file.

25. Kramer with Coffey, *Mad, Mad, Mad, Mad World*, 181; Shale, "Conflicts of Law," 999–1000; Broch, "Film *Judgment at Nuremberg* Time Bomb."

26. Kramer, quoted in Steven Bach, *Marlene Dietrich: Life and Legend* (New York: William Morrow, 1992), 408.

27. Donald Spoto, *Blue Angel: The Life of Marlene Dietrich* (New York: Cooper Square, 2000), 279, 278 (quotation); Ean Wood, *Dietrich, a Biography* (London: Sanctuary, 2002), 226; Annette Insdorf, *Indelible Shadows: Film and the Holocaust*, 3rd ed. (Cambridge: Cambridge University Press, 2003), 9.

28. Henry Gonshak, "Does *Judgment at Nuremberg* Accurately Depict the Nazi War Crimes Trial?" *Journal of American Culture* 31, no. 2 (2008): 155; Quigly, "Salutary Clangers," 928.

29. Kramer with Coffey, *Mad, Mad, Mad, Mad World*, 181; audience preview cards, San Francisco, August 1961, box 40, Kramer Papers.

30. Lambert, "*Judgment at Nuremberg* Review," 52; audience preview cards, San Francisco, August 1961, box 40, Kramer Papers; Clift, quoted in Vernon Scott, "Clift Refuses $100,000 for Role, Does It Free," *World-Telegram and Sun Feature Magazine Section*, 25 March 1961, news clipping, C-R Enterprises Title Protest–"JAN," folder 36, Kramer Papers.

31. Kramer with Coffey, *Mad, Mad, Mad, Mad World*, 182–183; Gonshak, "*Judgment at Nuremberg*," 155; Thomas Doherty, "Homevideo: *Judgment at Nuremberg*," *Cineaste*, Spring 2005, 58.

32. Gabrielle M. Spiegel, "The Final Phase?" *History and Theory* 51 (October 2012): 431; Carolyn J. Dean, *Aversion and Erasure: The Fate of the Victim after the Holocaust* (Ithaca, N.Y.: Cornell University Press, 2010), 134, 113.

33. Schell, quoted/attributed in Al Horwits Release, Widmark, quoted/attributed in "The Importance of Being Earnest," Al Horwits Release, and official PR materials, Publicity–"JAN" Al Horwits–Releases folder, box 38, Kramer Papers.

34. Mann, quoted in *Judgment at Nuremberg* Program, *JAN* Clippings file, 99; Rosenstone, *Visions of the Past*, 72–73.

35. Powers, "*Judgment at Nuremberg* Moving, Important"; Kramer, quoted in Bawden, "Stanley Kramer," 70; Mann, quoted in Mae Tinee, "*Nuremberg* Earns Oscar for Writing," *Chicago Tribune*, 13 May 1962, G12.

36. Shale, "Conflicts of Law," 996–997. Books included Peter Calvocoressi, *Nuremberg: The Facts, the Law, and the Consequences* (1947); Gustave M. Gilbert, *Nuremberg Diary* (1948); and John P. Kenny, *Moral Aspects of Nuremberg* (1949). See Mann Contract folder.

37. Jeffrey Shandler, *While America Watches: Televising the Holocaust* (New York: Oxford University Press, 1999), 72; Shale, "Conflicts of Law," 1008.

38. Shale, "Conflicts of Law," 995–996; Windham, "Trials of Representation," 96–98.

39. Gunther H. Schiff, "Conversation with Judge James T. Brand," 22 February 1961, Brand folder; Telford Taylor to Robert S. Benjamin, 13 February 1961 and 10 February 1961, Taylor folder.

40. Rosenstone, *Visions of the Past*, 72.

41. Telford Taylor to Robert S. Benjamin, 9 March 1961 and 10 February 1961, Taylor folder.

42. Lambert, "*Judgment at Nuremberg* Review," 52; audience preview cards, San Francisco, August 1961, box 40, Kramer Papers; Shale, "Conflicts of Law," 1012.

43. Hayden White, "Historiography and Historiophoty," *American Historical Review* 93 (December 1988): 1198–1199.

44. Gunther H. Schiff to Telford Taylor, 28 February 1961, and Telford Taylor to Gunther H. Schiff, 9 March 1961, Taylor folder.

45. Abby Mann, *Judgment at Nuremberg*, in Sam Thomas, ed., *Best American Screenplays 2* (New York: Crown, 1990), 324; "*Judgment at Nuremberg*," *Variety*, 18 October 1961, *JAN* Clippings file.

46. Mann, quoted in Shale, "Conflicts of Law," 1007n45; James T. Brand to Gunther H. Schiff, 17 March 1961, Brand folder.

47. "*Judgment at Nuremberg*," *I. F. Stone's Weekly*, 15 January 1962, 2; Ronald Steel, "Kramer's Nuremberg," *Christian Century*, 14 March 1962, clipping in *Judgment at Nuremberg* file, PCA Records.

48. William Henry Chamberlin, "The Revival of Anti-Germanism," *Modern Age* 6 (Summer 1962): 280; *Life* magazine, quoted in Alan Mintz, *Popular Culture and the Shaping of Holocaust Memory in America* (Seattle: University of Washington Press, 2001), 101.

49. Audience preview cards, San Francisco, August 1961, box 40, Kramer Papers; Norbert Muhlen, "The U.S. Image of Germany, 1962, as Reflected in American Books," *Modern Age* 6 (Fall 1962): 424.

50. Mann, paraphrased in Gunther H. Schiff, "Conversation with Judge James T. Brand," 22 February 1961, Brand folder.

51. Barraclough, quoted in Rosenfeld, "Reception of William L. Shirer's

The Rise and Fall of the Third Reich," 105; Telford Taylor, "Large Questions in the Eichmann Case," *New York Times,* 22 January 1961, 23.

52. Ian Buruma, "The Twisted Art of Documentary," *New York Review of Books,* 25 November 2010, 44; Deborah E. Lipstadt, "America and the Memory of the Holocaust, 1950–1965," *Modern Judaism* 16, no. 3 (1996): 200; Diner, *We Remember,* 218.

53. Carol J. Glover, "'God Bless Juries!'" in Nick Browne, ed., *Refiguring American Film Genres: History and Theory* (Berkeley: University of California Press, 1998), 255–277.

54. Pierre Sorlin, *The Film in History: Restaging the Past* (Totowa, N.J.: Barnes and Noble, 1980), 71; White, "Historiography and Historiophoty," 1193–1199.

55. Deborah Lipstadt, *The Eichmann Trial* (New York: Schocken, 2011), 55.

56. Geoffrey M. Shurlock to SK, 14 December 1960, and SK to Geoffrey M. Shurlock, 15 December 1960, *Judgment at Nuremberg* file, PCA Records; Thomas Doherty, *Hollywood's Censor: Joseph I. Breen and the Production Code Administration* (New York: Columbia University Press, 2007).

57. Abby Mann, revised final script, January 1961, 117, Scripts, box 35, Kramer Papers; Robert H. Abzug, *Inside the Vicious Heart: Americans and the Liberation of Nazi Concentration Camps* (New York: Oxford University Press, 1985), ix.

58. Marsha Orgeron, "Liberating Images? Samuel Fuller's Film of Falkenau Concentration Camp," *Film Quarterly* 60 (Winter 2006–2007): 43.

59. William O. Douglas to SK, 10 November 1960, and SK to William O. Douglas, 4 November 1960, Justice William O. Douglas–"JAN" folder, box 37, Kramer Papers.

60. Lambert, "*Judgment at Nuremberg* Review," 52; Insdorf, *Indelible Shadows,* 8, 37; Shandler, *While America Watches,* 12; Abzug, *Inside the Vicious Heart,* 27–30.

61. Steel, "Kramer's Nuremberg"; Abby Mann, revised final script, January 1961, 117–118, Scripts, box 35, Kramer Papers.

62. Toby Haggith, "Filming the Liberation of Bergen-Belsen," in Toby Haggith and Joanna Newman, eds., *Holocaust and the Moving Image: Representations in Film and Television since 1933* (London: Wallflower, 2005), 45; Insdorf, *Indelible Shadows,* 8; Lawrence Douglas, *The Memory of Judgment: Making Law and History in the Trials of the Holocaust* (New Haven, Conn.: Yale University Press, 2001), 23; Abzug, *Inside the Vicious Heart,* 27–30.

63. Steel, "Kramer's Nuremberg"; Shandler, *While America Watches,* 75–77; Gonshak, "*Judgment at Nuremberg,*" 161.

64. Chamberlin, "Revival of Anti-Germanism," 280; "Cinema: Show Trial," *Time*, 15 December 1961, 87; Epstein, from Dienstfrey and Epstein, "Two Views of *Judgment at Nuremberg*," 62; Shale, "Conflicts of Law," 1001n31.

65. Audience preview cards, San Francisco, August 1961, box 40, Kramer Papers.

66. Shandler, *While America Watches*, 12, 14.

67. Haggith, "Filming the Liberation of Bergen-Belsen," 34; Ilan Avisar, *Screening the Holocaust: Cinema's Images of the Unimaginable* (Bloomington: Indiana University Press, 1988), 133; Kramer with Coffey, *Mad, Mad, Mad, Mad World*, 179.

68. Dienstfrey, from Dienstfrey and Epstein, "Two Views of *Judgment at Nuremberg*," 58; Gunther H. Schiff, "Conversation with Judge James T. Brand," 22 February 1961, and Gunther H. Schiff to James T. Brand, 16 March 1961, Brand folder; Lipstadt, *Eichmann Trial*, 53.

69. Mann, *Judgment at Nuremberg*, 326; Lipstadt, *Eichmann Trial*, 127–128.

70. "History and Mr. Kramer," *Los Angeles Examiner*, 3 December 1961, news clipping, Kramer Clippings file.

71. Mann, *Judgment at Nuremberg*, 316, 289; "Cinema: Show Trial," *Time*, 15 December 1961, 87; Mosely, "Face in the Film"; Chamberlin, "Revival of Anti-Germanism," 280; Kramer, quoted in Spoto, *Stanley Kramer*, 229.

72. Hollis Alpert, "Haunting Question," *Saturday Review*, 2 December 1961, 43, news clipping, *Judgment at Nuremberg* file, PCA Records; Shoshana Goldman, "*Judgment in Nuremberg* in Front of Millions of Viewers," *Herut*, 17 November 1961, 6, translated for the author by Ayelet Zoran-Rosen; Powers, "*Judgment at Nuremberg* Moving, Important."

73. Steel, "Kramer's Nuremberg"; Eleanor Roosevelt, "Nuremberg Revisited," *New York Post*, 2 November 1961, news clipping, *JAN* Comments folder.

74. Audience preview cards, San Francisco, August 1961, box 40, Kramer Papers.

75. Kramer and Widmark, paraphrased in Harold Myers, "Emotional *Nuremberg* Premiere," *Variety*, 20 December 1961, and Broch, "*Nuremberg* Premiere in Berlin Was Grim Lesson," *JAN* Clippings file.

76. Doneson, *Holocaust in American Film*, 100; Kramer, quoted in Peter Cowie, "The Defiant One," *Films and Filming*, March 1963, 19.

77. Mann, *Judgment at Nuremberg*, 327–328; Analysis of Film Content, *Judgment at Nuremberg* file, PCA Records.

78. "*Judgment at Nuremberg*," *Cue*, 23 December 1961, *JAN* Clippings file; Gillett, "*Judgment at Nuremberg*," 41; audience preview cards, San Francisco, August 1961, box 40, Kramer Papers; Steel, "Kramer's Nuremberg."

79. Peter Novick, *The Holocaust in American Life* (New York: Houghton Mifflin, 1999), 13.

80. Mann, *Judgment at Nuremberg*, 283; "Cinema: Show Trial," *Time*, 15 December 1961, 87.

81. Knight, "Producer-Director at Work," 45; Epstein, from Dienstfrey and Epstein, "Two Views of *Judgment at Nuremberg*," 61; Alpert, "Haunting Question," 44.

82. Mann, quoted and paraphrased in Shale, "Conflicts of Law," 1007n45; Kramer, quoted in Crowther, "Hollywood's Producer of Controversy," SM80; Mann, *Judgment at Nuremberg*, 335.

83. Kramer, quoted in Cowie, "Defiant One," 19; Doneson, *Holocaust in American Film*, 99–100, 102–103; Gonshak, "*Judgment at Nuremberg*," 161.

84. Heberer and Matthäus, *Atrocities on Trial*, xvi; Norman Nadel, "Director Kramer Readies *Judgment at Nuremberg*," *Citizen-Journal*, 6 March 1961, clipping, C-R Enterprises Title Protest—"JAN" folder, box 36, Kramer Papers.

85. Avisar, *Screening the Holocaust*, 181; Mann, paraphrased in Shale, "Conflicts of Law," 1006n44.

86. Schumach, "Hollywood Trial," X9.

87. Moses M. Berlin to SK, 10 January 1962, *JAN* Comments folder; untitled review, *Judgment at Nuremberg* file, PCA Records.

88. United Artists Press Release, 23 July 1962, Publicity—"JAN" UA Releases folder, box 38, and Jewish Interest award, Awards SEK—"JAN" folder, box 35, Kramer Papers; Mintz, *Popular Culture and the Shaping of Holocaust Memory*, 103.

89. Tobias Ebbrecht, "Migrating Images: Iconic Images of the Holocaust and the Representation of War in Popular Film," *Shofar: An Interdisciplinary Journal of Jewish Studies* 28 (Summer 2010): 87.

90. Goldman, "*Judgment in Nuremberg* in Front of Millions," *Davar*, 2 January 1962, R. Gavrielit, "In the Cinema: The Past, Mirroring in the Present," *Davar*, 2 January 1962, 5, and Zeev Rav-Nof, "The Floating World," *Davar*, 26 November 1965, 13, translated for the author by Ayelet Zoran-Rosen.

91. Sol Lesser to SK, 16 February 1962, and Meyer W. Weisgal to SK, 13 October 1961, *JAN* Comments folder.

92. Audience preview cards, San Francisco, August 1961, box 40, Kramer Papers.

93. W. J. Weatherby, "*Judgment at Nuremberg*," *Guardian*, 15 December 1961, 9.

94. Lawrence Baron, "The First Wave of American 'Holocaust' Films, 1945–1959," *American Historical Review* 115 (February 2010): 90–114;

"*Judgment at Nuremberg,*" *I. F. Stone's Weekly,* 15 January 1962, 2; Hilene Flanzbaum, ed., *The Americanization of the Holocaust* (Baltimore, Md.: John Hopkins University Press, 1999), 3.

95. Lawrence L. Langer, "The Americanization of the Holocaust on Stage and Screen," reprinted in *Admitting the Holocaust: Collected Essays* (New York: Oxford University Press, 1995), 158; Alvin H. Rosenfeld, "The Americanization of the Holocaust," *Commentary,* 1 June 1995, 37.

96. Harry Golden, "A Letter from Berlin: The Movie Started a Controversy," *Maariv,* 29 December 1961, 21, translated for the author by Ayelet Zoran-Rosen.

97. John C. Satterfield, President, American Bar Association, to SK, 23 June 1962, Awards SEK–"JAN" folder, box 35, Kramer papers; Roosevelt, "Nuremberg Revisited."

98. Avisar, *Screening the Holocaust,* 133; Hatch, "Films," 19.

99. Brendan Gill, "The Current Cinema: Out of Evil," *New Yorker,* 23 December 1961, 68; Albert Maltz, San Angel, Mexico, to SK, 5 January 1961, *JAN* Comments folder.

100. Diner, *We Remember,* 233; Mann to SK, 16 June 1961, Mann Contract folder; Mann, quoted in Shale, "Conflicts of Law," 1007n45.

101. Brand, paraphrased in Gunther H. Schiff, "Conversation with Judge James T. Brand," 22 February 1961, Brand folder; Michael A. Musmanno to SK, 2 December 1961 and 30 November 1961, Musmanno folder.

102. Audience preview cards, San Francisco, August 1961, box 40, Kramer Papers; Abby Mann to SK, 16 June 1961, Mann Contract folder.

103. SK to Michael A. Musmanno, 11 December 1961, Musmanno folder; audience preview cards, San Francisco, August 1961, box 40, Kramer Papers.

104. Untitled review, *Judgment at Nuremberg* file, PCA Records; Golden, "Letter from Berlin," 21; Hatch, "Films," 20.

105. Audience preview cards, San Francisco, August 1961, box 40, Kramer Papers.

106. Balio, *United Artists,* 2:145; Kramer with Coffey, *Mad, Mad, Mad, Mad World,* 187.

107. "*Judgment at Nuremberg,*" *Variety,* 18 October 1961, *JAN* Clippings File.

108. Audience preview cards, San Francisco, August 1961, box 40, Kramer Papers.

109. Stanley Kauffmann, "Hollywood's Germany," *New Republic,* 11 December 1961, 26, 28; Quigly, "Salutary Clangers," 928.

110. Audience preview cards, San Francisco, August 1961, box 40, Kramer Papers.

111. Alpert, "Haunting Question," 43; Dan Taradash to SK, [October 1961], *JAN* Comments folder.

112. Mann, quoted in Susan King, "Abby Mann, 1927–2008," *Los Angeles Times*, 1 April 2008, A2.

113. Crowther, "Hollywood's Producer of Controversy," SM76; Goldman, "*Judgment at Nuremberg* in Front of Millions," 6.

Chapter 6. Cinematic Diplomacy in Cold War Moscow

1. Dina Iordanova, *Cinema of the Other Europe: The Industry and Artistry of East Central European Film* (London: Wallflower, 2003), 9; Jeremy Suri, "Conflict and Co-operation in the Cold War: New Directions in Contemporary Historical Research," *Journal of Contemporary History* 46, no. 1 (2011): 8.

2. Yale Richmond, *Cultural Exchange and the Cold War: Raising the Iron Curtain* (University Park: Pennsylvania State University Press, 2003), 130.

3. Penny M. Von Eschen, *Satchmo Blows Up the World: Jazz Ambassadors Play the Cold War* (Cambridge, Mass.: Harvard University Press, 2004), 11.

4. Kramer, quoted in Bosley Crowther, "Hollywood's Producer of Controversy," *New York Times*, 10 December 1961, SM82.

5. Milton Cummings, *Cultural Diplomacy and the United States Government: A Survey* (Washington, DC: Center for Arts and Culture, 2003), 1; Kramer, quoted in *Pravda* interview; William Benton, "Should We Continue the Cultural Exchanges with the USSR?" *Saturday Review*, 27 October 1962, 40.

6. "Kramer Irritated by State Dept. Snub of Moscow Fest," *Variety*, 4 August 1971, 3, *BBC* Moscow festival folder; SK to L. Pogojeva, Editor in Chief, *Iskusstvo Kino*, 28 May 1961, Russia Correspondence folder.

7. SK to Mr. Y. Volsky, Cultural Counselor, Embassy of the USSR, Washington, 14 September 1960, Russia Correspondence folder; Frank A. Ninkovich, *The Diplomacy of Ideas: U.S. Foreign Policy and Cultural Relations, 1938–1950* (Cambridge: Cambridge University Press, 1981), 119; Kramer, quoted in *Pravda* interview.

8. "Editor's Corner: Culture Cult" and "Editor's Corner: Movie Note," *American Legion Magazine*, April 1959, 6–7.

9. Hy Hollinger, "Mixed Emotions of a Disunited Industry Facing Renewed Slurs On Commie-Angled Scripters," *Variety*, n.d., American Legion Clippings folder; G. J. Schaefer, President of Selected Pictures Corp., New York, New York, to SK, 7 March 1960, American Legion Correspondence folder.

10. Donald T. Critchlow, *Phyllis Schlafly and Grassroots Conservatism: A Woman's Crusade* (Princeton, N.J.: Princeton University Press, 2005), 87.

11. Mr. Dangulov, Deputy Chief Editor, *Editors Foreign Language Magazine*, to SK, 27 November 1959, and SK to Mr. Dangulov, 30 November 1959, Russia Correspondence folder.

12. *OTB* Press Conference transcript, 17 December 1959, *OTB* Comments folder; Tony Shaw and Denise J. Youngblood, *Cinematic Cold War: The American and Soviet Struggle for Hearts and Minds* (Lawrence: University Press of Kansas, 2010), 53; "Film Festivals: A 'Circus' in Moscow . . . a 'Soft Wave' in Berlin," *Christian Science Daily Monitor*, 6 August 1971, 15, *BBC* Moscow festival folder.

13. Kramer with Thomas M. Coffey, *A Mad, Mad, Mad, Mad World: A Life in Hollywood* (New York: Harcourt Brace, 1997), 1–2.

14. William Henry Chamberlin, "The Revival of Anti-Germanism," *Modern Age* 6 (Summer 1962): 280.

15. Vladich Alekseevich Nedelin, *Stanley Kramer* (Moscow: Iskusstvo, 1969), 5, 8, 42, 219, translated for the author by Natalia Galvin. See also Frank Costigliola, "'Unceasing Pressure for Penetration': Gender, Pathology, and Emotion in George Kennan's Formation of the Cold War," *Journal of American History* 83, no. 4 (March 1997): 1309–1339.

16. "Russian Paper Blasts Sexy Foreign Movies," *Los Angeles Times*, 19 April 1968, D14; George Faraday, *Revolt of the Filmmakers: The Struggle for Artistic Autonomy and the Fall of the Soviet Film Industry* (University Park: Pennsylvania State University Press, 2000), 6, 12, 50; Sergei Zhuk, "Hollywood's Insidious Charms: The Impact of American Cinema and Television on the Soviet Union during the Cold War," *Cold War History* 14, no. 4 (2014): 607, 598.

17. Nedelin, *Stanley Kramer*, 136–137, 38–40; Kramer with Coffey, *Mad, Mad, Mad, Mad World*, 1.

18. Faraday, *Revolt of the Filmmakers*, 73; Iordanova, *Cinema of the Other Europe*, 37–38.

19. John Russell Taylor, "How Russians See West's Films," *Globe and Mail*, newspaper clipping, 8 September 1967, Russia Correspondence folder; Mary Blume, "Hero Rating for Stanley Kramer," *Los Angeles Times*, 29 July 1971, 14.

20. Kramer, quoted in Bob Thomas, "Kramer Meets Russians on Own Ground," *Los Angeles Herald-Examiner*, 13 August 1971, B6, *BBC* Moscow festival folder, and in Stephen Klain, "Kramer Is Elated as Moscow Blesses Film," *Motion Picture Daily*, 30 July 1971, 1, 4, "BBC" Trade Clips folder, box 136, Kramer Papers; Leonid Heller, "A World of Prettiness: Socialist Realism and Its Aesthetic Categories," in Thomas Lahusen and Evgeny Dobrenko, eds., *Socialist Realism without Shores* (Durham, N.C.: Duke University Press, 1997), 53; Faraday, *Revolt of the Filmmakers*, 78–80; Iordanova, *Cinema of the Other Europe*, 35.

21. Shneiderov, quoted in Zhuk, "Hollywood's Insidious Charms," 599.

22. Raisa Orlova, quoted in "The Young Man of the Mid-20th Century," *Anglo-Soviet Journal*, Summer 1961, 36; Nedelin, *Stanley Kramer*, 71, 105, 59.

23. Gerasimov, paraphrased in Embassy Moscow to Secretary of State, 19 December 1959, State Department *OTB* Premiere file.

24. Chakovskii, quoted in "Russ Hail Acting in *On the Beach*," *Los Angeles Mirror News*, 25 December 1959, Paxton Publicity folder; Patrick Major, "Future Perfect? Communist Science Fiction in the Cold War," *Cold War History* 4 (2003): 1, 71, 73. See also Katerina Clark, "Socialist Realism with Shores: The Conventions for the Positive Hero," in Lahusen and Dobrenko, *Socialist Realism without Shores*, 28.

25. Kramer, quoted in Charles Champlin, "Film Festivals a Window to World," *Los Angeles Times*, 14 August 1967, D24; Kramer, quoted in Thomas, "Kramer Meets Russians on Own Ground," B6; Zhuk, "Hollywood's Insidious Charms," 608–609; Stanley Kauffman, "Waiting for the End," *New Republic*, 14 December 1959, 22.

26. Kramer, quoted in Thomas, "Kramer Meets Russians on Own Ground," B6; Harry Trimborn, "Individualism Returns as Part of Russ Renaissance," *Los Angeles Times*, 28 October 1967, A6; Nedelin, *Stanley Kramer*, 136–137.

27. Kramer, quoted in Thomas, "Kramer Meets Russians on Own Ground," B6; F. Burlatsky, "This Must Not Be Repeated: Sociological Notes on Films about Fascism," *Pravda*, 14–16 February 1966, 4, translated and reprinted in *Current Digest of the Soviet Press*, 9 March 1966, 18; Nedelin, *Stanley Kramer*, 158.

28. Ivan Piriev and Serguey Youtkevitch, President and Vice President of the Association of Film Makers of the USSR, to SK, 25 December 1962 and 13 December 1962, Russia Correspondence folder.

29. Myer P. Beck to SK, 21 August 1959, *OTB* Comments folder; Larry Glenn, "Russ OK on *Beach* Preem in Moscow May Be Sign of Thaw," *Variety*, 30 November 1959, *OTB* Clippings file.

30. Louella O. Parsons, "Elvis Asks Quiet Welcome in April," *New York Journal-American*, 2 December 1959, 23, *OTB* Clippings file.

31. Glenn, "Russ OK on *Beach* Preem"; Nedelin, *Stanley Kramer*, 117, 109, 130.

32. Department of State to American Embassy Moscow, 21 December 1959, and Embassy Moscow to Secretary of State, 19 December 1959, State Department *OTB* Premiere file.

33. "Gregory Peck Sees His Film in Moscow," *New York Times*, 18 December 1959, 34; "Global Reactions to *On the Beach*," *Variety*, 23 December

1959, Kramer Clippings files; Army Archerd, "*Beach* Is Controversial Hit with Raps and Raves on Preems: Peck at Moscow Bow," *Variety*, 21 December 1959, Paxton Publicity folder.

34. Embassy Moscow to Secretary of State, 19 December 1959, State Department *OTB* Premiere file.

35. Ibid.

36. Ninkovich, *Diplomacy of Ideas*, 8, 22. Scott Lucas shows how US cultural diplomacy was the product of a "State-private network" in *Freedom's War: The US Crusade against the Soviet Union, 1945–56* (Manchester, UK: Manchester University Press, 1999).

37. "Moscow Film Fest Not Yet 'Official' to State; Yankees Ponder Pitch," *Variety*, 27 May 1959, 1959 Moscow Festival Clippings file; SK to Edward R. Murrow, Director, USIA, 7 April 1961, and Murrow to SK, 17 April 1961, Russia Correspondence folder.

38. L. Pogojeva, Editor in Chief, *Iskusstvo Kino*, to SK, 5 March 1961, SK to L. Pogojeva, 28 May 1961, SK to Turner B. Shelton, Director Motion Picture Service, USIA, 28 April 1961, and Turner B. Shelton to SK, 11 May 1961, Russia Correspondence folder.

39. Kramer, quoted in "Lew Irwin Reports," transcript, KABC-TV, 15 October 1959, AMPTP Records.

40. Shelton to SK, 31 May 1961, 21 June 1961, and 29 January 1962, and SK to Shelton, 1 February 1962, Russia Correspondence folder.

41. SK to Mr. Surkov, *Moscow Literary Gazette*, 5 July 1961, and Sergei Gerasimov to SK, n.d., Russia Correspondence folder.

42. Tony Shaw, *Hollywood's Cold War* (Amherst: University of Massachusetts Press, 2007), 176; Richard L. Coe, "Film Festivals Burgeon All Over," *Los Angeles Times*, 7 July 1963, D9.

43. George Stevens, Jr., *Conversations with the Great Moviemakers of Hollywood's Golden Age* (New York: Knopf, 2006), 558–559; David Caute, *The Dancer Defects: The Struggle for Cultural Supremacy during the Cold War* (New York: Oxford University Press, 2003), 238.

44. Kramer, quoted in Marian Dern, "Kramer in Moscow: A New Approach to the American Image," *Beverly Hills Times*, 18 October 1963, news clipping, Russia Correspondence folder; Jonathan Rosenberg, "Let Freedom Swing," *Diplomatic History* 35 (January 2011): 92; Laura A. Belmonte, *Selling the American Way: U.S. Propaganda and the Cold War* (Philadelphia: University of Pennsylvania Press, 2008), 4; Walter L. Hixon, *Parting the Curtain: Propaganda, Culture, and the Cold War, 1945–1961* (London: Macmillan, 1997), xv.

45. Stanley Kramer, "Politics, Social Comment and My Emotions," *Films and Filming*, June 1960, 7–8; Kramer, quoted in Dern, "Kramer in Moscow";

Nicholas J. Cull, "'The Man Who Invented Truth': The Tenure of Edward R. Murrow as Director of the United States Information Agency during the Kennedy Years," in Rana Mitter and Patrick Major, eds., *Across the Blocs: Cold War Cultural and Social History* (London: Frank Cass, 2004), 23; Eric Pleskow, UA, to SK, 4 April 1963, SK to Eric Pleskow, UA, 13 April 1963, and Myer P. Beck to SK, 12 June 1963, Russia Correspondence folder.

46. "Briefing Note: The Third Moscow Film Festival, April 30, 1963," Khrushchev speech, "High Ideological Content and Artistic Mastery Constitute the Great Strength of Soviet Literature and Art," 8 March 1963, and SK to George Stevens, Jr., 29 March 1963 and 16 May 1963, Russia Correspondence folder; Theodore Shabad, "Kramer to Serve Soviet Film Fete," *New York Times*, 24 April 1963, 32.

47. "Report of the United States Delegation to the III International Film Festival at Moscow, USSR, July 7 through July 21, 1963," 1, USIA Moscow 1963 Festival file.

48. Fred Hift, "Is Moscow Film Fest Circusy Stunt to 'Distract' from U.S. Expo There?" *Variety*, 8 July 1959, "U.S. Is 'Limited' Entry in Russ Fest," and "Russia Fest Edict Fall to Skouras," *Variety*, 12 August 1959, 1959 Moscow Festival Clippings file; Hixon, *Parting the Curtain*, xiv.

49. David Stewart Hall, "Verdict on Moscow," *Guardian*, 26 July 1961, 7; Seymour Topping, "Moscow in Retrospect," *New York Times*, 30 July 1961, X5; Gerald Pratley, *Pratley at the Movies*, Canadian Broadcasting Corporation, 10 August 1963, Russia Correspondence folder.

50. Marsha Siefert, "From Cold War to Wary Peace: American Culture in the USSR and Russia," in Alexander Stephan, ed., *The Americanization of Europe: Culture, Diplomacy, and Anti-Americanism after 1945* (New York: Berghahn, 2006), 185.

51. Stevens, paraphrased in "Large Hollywood Turnout for Moscow Movie Festival," *Los Angeles Times*, 22 June 1963, B6; Marijke de Valck, *Film Festivals: From European Geopolitics to Global Cinephilia* (Amsterdam: Amsterdam University Press, 2007), 24, 157.

52. Kramer, quoted in Champlin, "Film Festivals a Window," D24.

53. Kramer, quoted in Henry Tanner, "Moscow Film Fete: Ideas in Motion," *New York Times*, 28 July 1963, 75.

54. *Pravda* review, quoted in Eugene S. Staples, Counselor for Cultural Affairs, for the Ambassador, American Embassy Moscow, to Secretary of State, 19 July 1963, State Department Moscow Festival file.

55. Dern, "Kramer in Moscow"; "Soviet Critic Doesn't Like US War Film," *Los Angeles Times*, 12 July 1963, D14; American Embassy Moscow to Secretary of State, 27 May 1963, State Department Moscow Festival file.

56. Stevens, *Conversations with the Great Moviemakers*, 559; Kramer,

quoted in Michael Singer, *A Cut Above: 50 Film Directors Talk about Their Craft* (Los Angeles: Lone Eagle, 1998), 161.

57. Stevens presentation; Foy D. Kohler, American Embassy Moscow, to Secretary of State, 22 July 1963, State Department Moscow Festival file; Harold Myers, "Moscow Fest, Sans Airconditioning, Pro Ordeal but Worth While to Americans," *Variety*, 31 September 1963, 1963 Moscow Festival Clippings file.

58. Harold Myers, "H'Wood in Early Moscow Fest Triumph; Big Hand for Kramer," *Variety*, 15 July 1963, 1963 Moscow Festival Clippings file.

59. Thomas Hischak, *The Oxford Companion to the American Musical: Theatre, Film, and Television* (New York: Oxford University Press, 2008), 789.

60. "U.S. Film Is Noticed by Soviet–At Last," *New York Times*, 15 July 1963, 24; Benton, "Should We Continue the Cultural Exchanges with the USSR?" 18.

61. Jim Lovensheimer, "Stephen Sondheim and the Musical of the Outsider," in William A. Everett and Paul R. Laird, eds., *The Cambridge Companion to the Musical*, 2nd ed. (Cambridge: Cambridge University Press, 2008), 206; John Bush Jones, *Our Musicals, Ourselves: A Social History of the American Musical Theatre* (Waltham, Mass.: Brandeis University Press, 2003), 193–194; Marc Bauch, *The American Musical: A Literary Study* (Marburg, Germany: Tectum Verlag, 2003), 67–107, quotation on 83.

62. Kramer, quoted in Foy D. Kohler to Secretary of State, 8 July 1963, State Department Moscow Festival file.

63. Kramer, paraphrased in Don Harrison, "Kramer Cites Propaganda Value in Criticism of Self," *UCLA Daily Bruin*, 10 October 1963, Russia Correspondence folder; Kramer, quoted in "*West Side Story* Is Applauded in Soviet Film Festival Showing," *New York Times*, 9 July 1963, 28.

64. Kramer, quoted in Foy D. Kohler to Secretary of State, 8 July 1963, State Department Moscow Festival file.

65. Foy D. Kohler to Secretary of State, 8 July 1963, State Department Moscow Festival file; Myer P. Beck to SK, Moscow, July 9, 1963, Russia Correspondence folder.

66. Foy D. Kohler to Secretary of State, 21 June 1963, Department of State to American Embassy Moscow, 19 June 1963, and George Ball, Department of State, to American Embassy Moscow, 24 June 1963, State Department Moscow Festival file; "Rejoinder: Duet without Words," translated and reprinted in *Current Digest of the Soviet Press*, 7 August 1963, 47.

67. "Izvestia Sees Political Angle in Film Incident," *Los Angeles Times*, 10 July 1963, 17; American Embassy Moscow to Secretary of State, 26 July 1963, State Department Moscow Festival file.

68. Kramer, quoted in Foy D. Kohler to Secretary of State, 15 July 1963, State Department Moscow Festival file; "Footnotes to Moscow Fest," *Variety*,

24 July 1963, and Myers, "Moscow Fest, Sans Airconditioning," 1963 Moscow Festival Clippings file; Caute, *Dancer Defects*, 238.

69. Kramer, quoted in Foy D. Kohler to Secretary of State, 15 July 1963, and *Izvestia* and *Komsomolskaya Pravda*, quoted in American Embassy Moscow to Secretary of State, 26 July 1963, State Department Moscow Festival file; Dern, "Kramer in Moscow."

70. Kramer, paraphrased in Foy D. Kohler to Secretary of State, 17 July 1963, State Department Moscow Festival file; Mann, quoted in Philip K. Scheuer, "Mann Tells Soviets to 'Let Chips Fly,'" *Los Angeles Times*, 17 July 1963, D9; Belmonte, *Selling the American Way*, 5, 97.

71. Mr. George Stevens, Jr.'s Remarks on United States Participation in the Moscow International Film Festival, 7–21 July 1963, [20], USIA Moscow 1963 Festival file.

72. "Soviet (Natch!) Film Wins Fest Staged in Moscow," *Hollywood Reporter*, 19 August 1959, and "It's No Surprise: Home Film Wins in Moscow Fest," *Hollywood Citizen-News*, 18 August 1959, 1959 Moscow Festival Clippings file.

73. Tanner, "Moscow Film Fete," 75; Mark Frankland, "Festival versus Party Line," *Observer*, 14 July 1963, 26.

74. Tanner, "Moscow Film Fete," 75; Bruce Renton "*8½*: Moscow Award-Winner Nyet for Soviet Eye," *Los Angeles Times*, 25 August 1963, E3; "Soviets Hail *8½* as Best at Festival," *Chicago Tribune*, 22 July 1963, A3; Jan Prochaska, quoted in "Italy Film Gets Disputed Russia Festival Award," *Los Angeles Times*, 22 July 1963, 21.

75. Costigliola, "'Unceasing Pressure for Penetration,'" 1328; Foy D. Kohler to Secretary of State, 22 July 1963, State Department Moscow Festival file; "Moscow International Film Festival," 1, File MV 8 Festival, Box 3 Moscow Film Festival, Entry 166, Record Group 306, National Archives, College Park, Maryland.

76. Renton, "*8½*," E3; Stevens presentation, 28–29.

77. Jury, quoted in "Soviets Hail *8½* as Best," A3; Romanov and Fellini, quoted in Renton, "*8½*," E3; Stevens presentation, 28–29; Furtseva, paraphrased in "*8½* Not Communistic Bloc Notion of 'Peace, Friendship, Humanism,'" *Variety*, 31 July 1963, 1963 Moscow Festival Clippings file; Eugene S. Staples to Secretary of State, 26 July 1963, State Department Moscow Festival file.

78. "Romanov's Press Conference: For the Further Strengthening of Friendly Contacts," *Pravda*, 30 July 1963, translated and reprinted in *Current Digest of the Soviet Press*, 21 August 1963, 6; Bosley Crowther, "Headache in Moscow," *New York Times*, 4 August 1963, 85; Stevens presentation, 29.

79. Kramer, paraphrased in Jim Becker, "Kramer Says US Denting Russian Armor," *Chicago Tribune*, 23 July 1963, A4; "Stanley Kramer Defies

Soviets on Race Issue," 20 July 1963, news clipping, Kramer Clippings file; Foy D. Kohler to Secretary of State, 17 July 1963, State Department Moscow Festival file; Belmonte, *Selling the American Way*, 160–161; Hixon, *Parting the Curtain*, 195.

80. Stanley Kramer, "Soviets React to US Candor," *Los Angeles Times*, 18 August 1963, L3; Tanner, "Moscow Film Fete," 75.

81. Stevens, *Conversations with the Great Moviemakers*, 560; Aram Goudsouzian, *Sidney Poitier: Man, Actor, Icon* (Chapel Hill: University of North Carolina Press, 2004), 209.

82. Nedelin, *Stanley Kramer*, 59, 71, 105, 66; Kramer, paraphrased in Dern, "Kramer in Moscow."

83. Tanner, "Moscow Film Fete," 75; Stanley Kramer, "Films Can Improve U.S. Image Abroad," *Washington Post*, 22 August 1963, D20.

84. Eugene S. Staples to Secretary of State, 26 July 1963, State Department Moscow Festival file.

85. "Film Workers' Congress: One Review of Screen Trends," translated and reprinted in *Current Digest of the Soviet Press*, 16 March 1966, 19; Burlatsky, "This Must Not Be Repeated," 18.

86. Telegram from Dean Rusk, Department of State, to American Embassy Moscow, 23 July 1963, State Department Post–Moscow Festival file.

87. Foy D. Kohler to Department of State, 22 July 1963, State Department Moscow Festival file.

88. Foy D. Kohler, quoted in Philip K. Scheuer, "Comedian Berman Essays First Movie," *Los Angeles Times*, 2 September 1963, D11.

89. Foy D. Kohler to Secretary of State, 22 July 1963, State Department Moscow Festival file; Foy D. Kohler to Edward R. Murrow, director USIA, 2 August 1963, Russia Correspondence folder.

90. Murrow to SK, 27 August 1963, Russia Correspondence folder; USIA Certificate of Merit, Awards SEK–"JAN" folder, box 35, Kramer Papers; Pratley, *Pratley at the Movies*.

91. Stevens to Tom Pryor, *Variety* Editor, 30 August 1963, Russia Correspondence folder; Stevens and Kramer, paraphrased in "Kramer Sees Festival Russia Breakthrough," *Film Daily*, 5 August 1963, Kramer Clippings file.

92. Kramer, "Soviets React to U.S. Candor," L3; Kramer, quoted in Dern, "Kramer in Moscow."

93. Ninkovich, *Diplomacy of Ideas*, 170; Scheuer, "Kramer Tells Russ to Face Criticism," C9.

94. Stevens, *Conversations with the Great Moviemakers*, 560.

95. The phrase is Jessica C. E. Gienow-Hecht's, from her article "The World Is Ready to Listen: Symphony Orchestras and the Global Performance of America," *Diplomatic History* 36 (January 2012): 18.

Chapter 7. An Old Liberal in New Hollywood

1. Amy Swerdlow, "Ladies' Day at the Capitol: Women Strike for Peace versus HUAC," *Feminist Studies* 8 (Autumn 1982): 499; Deborah E. Lipstadt, "America and the Memory of the Holocaust, 1950–1965," *Modern Judaism* 16, no. 3 (1996): 208.

2. Paul Monaco, *The Sixties: 1960–1969*, vol. 8 of *History of the American Cinema*, ed. Charles Harpole (Berkeley: University of California Press, 2001), 11.

3. Kramer, quoted in *Stage and Screen: Interviews by Donald McDonald with Walter Kerr and Stanley Kramer* (Nashville, Tenn.: Center for the Study of Democratic Institutions, 1962), 33–34.

4. Thomas Doherty, *Hollywood's Censor: Joseph I. Breen and the Production Code Administration* (New York: Columbia University Press, 2007), 346; "Stan Kramer Lauds MPAA Ratings," *Variety*, 15 June 1970, news clipping, Kramer Clippings file.

5. SK to L. Pogojeva, Editor in Chief, *Iskusstvo Kino*, 28 May 1961, Russia Correspondence folder; *Film Daily* review [1963], news clipping, *It's a Mad, Mad, Mad, Mad World* file, PCA Records.

6. Kramer, quoted in *Stage and Screen*, 33–34, excerpted in "Kramer Hopeful of Films' Future," *New York Times*, 30 April 1962, 30.

7. Geoff King, *New Hollywood Cinema: An Introduction*, reprint (London: I. B. Tauris, 2002, 2007), 60.

8. Kramer, quoted in Art Ryon, "Kramer Says Producers Can Blame Themselves for Rising Film Costs," *Los Angeles Times*, 14 November 1962, A1; Kramer, quoted in Walter Wagner, *You Must Remember This: Oral Reminiscences of the Real Hollywood* (New York: G. P. Putnam's Sons, 1975), 291; "An Actors' Director," *Films and Filming*, January 1962, 10.

9. Philip R. Davey, *When Hollywood Came to Melbourne: The Story of the Making of Stanley Kramer's On the Beach* (Melbourne: P. R. Davey, 2005), 161; Perkins, quoted in Charles Winecoff, *Anthony Perkins: Split Image* (New York: Advocate, 2006), 164; Tracy, quoted in "An Actors' Director," 10.

10. Larry M. Wertheim, "Nedrick Young, et al. v. MPAA, et al.: The Fight against the Hollywood Blacklist," *Southern California Quarterly* 57 (Winter 1975): 383–418.

11. Larry Ceplair and Christopher Trumbo, *Dalton Trumbo: Blacklisted Hollywood Radical* (Lexington: University Press of Kentucky, 2014), 414–415; Murray Schumach, "Hollywood Trial," *New York Times*, 8 January 1961, X7.

12. Young, quoted in *The Defiant One*, written and directed by Jan Johnson and Pat Wright (Fayetteville, N.C.: GroundSwell Pictures, 2014), DVD.

13. Wertheim, "Nedrick Young, et al. v. MPAA, et al.," 411; Peter Bart, "Liberals vs. Their Movies," *New York Times*, 29 August 1965, X9. See Young's obituary in *New York Times*, 18 September 1968, 44.

14. Kramer, quoted in *Stage and Screen*, 42, excerpted in "Kramer Hopeful of Films' Future," 30; Kramer, quoted in Bosley Crowther, "Hollywood's Producer of Controversy," *New York Times*, 10 December 1961, SM82.

15. Duncan Petrie and Rod Stoneman, *Educating Film-makers: Past, Present and Future* (Bristol, UK: Intellect Books, 2014), 59; Stanley Kramer, "Sending Myself the Message," *Films and Filming*, February 1964, 8.

16. Kramer, "Sending Myself the Message," 8; Cornfield, quoted in Albert Johnson, "Interviews with Hubert Cornfield and Paul Wendkos," *Film Quarterly* 15 (Spring 1962): 41, 43.

17. Harvey Roy Greenberg, *Screen Memories: Hollywood Cinema on the Psychoanalytic Couch* (New York: Columbia University Press, 1993), 36; Ellen Herman, *The Romance of American Psychology: Political Culture in the Age of Experts* (Berkeley: University of California Press, 1995), 261; Kramer, "Sending Myself the Message," 8; Kramer with Thomas M. Coffey, *A Mad, Mad, Mad, Mad World: A Life in Hollywood* (New York: Harcourt Brace, 1997), 154.

18. David Marriott, *Haunted Life: Visual Culture and Black Modernity* (Brunswick, N.J.: Rutgers University Press, 2007), 181–206; Andrea Slane, "Pressure Points: Political Psychology, Screen Adaptation, and the Management of Racism in the Case-History Genre," *Camera Obscura* 45 (2000): 70–113.

19. Kramer, "Sending Myself the Message," 8; Philip K. Scheuer, "*Pressure Point* Grim Drama of Race Hatred," *Los Angeles Times*, 20 September 1962, C9.

20. Poitier, quoted in Philip K. Scheuer, "Race Switch Fought by Diahann Carroll," *Los Angeles Times*, 15 November 1962, A11; Lester J. Keyser and Andre H. Ruszkowski, *The Cinema of Sidney Poitier: The Black Man's Changing Role on the American Screen* (San Diego: A. S. Barnes, 1980), 70; Murray Schumach, "Hollywood's Negro Crisis," *New York Times*, 30 June 1963, 65.

21. Raymond Carney, *American Dreaming: The Films of John Cassavetes and the American Experience* (Berkeley: University of California Press, 1985), 81; Kramer, "Sending Myself the Message," 8.

22. Kramer and Cassavetes, quoted/paraphrased in Donald Spoto, *Stanley Kramer, Film Maker* (Hollywood, Calif.: Samuel French, 1978), 246; George Kouvaros, *Where Does It Happen?: John Cassavetes and Cinema at the Breaking Point* (Minneapolis: University of Minnesota Press, 2004), 12.

23. Carney, *American Dreaming*, 77; Ray Carney, *The Films of John Cassavetes: Pragmatism, Modernism, and the Movies* (Cambridge: Cambridge University Press, 1994), 74; Kramer, quoted in James Bawden, "Stanley Kramer: Hollywood Liberal," *Classic Images*, February 2011, 72–73.

24. Tino T. Balio, *United Artists: The Company That Changed the Film Industry*, vol. 2, *1951–1978* (Madison: University of Wisconsin Press, 2009), 145–146, 160; Jason Apuzzo, "The Ultimate Southern California Movie: Criterion Restores *It's a Mad, Mad, Mad, Mad World* to Its Full Glory," *Huffington Post*, 3 March 2014, http://www.huffingtonpost.com/jason-apuzzo/the-ultimate-southern-cal_b_4888024.html.

25. "Talk with the Director," *Newsweek*, 17 October 1960, 114; Howard Thompson, "Stanley Kramer Turns to Humor," *New York Times*, 10 September 1960, 10.

26. Kramer, quoted in Philip K. Scheuer, "Cameras Will Roll on Kramer's *Mad*," *Los Angeles Times*, 26 April 1962, A11; Kramer with Coffey, *Mad, Mad, Mad, Mad World*, 192.

27. Thompson, "Stanley Kramer Turns to Humor," 10; Hedda Hopper, "Looking at Hollywood," *Chicago Daily Tribune*, 27 January 1962, N6; Kramer with Coffey, *Mad, Mad, Mad, Mad World*, 189.

28. Scheuer, "Cameras Will Roll on Kramer's *Mad*," A11.

29. James Harvey, *Movie Love in the Fifties* (New York: Knopf, 2001), 222; Kramer, quoted in Bawden, "Stanley Kramer," 73.

30. *Our Sunday Visitor*, review, 5 April 1964, and *New Yorker* review [1963], news clippings, *It's a Mad, Mad, Mad, Mad World* file, PCA Records.

31. Hollis Alpert, "Crazy, Man," *Saturday Review*, 9 November 1963, 33; Paul Nelson, "*It's a Mad, Mad, Mad, Mad World*," *Film Quarterly* 17 (Spring 1964): 43; *Film Daily* review [1963], news clippings, *It's a Mad, Mad, Mad, Mad World* file, PCA Records.

32. Aleksandr Mikhalevich, "Notes of a Publicist: It's a Sane, Sane, Sane World," *Izvestia*, 27 March 1966, 3, translated and reprinted in *Current Digest of the Soviet Press*, 20 April 1966, 23; Vladimir Solodovnik, quoted in Sergei I. Zhuk, "Détente and Western Cultural Products in Soviet Ukraine during the 1970s," in William Jay Risch, ed., *Youth and Rock in the Soviet Bloc: Youth Cultures, Music, and the State Russia and Eastern Europe* (Lanham, Md.: Lexington, 2015), 134.

33. Porter, quoted in Philip K. Scheuer, "*Ship of Fools* Under Way with Kramer at the Helm," *Los Angeles Times*, 2 August 1964, B3.

34. Abby Mann, "Long Voyage for *Ship of Fools*," *Los Angeles Times*, 25 July 1965, K10; Philip K. Scheuer, "*Ship of Fools*—Ark of Talent," *Los Angeles Times*, 18 July 1965, K1.

35. Mann, paraphrased in Peter Bart, "Filming Starts on *Ship of Fools* after Two Years of Preparation," *New York Times*, 14 July 1964, 28; Annette Insdorf, *Indelible Shadows: Film and the Holocaust*, 3rd ed. (Cambridge: Cambridge University Press, 2003), 3.

36. Simone Signoret, *Nostalgia Isn't What It Used to Be* (New York: Harper & Row, 1978), 281, and quoted in Susan Hayward, *Simone Signoret: The Star as Cultural Sign* (New York: Continuum, 2004), 149.

37. Mann, "Long Voyage for *Ship of Fools*," K10; Scheuer, "*Ship of Fools*," K1; Kramer, quoted in Bart, "Filming Starts on *Ship of Fools*," 28; Kramer, "Sending Myself the Message," 7.

38. Scheuer, "*Ship of Fools*," K1; Arthur Knight, "What Fools These Mortals Be," *Saturday Review*, 3 July 1965, 19.

39. "Cinema: Rough Crossing," *Time*, 6 August 1965, 85; Shmuel Or, "Fools' Illusions," *Herut*, 3 December 1965, 7, translated for the author by Ayelet Zoran-Rosen.

40. Midge Decter, "Movies and Messages," *Commentary*, November 1965, 77–78; Joan Shelley Rubin, *The Making of Middlebrow Culture* (Chapel Hill: University of North Carolina Press, 1992); Peter Cowie, "The Defiant One," *Films and Filming*, March 1963, 19.

41. Stanley Kauffmann, "O Come, All Ye Faithful," *New Republic*, 31 October 1960, 30; Peter Roffman and Jim Purdy, *The Hollywood Social Problem Film: Madness, Despair and Politics from the Depression to the Fifties* (Bloomington: Indiana University Press, 1981), 305.

42. Pauline Kael, "The Intentions of Stanley Kramer," in *Kiss Kiss Bang Bang* (London: Calder & Boyars, 1970), 203–214; Pauline Kael, "The Current Cinema," *New Yorker*, 13 June 1983, 122, and 8 January 1972, 77.

43. Kramer with Coffey, *Mad, Mad, Mad, Mad World*, 216–217; Bart, "Liberals vs. Their Movies," X9; fund-raiser invitation and receipt in Student Non-Violent Coordinating Committee folder, box 268, Kramer Papers.

44. See Mark Harris, *Pictures at a Revolution: Five Movies and the Birth of the New Hollywood* (New York: Penguin, 2008) and Susan Courtney, *Hollywood Fantasies of Miscegenation: Spectacular Narratives of Gender and Race: 1903–1967* (Princeton, N.J.: Princeton University Press, 2005), 250–294.

45. Tracy, quoted in Harris, *Pictures at a Revolution*, 308; Kramer, quoted in Michael Singer, *A Cut Above: 50 Film Directors Talk about Their Craft* (Los Angeles: Lone Eagle, 1998), 163.

46. Bosley Crowther, "Screen: *Guess Who's Coming to Dinner* Arrives," *New York Times*, 12 December 1967, 56; Charles Champlin, "Movie Reviews: *Dinner, Cold Blood* to Bow," *Los Angeles Times*, 17 December 1967, D14.

47. Roland Forte, "This, That and the Other," *Call and Post*, 24 February 1968, 10B.

48. "Council of Churches Honors Kramer for Interracial Film," *Los Angeles Times*, 14 March 1968, B1; Julian Hartt, "Film Producer Kramer Given Hollzer Award," *Los Angeles Times*, 22 January 1968, 23.

49. Kramer with Coffey, *Mad, Mad, Mad, Mad World*, 218; Renee C. Romano, *Race Mixing: Black-White Marriage in Postwar America* (Cambridge, Mass.: Harvard University Press, 2003); Alex Lubin, *Romance and Rights: The Politics of Interracial Intimacy, 1945–1954* (Jackson: University Press of Mississippi, 2005).

50. A. S. Doc Young, "A Hollywood Break-Through," *Los Angeles Sentinel*, 22 November 1967, D1; Bill Lane, "The Inside Story," *Los Angeles Sentinel*, 14 December 1967, D2; Forte, "This, That and the Other."

51. Robert Hofler, "He Gambled on Aud's Good Taste," *Daily Variety*, 1 February 2008, Kramer Clippings file; Stanley Kramer, "Guess Who Didn't Dig *Dinner*," *New York Times*, 26 May 1968, D21.

52. See letters to SK in Crank Letters folder, box 82, Kramer Papers; Anne Gray Perrin, "*Guess Who's Coming to Dinner:* The Web of Racial, Class, and Gender Constructions in Late 1960s America," *Journal of Popular Culture* 45, no. 4 (2012): 847; Glen Anthony Harris and Robert Brent Toplin, "*Guess Who's Coming to Dinner?* A Clash of Interpretations Regarding Stanley Kramer's Film on the Subject of Interracial Marriage," *Journal of Popular Culture* 40, no. 4 (2007): 712; Kim Cary Warren, "'You'd be criminals!': Transgression, Legal Union, and Interracial Marriage in 1967 Film and Law," in Ian Gregory Strachan and Mia Mask, eds., *Poitier Revisited: Reconsidering a Black Icon in the Obama Age* (New York: Bloomsbury, 2015), 152.

53. Poitier, quoted in Spoto, *Stanley Kramer*, 277.

54. Clifford Mason, "Why Does America Love Sidney Poitier So?" *New York Times*, 10 September 1967, 123; Andrea Levine, "Sidney Poitier's Civil Rights: Rewriting the Mystique of White Womanhood in *Guess Who's Coming to Dinner* and *In the Heat of the Night*," *American Literature* 73 (June 2001): 382.

55. Renata Adler, "The Negro That Movies Overlook," *New York Times*, 3 March 1968, D10; William Barry Furlong, "Interracial Marriage Is a Sometime Thing," *New York Times*, 9 June 1968, SM44; Perrin, "*Guess Who's Coming to Dinner*," 859.

56. Stanley Kauffmann, "Recent Wars," *New Republic*, 16 December 1967, 19, 30; Kramer, quoted in Charles Champlin, "Students Quiz the New Hollywood," *Los Angeles Times*, 14 January 1968, D18.

57. "Baldwin Blasts Poitier's Hit Role," *Los Angeles Sentinel*, 11 July 1968, B10; James Baldwin, *The Devil Finds Work* (London: Michael Joseph, 1976), 75; Kramer, quoted in George Stevens, Jr., *Conversations with the Great Moviemakers of Hollywood's Golden Age* (New York: Knopf, 2006), 563; Kramer with Coffey, *Mad, Mad, Mad, Mad World*, 228; Elliston, quoted in Aram Goudsouzian, *Sidney Poitier: Man, Actor, Icon* (Chapel Hill: University of North Carolina Press, 2004), 286.

58. Charles Champlin, *"Dinner, Cold Blood* to Bow," *Los Angeles Times,* 17 December 1967, D14.

59. Student and Kramer, quoted in Richard L. Coe, "Mr. Kramer Goes to Class," *Washington Post,* 11 January 1968, B6.

60. Levine, "Sidney Poitier's Civil Rights," 373; Diana Goldsborough, "Mixed Marriage—Hollywood Style," *Star Weekly,* 27 January 1968, 44, Guess Who's Coming to Dinner Stanley Kramer Tour—Clippings folder, box 87, Kramer Papers; Harris and Toplin, *"Guess Who's Coming to Dinner,"* 704.

61. Kauffmann, "Recent Wars," 19, 30; Kramer with Coffey, *Mad, Mad, Mad, Mad World,* 226; Kramer, quoted in Bawden, "Stanley Kramer," 74.

62. "Cinema: Integrated Hearts and Flowers," *Time,* 15 December 1967, 108; *Glamour,* October 1968, news clipping, "Guess Who's Coming to Dinner" Magazine Clippings folder, box 87, Kramer Papers; students, quoted in Kramer, "Guess Who Didn't Dig *Dinner,*" D21; Baldwin, *Devil Finds Work,* 75.

63. Richard Schickel, "Sorry Stage for Tracy's Last Bow," *Life, Guess Who's Coming to Dinner* Clippings file, Herrick Library; Warren, "'You'd be criminals,'" 155.

64. Adler, "Negro That Movies Overlook," D10; Levine, "Sidney Poitier's Civil Rights," 372; student and Kramer, quoted in Champlin, "Students Quiz the New Hollywood," D18.

65. Houghton, quoted in Harris, *Pictures at a Revolution,* 300.

66. Kramer, quoted in Spoto, *Stanley Kramer,* 277.

67. Baldwin, *Devil Finds Work,* 74–75.

68. *Glamour,* October 1968, news clipping.

69. Baldwin, *Devil Finds Work,* 70; student, quoted in Wayne Robinson, "Temple Students Quiz Man from Hollywood," *Philadelphia Evening Bulletin,* 12 January 1968, 26, Universities—General Correspondence folder, box 254, Kramer Papers.

70. Kramer, quoted in Milton Berliner, "'Student Power': Director Kramer Runs into a Generation Gap in Films," *Washington Daily News,* 12 January 1968, Guess Who's Coming to Dinner Stanley Kramer Tour—Clippings folder, box 87, Kramer Papers. Hernán Vera and Andrew M. Gordon convincingly analyze the movie as a "crisis of the white patriarch," in *Screen Saviors: Hollywood Fictions of Whiteness* (Lanham, Md.: Rowman & Littlefield, 2003), 90–92.

71. Kramer, quoted in Stevens, *Conversations with the Great Moviemakers,* 569.

72. Spoto, *Stanley Kramer,* 280; Harris, *Pictures at a Revolution,* 398; Harris and Toplin, *"Guess Who's Coming to Dinner,"* 705.

73. Stanley Kramer, "Nine Times across the Generation Gap," *Action! The Magazine of the Directors Guild of America,* March–April 1968, 11–13, revised and reprinted as "Guess Who Didn't Dig *Dinner.*"

74. Stephen Powers, David J. Rothman, and Stanley Rothman, *Hollywood's America: Social and Political Themes in Motion Pictures* (New York: Westview, 1996), 25–26; Kramer, "Guess Who Didn't Dig *Dinner*," D21; Kramer, quoted in Coe, "Mr. Kramer Goes to Class," B6.

75. Bernard F. Dick, ed., *Columbia Pictures: Portrait of a Studio* (Lexington: University Press of Kentucky, 1992), 21; Kramer, quoted in Robinson, "Temple Students Quiz Man from Hollywood," 26.

76. Kramer, "Nine Times across the Generation Gap," 11; Kramer, quoted in Wayne Warga, "Stanley Kramer Swims Away from His Own Doubts," *Los Angeles Times*, 19 October 1969, U16.

77. Kramer with Coffey, *Mad, Mad, Mad, Mad World*, 215; Kramer, quoted in Sam Lesner, "So What's the Problem?" *Panorama–Chicago Daily News*, 20 January 1968, 12; Donald Bogle, *Toms, Coons, Mulattos, Mammies, and Bucks: An Interpretative History of Blacks in American Film*, updated and expanded 5th ed. (New York: Bloomsbury, 2016), 196.

78. Kramer, quoted in Rick Setlowe, "Modern Youth Takes Itself Big," *Variety*, 10 January 1968, news clipping, Kramer Clippings file; Kramer, "Guess Who Didn't Dig *Dinner*," D21; Kramer, quoted in Dave Smith, "English Teachers Give Stanley Kramer a Quiz," *Los Angeles Times*, 3 March 1968, G6.

79. Kramer with Coffey, *Mad, Mad, Mad, Mad World*, 214; Warga, "Stanley Kramer Swims Away," U16; Pauline Kael, "The Current Cinema: Private Worlds," *New Yorker*, 1 November 1969, 140.

80. Kramer, quoted in Warga, "Stanley Kramer Swims Away," U16.

81. David B. Hinton, *Celluloid Ivy: Higher Education in the Movies, 1960–1990* (Methuchen, N.J.: Scarecrow, 1994), 25; Pauline Kael, "The Current Cinema: Numbing the Audience," *New Yorker*, 3 October 1970, 78.

82. Arthur Knight, "SR Goes to the Movies," *Saturday Review*, 19 September 1970, 58; John Torzilli, "Con," *World Cinema*, 16 October 1970, and Glenn Padnick, "Low Marks for *RPM*," *Boston After Dark*, 6 October 1970, news clippings, *R.P.M.* Clippings File, Herrick Library; Spoto, *Stanley Kramer*, 298; Stephen Farber, "Movies from Behind the Barricades," *Film Quarterly* 24 (Winter 1970–1971): 26.

83. Charles Champlin, "*R.P.M.* Spells Plight of the Lost Liberal," *Los Angeles Times*, 4 October 1970, Q22; *R.P.M.* review, *Motion Picture Herald*, 23 September 1970, news clipping, *R.P.M.* Clippings File, Herrick Library; Kramer, quoted in Stevens, *Conversations with the Great Moviemakers*, 582.

84. Kramer with Coffey, *Mad, Mad, Mad, Mad World*, 215; Kramer, quoted in Kenneth Turan, "Movie Message Maker," *Washington Post*, 5 July 1971, D2; *Bless the Beasts and the Children*, review, *Variety*, 8 July 1971, 3, BBC Moscow festival folder.

85. Kramer with Coffey, *Mad, Mad, Mad, Mad World*, 215; Christopher Hudson, "Cinema," *Spectator*, 26 October 1973, 22; Gregg Kilday, "Guess Who's Coming at a New Film Concept," *Los Angeles Times*, 7 January 1973, 1.

86. Natalie Yakovleva, "Stanley Kramer's Moscow Triumph," *Hollywood Reporter*, 9 October 1971, 1; S. Kondrashov, "Art Abroad: A Tour of New York Movie Houses," *Izvestia*, 28 November 1967, 5, translated and reprinted in *Current Digest of the Soviet Press*, 20 December 1967, 15.

87. Kramer, paraphrased in Dan Lewis, "Stanley Kramer Sticks to the Old School," *Record*, 8 July 1968, 26, news clipping, Columbia Pictures Corp.– Correspondence, "Guess" folder, box 80, Kramer Papers; Yakovleva, "Stanley Kramer's Moscow Triumph," 1.

88. Report of the United States Delegation to the V. International Film Festival, Moscow, USSR, July 5–July 20, 1967, submitted to the Secretary of State, by Jack Valenti, Chairman, United States Delegation, Russia Correspondence folder.

89. "Moscow Trip Canceled by Burtons," *Los Angeles Times*, 28 June 1967, E10; "Moscow Festival Underway; U.S. Delegation Due Sunday," *Film Daily*, 7 July 1967, Moscow Film Festival, 1967 Clipping File, Herrick Library.

90. Kramer, quoted in Charles Champlin, "Film Festivals a Window to World," *Los Angeles Times*, 14 August 1967, D24.

91. "Kramer Irritated by State Dept. Snub of Moscow Fest," *Variety*, 4 August 1971, 3, and Yevtushenko, quoted in "Kramer *Children* a Moscow Fest Hit," *Variety*, 27 July 1971, 2, *BBC* Moscow festival folder.

92. Kramer, quoted in Mary Blume, "Hero Rating for Stanley Kramer," *Los Angeles Times*, 29 July 1971, E1; Kramer, quoted in "Stanley Kramer's Aim Is Self-Satisfaction," *Sarasota Journal*, 26 December 1969, 21.

Conclusion: Legacies of a Hollywood Liberal

1. Spacey, quoted in David Robb, "Golden Globes' Most Touching Moment," *Deadline*, 12 January 2015, http://deadline.com/2015/01/kevin-spacey -golden-globes-stanley-kramer-speech-karen-kramer-1201348413/ and in Roger Moore, "The Life of Kevin Spacey," *Orlando Sentinel*, 16 February 2003, http://articles.orlandosentinel.com/2003-02-16/news/0302140651_1 _kevin-spacey-laura-linney-stanley-kramer.

2. Johnson, quoted in David Robb, "Kevin Spacey's Tribute Revives Angry Feud over Stanley Kramer's Role in the Blacklist," *Deadline*, 22 January 2015, http://deadline.com/2015/01/stanley-kramer-kevin-spacey-blacklist -richard-johnson-1201355771/.

3. *Darkness at High Noon: The Carl Foreman Documents* (2002), quoted in Larry Ceplair, "Shedding Light on *Darkness at High Noon*," *Cineaste* 27

(Fall 2002), 20; Chetwynd, quoted in Ed Rampell, "*High Noon*: The Rewrite," *Nation*, 7 October 2002, 34.

4. Ceplair, "Shedding Light," 21, 22; Glenn Frankel, *High Noon: The Hollywood Blacklist and the Making of an American Classic* (New York: Bloomsbury, 2017), 307–308.

5. Michael Denning, *The Cultural Front: The Laboring of American Culture in the Twentieth Century* (London: Verso, 1996), 92.

6. Jennifer A. Delton, *Rethinking the 1950s: How Anticommunism and the Cold War Made America Liberal* (New York: Cambridge University Press, 2013), 32.

7. Kramer, quoted in Gregg Kilday, "Guess Who's Coming at a New Film Concept," *Los Angeles Times*, 7 January 1973, 1, in "Stanley Kramer's Aim Is Self-Satisfaction," *Sarasota Journal*, 26 December 1969, 39, and in Walter Wagner, *You Must Remember This: Oral Reminiscences of the Real Hollywood* (New York: G. P. Putnam's Sons, 1975), 296.

8. Kramer, quoted in Harry Tessel, "Kramer Has Played the Movie Odds Right—Mostly," *Chicago Tribune*, 13 September 1976, B2; Roderick Mann, "Guess Who's Returning to Film Making at 73," *Los Angeles Times*, 21 September 1986, Q26.

9. Wagner, *You Must Remember This*, 284; Kramer, quoted in Tom Buckley, "At the Movies," *New York Times*, 24 November 1978, C6.

10. Kramer, quoted in Roger Ebert, "Kramer: Living a Nice Life, Thank You," *Los Angeles Times*, 26 August 1983, G18, and in Michael Singer, *A Cut Above: 50 Film Directors Talk about Their Craft* (Los Angeles: Lone Eagle, 1998), 160.

11. Kramer, quoted in Nina Darnton, "At the Movies," *New York Times*, 15 May 1987, C8; Mann, "Guess Who's Returning to Film Making," Q26.

12. Kramer, quoted in James Bawden, "Stanley Kramer: Hollywood Liberal," *Classic Images*, February 2011, 170; Kramer, quoted in Leo Verswijver, *"Movies Were Always Magical": Interviews with 19 Actors, Directors and Producers from the Hollywood of the 1930s through the 1950s* (Jefferson, N.C.: McFarland, 2003), 81; Kramer, quoted in Singer, *Cut Above*, 161–163; Kramer with Thomas M. Coffey, *A Mad, Mad, Mad, Mad World: A Life in Hollywood* (New York: Harcourt Brace, 1997), 175.

13. "Aretha Franklin to Receive Vanguard Award at the 39th Annual NAACP Image Awards," 8 January 2008. Award description cited in http://www.naacp .org/latest/aretha-franklin-to-receive-vanguard-award-at-the-39th-annual -naacp-image-awards/.

14. Spielberg, quoted in Verswijver, *"Movies Were Always Magical,"* 75.

15. Poitier, quoted in Donald Spoto, *Stanley Kramer, Film Maker* (Hollywood, Calif.: Samuel French, 1978), 203, and in Kramer with Coffey, *Mad,*

Mad, Mad, Mad World, 152; Poitier, quoted in "Sir Sidney Poitier–BAFTA Fellowship in 2016," http://www.bafta.org/film/awards/sir-sidney-poitier -bafta-fellowship-in-2016.

16. Rick Lyman, "Stanley Kramer, Filmmaker with Social Bent, Dies at 87," *New York Times,* 21 February 2001, A1; Ronald Bergan, "Stanley Kramer," *Guardian,* 21 February 2001, 24; David Thomson, *The New Biographical Dictionary of Film,* 5th ed. (New York: Knopf, 2010), 534.

17. David Walsh, "Why Was Stanley Kramer So Unfashionable at the Time of His Death?" *World Socialist Web Site,* 26 February 2001, https://www .wsws.org/en/articles/2001/02/kram-f26.html.

18. Peter Roffman and Jim Purdy, *The Hollywood Social Problem Film: Madness, Despair and Politics from the Depression to the Fifties* (Bloomington: Indiana University Press, 1981), 301.

19. Charles Isherwood, *Variety,* 27 March 2001, *JAN* Clippings file; Ean Wood, *Dietrich, a Biography* (London: Sanctuary, 2002), 308; Andrew Sarris, *The American Cinema: Directors and Directions, 1929–1968* (New York: E. P. Dutton, 1968), 260.

20. David Robb, "Celebrating Stanley Kramer's Scopes Monkey Trial Masterpiece," *Hollywood Reporter,* 23 September 2010, 11; Terry Christensen, *Reel Politics: American Political Movies from Birth of a Nation to Platoon* (Oxford: Basil Blackwell, 1987), 104–105.

21. Michael Wilmington, "Stanley Kramer: 1913–2001," *Chicago Tribune,* 23 February 2001, http://articles.chicagotribune.com/2001-02-23/features /0102230014_1_high-noon-stanley-kramer-movies; Kramer with Coffey, *Mad, Mad, Mad, Mad World,* 232; Kramer, quoted in Verswijver, *"Movies Were Always Magical,"* 88.

INDEX